THE POEMS OF

JOHN DRYDEN

EDITED BY

JAMES KINSLEY

VOLUME I

OXFORD
AT THE CLARENDON PRESS
1958

PRINTED IN GREAT BRITAIN

WALTER SCOTT
HISTORICO POETAE EDITORI
SCHOLAE REGIAE EDINENSIS
ALUMNO

PREFACE

THE main purpose of this edition is to provide, for the first time, a complete text of Dryden's original poems and verse translations based on a critical review of all the early printings. It includes poems of which he was part author; prologues, epilogues, and songs from plays in which he collaborated with others; and a few poems attributed to him on evidence which, though inconclusive, has found some favour with modern scholars. For convenience these have been given their appropriate place in the text, and the evidence for attributing them to Dryden is discussed in the commentary.

The copy-text chosen for each poem is normally the first edition, collated with all subsequent editions published in Dryden's lifetime. Apparently authoritative variants from these have been admitted, and silently brought into conformity with the style of the copy-text. The text of the original poems has been prepared mainly from copies in the Bodleian Library and the library of Worcester College; that of the translations, mainly from my own copies. I have examined as many copies of each edition as possible. The typography of titles is standardized; and for short poems originally printed in italics the type has been reversed. Long 's' and merely typographical devices have been discarded. Errors of spacing and numbering, turned letters, wrong founts, obvious misprints, and irregularities in the use of 'æ' and 'œ' in classical names and quotations have been silently corrected; the distinction between italicized plurals in —*'s* and possessives in roman —'s has been regularized; proper names in roman type have been italicized in some contexts: otherwise all changes in the accidentals of the copy-text are recorded. Apart from differences in punctuation which involve differences of meaning or emphasis, and a few spellings of possible interest to the philologist, the textual apparatus is restricted to substantive variants. I have examined all seventeenth-century transcripts and miscellany reprints accessible to me, but variants from these are recorded only when they seem significant.

No arrangement of Dryden's varied and extensive writing is without its inconveniences. In this edition the poems follow the order in which they first appeared in print; and it is hoped that this arrangement, although it displaces a number of minor poems which were not immediately published, will facilitate the study of Dryden's professional career.

The commentary is an attempt to explain the occasion of each poem, elucidate the text, identify quotations and adaptations, and illustrate the more important of Dryden's literary and intellectual affinities. My debts to my predecessors will be everywhere apparent. I owe most to Sir Walter Scott, still the wisest and most richly endowed of Dryden's annotators, and to W. D. Christie, W. P. Ker, and G. R. Noyes.

Professor Nichol Smith read much of my commentary in draft; and I join the large company of Oxford editors who have profited immeasureably by his scholarship, judgement, and unfailing kindness. To the wealth of learning which he made available to students of Dryden in 1939, Mr. Hugh Macdonald has added his constant criticism and encouragement. Mr. John Hayward gave me much initial advice, and passed on a collection of transcripts and photostats which greatly reduced the labour of constructing a working text. The late Professor E. N. Hooker, who until his death in 1956 was responsible for the edition of Dryden now in progress at Los Angeles, gave me more assistance than professional rivalry and 'seas between us braid' would have allowed from a less magnanimous scholar and friend. I owe debts of gratitude to my wife, for her patient help in collation and in the interpretation of some passages in the poems; and to my colleague Professor Gwyn Jones, for his sustaining interest and a generous loan of books.

I have many other debts to acknowledge: to Sir Walter Greg, Dr. Percy Simpson, Dr. Herbert Davis, Dr. J. G. McManaway, Dr. Vinton Dearing, and Professor Thomas Jones, for help with textual problems; to Dr. C. T. Onions, for information on difficult points of vocabulary and syntax; to Col. C. H. Wilkinson, for help with literary references and for the freedom of Worcester College Library; to Sir George Clark, Professor D. B. Quinn, Mr. James Laver, Professor E. M. Wilson, Mr. S. H. F. Johnston, and Mr. William Urry, for advice on historical questions; to the Rev. Professor Norman Sykes, Father T. Corbishley, and Dr. John Mackay, for advice on points of ecclesiastical history; to the Very Rev. Dr. John Baillie and Professor R. I. Aaron for help with philosophical passages; to Sir Herbert Grierson, Dr. Catherine Ing, and Dr. O. R. Taylor, for help with literary allusions; to Mr. Alun Hudson-Williams and Dr. B. R. Rees, for answering many questions on Dryden's classical scholarship; to Professor Roberto Weiss, Mr. John Purves, Professor H. G. Wright, and Dr. Josef Raith, for guidance on Dryden's Italian reading; to the late Dr. John Allan, for information on the Whig medal; to Dr. C. H. Josten, for criticism of my notes on astrological passages; to the Very Rev. Dr. A. C. Don, the Rev. G. B. Ashburne, the Rev. W. J. Davies, and my sister, Mrs. Catherine Herriott, for collating lapidary inscriptions; and to Professor G. B. Kerferd, for help in reading proofs. I am deeply indebted to the Leverhulme Trustees, for a generous award without which my work would have been seriously retarded. Finally, it is a pleasure to acknowledge the constant courtesy and resourcefulness of the Secretary and staff of the Clarendon Press, and of the librarians and staff of the Bodleian Library, the National Library of Scotland, the British Museum, Edinburgh University Library, the National Library of Wales, the Folger Shakespeare Library, the William Andrews Clark Memorial Library, the Huntington Library, and the college libraries of the University of Wales.

J. K.

University College of Swansea
March 1958

CONTENTS

VOLUME I

VOLUME II

VOLUME III

REFERENCES AND ABBREVIATIONS

Aubrey	*Aubrey's Brief Lives*, ed. O. L. Dick, 1950
Boswell	Eleanore Boswell, *The Restoration Court Stage (1660–1702)*, 1932
Brown	L. F. Brown, *The First Earl of Shaftesbury*, 1933
Browning	*English Historical Documents 1660–1714*, ed. Andrew Browning, 1953
Bryant	Arthur Bryant, *King Charles II*, 1931
Burnet	*Bishop Burnet's History of His Own Time*, 2 vols., 1724–34
Burnet–Airy	*Burnet's History*, ed. Osmund Airy, 2 vols., 1897
Burnet–Foxcroft	*A Supplement to Burnet's History*, ed. H. C. Foxcroft, 1902
Burton	Robert Burton, *The Anatomy of Melancholy*, 1660
Christie	*The Poetical Works of John Dryden*, ed. W. D. Christie, 1907; rev. C. H. Firth, 1911
Cibber	*An Apology for the Life of Mr. Colley Cibber*, 1740
Clark	G. N. Clark, *The Later Stuarts, 1660–1714*, 1947
Clarke	*The Life of James II . . . collected out of Memoirs writ of his own Hand*, ed. J. S. Clarke, 2 vols., 1816
CSP	*Calendar of State Papers*
Day	*The Songs of John Dryden*, ed. C. L. Day, 1932
Dennis	*The Critical Works of John Dennis*, ed. E. N. Hooker, 2 vols., 1939–43
DNB	*The Dictionary of National Biography*
Downes	John Downes, *Roscius Anglicanus*, ed. Montague Summers, 1929
D'Oyley	Elizabeth D'Oyley, *James Duke of Monmouth*, 1938
EETS	The Early English Text Society
EHR	*The English Historical Review*
ELH	*A Journal of English Literary History*
ES	*English Studies* (Amsterdam)
ESt	*Englische Studien*
Evelyn, *Diary*	Ed. E. S. de Beer, 6 vols., 1955
Gardner	*The Prologues and Epilogues of John Dryden*, ed. W. B. Gardner, 1951
Grammont	Anthony Hamilton, *Memoirs of Count Grammont*, ed. Walter Scott, 1905
Harl. Misc.	*The Harleian Miscellany*, 8 vols., 1744–6
HLQ	*The Huntington Library Quarterly*
HMC	The Historical Manuscripts Commission

Hotson	Leslie Hotson, *The Commonwealth and Restoration Stage*, 1928
JEGP	*A Journal of English and Germanic Philology*
Johnson	Samuel Johnson, *Lives of the English Poets*, ed. G. B. Hill, 3 vols., 1905
Jonson	*Ben Jonson*, ed. C. H. Herford and Percy and Evelyn Simpson, 11 vols., 1925–52
Ker	*Essays of John Dryden*, ed. W. P. Ker, 2 vols., 1926
Lane	Jane Lane, *Titus Oates*, 1949
Luttrell	Narcissus Luttrell, *A Brief Historical Relation of State Affairs 1678–1714*, 6 vols., 1857
Macdonald	Hugh Macdonald, *John Dryden. A Bibliography of Early Editions and of Drydeniana*, 1939
Malone	*The Critical and Miscellaneous Prose Works of John Dryden*, ed. Edmond Malone, 3 vols., 1800
MLN	*Modern Language Notes*
MLQ	*The Modern Language Quarterly*
MLR	*The Modern Language Review*
MP	*Modern Philology*
Nichol Smith	*Dryden: Poetry and Prose*, ed. D. Nichol Smith, 1951
Nicoll	Allardyce Nicoll, *A History of English Drama: I. Restoration Drama 1660–1700*, 1952
North	Roger North, *Examen: or, An Enquiry into the Credit and Veracity of a Pretended Complete History*, 1740
Noyes	*The Poetical Works of Dryden*, ed. G. R. Noyes, 1950
NQ	*Notes and Queries*
OED	*The Oxford English Dictionary*
Ogg	David Ogg, *England in the Reign of Charles II*, 2 vols., 1955
Pepys, *Diary*	Ed. H. B. Wheatley, 8 vols., 1949
PMLA	*Publications of the Modern Language Association of America*
POAS	*Poems on Affairs of State* (see Macdonald, pp. 316–22)
Pollock	John Pollock, *The Popish Plot*, 1903
PQ	*The Philological Quarterly*
RES	*The Review of English Studies*
Saintsbury	*Minor Poets of the Caroline Period*, ed. George Saintsbury, 3 vols., 1905–21
SB	*Studies in Bibliography* (University of Virginia)
Scott	*The Works of John Dryden*, ed. Walter Scott, 18 vols., 1808
SHR	*The Scottish Historical Review*
Somers Tracts	*A Collection of Tracts selected from . . . Libraries, particularly that of the late Lord Somers*, revised by Walter Scott, 13 vols., 1809–15

SP	*Studies in Philology*
Spingarn	*Critical Essays of the Seventeenth Century*, ed. J. E. Spingarn, 3 vols., 1908–9
SR	*A Transcript of the Registers of the Worshipful Company of Stationers for 1640–1708* (Roxburghe Club), 3 vols., 1913–14
Summers	*Dryden. The Dramatic Works*, ed. Montague Summers, 6 vols., 1931–2
TC	*The Term Catalogues, 1668–1709 (1711)*, ed. Edward Arber, 3 vols., 1903–6
Tilley	M. P. Tilley, *A Dictionary of the Proverbs in England in the Sixteenth and Seventeenth Centuries*, 1950
TLS	*The Times Literary Supplement*
Turner	F. C. Turner, *James II*, 1948
Ward	*The Letters of John Dryden*, ed. C. E. Ward, 1942
Wiley	A. N. Wiley, *Rare Prologues and Epilogues 1642–1700*, 1940
Wood, *Ath. Ox.*	Anthony Wood, *Athenae Oxonienses*, 2 vols., 1721
Wood, *Life and Times*	Ed. Andrew Clark, 5 vols., 1891–1900

Note. Passages from Dryden's plays and prefaces are normally quoted from the collected edition of 1701. Quotations from seventeenth-century authors are normally given from the standard editions.

Upon the death of the Lord *HASTINGS*

MUST Noble *Hastings* Immaturely die,
(The Honour of his ancient Family?)
Beauty and Learning thus together meet,
To bring a *Winding* for a *Wedding-sheet*?
Must *Vertue* prove *Death*'s Harbinger? Must She,
With him expiring, feel Mortality?
Is *Death* (Sin's wages) Grace's now? shall Art
Make us more Learned, onely to depart?
If Merit be Disease, if Vertue Death;
To be Good, Not to be; who'd then bequeath
Himself to Discipline? Who'd not esteem
Labour a Crime, Study Self-murther deem?
Our *Noble Youth* now have pretence to be
Dunces securely, Ign'rant healthfully.
Rare Linguist! whose Worth speaks it self, whose Praise,
Though not his Own, all Tongues Besides do raise:
Then Whom, Great *Alexander* may seem Less;
Who conquer'd Men, but not their Languages.
In his mouth Nations speak; his Tongue might be
Interpreter to *Greece*, *France*, *Italy*.
His native Soyl was the Four parts o' th' Earth;
All *Europe* was too narrow for his Birth.
A young Apostle; and (with rev'rence may
I speak'it) inspir'd with gift of Tongues, as They.
Nature gave him, a Childe, what Men in vain
Oft strive, by Art though further'd, to obtain.
His Body was an Orb, his sublime Soul
Did move on Vertue's and on Learning's Pole:
Whose Reg'lar Motions better to our view,
Then *Archimedes* Sphere, the Heavens did shew.
Graces and Vertues, Languages and Arts,
Beauty and Learning, fill'd up all the parts.
Heav'ns Gifts, which do, like falling Stars, appear
Scatter'd in Others; all, as in their Sphear,
Were fix'd and conglobate in 's Soul; and thence
Shone th'row his Body, with sweet Influence;

Upon the death, &c. Text from Lachrymæ Musarum; The Tears of the Muses, *1649*

Letting their Glories so on each Limb fall,
The whole Frame render'd was Celestial.
Come, learned *Ptolomy*, and trial make,
If thou this Hero's Altitude canst take;
But that transcends thy skill; thrice happie all,
Could we but prove thus Astronomical.
Liv'd *Tycho* now, struck with this Ray, (which shone
More bright i' th' Morn, then others beam at Noon)
He'd take his *Astrolabe*, and seek out here
What new Star 't was did gild our Hemisphere.
Replenish'd then with such rare Gifts as these,
Where was room left for such a Foul Disease?
The Nations sin hath drawn that Veil, which shrouds
Our Day-spring in so sad benighting Clouds.
Heaven would no longer trust its Pledge; but thus
Recall'd it; rapt its *Ganymede* from us.
Was there no milder way but the Small Pox,
The very Filth'ness of *Pandora*'s Box?
So many Spots, like *næves*, our *Venus* soil?
One Jewel set off with so many a Foil?
Blisters with pride swell'd; which th'row 's flesh did sprout
Like Rose-buds, stuck i' th' Lily-skin about.
Each little Pimple had a Tear in it,
To wail the fault its rising did commit:
Who, Rebel-like, with their own Lord at strife,
Thus made an Insurrection 'gainst his Life.
Or were these Gems sent to adorn his Skin,
The Cab'net of a richer Soul within?
No Comet need foretel his Change drew on,
Whose Corps might seem a *Constellation.*
O had he di'd of old, how great a strife
Had been, who from his Death should draw their Life?
Who should, by one rich draught, become what ere
Seneca, *Cato*, *Numa*, *Cæsar*, were:
Learn'd, Vertuous, Pious, Great; and have by this
An universal *Metempsuchosis.*
Must all these ag'd Sires in one Funeral
Expire? All die in one so young, so small?
Who, had he liv'd his life out, his great Fame
Had swoln 'bove any *Greek* or *Romane* Name.

But hasty Winter, with one blast, hath brought
The hopes of Autumn, Summer, Spring, to nought.
Thus fades the Oak i' th' sprig, i' th' blade the Corn;
Thus, without Young, this *Phœnix* dies, new born.
Must then old three-legg'd gray-beards with their Gout,
Catarrhs, Rheums, Aches, live three Ages out?
Times Offal, onely fit for th' Hospital,
Or t' hang an Antiquaries room withal;
Must Drunkards, Lechers, spent with Sinning, live
With such helps as Broths, Possits, Physick give?
None live, but such as should die? Shall we meet
With none but Ghostly Fathers in the Street?
Grief makes me rail; Sorrow will force its way;
And, Show'rs of Tears, Tempestuous Sighs best lay.
The Tongue may fail; but over-flowing Eyes
Will weep out lasting streams of *Elegies*.

But thou, O *Virgin-Widow*, left alone,
Now thy belov'd, heaven-ravisht *Spouse* is gone,
(Whose skilful Sire in vain strove to apply
Med'cines, when thy Balm was no Remedy)
With greater then *Platonick* love, O wed
His Soul, though not his Body, to thy Bed:
Let that make thee a Mother; bring thou forth
Th' *Idea's* of his Vertue, Knowledge, Worth;
Transcribe th' Original in new Copies; give
Hastings o' th' better part: so shall he live
In 's Nobler Half; and the great Grandsire be
Of an Heroick Divine Progenie:
An Issue, which t' Eternity shall last,
Yet but th' Irradiations which he cast.
Erect no *Mausolæums*: for his best
Monument is his Spouses Marble brest.

To his friend the Authour, on his divine Epigrams

THOU hast inspir'd me with thy soul, and I
Who ne're before could ken of Poetry
Am grown so good proficient, I can lend
A line in commendation of my friend;
Yet 'tis but of the second hand, if ought
There be in this, 'tis from thy fancy brought.
Good thief who dar'st Prometheus-like aspire,
And fill thy poems with Celestiall fire:
Enliven'd by these sparks divine, their rayes
Adde a bright lustre to thy crown of bayes.
Young Eaglet who thy nest thus soon forsook,
So lofty and divine a course hast took
As all admire, before the down begin
To peep, as yet, upon thy smoother Chin;
And, making heaven thy aim, hast had the grace
To look the sunne of righteousnesse ith' face.
What may we hope, if thou go'st on thus fast!
Scriptures at first; Enthusiasmes at last!
Thou hast commenc'd, betimes, a saint: go on,
Mingling Diviner streams with Helicon:
That they who view what Epigrams here be
May learn to make like, in just praise of thee.
Reader, I've done, nor longer will withhold
Thy greedy eyes; looking on this pure gold
Thou'lt know adult'rate copper, which, like this,
Will onely serve to be a foil to his.

To his friend the Authour. Text from John Hoddesdon's Sion and Parnassus, Or Epigrams On severall texts of the Old and New Testament, *1650*

TO HONOR DRYDEN

To the faire hands of Madame Honor Dryden these crave admittance.

Madame

If you have received the lines I sent by the reverend Levite, I doubt not but they have exceedingly wrought vpon you; for beeing so longe in a Clergy-mans pocket, assuredly they have acquired more Sanctity then theire Authour meant them. Alasse Madame for ought I know they may become a Sermon ere they could arrive at you; and believe it haveing you for the text it could scarcely proove bad, if it light vpon one that could handle it indifferently. but I am so miserable a preacher that though I have so sweet and copious a subject, I still fall short in my expressions. And in stead of an vse of thanksgiveing I am allways makeing one of comfort, that I may one day againe have the happinesse to kisse your faire hand. but that is a Message I would not so willingly do by letter as by word of mouth. This is a point I must confesse I could willingly dwell longer on, and in this case what ever I say you may confidently take for gospell. But I must hasten. And indeed Madame (Beloved I had almost sayd) hee had need hasten who treats of you; for to speake fully to every part of your excellencyes requires a longer houre then most persons have allotted them. But in a word your selfe hath been the best Expositor vpon the text of your own worth, in that admirable Comment you wrote vpon it, I meane your incomparable letter. By all thats good (and you Madame are a great part of my Oath) it hath put mee so farre besides my selfe that I have scarce patience to write prose. and my pen is stealing into verse every time I kisse your letter. I am sure the poore paper smarts for my Idolatry, which by wearing it continually neere my brest will at last bee burnt and Martyrd in those flames of adoration it hath kindled in mee. But I forgett Madame, what rarityes your letter came fraught with besides words; You are such a Deity that commands worship by provideing the Sacrifice: you are pleasd Madame to force mee to write by sending mee Materialls, and compell mee to my greatest happinesse. Yet though I highly vallue your Magnificent presents, pardon mee if I must tell the world they are but imperfect Emblemes of your beauty; For the white and red of waxe and paper are but shaddowes of that vermillion and Snowe in your lips and forehead. And the Silver of the Inkehorne if it

To Honor Dryden. Text from letter in the William Andrews Clark Memorial Library. See Commentary

presume to vye whitenesse with your purer skinne, must confesse it selfe blacker then the liquour it containes. What then do I more then retrieve your own guifts? and present you that paper adulterated with blotts which you gave spotlesse?

For since t'was mine the white hath lost its hiew
To show t'was n'ere it selfe but whilst in you;
The Virgin Waxe hath blusht it selfe to red
Since it with mee hath lost its Maydenhead.
You (fairest Nymph) are waxe; oh may you bee
As well in softnesse so as purity;
Till fate and your ow[n] happy choise reveale
Whom you so farre shall blesse to make your Seale.

Fairest Valentine the vnfeigned
wishe of yo[r] humble Votary.
Jo: Dryden.

Cambridge
May the 23[d]
16[53?]

Heroique Stanza's, Consecrated to the Glorious Memory of his most Serene and Renowned Highnesse OLIVER Late *LORD PROTECTOR* of this Common-Wealth, &c.

Written after the Celebration of his Funerall

I

AND now 'tis time; for their Officious haste,
Who would before have born him to the sky,
Like *eager Romans* ere all Rites were past
Did let too soon the *sacred Eagle* fly.

Heroique Stanza's. Text from Three Poems Upon the Death of his late Highnesse Oliver, *1659, collated with the reprint of* c. *1691. See Commentary*
Heading. Glorious *om. 91* most Serene and Renowned *om. 91* *Celebration*] Celebrating *91*

2

Though our best notes are treason to his fame
Joyn'd with the loud applause of publique voice;
Since Heav'n, what praise we offer to his name,
Hath render'd too authentick by its choice:

3

Though in his praise no Arts can liberall be,
Since they whose muses have the highest flown
Add not to his immortall Memorie,
But do an act of friendship to their own:

4

Yet 'tis our duty and our interest too
Such monuments as we can build to raise;
Lest all the World prevent what we should do
And claime a *Title* in him by their praise.

5

How shall I then begin, or where conclude
To draw a *Fame* so truly *Circular*?
For in a round what order can be shew'd,
Where all the parts so *equall perfect* are?

6

His *Grandeur* he deriv'd from Heav'n alone,
For he was great e're Fortune made him so;
And Warr's like mists that rise against the Sunne
Made him but greater seem, not greater grow.

7

No borrow'd Bay's his *Temples* did adorne,
But to our *Crown* he did fresh *Jewells* bring,
Nor was his Vertue poyson'd soon as born
With the too early thoughts of being King.

12 own:] own. *59 91*

8

Fortune (that easie Mistresse of the young
But to her auncient servants coy and hard)
Him at that age her favorites rank'd among
When she her best-lov'd *Pompey* did discard.

9

He, private, mark'd the faults of others sway,
And set as *Sea-mark's* for himself to shun;
Not like rash *Monarch's* who their youth betray
By Acts their Age too late would wish undone.

10

And yet *Dominion* was not his Designe,
We owe that blessing not to him but Heaven,
Which to faire Acts unsought rewards did joyn,
Rewards that lesse to him than us were given.

11

Our former Cheifs like sticklers of the Warre
First sought t'inflame the Parties, then to poise;
The quarrell lov'd, but did the cause abhorre,
And did not strike to hurt but make a noise.

12

Warre our consumption was their gainfull trade,
We inward bled whilst they prolong'd our pain:
He fought to end our fighting, and assaid
To stanch the blood by breathing of the vein.

13

Swift and resistlesse through the Land he past
Like that bold *Greek* who did the East subdue;
And made to battails such Heroick haste
As if on wings of victory he flew.

14

He fought secure of fortune as of fame,
Till by *new maps* the Island might be shown,
Of Conquests which he strew'd where e're he came
Thick as the *Galaxy* with starr's is sown.

15

His *Palmes* though under weights they did not stand,
Still thriv'd; no *Winter* could his *Laurells* fade;
Heav'n in his Portraict shew'd a Workman's hand
And drew it perfect yet without a shade.

16

Peace was the Prize of all his toyles and care,
Which Warre had banisht and did now restore;
Bolognia's Walls thus mounted in the Ayre
To seat themselves more surely then before.

17

Her safety rescu'd *Ireland* to him owes;
And Treacherous *Scotland* to no int'rest true,
Yet blest that fate which did his Armes dispose
Her Land to Civilize as to subdue.

18

Nor was he like those *starr's* which only shine
When to pale *Mariners* they stormes portend,
He had his calmer influence; and his Mine
Did Love and Majesty together blend.

19

'Tis true, his Count'nance did imprint an awe,
And naturally all souls to his did bow;
As *Wands of Divination* downward draw
And point to Beds where Sov'raign Gold doth grow.

56 is] are *91*   61 toyles] Toil *91*   63 Walls *91*: wall *59*   65 owes; *91*: owes *59*

20

When past all Offerings to *Feretrian Jove*
He *Mars* depos'd, and Arms to Gowns made yield,
Successefull Councells did him soon approve
As fit for close *Intrigues*, as open field.

21

To suppliant *Holland* he vouchsaf'd a peace,
Our once bold Rivall in the *British Main*
Now tamely glad her unjust claime to cease,
And buy our Friendship with her Idoll gaine.

22

Fame of th' asserted Sea through *Europe* blown
Made *France* and *Spaine* ambitious of his Love;
Each knew that side must conquer he would own
And for him fiercely as for Empire strove.

23

No sooner was the *French man*'s cause embrac'd
Than the leight *Mounsire* the grave *Don* outwaigh'd,
His fortune turn'd the Scale where it was cast,
Though *Indian Mines* were in the other layd.

24

When absent, yet we conquer'd in his right;
For though some meaner Artist's skill were shown
In mingling colours, or in placing light,
Yet still the *faire Designment* was his own.

25

For from all tempers he could service draw,
The worth of each with its alloy he knew;
And as the *Confident* of *Nature* saw
How she Complexions did divide and brew.

81 peace, *91*: peace *59*

26

Or he their single vertues did survay
By *intuition* in his own large brest,
Where all the rich *Idea's* of them lay,
That were the rule and measure to the rest.

27

When such *Heröique Vertue* Heav'n sets out,
The Starrs like *Commons* sullenly obey;
Because it draines them when it comes about,
And therefore is a taxe they seldome pay.

28

From this high-spring our forraign-Conquests flow
Which yet more glorious triumphs do portend,
Since their Commencement to his Armes they owe,
If Springs as high as Fountaines may ascend.

29

He made us *Freemen* of the *Continent*
Whom Nature did like Captives treat before,
To nobler prey's the *English Lyon* sent,
And taught him first in *Belgian walks* to rore.

30

That old unquestion'd Pirate of the Land
Proud *Rome*, with dread, the fate of *Dunkirk* har'd;
And trembling wish't behind more *Alpes* to stand,
Although an *Alexander* were her guard.

31

By his command we boldly crost the Line
And bravely fought where *Southern Starrs* arise,
We trac'd the farre-fetchd Gold unto the mine
And that which brib'd our fathers made our prize.

32

Such was our Prince; yet own'd a soul above
The highest Acts it could produce to show:
Thus poor *Mechanique Arts* in publique moove
Whilst the deep Secrets beyond practice goe.

33

Nor dy'd he when his ebbing Fame went lesse,
But when fresh Lawrells courted him to live;
He seem'd but to prevent some new successe;
As if above what triumphs Earth could give.

34

His latest Victories still thickest came
As, near the *Center*, *Motion* does increase;
Till he, pres'd down by his own weighty name,
Did, like the *Vestall*, under spoyles decease.

35

But first the *Ocean* as a tribute sent
That Gyant *Prince* of all her watery Heard;
And th' *Isle* when her *Protecting Genius* went
Upon his *Obsequies* loud sighs confer'd.

36

No Civill broyles have since his death arose,
But *Faction* now by *Habit* does obey:
And *Warrs* have that respect for his repose,
As *Winds* for *Halcyons* when they breed at Sea.

37

His Ashes in a peacefull Urne shall rest,
His Name a great example stands to show
How strangely high endeavours may be blest,
Where *Piety* and *valour* joyntly goe.

138 Heard; *91*: Heard, *59*

To my Honored Friend,
S[r] ROBERT HOWARD,
On his Excellent Poems

As there is Musick uninform'd by Art
In those wild Notes, which with a merry heart
The Birds in unfrequented shades expresse,
Who better taught at home, yet please us lesse:
So in your Verse, a native sweetnesse dwells,
Which shames Composure, and its Art excells.
Singing, no more can your soft numbers grace
Then Paint adds charms unto a beauteous Face.
Yet as when mighty Rivers gently creep,
Their even calmnesse does suppose them deep,
Such is your Muse: no Metaphor swell'd high
With dangerous boldnesse lifts her to the sky;
Those mounting Fancies when they fall again,
Shew sand and dirt at bottom do remain.
So firm a strength, and yet withall so sweet,
Did never but in *Sampson*'s Riddle meet.
'Tis strange each line so great a weight should bear,
And yet no signe of toil, no sweat appear.
Either your Art hides Art, as Stoicks feign
Then least to feel, when most they suffer pain;
And we, dull souls, admire, but cannot see
What hidden springs within the Engine be:
Or 'tis some happinesse that still pursues
Each act and motion of your gracefull muse.
Or is it Fortune's work, that in your head
The curious* Net that is for fancies spread,
Let's through its Meshes every meaner thought,
While rich Idea's there are onely caught?
Sure that's not all; this is a piece too fair
To be the child of Chance, and not of Care.
No Atoms casually together hurl'd
Could e're produce so beautifull a world.

**Rete Mirabile*

To my Honored Friend. Text from Poems . . . By the Honorable S[r] Robert Howard, *1660, collated with the edition of 1696 and* A Collection of Poems by Several Hands, *1693*
21 souls,] souls *93*   28 caught?] caught. *60 93 96*

Nor dare I such a doctrine here admit,
As would destroy the providence of wit.
'Tis your strong Genius then which does not feel
Those weights would make a weaker spirit reel:
To carry weight and run so lightly too
Is what alone your *Pegasus* can do.
Great *Hercules* himself could ne're do more
Than not to feel those Heav'ns and gods he bore.
Your easier Odes, which for delight were penn'd,
Yet our instruction make their second end,
We're both enrich'd and pleas'd, like them that woo
At once a Beauty and a Fortune too.
Of Morall Knowledge Poesie was Queen,
And still she might, had wanton wits not been;
Who like ill Guardians liv'd themselves at large,
And not content with that, debauch'd their charge:
Like some brave Captain, your successfull Pen
Restores the Exil'd to her Crown again;
And gives us hope, that having seen the days
When nothing flourish'd but Fanatique Bays,
All will at length in this opinion rest,
"A sober Prince's Government is best."
This is not all; your Art the way has found
To make improvement of the richest ground,
That soil which those immortall Lawrells bore,
That once the sacred *Maro*'s temples wore.
Elisa's griefs, are so exprest by you,
They are too eloquent to have been true.
Had she so spoke, *Æneas* had obey'd
What *Dido* rather then what *Jove* had said.
If funerall Rites can give a Ghost repose,
Your Muse so justly has discharged those,
Elisa's shade may now its wandring cease,
And claim a title to the fields of peace.
But if *Æneas* be oblig'd, no lesse
Your kindnesse great *Achilles* doth confesse,
Who dress'd by *Statius* in too bold a look,
Did ill become those Virgin's Robes he took.
To understand how much we owe to you,

58 wore.] wore *60 93 96* 64 those,] those. *60 93 96*

We must your Numbers with your Author's view;
Then we shall see his work was lamely rough,
Each figure stiffe as if design'd in buffe;
His colours laid so thick on every place,
As onely shew'd the paint, but hid the face:
But as in Perspective we Beauties see,
Which in the Glasse, not in the Picture be;
So here our sight obligeingly mistakes
That wealth which his your bounty onely makes.
Thus vulgar dishes are by Cooks disguis'd,
More for their dressing than their substance priz'd.
Your curious *Notes so search into that Age,
When all was fable but the sacred Page,
That since in that dark night we needs must stray,
We are at least misled in pleasant way.
But what we most admire, your Verse no lesse
The Prophet than the Poet doth confesse.
Ere our weak eyes discern'd the doubtfull streak
Of light, you saw great *Charls* his morning break.
So skilfull Sea-men ken the Land from far,
Which shews like mists to the dul Passenger.
To *Charls* your Muse first pays her dutious love,
As still the Antients did begin from *Jove*.
With *Monck* you end, whose name preserv'd shall be,
As *Rome* recorded †*Rufus* memory,
Who thought it greater honor to obey
His Countrey's interest than the world to sway.
But to write worthy things of worthy men
Is the peculiar talent of your Pen:
Yet let me take your Mantle up, and I
Will venture in your right to prophesy.

"This Work by merit first of Fame secure
"Is likewise happy in its Geniture:
"For since 'tis born when *Charls* ascends the Throne,
"It shares at once his Fortune and its own."

* *Annotations on* Statius

† Hîc situs est *Rufus* qui pulso vindice quondam, Imperium asseruit non sibi sed Patriæ

Astræa Redux
A POEM On the Happy Restoration and Return Of His Sacred Majesty Charles the Second

Iam Redit & Virgo, Redeunt Saturnia Regna. Virgil.

Now with a general Peace the World was blest,
While Ours, a World divided from the rest,
A dreadful Quiet felt, and worser farre
Then Armes, a sullen Intervall of Warre:
Thus when black Clouds draw down the lab'ring Skies,
Ere yet abroad the winged Thunder flyes
An horrid Stillness first invades the ear,
And in that silence Wee the Tempest fear.
Th' Ambitious *Swede* like restless Billowes tost,
On this hand gaining what on that he lost,
Though in his life he Blood and Ruine breath'd,
To his now guideless Kingdome Peace bequeath'd.
And Heaven that seem'd regardless of our Fate,
For *France* and *Spain* did Miracles create,
Such mortal Quarrels to compose in Peace
As Nature bred and Int'rest did encrease.
We sigh'd to hear the fair *Iberian* Bride
Must grow a Lilie to the Lilies side,
While Our cross Stars deny'd us *Charles* his Bed
Whom Our first Flames and Virgin Love did wed.
For his long absence Church and State did groan;
Madness the Pulpit, Faction seiz'd the Throne:
Experienc'd Age in deep despair was lost
To see the Rebel thrive, the Loyal crost:
Youth that with Joys had unacquainted been
Envy'd gray hairs that once good days had seen:
We thought our Sires, not with their own content,
Had ere we came to age our Portion spent.
Nor could our Nobles hope their bold Attempt

Astræa Redux. Text from the first edition of 1660, collated with the second edition, 1688
11 breath'd, *88*: breath'd *60*

Who ruin'd Crowns would Coronets exempt:
For when by their designing Leaders taught
To strike at Pow'r which for themselves they sought,
The Vulgar gull'd into Rebellion, arm'd,
Their blood to action by the Prize was warm'd.
The Sacred Purple then and Scarlet Gown
Like sanguine Dye to Elephants was shown.
Thus when the bold *Typhoeus* scal'd the Sky,
And forc'd great *Jove* from his own Heaven to fly,
(What King, what Crown from Treasons reach is free,
If *Jove* and *Heaven* can violated be?)
The lesser Gods that shar'd his prosp'rous State
All suffer'd in the Exil'd Thund'rers Fate.
The Rabble now such Freedom did enjoy,
As Winds at Sea that use it to destroy:
Blind as the *Cyclops*, and as wild as he,
They own'd a lawless salvage Libertie,
Like that our painted Ancestours so priz'd
Ere Empires Arts their Breasts had Civiliz'd.
How Great were then Our *Charles* his Woes, who thus
Was forc'd to suffer for Himself and us!
He toss'd by Fate, and hurried up and down,
Heir to his Fathers Sorrows, with his Crown,
Could tast no sweets of youths desired Age,
But found his life too true a Pilgrimage.
Unconquer'd yet in that forlorne Estate
His Manly Courage overcame his Fate.
His wounds he took like *Romans* on his brest,
Which by his Vertue were with Lawrells drest.
As Souls reach Heav'n while yet in Bodies pent,
So did he live above his Banishment.
That Sun which we beheld with cous'ned eyes
Within the water, mov'd along the skies.
How easie 'tis when Destiny proves kind
With full spread Sails to run before the wind,
But those that 'gainst stiff gales laveering go
Must be at once resolv'd and skilful too.
He would not like soft *Otho* hope prevent
But stay'd and suffer'd Fortune to repent.
These Vertues *Galba* in a stranger sought;

And *Piso* to Adopted Empire brought.
How shall I then my doubtful thoughts express
That must his suff'rings both regret and bless!
For when his early Valour Heav'n had crost,
And all at *Worc'ster* but the honour lost,
Forc'd into exile from his rightful Throne
He made all Countries where he came his own.
And viewing Monarchs secret Arts of sway
A Royal Factor for their Kingdomes lay.
Thus banish'd *David* spent abroad his time,
When to be Gods Anointed was his Crime;
And when restor'd made his proud Neighbours rue
Those choice Remarques he from his Travels drew:
Nor is he onely by afflictions shown
To conquer others Realms but rule his own:
Recov'ring hardly what he lost before,
His right indears it much, his purchase more.
Inur'd to suffer ere he came to raigne
No rash procedure will his actions stain.
To bus'ness ripened by digestive thought
His future rule is into Method brought:
As they who first Proportion understand
With easie Practice reach a Masters hand.
Well might the Ancient Poets then confer
On Night the honour'd name of *Counseller*,
Since struck with rayes of prosp'rous fortune blind
We light alone in dark afflictions find.
In such adversities to Scepters train'd
The name of *Great* his famous Grandsire gain'd:
Who yet a King alone in Name and Right,
With hunger, cold and angry *Jove* did fight;
Shock'd by a Covenanting Leagues vast Pow'rs
As holy and as Catholique as ours:
Till Fortunes fruitless spight had made it known
Her blowes not shook but riveted his Throne.
  Some lazy Ages lost in sleep and ease
No action leave to busie Chronicles;
Such whose supine felicity but makes

79 time, *88*: time. *60* 80 Crime;] Crime *60*: Crime, *88* 82 drew: *88*: drew, *60* 85 before, *88*: before *60*

In story *Chasmes*, in *Epoche's* mistakes;
O're whom *Time* gently shakes his wings of Down
Till with his silent sickle they are mown:
Such is not *Charles* his too too active age,
Which govern'd by the wild distemper'd rage
Of some black Star infecting all the Skies,
Made him at his own cost like *Adam* wise.
Tremble ye Nations who secure before
Laught at those Armes that 'gainst our selves we bore;
Rous'd by the lash of his own stubborn tail
Our Lyon now will forraign Foes assail.
With *Alga* who the sacred altar strowes?
To all the Sea-Gods *Charles* an Off'ring owes:
A Bull to thee *Portunus* shall be slain,
A Lamb to you the Tempests of the Main:
For those loud stormes that did against him rore
Have cast his shipwrack'd Vessel on the shore.
Yet as wise Artists mix their colours so
That by degrees they from each other go,
Black steals unheeded from the neighb'ring white
Without offending the well cous'ned sight:
So on us stole our blessed change; while we
Th' effect did feel but scarce the manner see.
Frosts that constrain the ground, and birth deny
To flow'rs, that in its womb expecting lye,
Do seldom their usurping Pow'r withdraw,
But raging floods pursue their hasty thaw:
Our thaw was mild, the cold not chas'd away
But lost in kindly heat of lengthned day.
Heav'n would no bargain for its blessings drive
But what we could not pay for, freely give.
The Prince of Peace would like himself confer
A gift unhop'd without the price of war.
Yet as he knew his blessings worth, took care
That we should know it by repeated pray'r;
Which storm'd the skies and ravish'd *Charles* from thence
As Heav'n it self is took by violence.
Booth's forward Valour only serv'd to show
He durst that duty pay we all did owe:

121 slain, *88*: slain *60*

Th' Attempt was fair; but Heav'ns prefixed hour
Not come; so like the watchful travellour
That by the Moons mistaken light did rise,
Lay down again, and clos'd his weary eyes.
'Twas *MONCK* whom Providence design'd to loose
Those real bonds false freedom did impose.
The blessed Saints that watch'd this turning Scene
Did from their Stars with joyful wonder leane,
To see small clues draw vastest weights along,
Not in their bulk but in their order strong.
Thus Pencils can by one slight touch restore
Smiles to that changed face that wept before.
With ease such fond *Chymæra's* we pursue
As fancy frames for fancy to subdue,
But when our selves to action we betake
It shuns the Mint like gold that Chymists make:
How hard was then his task, at once to be
What in the body natural we see
Mans Architect distinctly did ordain
The charge of Muscles, Nerves, and of the Brain;
Through viewless Conduits Spirits to dispense,
The Springs of Motion from the Seat of Sense.
'Twas not the hasty product of a day,
But the well ripened fruit of wise delay.
He like a patient Angler, e're he strooke
Would let them play a while upon the hook.
Our healthful food the Stomach labours thus,
At first embracing what it strait doth crush.
Wise Leeches will not vain Receipts obtrude,
While growing pains pronounce the humours crude;
Deaf to complaints they wait upon the ill
Till some safe *Crisis* authorise their skill.
Nor could his Acts too close a vizard wear
To scape their eyes whom guilt had taught to fear,
And guard with caution that polluted nest
Whence Legion twice before was dispossest,
Once sacred house which when they enter'd in
They thought the place could sanctifie a sin;

151 loose *60 (some copies) 88*: lose *60 (some copies)* 166 Brain; *60 (some copies)*: Brain, *60 (some copies) 88* 182 dispossest,] dispossest. *60 88*

Like those that vainly hop'd kind Heav'n would wink
While to excess on Martyrs tombs they drink.
And as devouter *Turks* first warn their souls
To part, before they tast forbidden bowls,
So these when their black crimes they went about
First timely charm'd their useless conscience out.
Religions name against it self was made;
The shadow serv'd the substance to invade:
Like Zealous Missions they did care pretend
Of souls in shew, but made the Gold their end.
Th' incensed Pow'rs beheld with scorn from high
An Heaven so far distant from the sky,
Which durst with horses hoofs that beat the ground
And Martial brass bely the thunders sound.
'Twas hence at length just Vengeance thought it fit
To speed their ruine by their impious wit.
Thus *Sforza* curs'd with a too fertile brain
Lost by his wiles the Pow'r his wit did gain.
Henceforth their Fogue must spend at lesser rate
Then in its flames to wrap a Nations Fate.
Suffer'd to live, they are like *Helots* set
A vertuous shame within us to beget.
For by example most we sinn'd before,
And glass-like, clearness mixt with frailty bore.
But since reform'd by what we did amiss,
We by our suff'rings learn to prize our bliss:
Like early Lovers whose unpractis'd hearts
Were long the May-game of malicious arts,
When once they find their Jealousies were vain
With double heat renew their fires again.
'Twas this produc'd the joy that hurried o're
Such swarmes of *English* to the Neighb'ring shore,
To fetch that prize, by which *Batavia* made
So rich amends for our impoverish'd Trade.
Oh had you seen from *Schevelines* barren shore
(Crowded with troops, and barren now no more,)
Afflicted *Holland* to his farewell bring

195 beheld *60 (some copies) 88*: behold *60 (some copies)* 208 And glass-like,] And glass-like *60 (some copies) 88*: Like glass we *60 (some copies)* 210 bliss: *60 (some copies)*: bliss. *60 (some copies) 88*

True Sorrow, *Holland* to regret a King;
While waiting him his Royal Fleet did ride
And willing winds to their low'rd sayles deny'd.
The wavering Streamers, Flags, and Standart out,
The merry Seamens rude but chearful shout,
And last the Cannons voice that shook the skies
And, as it fares in sudden Extasies
At once bereft us both of ears and eyes.
The *Naseby* now no longer *Englands* shame
But better to be lost in *Charles* his name
(Like some unequal Bride in nobler sheets)
Receives her Lord: the joyful *London* meets
The Princely *York*, himself alone a freight;
The *Swift-sure* groans beneath Great *Gloc'sters* weight.
Secure as when the *Halcyon* breeds, with these
He that was born to drown might cross the Seas.
Heav'n could not own a Providence and take
The wealth three Nations ventur'd at a stake.
The same indulgence *Charles* his Voyage bless'd
Which in his right had Miracles confess'd.
The winds that never Moderation knew
Afraid to blow too much, too faintly blew;
Or out of breath with joy could not enlarge
Their straightned lungs, or conscious of their Charge.
The British *Amphitryte* smooth and clear
In richer Azure never did appear;
Proud her returning Prince to entertain
With the submitted Fasces of the Main.

And welcome now (*Great Monarch*) to your own;
Behold th' approaching cliffes of *Albion*;
It is no longer Motion cheats your view,
As you meet it, the Land approacheth you.
The Land returns, and in the white it wears
The marks of penitence and sorrow bears.
But you, whose goodness your discent doth show,
Your Heav'nly Parentage and earthly too;
By that same mildness which your Fathers Crown
Before did ravish, shall secure your own.

225 out, *88*: out *60*

Not ty'd to rules of Policy, you find
Revenge less sweet then a forgiving mind.
Thus when th' Almighty would to *Moses* give
A sight of all he could behold and live;
A voice before his entry did proclaim
Long-Suff'ring, *Goodness*, *Mercy* in his Name.
Your Pow'r to Justice doth submit your Cause,
Your Goodness only is above the Laws;
Whose rigid letter while pronounc'd by you
Is softer made. So winds that tempests brew
When through *Arabian* Groves they take their flight
Made wanton with rich Odours, lose their spight.
And as those Lees that trouble it, refine
The agitated Soul of Generous Wine,
So tears of joy for your returning spilt,
Work out and expiate our former guilt.
Methinks I see those Crowds on *Dovers* Strand
Who in their hast to welcome you to Land
Choak'd up the Beach with their still growing store,
And made a wilder Torrent on the shore.
While spurr'd with eager thoughts of past delight
Those who had seen you, court a second sight;
Preventing still your steps, and making hast
To meet you often where so e're you past.
How shall I speak of that triumphant Day
When you renew'd the expiring Pomp of *May*!
(A Month that owns an Intrest in your Name:
You and the Flow'rs are its peculiar Claim.)
That Star that at your Birth shone out so bright
It stain'd the duller Suns Meridian light,
Did once again its potent Fires renew
Guiding our eyes to find and worship you.
   And now times whiter Series is begun
Which in soft Centuries shall smoothly run;
Those Clouds that overcast your Morne shall fly
Dispell'd to farthest corners of the sky.
Our Nation with united Int'rest blest
Not now content to poize, shall sway the rest.
Abroad your Empire shall no Limits know,
But like the Sea in boundless Circles flow.

Your much lov'd Fleet shall with a wide Command
Besiege the petty Monarchs of the Land:
And as Old Time his Off-spring swallow'd down
Our Ocean in its depths all Seas shall drown.
Their wealthy Trade from Pyrates Rapine free
Our Merchants shall no more Advent'rers be:
Nor in the farthest East those Dangers fear
Which humble *Holland* must dissemble here.
Spain to your Gift alone her *Indies* owes;
For what the Pow'rful takes not he bestowes.
And *France* that did an Exiles presence fear
May justly apprehend you still too near.
At home the hateful names of Parties cease
And factious Souls are weary'd into peace.
The discontented now are only they
Whose Crimes before did your Just Cause betray:
Of those your Edicts some reclaim from sins,
But most your Life and Blest Example wins.
Oh happy Prince whom Heav'n hath taught the way
By paying Vowes, to have more Vowes to pay!
Oh Happy Age! Oh times like those alone
By Fate reserv'd for Great *Augustus* Throne!
When the joint growth of Armes and Arts foreshew
The World a Monarch, and that Monarch *You*.

TO HIS SACRED MAIESTY, A PANEGYRICK ON HIS CORONATION

IN that wild Deluge where the World was drownd,
When life and sin one common tombe had found,
The first small prospect of a rising hill
With various notes of Joy the Ark did fill:
Yet when that flood in its own depths was drownd
It left behind it false and slipp'ry ground;
And the more solemn pomp was still deferr'd
Till new-born Nature in fresh looks appear'd:

To His Sacred Maiesty. Text from the first edition of 1661, collated with the editions of 1662 and 1688. See Commentary

Thus (Royall Sir) to see you landed here
Was cause enough of triumph for a year:
Nor would your care those glorious Joyes repeat
Till they at once might be secure and great:
Till your kind beams by their continu'd stay
Had warm'd the ground, and call'd the Damps away.
Such vapours while your pow'rfull influence dryes
Then soonest vanish when they highest rise.
Had greater hast these sacred rights prepar'd
Some guilty Moneths had in your triumphs shar'd:
But this untainted year is all your own,
Your glory's may without our crimes be shown.
We had not yet exhausted all our store
When you refresh'd our joyes by adding more:
As Heav'n of old dispenc'd Cælestial dew,
You give us Manna and still give us new.
   Now our sad ruines are remov'd from sight,
The Season too comes fraught with new delight;
Time seems not now beneath his years to stoop
Nor do his wings with sickly feathers droop:
Soft western winds waft ore the gaudy spring
And opend Scenes of flow'rs and blossoms bring
To grace this happy day, while you appear
Not King of us alone but of the year.
All eyes you draw, and with the eyes the heart,
Of your own pomp your self the greatest part:
Loud shouts the Nations happiness proclaim
And Heav'n this day is feasted with your name.
Your Cavalcade the fair Spectators view
From their high standings, yet look up to you.
From your brave train each singles out a prey,
And longs to date a Conquest from your day.
Now charg'd with blessings while you seek repose,
Officious slumbers hast your eyes to close:
And glorious dreams stand ready to restore
The pleasing shapes of all you saw before.
Next to the sacred Temple you are led,
Where waites a Crown for your more sacred Head:
How justly from the Church that Crown is due,

32 Not . . . alone *61* (*some copies*) *88*: Not only King of us *61* (*some copies*) *62*

Preserv'd from ruine and restor'd by you!
The gratefull quire their harmony employ
Not to make greater but more solemn joy.
Wrapt soft and warm your Name is sent on high,
As flames do on the wings of Incense fly:
Musique her self is lost, in vain she brings
Her choisest notes to praise the best of Kings:
Her melting strains in you a tombe have found,
And lye like Bees in their own sweetnesse drown'd.
He that brought peace and discord could attone,
His Name is Musick of it self alone.
Now while the sacred Oyl annoints your head,
And fragrant scents, begun from you, are spread
Through the large Dome, the peoples joyful sound
Sent back, is still preserv'd in hallow'd ground:
Which in one blessing mixt descends on you,
As heightned spirits fall in richer dew.
Not that our wishes do increase your store,
Full of your self you can admit no more:
We add not to your glory, but employ
Our time like Angels in expressing joy.
Nor is it duty or our hopes alone
Create that joy, but full fruition;
We know those blessings which we must possesse,
And judge of future by past happinesse.
No promise can oblige a Prince so much
Still to be good as long to have been such.
A noble Emulation heats your breast,
And your own fame now robbs you of your rest:
Good actions still must be maintain'd with good,
As bodies nourish'd with resembling food.
You have already quench'd seditions brand;
And zeal (which burnt it) only warms the Land.
The jealous Sects that dare not trust their cause
So farre from their own will as to the Laws,
You for their Umpire and their Synod take,
And their appeal alone to *Cæsar* make.
Kind Heav'n so rare a temper did provide
That guilt repenting might in it confide.

78 *Text ends in 62 (some copies)*

Among our crimes oblivion may be set,
But 'tis our Kings perfection to forget.
Virtues unknown to these rough Northern climes
From milder heav'ns you bring, without their crimes:
Your calmnesse does no after storms provide,
Nor seeming patience mortal anger hide.
When Empire first from families did spring,
Then every Father govern'd as a King;
But you that are a Soveraign Prince, allay
Imperial pow'r with your paternal sway.
From those great cares when ease your soul unbends
Your pleasures are design'd to noble ends:
Born to command the Mistress of the Seas,
Your thoughts themselves in that blue Empire please.
Hither in Summer ev'nings you repair
To take the fraischeur of the purer air:
Vndaunted here you ride when Winter raves,
With *Cæsars* heart that rose above the waves.
More I could sing but fear my Numbers stayes;
No Loyal Subject dares that courage praise.
In stately Frigats most delight you find,
Where well-drawn Battels fire your martial mind.
What to your cares we owe is learnt from hence,
When ev'n your pleasures serve for our defence.
Beyond your Court flows in th' admitted tide,
Where in new depths the wondring fishes glide:
Here in a Royal bed the waters sleep,
When tir'd at Sea within this bay they creep.
Here the mistrustfull foul no harm suspects,
So safe are all things which our King protects.
From your lov'd *Thames* a blessing yet is due,
Second alone to that it brought in you;
A Queen, from whose chast womb, ordain'd by Fate,
The souls of Kings unborn for bodies wait.
It was your Love before made discord cease:
Your love is destin'd to your Countries peace.
Both *Indies* (Rivalls in your bed) provide
With Gold or Jewels to adorn your Bride.
This to a mighty King presents rich ore,
While that with Incense does a God implore.

Two Kingdomes wait your doom, and as you choose,
This must receive a Crown, or that must loose.
Thus from your Royal Oke, like *Jove*'s of old,
Are answers sought, and destinies fore-told:
Propitious Oracles are beg'd with vows,
And Crowns that grow upon the sacred boughs.
Your Subjects, while you weigh the Nations fate,
Suspend to both their doubtfull love or hate:
Choose only, (Sir,) that so they may possesse
With their own peace their Childrens happinesse.

TO MY LORD CHANCELLOR
Presented on New-years-day

My Lord,

WHILE flattering crouds officiously appear
To give themselves, not you, an happy year;
And by the greatness of their Presents prove
How much they hope, but not how well they love;
The Muses (who your early courtship boast,
Though now your flames are with their beauty lost)
Yet watch their time, that if you have forgot
They were your Mistresses, the World may not:
Decay'd by time and wars, they only prove
Their former beauty by your former love;
And now present, as antient Ladies do
That courted long at length are forc'd to woo.
For still they look on you with such kind eyes
As those that see the Churches Soveraign rise
From their own Order chose, in whose high State
They think themselves the second choice of Fate.
When our Great Monarch into Exile went
Wit and Religion suffer'd banishment:
Thus once when *Troy* was wrapt in fire and smoak
The helpless Gods their burning shrines forsook;
They with the vanquisht Prince and party go,
And leave their Temples empty to the fo:

To My Lord Chancellor. Text from the first edition, 1662, collated with the edition of 1688

At length the Muses stand restor'd again
To that great charge which Nature did ordain;
And their lov'd Druyds seem reviv'd by Fate
While you dispence the Laws and guide the State.
The Nations soul (our Monarch) does dispence
Through you to us his vital influence;
You are the Chanel where those spirits flow,
And work them higher as to us they go.
  In open prospect nothing bounds our eye
Until the Earth seems joyn'd unto the Sky:
So in this Hemisphær our utmost view
Is only bounded by our King and you:
Our sight is limited where you are joyn'd
And beyond that no farther Heav'n can find.
So well your Vertues do with his agree
That though your Orbs of different greatness be,
Yet both are for each others use dispos'd,
His to inclose, and yours to be inclos'd.
Nor could another in your room have been
Except an Emptinesse had come between.
Well may he then to you his Cares impart,
And share his burden where he shares his heart.
In you his sleep still wakes; his pleasures find
Their share of bus'nesse in your lab'ring mind:
So when the weary Sun his place resigns
He leaves his light and by reflection shines.
  Justice that sits and frowns where publick Laws
Exclude soft mercy from a private cause,
In your Tribunal most her self does please;
There only smiles because she lives at ease;
And like young *David* finds her strength the more
When disincumberd from those arms she wore:
Heav'n would your Royal Master should exceed
Most in that Vertue which we most did need,
And his mild Father (who too late did find
All mercy vain but what with pow'r was joyn'd,)
His fatal goodnesse left to fitter times,
Not to increase but to absolve our Crimes:
But when the Heir of this vast treasure knew

29 flow, *88*: flow *62*   43 impart, *88*: impart *62*

How large a Legacy was left to you,
(Too great for any Subject to retain)
He wisely ti'd it to the Crown again:
Yet passing through your hands it gathers more,
As streams through Mines bear tincture of their Ore.
While Emp'rique politicians use deceipt,
Hide what they give, and cure but by a cheat;
You boldly show that skill which they pretend,
And work by means as noble as your end:
Which, should you veil, we might unwind the clue
As men do Nature, till we came to you.
And as the *Indies* were not found before
Those rich perfumes, which from the happy shore
The winds upon their balmy wings convay'd,
Whose guilty sweetnesse first their World betray'd;
So by your Counsels we are brought to view
A rich and undiscover'd World in you.
By you our Monarch does that fame assure
Which Kings must have or cannot live secure:
For prosp'rous Princes gain their Subjects heart,
Who love that praise in which themselves have part:
By you he fits those Subjects to obey,
As Heavens Eternal Monarch does convey
His pow'r unseen, and man to his designs,
By his bright Ministers the Stars, inclines.
  Our setting Sun from his declining seat
Shot beams of kindnesse on you, not of heat:
And when his love was bounded in a few,
That were unhappy that they might be true;
Made you the favo'rite of his last sad times,
That is a suff'rer in his Subjects crimes:
Thus those first favours you receiv'd were sent
Like Heav'ns rewards, in earthly punishment.
Yet Fortune conscious of your destiny
Ev'n then took care to lay you softly by:
And wrapt your fate among her precious things,
Kept fresh to be unfolded with your Kings.
Shown all at once you dazled so our eyes,
As new-born *Pallas* did the Gods surprise;

74 perfumes, *88*: perfumes *62*   81 their *88*: the *62*

When springing forth from *Jove*'s new-closing wound
She struck the Warlick Spear into the ground;
Which sprouting leaves did suddenly inclose,
And peaceful Olives shaded as they rose.
How strangely active are the arts of Peace,
Whose restlesse motions lesse than Wars do cease!
Peace is not freed from labour but from noise;
And War more force but not more pains employs;
Such is the mighty swiftnesse of your mind
That (like the earth's) it leaves our sence behind;
While you so smoothly turn and roul our Sphear,
That rapid motion does but rest appear.
For as in Natures swiftnesse, with the throng
Of flying Orbs while ours is born along,
All seems at rest to the deluded eye:
(Mov'd by the Soul of the same harmony)
So carry'd on by your unwearied care
We rest in Peace and yet in motion share.
Let Envy then those Crimes within you see
From which the Happy never must be free;
(Envy that does with misery reside,
The joy and the revenge of ruin'd Pride;)
Think it not hard if at so cheap a rate
You can secure the constancy of Fate,
Whose kindnesse sent, what does their malice seem,
By lesser ills the greater to redeem.
Nor can we this weak show'r a tempest call
But drops of heat that in the Sun-shine fall.
You have already weary'd Fortune so
She can not farther be your friend or fo;
But sits all breathlesse, and admires to feel
A Fate so weighty that it stops her wheel.
In all things else above our humble fate
Your equal mind yet swells not into state,
But like some mountain in those happy Isles
Where in perpetual Spring young Nature smiles,
Your greatnesse shows: no horrour to afright
But Trees for shade, and Flow'rs to court the sight;
Sometimes the Hill submits itself a while
In small descents, which do its height beguile;

And sometimes mounts, but so as billows play
Whose rise not hinders but makes short our way.
Your brow which does no fear of thunder know
Sees rouling tempests vainly beat below;
And (like *Olympus* top,) th' impression wears
Of Love and Friendship writ in former years.
Yet unimpair'd with labours or with time
Your age but seems to a new youth to climb.
Thus Heav'nly bodies do our time beget;
And measure Change, but share no part of it.
And still it shall without a weight increase,
Like this New-year, whose motions never cease;
For since the glorious Course you have begun
Is led by *CHARLS*, as that is by the Sun,
It must both weightlesse and immortal prove,
Because the Center of it is above.

To my Honour'd Friend, Dr Charleton, *on his learned and useful Works; and more particularly this of* STONE-HENG, *by him Restored to the true Founders*

THE longest Tyranny that ever sway'd,
Was that wherein our Ancestors betray'd
Their free-born *Reason* to the *Stagirite*,
And made his Torch their universal Light.
So *Truth*, while onely one suppli'd the State,
Grew scarce, and dear, and yet sophisticate,
Until 'twas bought, like Emp'rique Wares, or Charms,
Hard words seal'd up with *Aristotle*'s Armes.
Columbus was the first that shook his Throne;
And found a *Temp'rate* in a *Torrid* Zone:
The fevrish aire fann'd by a cooling breez,
The fruitful Vales set round with shady Trees;

To my Honour'd Friend, Dr Charleton. Text from Charleton's Chorea Gigantum, *1663, collated with* Poetical Miscellanies: The Fifth Part, *1704*

Heading. and more particularly this] But more particularly his Treatise *04* 6 sophisticate,] sophisticate. *63 04* 7 Until 'twas] 'Till it was *04*

And guiltless *Men*, who danc'd away their time,
Fresh as their *Groves*, and *Happy* as their *Clime*.
Had we still paid that homage to a *Name*,
Which onely *God* and *Nature* justly claim;
The *Western* Seas had been our utmost bound,
Where *Poets* still might dream the *Sun* was drown'd:
And all the *Starrs*, that shine in *Southern* Skies,
Had been admir'd by none but *Salvage* Eyes.
  Among th' *Assertors* of free Reason's claim,
Th' *English* are not the least in Worth, or Fame.
The World to *Bacon* does not onely owe
Its *present* Knowledge, but its *future* too.
Gilbert shall live, till *Load-stones* cease to draw,
Or *British* Fleets the boundless Ocean awe.
And noble *Boyle*, not less in *Nature* seen,
Than his great *Brother* read in *States* and *Men*.
The *Circling* streams, once thought but pools, of blood
(Whether Life's fewel, or the Bodie's food)
From dark Oblivion *Harvey*'s name shall save;
While *Ent* keeps all the honour that he gave.
Nor are *You*, Learned Friend, the least renown'd;
Whose Fame, not circumscrib'd with *English* ground,
Flies like the nimble journeys of the Light;
And is, like that, unspent too in its flight.
What ever *Truths* have been, by *Art*, or *Chance*,
Redeem'd from *Error*, or from *Ignorance*,
Thin in their *Authors*, (like rich veins of Ore)
Your Works unite, and still discover more.
Such is the healing virtue of Your Pen,
To perfect Cures on *Books*, as well as *Men*.
Nor is This Work the least: You well may give
To *Men* new vigour, who make *Stones* to live.
Through You, the *DANES* (their short Dominion lost)
A longer Conquest than the *Saxons* boast.
STONE-HENG, once thought a *Temple*, You have found
A *Throne*, where Kings, our Earthly Gods, were Crown'd,
Where by their wondring Subjects They were seen,

13 who *63 (some copies) 04*: that *63 (some copies)* 22 Th' *English* are not the least *63 (some copies)*: The *English* are not least *63 (some copies)*: Our Nation's not the least *04* 39 of *63 (some copies) 04*: in *63 (some copies)* 48 Crown'd,] Crown'd. *63 04* 49 wondring] wandring *04*

Joy'd with their Stature, and their Princely meen.
Our *Soveraign* here above the rest might stand;
And here be chose again to rule the Land.
  These Ruines sheltred once *His* Sacred Head,
Then when from *Wor'sters* fatal Field *He* fled;
Watch'd by the Genius of this Royal place,
And mighty Visions of the *Danish* Race.
His *Refuge* then was for a *Temple* shown:
But, *He* Restor'd, 'tis now become a *Throne*.

PROLOGUE To the RIVAL-LADIES

'TIS much Desir'd, you Judges of the Town
Would pass a Vote to put all *Prologues* down;
For who can show me, since they first were Writ,
They e'r Converted one hard-hearted Wit?
Yet the World 's mended well; in former Days
Good *Prologues* were as scarce, as now good *Plays*.
For the reforming Poets of our Age,
In this first Charge, spend their Poetique rage:
Expect no more when once the *Prologue*'s done;
The Wit is ended e'r the *Play* 's begun.
You now have Habits, Dances, Scenes, and Rhymes;
High Language often; I, and Sense, sometimes:
As for a clear Contrivance doubt it not;
They blow out Candles to give Light to th' Plot.
And for Surprize, two Bloody-minded Men
Fight till they Dye, then rise and Dance agen:
Such deep Intrigues you'r welcome to this Day:
But blame your Selves, not him who Writ the Play;
Though his Plot 's Dull, as can be well desir'd,
Wit stiff as any you have e'r admir'd:
He 's bound to please, not to Write well; and knows
There is a mode in Plays as well as Cloaths:
Therefore kind Judges——

50 Joy'd with *63 (some copies) 04*: Chose by *63 (some copies)*   52 rule *63 (some copies) 04*: sway *63 (some copies)*   54 Then . . . fled] When *He* from *Wor'sters* fatal Battle fled *04*   55 Royal *63 (some copies) 04*: Kingly *63 (some copies)*
Prologue. Text from The Rival Ladies. A Tragi-Comedy, *1664, collated with the editions of 1669, 1675, 1693*

A SECOND PROLOGUE
Enters.

2.——Hold; Would you admit
For Judges all you see within the Pit?
1. Whom would he then Except, or on what Score?
2. All, who (like him) have Writ ill Plays before:
For they, like Thieves condemn'd, are Hang-men made,
To execute the Members of their Trade.
All that are Writing now he would disown;
But then he must Except, ev'n all the Town.
All Chol'rique, losing Gamesters, who in spight
Will Damn to Day, because they lost last Night.
All Servants whom their Mistress's scorn upbraids;
All Maudlin Lovers, and all Slighted Maids:
All who are out of Humour, or Severe;
All, that want Wit, or hope to find it here.

PROLOGUE, EPILOGUE and SONGS from *THE INDIAN-QUEEN, A Tragedy*

PROLOGUE

As the Musick plays a soft Air, the Curtain rises softly, and discovers an Indian *Boy and Girl sleeping under two Plantain-Trees; and when the Curtain is almost up, the Musick turns into a Tune expressing an Alarm, at which the Boy wakes and speaks.*

Boy. WAKE, wake, *Quevira*; our soft Rest must cease,
And fly together with our Country's Peace;
No more must we sleep under Plantain shade,
Which neither Heat could pierce, nor Cold invade;

Prologue, Epilogue and Songs. Text from Four New Plays . . . Written by the Honourable Sir Robert Howard, *1665, collated with* Five New Plays, *1692. See Commentary*

Where bounteous Nature never feels decay,
And op'ning Buds drive falling Fruits away.
Que. Why should men quarrel here, where all possess
As much as they can hope for by success?
None can have most, where Nature is so kind
As to exceed Man's Use, though not his Mind.
Boy. By ancient Prophesies we have been told
Our World shall be subdu'd by one more old;
And see that World already's hither come.
Que. If these be they, we welcom then our Doom.
Their Looks are such, that Mercy flows from thence,
More gentle than our Native Innocence.
Boy. Why should we then fear these are Enemies,
That rather seem to us like Deities?
Que. By their protection let us beg to live;
They came not here to Conquer, but Forgive.
If so, your Goodness may your Pow'r express;
And we shall judg both best by our success.

EPILOGUE TO THE INDIAN QUEEN

Spoken by Montezuma

YOU see what Shifts we are inforc'd to try
To help out Wit with some Variety;
Shows may be found that never yet were seen,
'Tis hard to finde such Wit as ne're has been:
You have seen all that this old World cou'd do,
We therefore try the fortune of the new,
And hope it is below your aim to hit
At untaught Nature with your practic'd Wit:
Our naked Indians then, when Wits appear,
Wou'd as soon chuse to have the Spaniards here:
'Tis true, y'have marks enough, the Plot, the Show,
The Poets Scenes, nay, more the Painters too:
If all this fail, considering the cost,
'Tis a true Voyage to the Indies lost:
But if you smile on all, then these designs,
Like the imperfect Treasure of our Mindes,

'Twill pass for currant wheresoe're they go,
When to your bounteous hands their stamps they owe.

SONGS

I

Ism. YOU twice Ten Hundred Deities,
To whom we daily Sacrifice;
You Powers that dwell with Fate below,
And see what men are doom'd to do;
Where Elements in discord dwell;
Thou God of Sleep arise and tell
Great *Zempoalla* what strange Fate
Must on her dismal Vision wait.

By the croaking of the Toad,
In their Caves that make aboad,
Earthy *Dun* that pants for breath,
With her swell'd sides full of death;
By the Crested Adders Pride
That along the Clifts do glide;
By thy visage fierce and black;
By the Deaths-head on thy Back;
By the twisted Serpents plac'd
For a Girdle round thy Waste.
By the Hearts of Gold that deck
Thy Brest, thy Shoulders, and thy Neck:
From thy sleepy Mansion rise,
And open thy unwilling Eyes,
While bubling Springs their Musick keep,
That use to lull thee in thy sleep.

II

SONG is suppos'd sung by Aerial-Spirits

POOR Mortals that are clog'd with Earth below
Sink under Love and Care,
While we that dwell in Air
Such heavy Passions never know.

Why then shou'd Mortals be
Unwilling to be free
From Blood, that sullen Cloud,
Which shining Souls does shroud?
Then they'l shew bright,
And like us light,
When leaving Bodies with their Care,
They slide to us and Air.

III

SONG

YOU to whom Victory we owe,
Whose glories rise
By sacrifice,
And from our fates below;
Never did yet your Altars shine
Feasted with Blood so nere divine;
Princes to whom we bow,
As they to you,
These you can ravish from a throne,
And by their loss of power declare your own.

PROLOGUE, EPILOGUE and SONGS from *THE INDIAN EMPEROUR*

PROLOGUE

ALMIGHTY Critiques! whom our *Indians* here
Worship, just as they do the Devil, for fear.
In reverence to your pow'r I come this day
To give you timely warning of our Play.

Songs. III. 9 These] Thus *92*
Prologue, Epilogue and Songs. Text from The Indian Emperour, or, The Conquest of Mexico by the Spaniards, *1667, collated with the editions of 1668, 1670, 1681, 1686, 1692, 1694, 1696*

The Scenes are old, the Habits are the same,
We wore last year, before the *Spaniards* came.
Now if you stay, the blood that shall be shed
From this poor Play, be all upon your head.
We neither promise you one Dance, or Show,
Then Plot and Language they are wanting too:
But you, kind Wits, will those light faults excuse:
Those are the common frailties of the Muse;
Which who observes he buyes his place too dear:
For 'tis your business to be couz'ned here.
These wretched spies of wit must then confess
They take more pains to please themselves the less.
Grant us such Judges, *Phœbus* we request,
As still mistake themselves into a jest;
Such easie Judges, that our Poet may
Himself admire the fortune of his Play.
And arrogantly, as his fellows do,
Think he writes well, because he pleases you.
This he conceives not hard to bring about
If all of you would join to help him out.
Would each man take but what he understands,
And leave the rest upon the Poets hands.

EPILOGUE

By a Mercury

To all and singular in this full meeting,
Ladies and Gallants, *Phœbus* sends me greeting.
To all his Sons by what e're Title known,
Whether of Court, of Coffee-house, or Town;
From his most mighty Sons, whose confidence
Is plac'd in lofty sound, and humble sence,
Ev'n to his little Infants of the Time
Who Write new Songs, and trust in Tune and Rhyme.

Prologue. Additional after l. 6 in 67 only:
Our Prologue, th'old-cast too—
For to observe the new it should at least
Be spoke, by some ingenious Bird or Beast.
See Commentary
Epilogue. 2 me] you *92 94 96* 8 Who *68–96*: That *67*

Be't known that *Phœbus* (being daily griev'd
To see good Plays condemn'd, and bad receiv'd,)
Ordains your judgement upon every Cause,
Henceforth be limited by wholesome Laws.
He first thinks fit no Sonnettier advance
His censure, farther then the Song or Dance.
Your Wit Burlesque may one step higher climb,
And in his sphere may judge all Doggrel Rhyme:
All proves, and moves, and Loves, and Honours too:
All that appears high sence, and scarce is low.
As for the Coffee-wits he says not much,
Their proper bus'ness is to Damn the *Dutch*:
For the great *Dons* of Wit—
Phœbus gives them full priviledge alone
To Damn all others, and cry up their own.
Last, for the Ladies, 'tis *Apollo*'s will,
They should have pow'r to save, but not to kill:
For Love and He long since have thought it fit,
Wit live by Beauty, Beauty raign by Wit.

SONGS

I

Kalib *ascends all in White in the shape of a Woman and Sings*

Kalib. I LOOK'D and saw within the Book of Fate,
Where many days did lower,
When lo one happy hour
Leapt up, and smil'd to save thy sinking State;
A day shall come when in thy power
Thy cruel Foes shall be;
Then shall thy Land be free,
And thou in Peace shalt Raign:
But take, O take that opportunity,
Which once refus'd will never come again.

Songs. I. 8 shalt *68–96*: shall *67*

II

A pleasant Grotto discover'd: in it a Fountain spouting; round about it Vasquez, Pizarro, *and other* Spaniards *lying carelessly un-arm'd, and by them many* Indian *Women, one of which Sings the following Song.*

SONG

AH fading joy, how quickly art thou past?
Yet we thy ruine haste:
As if the cares of Humane Life were few
We seek out new:
And follow Fate which would too fast pursue.

See how on every bough the Birds express
In their sweet notes their happiness.
They all enjoy, and nothing spare;
But on their Mother Nature lay their care:
Why then should Man, the Lord of all below
Such troubles chuse to know
As none of all his Subjects undergo?

Hark, hark, the Waters fall, fall, fall;
And with a Murmuring sound
Dash, dash, upon the ground,
To gentle slumbers call.

After the Song two Spaniards *arise and Dance a* Saraband *with* Castanieta'*s* . . .

Songs. II. 5 which would *68–96*: that does *67*

ANNUS MIRABILIS

The Year of WONDERS, 1666.

AN HISTORICAL POEM: CONTAINING

The Progress and various Successes of our Naval War with *Holland*, under the Conduct of His Highness Prince RUPERT, and His Grace the Duke of ALBEMARL. And describing THE FIRE OF LONDON

Multum interest res poscat, an homines latius imperare velint.
TRAJAN. Imperator. ad Plin.

Urbs antiqua ruit, multos dominata per annos. VIRG.

TO THE METROPOLIS OF GREAT BRITAIN,

The most Renowned and late Flourishing CITY of LONDON, In its REPRESENTATIVES *The* LORD MAYOR *and Court of* ALDERMEN, *the* SHERIFS *and* COMMON COUNCIL *of it*

As perhaps I am the first who ever presented a work of this nature to the Metropolis of any Nation, so is it likewise consonant to Justice, that he who was to give the first Example of such a Dedication should begin it with that City, which has set a pattern to all others of true Loyalty, invincible Courage and unshaken Constancy. Other Cities have been prais'd for the same Virtues, but I am much deceiv'd if any have so dearly purchas'd their reputation; their fame has been won them by cheaper trials then an expensive, though necessary, War, a consuming Pestilence, and a more consuming Fire. To submit your selves with that humility to the Judgments of Heaven, and at the same time to raise your selves with that vigour above all humane Enemies; to be combated at once from above and from below, to be struck

Annus Mirabilis. Text from the first edition, 1667, collated with the editions of 1668 and 1688.
To The Metropolis. 2 is it] it is *88*

down and to triumph; I know not whether such trials have been ever parallel'd in any Nation, the resolution and successes of them never can be. Never had Prince or People more mutual reason to love each other, if suffering for each other can indear affection. You have come together a pair of matchless Lovers, through many difficulties; He, through a long Exile, various traverses of Fortune, and the interposition of many Rivals, who violently ravish'd and with-held You from Him: And certainly you have had your share in sufferings. But Providence has cast upon you want of Trade, that you might appear bountiful to your Country's necessities; and the rest of your afflictions are not more the effects of God's displeasure, (frequent examples of them having been in the Reign of the most excellent Princes) then occasions for the manifesting of your Christian and Civil virtues. To you therefore this Year of Wonders is justly dedicated, because you have made it so: You who are to stand a wonder to all Years and Ages, and who have built your selves an immortal Monument on your own ruines. You are now a *Phœnix* in her ashes, and, as far as Humanity can approach, a great Emblem of the suffering Deity. But Heaven never made so much Piety and Vertue to leave it miserable. I have heard indeed of some vertuous persons who have ended unfortunately, but never of any vertuous Nation: Providence is engag'd too deeply, when the cause becomes so general. And I cannot imagine it has resolv'd the ruine of that people at home, which it has blessed abroad with such successes. I am therefore to conclude, that your sufferings are at an end; and that one part of my Poem has not been more an History of your destruction, then the other a Prophecy of your restoration. The accomplishment of which happiness, as it is the wish of all true *English-men*, so is by none more passionately desired then by

The greatest of your Admirers, and
most humble of your Servants,
JOHN DRYDEN.

An account of the ensuing Poem, in a LETTER to the Honorable, Sir ROBERT HOWARD

SIR,

I Am so many ways oblig'd to you, and so little able to return your favours, that, like those who owe too much, I can onely live by getting farther into your debt.

27 so:] so. *67 68 88*

You have not onely been careful of my Fortune, which was the effect of your Nobleness, but you have been sollicitous of my Reputation, which is that of your Kindness. It is not long since I gave you the trouble of perusing a Play for me, and now, instead of an acknowledgment, I have given you a greater, in the correction of a Poem. But since you are to bear this persecution, I will at least give you the encouragement of a Martyr, you could never suffer in a nobler cause. For I have chosen the most heroick Subject which any Poet could desire: I have taken upon me to describe the motives, the beginning, progress and successes of a most just and necessary War; in it, the care, management and prudence of our King; the conduct and valour of a Royal Admiral, and of two incomparable Generals; the invincible courage of our Captains and Sea-men, and three glorious Victories, the result of all. After this I have, in the Fire, the most deplorable, but withall the greatest Argument that can be imagin'd: the destruction being so swift, so sudden, so vast and miserable, as nothing can parallel in Story. The former part of this Poem, relating to the War, is but a due expiation for my not serving my King and Country in it. All Gentlemen are almost oblig'd to it: And I know no reason we should give that advantage to the Commonalty of England to be formost in brave actions, which the Noblesse of France would never suffer in their Peasants. I should not have written this but to a Person, who has been ever forward to appear in all employments, whither his Honour and Generosity have call'd him. The latter part of my Poem, which describes the Fire, I owe first to the Piety and Fatherly Affection of our Monarch to his suffering Subjects; and, in the second placc, to the courage, loyalty and magnanimity of the City: both which were so conspicuous, that I have wanted words to celebrate them as they deserve. I have call'd my Poem Historical, not Epick, though both the Actions and Actors are as much Heroick, as any Poem can contain. But since the Action is not properly one, nor that accomplish'd in the last successes, I have judg'd it too bold a Title for a few Stanza's, which are little more in number then a single Iliad, or the longest of the Æneids. For this reason, (I mean not of length, but broken action, ti'd too severely to the Laws of History) I am apt to agree with those who rank Lucan rather among Historians in Verse, then Epique Poets: In whose room, if I am not deceiv'd, Silius Italicus, though a worse Writer, may more justly be admitted. I have chosen to write my Poem in Quatrains or Stanza's of four in alternate rhyme, because I have ever judg'd them more noble, and of greater dignity, both for the sound and number, then any other Verse in use amongst us; in which I am sure I have your approbation. The learned Languages have, certainly, a great advantage of us, in not being tied to the slavery of any Rhyme; and were less constrain'd in the quantity of

An account. 20 *formost 88*: *for most 67 68*   23 *latter*] *later 88*   37 *for 88*: *fro 67*: *from 68*

every syllable, which they might vary with Spondæes *or* Dactiles, *besides so many other helps of Grammatical Figures, for the lengthning or abbreviation of them, then the Modern are in the close of that one Syllable, which often confines, and more often corrupts the sense of all the rest. But in this necessity of our Rhymes, I have always found the couplet Verse most easie, (though not so proper for this occasion) for there the work is sooner at an end, every two lines concluding the labour of the Poet: but in Quattrains he is to carry it farther on; and not onely so, but to bear along in his head the troublesome sense of four lines together. For those who write correctly in this kind must needs acknowledge, that the last line of the Stanza is to be consider'd in the composition of the first. Neither can we give our selves the liberty of making any part of a Verse for the sake of Rhyme, or concluding with a word which is not currant* English, *or using the variety of Female Rhymes, all which our Fathers practis'd; and for the Female Rhymes, they are still in use amongst other Nations: with the* Italian *in every line, with the* Spaniard *promiscuously, with the* French *alternately, as those who have read the* Alarique, *the* Pucelle, *or any of their latter Poems, will agree with me. And besides this, they write in* Alexandrins, *or Verses of six feet, such as amongst us is the old Translation of* Homer, *by* Chapman; *all which, by lengthning of their Chain, makes the sphere of their activity the larger. I have dwelt too long upon the choice of my Stanza, which you may remember is much better defended in the Preface to* Gondibert, *and therefore I will hasten to acquaint you with my endeavours in the writing. In general I will onely say, I have never yet seen the description of any Naval Fight in the proper terms which are us'd at Sea; and if there be any such in another Language, as that of* Lucan *in the third of his* Pharsalia, *yet I could not prevail my self of it in the* English; *the terms of Arts in every Tongue bearing more of the Idiom of it then any other words. We hear, indeed, among our Poets, of the thundring of Guns, the smoke, the disorder and the slaughter; but all these are common notions. And certainly as those who, in a Logical dispute, keep in general terms, would hide a fallacy, so those who do it in any Poetical description would vail their ignorance.*

Descriptas servare vices operumque colores
Cur ego, si nequeo ignoroque, poeta salutor?

For my own part, if I had little knowledge of the Sea, yet I have thought it no shame to learn: and if I have made some few mistakes, 'tis onely, as you can bear me witness, because I have wanted opportunity to correct them, the whole Poem being first written, and now sent you from a place, where I have not so much as the converse of any Sea-man. Yet, though the trouble I had in writing it was great, it was more then recompens'd by the pleasure; I found my self so warm in

56 *latter*] *later 88*   66 *Arts*] *Art 88*

celebrating the praises of military men, two such especially as the Prince *and* General, *that it is no wonder if they inspir'd me with thoughts above my ordinary level. And I am well satisfi'd, that as they are incomparably the best subject I have ever had, excepting onely the* Royal Family; *so also, that this I have written of them is much better then what I have perform'd on any other. I have been forc'd to help out other Arguments, but this has been bountiful to me; they have been low and barren of praise, and I have exalted them, and made them fruitful: but here*—Omnia sponte suâ reddit justissima tellus. *I have had a large, a fair and a pleasant field, so fertile, that, without my cultivating, it has given me two Harvests in a Summer, and in both oppress'd the Reaper. All other greatness in subjects is onely counterfeit, it will not endure the test of danger; the greatness of Arms is onely real: other greatness burdens a Nation with its weight, this supports it with its strength. And as it is the happiness of the Age, so is it the peculiar goodness of the best of Kings, that we may praise his Subjects without offending him: doubtless it proceeds from a just confidence of his own vertue, which the lustre of no other can be so great as to darken in him: for the Good or the Valiant are never safely prais'd under a bad or a degenerate Prince. But to return from this digression to a farther account of my Poem, I must crave leave to tell you, that as I have endeavour'd to adorn it with noble thoughts, so much more to express those thoughts with elocution. The composition of all Poems is or ought to be of wit, and wit in the Poet, or wit writing, (if you will give me leave to use a School distinction) is no other then the faculty of imagination in the writer, which, like a nimble Spaniel, beats over and ranges through the field of Memory, till it springs the Quarry it hunted after; or, without metaphor, which searches over all the memory for the species or Idea's of those things which it designs to represent. Wit written, is that which is well defin'd, the happy result of thought, or product of that imagination. But to proceed from wit in the general notion of it, to the proper wit of an Heroick or Historical Poem, I judge it chiefly to consist in the delightful imaging of persons, actions, passions, or things. 'Tis not the jerk or sting of an Epigram, nor the seeming contradiction of a poor Antithesis, (the delight of an ill judging Audience in a Play of Rhyme) nor the gingle of a more poor* Paranomasia: *neither is it so much the morality of a grave sentence, affected by* Lucan, *but more sparingly used by* Virgil; *but it is some lively and apt description, dress'd in such colours of speech, that it sets before your eyes the absent object, as perfectly and more delightfully then nature. So then, the first happiness of the Poet's imagination is properly Invention, or finding of the thought; the second is Fancy, or the variation, deriving or moulding of that thought, as the judgment represents it proper to the subject; the third is Elocution, or the Art of clothing and adorning that thought so found and varied, in apt,*

91 *is it*] *it is 88* 105 *that* om. *88* 115 *deriving 88: driving 67 68*

significant and sounding words: the quickness of the Imagination is seen in the Invention, the fertility in the Fancy, and the accuracy in the Expression. For the two first of these Ovid *is famous amongst the Poets, for the latter* Virgil. Ovid *images more often the movements and affections of the mind, either combating between two contrary passions, or extremely discompos'd by one: his words therefore are the least part of his care, for he pictures Nature in disorder, with which the study and choice of words is inconsistent. This is the proper wit of Dialogue or Discourse, and, consequently, of the* Drama, *where all that is said is to be suppos'd the effect of sudden thought; which, though it excludes not the quickness of wit in repartees, yet admits not a too curious election of words, too frequent allusions, or use of Tropes, or, in fine, any thing that showes remoteness of thought, or labour in the Writer. On the other side,* Virgil *speaks not so often to us in the person of another, like* Ovid, *but in his own; he relates almost all things as from himself, and thereby gains more liberty then the other, to express his thoughts with all the graces of elocution, to write more figuratively, and to confess, as well the labour as the force of his imagination. Though he describes his* Dido *well and naturally, in the violence of her passions, yet he must yield in that to the* Myrrha, *the* Biblis, *the* Althæa, *of* Ovid*; for, as great an admirer of him as I am, I must acknowledge, that, if I see not more of their Souls then I see of* Dido's, *at least I have a greater concernment for them: and that convinces me that* Ovid *has touch'd those tender strokes more delicately then* Virgil *could. But when Action or Persons are to be describ'd, when any such Image is to be set before us, how bold, how masterly are the strokes of* Virgil*! we see the objects he represents us with in their native figures, in their proper motions; but we so see them, as our own eyes could never have beheld them so beautiful in themselves. We see the Soul of the Poet, like that universal one of which he speaks, informing and moving through all his Pictures,* Totamque infusa per artus mens agitat molem, & magno se corpore miscet; *we behold him embellishing his Images, as he makes* Venus *breathing beauty upon her son* Æneas.

—lumenque juventæ
Purpureum, & lætos oculis afflârat honores:
Quale manus addunt Ebori decus, aut ubi flavo
Argentum, Pariusve lapis circundatur auro.

See his Tempest, his Funeral Sports, his Combat of Turnus *and* Æneas, *and in his* Georgicks, *which I esteem the Divinest part of all his writings, the Plague, the Country, the Battel of Bulls, the labour of the Bees, and those many other excellent Images of Nature, most of which are neither great in themselves, nor*

120 *latter*] *later 88* 130 *own;*] *own, 67 68 88* 139 *be set 68 88*: *beset 67*
141 *we so*] *so we 88* 144 molem *88*: motem *67 68* 150 Pariusve *88*: pariusve *67 68*

have any natural ornament to bear them up: but the words wherewith he describes them are so excellent, that it might be well appli'd to him which was said by Ovid, Materiam superabat opus: *the very sound of his words has often somewhat that is connatural to the subject, and while we read him, we sit, as in a Play, beholding the Scenes of what he represents. To perform this, he made frequent use of Tropes, which you know change the nature of a known word, by applying it to some other signification; and this is it which* Horace *means in his Epistle to the* Pisos.

Dixeris egregie notum si callida verbum
Reddiderit junctura novum—

But I am sensible I have presum'd too far, to entertain you with a rude discourse of that Art, which you both know so well, and put into practise with so much happiness. Yet before I leave Virgil, *I must own the vanity to tell you, and by you the world, that he has been my Master in this Poem: I have followed him every where, I know not with what success, but I am sure with diligence enough: my Images are many of them copied from him, and the rest are imitations of him. My expressions also are as near as the Idioms of the two Languages would admit of in translation. And this, Sir, I have done with that boldness, for which I will stand accomptable to any of our little Criticks, who, perhaps, are not better acquainted with him then I am. Upon your first perusal of this Poem, you have taken notice of some words which I have innovated (if it be too bold for me to say refin'd) upon his* Latin; *which, as I offer not to introduce into* English *prose, so I hope they are neither improper, nor altogether unelegant in Verse; and, in this,* Horace *will again defend me.*

Et nova, fictaque nuper habebunt verba fidem, si
Græco fonte cadant, parcè detorta—

The inference is exceeding plain; for if a Roman *Poet might have liberty to coin a word, supposing onely that it was derived from the* Greek, *was put into a* Latin *termination, and that he us'd this liberty but seldom, and with modesty: How much more justly may I challenge that privilege to do it with the same præ-requisits, from the best and most judicious of* Latin *Writers? In some places, where either the fancy, or the words, were his, or any others, I have noted it in the Margin, that I might not seem a Plagiary: in others I have neglected it, to avoid as well the tediousness, as the affectation of doing it too often. Such descriptions or images, well wrought, which I promise not for mine, are, as I have said, the adequate delight of heroick Poesie, for they beget admiration, which is its proper object; as the images of the Burlesque, which is contrary to this, by the same reason beget laughter; for the one shows Nature beautified, as in the picture*

188 *well the tediousness*] *well tediousness 88*

of a fair Woman, which we all admire; the other shows her deformed, as in that of a Lazar, or of a fool with distorted face and antique gestures, at which we cannot forbear to laugh, because it is a deviation from Nature. But though the same images serve equally for the Epique Poesie, and for the Historique and Panegyrique, which are branches of it, yet a several sort of Sculpture is to be used in them: if some of them are to be like those of Juvenal, Stantes in curribus Æmiliani, *Heroes drawn in their triumphal Chariots, and in their full proportion; others are to be like that of* Virgil, Spirantia mollius æra: *there is somewhat more of softness and tenderness to be shown in them. You will soon find I write not this without concern. Some who have seen a paper of Verses which I wrote last year to her Highness the* Dutchess, *have accus'd them of that onely thing I could defend in them; they have said I did* humi serpere, *that I wanted not onely height of fancy, but dignity of words to set it off; I might well answer with that of* Horace, Nunc non erat his locus, *I knew I address'd them to a Lady, and accordingly I affected the softness of expression, and the smoothness of measure, rather then the height of thought; and in what I did endeavour, it is no vanity to say, I have succeeded. I detest arrogance, but there is some difference betwixt that and a just defence. But I will not farther bribe your candour, or the Readers. I leave them to speak for me, and, if they can, to make out that character, not pretending to a greater, which I have given them.*

Verses to her Highness *the* DUTCHESS, *on the memorable Victory gain'd by the* DUKE *against the* Hollanders, June *the* 3. 1665. *and on Her Journey afterwards into the North*

MADAM,

WHEN, for our sakes, your *Heroe* you resign'd
To swelling Seas, and every faithless wind;
When you releas'd his courage, and set free
A valour fatal to the Enemy,
You lodg'd your Countries cares within your breast;
(The mansion where soft Love should onely rest:)
And ere our foes abroad were overcome,
The noblest conquest you had gain'd at home.
Ah, what concerns did both your Souls divide!

204 *have* om. *88*　　206 erat] erit *68*　　his] hic *67 68 88*

Your Honour gave us what your Love deni'd:
And 'twas for him much easier to subdue
Those foes he fought with, then to part from you.
That glorious day, which two such Navies saw,
As each, unmatch'd, might to the world give Law,
Neptune, yet doubtful whom he should obey,
Held to them both the Trident of the Sea:
The winds were hush'd, the waves in ranks were cast,
As awfully as when God's people past:
Those, yet uncertain on whose sails to blow,
These, where the wealth of Nations ought to flow.
Then with the Duke your Highness rul'd the day:
While all the brave did his command obey,
The fair and pious under you did pray.
How pow'rful are chast vows! the wind and tyde
You brib'd to combat on the *English* side.
Thus to your much lov'd Lord you did convey
An unknown succour, sent the nearest way.
New vigour to his wearied arms you brought;
(So *Moses* was upheld while *Israel* fought.)
While, from afar, we heard the Canon play,
Like distant Thunder on a shiny day,
For absent friends we were asham'd to fear,
When we consider'd what you ventur'd there.
Ships, Men and Arms our Country might restore,
But such a Leader could supply no more.
With generous thoughts of conquest he did burn,
Yet fought not more to vanquish then return.
Fortune and Victory he did pursue,
To bring them, as his Slaves, to wait on you.
Thus Beauty ravish'd the rewards of Fame,
And the Fair triumph'd when the Brave o'rcame.
Then, as you meant to spread another way
By Land your Conquests far as his by Sea,
Leaving our Southern Clime, you march'd along
The stubborn North, ten thousand *Cupid's* strong.
Like Commons the Nobility resort
In crowding heaps, to fill your moving Court:
To welcome your approach the Vulgar run,

Verses. 14 Law,] Law. *67 68 88*   15 he] she *68*   22 obey, *88*: obey. *67 68*

Like some new Envoy from the distant Sun.
And Country Beauties by their Lovers go,
Blessing themselves, and wondring at the show.
So when the new-born *Phœnix* first is seen,
Her feather'd Subjects all adore their Queen.
And, while she makes her progress through the East,
From every grove her numerous train's increase:
Each Poet of the air her glory sings,
And round him the pleas'd Audience clap their wings.

And now, Sir, 'tis time I should relieve you from the tedious length of this account. You have better and more profitable employment for your hours, and I wrong the Publick to detain you longer. In conclusion, I must leave my Poem to you with all its faults, which I hope to find fewer in the printing by your emendations. I know you are not of the number of those, of whom the younger Pliny *speaks,* Nec sunt parum multi qui carpere amicos suos judicium vocant; *I am rather too secure of you on that side. Your candour in pardoning my errors may make you more remiss in correcting them; if you will not withall consider that they come into the world with your approbation, and through your hands. I beg from you the greatest favor you can confer upon an absent person, since I repose upon your management what is dearest to me, my Fame and Reputation; and therefore I hope it will stir you up to make my Poem fairer by many of your blots; if not, you know the story of the Gamester who married the rich man's daughter, and when her father denyed the portion, christned all the children by his sirname, that if, in conclusion, they must beg, they should do so by one name, as well as by the other. But since the reproach of my faults will light on you, 'tis but reason I should do you that justice to the Readers, to let them know that if there be any thing tolerable in this Poem, they owe the Argument to your choice, the writing to your encouragement, the correction to your judgment, and the care of it to your friendship, to which he must ever acknowledge himself to owe all things, who is,*

SIR,
The most obedient and most
faithful of your Servants,
JOHN DRYDEN.

From Charleton *in* Wiltshire,
Novem. 10. 1666.

49 Envoy *68 88*: Envoy' *67*   55 train's] trains *68*

ANNUS MIRABILIS

The YEAR of WONDERS, *MDCLXVI*

I

IN thriving Arts long time had *Holland* grown,
  Crouching at home, and cruel when abroad:
Scarce leaving us the means to claim our own.
  Our King they courted, and our Merchants aw'd.

2

Trade, which like bloud should circularly flow,
  Stop'd in their Channels, found its freedom lost
Thither the wealth of all the world did go,
  And seem'd but shipwrack'd on so base a Coast.

3

For them alone the Heav'ns had kindly heat,
  [a]In Eastern Quarries ripening precious Dew:
For them the *Idumæan* Balm did sweat,
  And in hot *Ceilon* Spicy Forrests grew.

(a) *In Eastern Quarries, &c. Precious Stones at first are Dew, condens'd and harden'd by the warmth of the Sun, or subterranean Fires.*

4

The Sun but seem'd the Lab'rer of their Year;
  [b]Each wexing Moon suppli'd her watry store,
To swell those Tides, which from the Line did bear
  Their brim-full Vessels to the *Belg'an* shore.

(b) *Each wexing, &c. according to their opinion, who think that great heap of waters under the Line is depressed into Tydes by the Moon, towards the Poles.*

13 their] the *88*

5

Thus mighty in her Ships, stood *Carthage* long,
And swept the riches of the world from far;
Yet stoop'd to *Rome*, less wealthy, but more strong:
And this may prove our second Punick War.

6

What peace can be where both to one pretend?
(But they more diligent, and we more strong)
Or if a peace, it soon must have an end
For they would grow too pow'rful were it long.

7

Behold two Nations then, ingag'd so far,
That each seav'n years the fit must shake each Land:
Where *France* will side to weaken us by War,
Who onely can his vast designs withstand.

8

See how he feeds th' [c]*Iberian* with delays,
To render us his timely friendship vain;
And, while his secret Soul on *Flanders* preys,
He rocks the Cradle of the Babe of *Spain*.

(c) *Th'* Iberian, *the* Spaniard.

9

Such deep designs of Empire does he lay
O're them whose cause he seems to take in hand:
And, prudently, would make them Lords at Sea,
To whom with ease he can give Laws by Land.

10

This saw our King; and long within his breast
His pensive counsels ballanc'd too and fro;
He griev'd the Land he freed should be oppress'd,
And he less for it then Usurpers do.

11

His gen'rous mind the fair Idea's drew
Of Fame and Honour which in dangers lay;
Where wealth, like fruit on precipices, grew,
Not to be gather'd but by Birds of prey.

12

The loss and gain each fatally were great;
And still his Subjects call'd aloud for war:
But peaceful Kings o'r martial people set,
Each others poize and counter-ballance are.

13

He, first, survey'd the charge with careful eyes,
Which none but mighty Monarchs could maintain;
Yet judg'd, like vapours that from Limbecks rise,
It would in richer showers descend again.

14

At length resolv'd t' assert the watry Ball,
He in himself did whole Armado's bring:
Him, aged Sea-men might their Master call,
And choose for General were he not their King.

15

It seems as every Ship their Sovereign knows,
His awful summons they so soon obey;
So hear the skaly Herd when [d]*Proteus* blows,
And so to pasture follow through the Sea.

(d) *When* Proteus *blows, or* Cæruleus Proteus immania ponti armenta, & magnas pascit sub gurgite Phocas. *Virg.*

43 on *67* (*errata*): an *67* (*text*) *(errata) 68*: poscit *67* (*text*) *88*   59 hear] here *67 68 88*   59 *note* pascit *67*

16

To see this Fleet upon the Ocean move
  Angels drew wide the Curtains of the skies:
And Heav'n, as if there wanted Lights above,
  For Tapers made two glareing Comets rise.

17

Whether they unctuous Exhalations are,
  Fir'd by the Sun, or seeming so alone,
Or each some more remote and slippery Star,
  Which looses footing when to Mortals shown.

18

Or one that bright companion of the Sun,
  Whose glorious aspect seal'd our new-born King;
And now a round of greater years begun,
  New influence from his walks of light did bring.

19

Victorious *York* did, first, with fam'd success,
  To his known valour make the *Dutch* give place:
Thus Heav'n our Monarch's fortune did confess,
  Beginning conquest from his Royal Race.

20

But since it was decreed, Auspicious King,
  In *Britain*'s right that thou should'st wed the Main,
Heav'n, as a gage, would cast some precious thing
  And therefore doom'd that *Lawson* should be slain.

21

Lawson amongst the formost met his fate,
  Whom Sea-green *Syrens* from the Rocks lament:
Thus as an off'ring for the *Grecian* State,
  He first was kill'd who first to Battel went.

63 there *68 88*: their *67*

22

*Their Chief blown up, in air, not waves expir'd,
To which his pride presum'd to give the Law:
The *Dutch* confess'd Heav'n present, and retir'd,
And all was *Britain* the wide Ocean saw.

* *The Admiral of* Holland.

23

To nearest Ports their shatter'd Ships repair,
Where by our dreadful Canon they lay aw'd:
So reverently men quit the open air
When thunder speaks the angry Gods abroad.

24

And now approach'd their Fleet from *India*, fraught
With all the riches of the rising Sun:
And precious Sand from [e]Southern Climates brought,
(The fatal Regions where the War begun.)

The attempt at Berghen.

(e) *Southern Climates*, Guinny.

25

Like hunted *Castors*, conscious of their store,
Their way-laid wealth to *Norway*'s coasts they bring:
There first the North's cold bosome Spices bore,
And Winter brooded on the Eastern Spring.

26

By the rich scent we found our perfum'd prey,
Which flanck'd with Rocks did close in covert lie:
And round about their murdering Canon lay,
At once to threaten and invite the eye.

27

Fiercer then Canon, and then Rocks more hard,
The *English* undertake th' unequal War:
Seven Ships alone, by which the Port is barr'd,
Besiege the *Indies*, and all *Denmark* dare.

28

These fight like Husbands, but like Lovers those:
These fain would keep, and those more fain enjoy:
And to such height their frantick passion grows,
That what both love, both hazard to destroy.

29

Amidst whole heaps of Spices lights a Ball,
And now their Odours arm'd against them flie:
Some preciously by shatter'd Porc'lain fall,
And some by Aromatick splinters die.

30

And though by Tempests of the prize bereft,
In Heavens inclemency some ease we find:
Our foes we vanquish'd by our valour left,
And onely yielded to the Seas and Wind.

31

Nor wholly lost we so deserv'd a prey;
For storms, repenting, part of it restor'd:
Which, as a tribute from the *Balthick* Sea,
The *British* Ocean sent her mighty Lord.

32

Go, Mortals, now, and vex your selves in vain
For wealth, which so uncertainly must come:
When what was brought so far, and with such pain,
Was onely kept to lose it neerer home.

106 undertake *67* (*errata*): undertook *67* (*text*)

33

The Son, who, twice three month's on th' Ocean tost,
Prepar'd to tell what he had pass'd before,
Now sees, in *English* Ships the *Holland* Coast,
And Parents arms in vain stretch'd from the shore.

34

This carefull Husband had been long away,
Whom his chast wife and little children mourn;
Who on their fingers learn'd to tell the day
On which their Father promis'd to return.

35

[f]Such are the proud designs of human kind,
And so we suffer Shipwrack every where!
Alas, what Port can such a Pilot find,
Who in the night of Fate must blindly steer!

(f) *Such are*, &c. *from* Petronius. Si, bene calculum ponas ubique fit naufragium.

36

The undistinguish'd seeds of good and ill
Heav'n, in his bosom, from our knowledge hides;
And draws them in contempt of human skill,
Which oft, for friends, mistaken foes provides.

37

Let *Munsters* Prelate ever be accurst,
In whom we seek the [g]*German* faith in vain:
Alas, that he should teach the *English* first
That fraud and avarice in the Church could reign!

(g) *The* German *faith*. Tacitus *saith of them*, Nullos mortalium fide aut armis ante Germanos esse.

137 *note* fit naufragium *67* (*errata*): naufragiunt est *67* (*text*) 146 note *them*, *68*: *them*. *67 88*

38

Happy who never trust a Strangers will,
  Whose friendship's in his interest understood!
Since money giv'n but tempts him to be ill
  When pow'r is too remote to make him good.

39

Till now, alone the Mighty Nations strove:
  The rest, at gaze, without the Lists did stand:
And threatning *France*, plac'd like a painted *Jove*,
  Kept idle thunder in his lifted hand.

War declar'd by France.

40

That Eunuch Guardian of rich *Hollands* trade,
  Who envies us what he wants pow'r t' enjoy!
Whose noisefull valour does no foe invade,
  And weak assistance will his friends destroy.

41

Offended that we fought without his leave,
  He takes this time his secret hate to show:
Which *Charles* does with a mind so calm receive
  As one that neither seeks, nor shuns his foe.

42

With *France*, to aid the *Dutch*, the *Danes* unite:
  France as their Tyrant, *Denmark* as their Slave.
But when with one three Nations joyn to fight,
  They silently confess that one more brave.

43

Lewis had chas'd the *English* from his shore;
  But *Charles* the *French* as Subjects does invite.
Would Heav'n for each some *Salomon* restore,
  Who, by their mercy, may decide their right.

44

Were Subjects so but onely by their choice,
And not from Birth did forc'd Dominion take,
Our Prince alone would have the publique voice;
And all his Neighbours Realms would desarts make.

45

He without fear a dangerous War pursues,
Which without rashness he began before.
As Honour made him first the danger choose,
So still he makes it good on virtues score.

46

The doubled charge his Subjects love supplies,
Who, in that bounty, to themselves are kind:
So glad *Egyptians* see their *Nilus* rise,
And in his plenty their abundance find.

47

With equal pow'r he does two Chiefs create,
Two such, as each seem'd worthiest when alone:
Each able to sustain a Nations fate,
Since both had found a greater in their own.

Prince Rupert *and Duke* Albemarl *sent to sea.*

48

Both great in courage, Conduct and in Fame,
Yet neither envious of the others praise;
Their duty, faith, and int'rest too the same,
Like mighty Partners equally they raise.

185 *Duke* Albemarl] *Duke of* Albemarl *68* 190 praise; *88*: praise. *67 68* 191 same, *68 88*: same. *67*

49

The Prince long time had courted Fortune's love,
But once possess'd did absolutely reign;
Thus with their *Amazons* the *Heroes* strove,
And conquer'd first those Beauties they would gain.

50

The Duke beheld, like *Scipio*, with disdain
That *Carthage*, which he ruin'd, rise once more:
And shook aloft the Fasces of the Main,
To fright those Slaves with what they felt before.

51

Together to the watry Camp they haste,
Whom Matrons passing, to their children show:
Infants first vows for them to Heav'n are cast,
And [h]future people bless them as they go.

(h) *Future people*, Examina infantium futurusque populus. Plin. Jun. in pan. ad Traj.

52

With them no riotous pomp, nor *Asian* train,
T' infect a Navy with their gawdy fears:
To make slow fights, and victories but vain;
But war, severely, like it self, appears.

53

Diffusive of themselves, where e'r they pass,
They make that warmth in others they expect:
Their valour works like bodies on a glass,
And does its Image on their men project.

197 Duke *88*: Duke, *67 68*

54

Our Fleet divides, and straight the *Dutch* appear,
  In number, and a fam'd Commander, bold:
The Narrow Seas can scarce their Navy bear,
  Or crowded Vessels can their Soldiers hold.

Duke of Albemarl'*s Battel, first day.*

55

The Duke, less numerous, but in courage more.
  On wings of all the winds to combat flies:
His murdering Guns a loud defiance roar,
  And bloudy Crosses on his Flag-staffs rise.

56

Both furl their sails, and strip them for the fight,
  Their folded sheets dismiss the useless air:
[i]Th' *Elean* Plains could boast no nobler sight,
  When strugling Champions did their bodies bare.

(i) *Th'* Elean, *&c. Where the Olimpick Games were celebrated.*

57

Born each by other in a distant Line,
  The Sea-built Forts in dreadful order move:
So vast the noise, as if not Fleets did joyn,
  [k]But Lands unfix'd, and floating Nations, strove.

(k) *Lands unfix'd, from* Virgil*: Credas innare revulsas Cycladas, &c.*

58

Now pass'd, on either side they nimbly tack,
  Both strive to intercept and guide the wind:
And, in its eye, more closely they come back
  To finish all the deaths they left behind.

219 a loud *67* (*errata*): aloud *67* (*text*)   226 dreadful *67* (*errata*): distant *67* (*text*)
228 note *revulsas 88*: *revultas 67 68*

59

On high-rais'd Decks the haughty *Belgians* ride,
  Beneath whose shade our humble Fregats go:
Such port the *Elephant* bears, and so defi'd
  By the *Rhinocero's* her unequal foe.

60

And as the built, so different is the fight;
  Their mounting shot is on our sails design'd:
Deep in their hulls our deadly bullets light,
  And through the yielding planks a passage find.

61

Our dreaded Admiral from far they threat,
  Whose batter'd rigging their whole war receives.
All bare, like some old Oak which tempests beat,
  He stands, and sees below his scatter'd leaves.

62

Heroes of old, when wounded, shelter sought,
  But he, who meets all danger with disdain,
Ev'n in their face his ship to Anchor brought,
  And Steeple high stood propt upon the Main.

63

At this excess of courage, all amaz'd,
  The foremost of his foes a while withdraw.
With such respect in enter'd *Rome* they gaz'd,
  Who on high Chairs the God-like Fathers saw.

64

And now, as where *Patroclus* body lay,
  Here *Trojan* Chiefs advanc'd, and there the *Greek*:
Ours o'r the Duke their pious wings display,
  And theirs the noblest spoils of *Britain* seek.

65

Mean time, his busie Marriners he hasts,
His shatter'd sails with rigging to restore:
And willing Pines ascend his broken Masts,
Whose lofty heads rise higher then before.

66

Straight to the *Dutch* he turns his dreadful prow,
More fierce th' important quarrel to decide.
Like Swans, in long array his Vessels show,
Whose creasts, advancing, do the waves divide.

67

They charge, re-charge, and all along the Sea
They drive, and squander the huge *Belgian* Fleet.
Berkley alone, who neerest Danger lay,
Did a like fate with lost *Creüsa* meet.

68

The night comes on, we, eager to pursue
The Combat still, and they asham'd to leave:
Till the last streaks of dying day withdrew,
And doubtful Moon-light did our rage deceive.

69

In th' *English* Fleet each ship resounds with joy,
And loud applause of their great Lead'rs fame.
In fiery dreams the *Dutch* they still destroy,
And, slumbring, smile at the imagin'd flame.

70

Not so the *Holland* Fleet, who tir'd and done,
Stretch'd on their decks like weary Oxen lie:
Faint sweats all down their mighty members run,
(Vast bulks which little souls but ill supply.)

267 who neerest Danger lay *67* (*some copies*) *88*: not making equal way *67* (*some copies*) *68*. *See Commentary*.
74 Lead'rs *67* (*some copies*) *88*: Leader's *67* (*some copies*) *68* 279 mighty] might *88*

71

In dreams they fearful precipices tread,
  Or, shipwrack'd, labour to some distant shore:
Or in dark Churches walk among the dead:
  They wake with horrour, and dare sleep no more.

72

The morn they look on with unwilling eyes,
  Till, from their Main-top, joyful news they hear
Of ships, which by their mould bring new supplies,
  And in their colours *Belgian* Lions bear.

Second days Battel.

73

Our watchful General had discern'd, from far,
  This mighty succour which made glad the foe.
He sigh'd, but, like a Father of the War,
  [1]His face spake hope, while deep his sorrows flow.

(l) *His face, &c.* Spem vultu simulat premit alto corde dolorem. *Virg.*

74

His wounded men he first sends off to shore:
  (Never, till now, unwilling to obey.)
They, not their wounds but want of strength deplore,
  And think them happy who with him can stay.

75

Then, to the rest, Rejoyce, (said he) to day
  In you the fortune of *Great Britain* lies:
Among so brave a people you are they
  Whom Heav'n has chose to fight for such a Prize.

76

If number *English* courages could quell,
  We should at first have shun'd, not met our foes;
Whose numerous sails the fearful onely tell:
  Courage from hearts, and not from numbers grows.

77

He said; nor needed more to say: with hast
  To their known stations chearfully they go:
And all at once, disdaining to be last,
  Sollicite every gale to meet the foe.

78

Nor did th' incourag'd *Belgians* long delay,
  But, bold in others, not themselves, they stood:
So thick, our Navy scarce could sheer their way,
  But seem'd to wander in a moving wood.

79

Our little Fleet was now ingag'd so far,
  That, like the Sword-fish in the Whale, they fought.
The Combat onely seem'd a Civil War,
  Till through their bowels we our passage wrought.

80

Never had valour, no not ours before,
  Done ought like this upon the Land or Main:
Where not to be o'rcome was to do more
  Then all the Conquests former Kings did gain.

81

The mighty Ghosts of our great *Harries* rose,
  And armed *Edwards* look'd, with anxious eyes,
To see this Fleet among unequal foes,
  By which fate promis'd them their *Charls* should rise.

311 sheer] steer *88*

82

Mean time the *Belgians* tack upon our Reer,
And raking Chace-guns through our sterns they send:
Close by, their Fire-ships, like *Jackals*, appear,
Who on their Lions for the prey attend.

83

Silent in smoke of Canons they come on:
(Such vapours once did fiery *Cacus* hide.)
In these the height of pleas'd revenge is shown,
Who burn contented by another's side.

84

Sometimes, from fighting Squadrons of each Fleet,
(Deceiv'd themselves, or to preserve some friend)
Two grapling *Ætna's* on the Ocean meet,
And *English* fires with *Belgian* flames contend.

85

Now, at each Tack, our little Fleet grows less;
And, like maim'd fowl, swim lagging on the Main.
Their greater loss their numbers scarce confess
While they lose cheaper then the *English* gain.

86

Have you not seen when, whistled from the fist,
Some Falcon stoops at what her eye design'd,
And, with her eagerness, the quarry miss'd,
Straight flies at check, and clips it down the wind,

87

The dastard Crow, that to the wood made wing,
And sees the Groves no shelter can afford,
With her loud Kaws her Craven kind does bring,
Who, safe in numbers cuff the noble Bird?

344 wind,] wind. *67 68 88* 348 Bird?] Bird. *67 68 88*

88

Among the *Dutch* thus *Albemarl* did fare:
He could not conquer, and disdain'd to flie.
Past hope of safety, 'twas his latest care,
Like falling *Cesar*, decently to die.

89

Yet pity did his manly spirit move
To see those perish who so well had fought:
And, generously, with his dispair he strove,
Resolv'd to live till he their safety wrought.

90

Let other Muses write his prosp'rous fate,
Of conquer'd Nations tell, and Kings restor'd:
But mine shall sing of his eclips'd estate,
Which, like the Sun's, more wonders does afford.

91

He drew his mighty Fregates all before,
On which the foe his fruitless force employes:
His weak ones deep into his Reer he bore,
Remote from Guns as sick men are from noise.

92

His fiery Canon did their passage guide,
And foll'wing smoke obscur'd them from the foe.
Thus *Israel* safe from the *Egyptian*'s pride,
By flaming pillars, and by clouds did go.

93

Elsewhere the *Belgian* force we did defeat,
But here our courages did theirs subdue:
So *Xenophon* once led that fam'd retreat,
Which first the *Asian* Empire overthrew.

364 are from] from the *88*

94

The foe approach'd: and one, for his bold sin,
Was sunk, (as he that touch'd the Ark was slain;)
The wild waves master'd him, and suck'd him in,
And smiling Eddies dimpled on the Main.

95

This seen, the rest at awful distance stood;
As if they had been there as servants set,
To stay, or to go on, as he thought good,
And not persue, but wait on his retreat.

96

So *Lybian* Huntsmen, on some sandy plain,
From shady coverts rouz'd, the Lion chace:
The Kingly beast roars out with loud disdain,
[m]And slowly moves, unknowing to give place.

(m) *The simile is* Virgil'*s*, Vestigia retro improperata refert, &c.

97

But if some one approach to dare his force,
He swings his tail, and swiftly turns him round:
With one paw seizes on his trembling Horse,
And with the other tears him to the ground.

98

Amidst these toils succeeds the balmy night,
Now hissing waters the quench'd guns restore;
[n]And weary waves, withdrawing from the fight,
Lie lull'd and panting on the silent shore.

(n) *Weary waves, from* Statius Sylv. Nec trucibus fluviis idem sonus: occidit horror æquoris, ac terris maria acclinata quiescunt.

391 *note* ac terris] ac tenis *67 68*: antennis *88*

99

The Moon shone clear on the becalmed floud,
  Where, while her beams like glittering silver play,
Upon the Deck our careful General stood,
  And deeply mus'd on the °succeeding day.

(o) *The third of* June, *famous for two former Victories.*

100

That happy Sun, said he, will rise again,
  Who twice victorious did our Navy see:
And I alone must view him rise in vain,
  Without one ray of all his Star for me.

101

Yet, like an *English* Gen'ral will I die,
  And all the Ocean make my spatious grave.
Women and Cowards on the Land may lie,
  The Sea 's a Tomb that 's proper for the brave.

102

Restless he pass'd the remnants of the night,
  Till the fresh air proclaim'd the morning nigh,
And burning ships, the Martyrs of the fight,
  With paler fires beheld the Eastern sky.

103

But now, his Stores of Ammunition spent,
  His naked valour is his onely guard:
Rare thunders are from his dumb Cannon sent,
  And solitary Guns are scarcely heard.

Third day.

104

Thus far had Fortune pow'r, here forc'd to stay,
  Nor longer durst with vertue be at strife:
This, as a Ransome *Albemarl* did pay
  For all the glories of so great a life.

105

For now brave *Rupert* from afar appears,
  Whose waving Streamers the glad General knows:
With full spread Sails his eager Navy steers,
  And every Ship in swift proportion grows.

106

The anxious Prince had heard the Cannon long,
  And from that length of time dire *Omens* drew
Of *English* over-match'd, and *Dutch* too strong,
  Who never fought three days but to pursue.

107

Then, as an Eagle, (who, with pious care,
  Was beating widely on the wing for prey)
To her now silent Eiry does repair,
  And finds her callow Infants forc'd away;

108

Stung with her love she stoops upon the plain,
  The broken air loud whistling as she flies:
She stops, and listens, and shoots forth again,
  And guides her pinions by her young ones cries:

417–20 For now . . . grows. *67 (some copies) 88*: *67 (some copies) and 68 have*:
For now brave *Rupert*'s Navy did appear,
Whose waving streamers from afar he knows:
As in his fate something divine there were,
Who dead and buried the third day arose.

See Commentary

428 away;] away. *67 68 88*   432 cries:] cries. *67 68 88*

109

With such kind passion hastes the Prince to fight,
And spreads his flying canvass to the sound:
Him, whom no danger, were he there, could fright,
Now, absent, every little noise can wound.

110

As, in a drought, the thirsty creatures cry,
And gape upon the gather'd clowds for rain,
And first the Martlet meets it in the sky,
And, with wet wings, joys all the feather'd train,

111

With such glad hearts did our dispairing men
Salute th' appearance of the Princes Fleet:
And each ambitiously would claim the Ken
That with first eyes did distant safety meet.

112

The *Dutch*, who came like greedy Hinds before,
To reap the harvest their ripe ears did yield,
Now look like those, when rowling thunders roar,
And sheets of Lightning blast the standing field.

113

Full in the Princes passage, hills of sand
And dang'rous flats in secret ambush lay,
Where the false tides skim o'r the cover'd Land,
And Sea-men with dissembled depths betray:

114

The wily *Dutch*, who, like fall'n Angels, fear'd
This new *Messiah*'s coming, there did wait,
And round the verge their braving Vessels steer'd,
To tempt his courage with so fair a bait.

435 were] where *88* 440 train,] train. *67 68 88*

115

But he, unmov'd, contemns their idle threat,
Secure of fame when ere he please to fight:
His cold experience tempers all his heat,
And inbred worth does boasting valour slight.

116

Heroique virtue did his actions guide,
And he the substance not th' appearance chose:
To rescue one such friend he took more pride
Than to destroy whole thousands of such foes.

117

But, when approach'd, in strict embraces bound,
Rupert and *Albemarl* together grow:
He joys to have his friend in safety found,
Which he to none but to that friend would owe.

118

The chearful Souldiers, with new stores suppli'd,
Now long to execute their spleenfull will;
And, in revenge for those three days they tri'd,
Wish one, like *Joshuah*'s, when the Sun stood still.

119

Thus re-inforc'd, against the adverse Fleet
Still doubling ours, brave *Rupert* leads the way.
With the first blushes of the Morn they meet,
And bring night back upon the new-born day.

Fourth days Battel.

120

His presence soon blows up the kindling fight,
And his loud Guns speak thick like angry men:
It seem'd as slaughter had been breath'd all night,
And death new pointed his dull dart agen.

460 does] doth *88*

121

The *Dutch*, too well his mighty Conduct knew,
And matchless Courage since the former fight:
Whose Navy like a stiff stretch'd cord did show
Till he bore in, and bent them into flight.

122

The wind he shares while half their Fleet offends
His open side, and high above him shows,
Upon the rest at pleasure he descends,
And, doubly harm'd, he double harms bestows.

123

Behind, the Gen'ral mends his weary pace,
And sullenly to his revenge he sails:
[p]So glides some trodden Serpent on the grass,
And long behind his wounded vollume trails.

(p) *So glides, &c. from* Virgil. Quum medii nexus, extremæque agmina caudæ solvuntur; tardosque trahit sinus ultimus orbes, &c.

124

Th' increasing sound is born to either shore,
And for their stakes the throwing Nations fear.
Their passions double with the Cannons roar,
And with warm wishes each man combats there.

125

Pli'd thick and close as when the fight begun,
Their huge unwieldy Navy wasts away:
So sicken waning Moons too neer the Sun,
And blunt their crescents on the edge of day.

495 passions] passion, *67 68 88*

126

And now reduc'd on equal terms to fight,
  Their Ships like wasted Patrimonies show:
Where the thin scatt'ring Trees admit the light,
  And shun each others shadows as they grow.

127

The warlike Prince had sever'd from the rest
  Two giant ships, the pride of all the Main;
Which, with his one, so vigorously he press'd,
  And flew so home they could not rise again.

128

Already batter'd, by his Lee they lay,
  In vain upon the passing winds they call:
The passing winds through their torn canvass play,
  And flagging sails on heartless Sailors fall.

129

Their open'd sides receive a gloomy light,
  Dreadful as day let in to shades below:
Without, grim death rides bare-fac'd in their sight,
  And urges ent'ring billows as they flow.

130

When one dire shot, the last they could supply,
  Close by the board the Prince's Main-mast bore:
All three now, helpless, by each other lie,
  And this offends not, and those fear no more.

131

So have I seen some fearful Hare maintain
  A Course, till tir'd before the Dog she lay:
Who, stretch'd behind her, pants upon the plain,
  Past pow'r to kill as she to get away.

517 one *67* (*errata*): own *67* (*text*) 518 board *88*: boar'd *67 68*

132

With his loll'd tongue he faintly licks his prey,
  His warm breath blows her flix up as she lies:
She, trembling, creeps upon the ground away,
  And looks back to him with beseeching eyes.

133

The Prince unjustly does his Stars accuse,
  Which hinder'd him to push his fortune on:
For what they to his courage did refuse,
  By mortal valour never must be done.

134

This lucky hour the wise *Batavian* takes,
  And warns his tatter'd Fleet to follow home:
Proud to have so got off with equal stakes,
  [q]Where 'twas a triumph not to be o'r-come.

(q) *From* Horace: Quos opimus fallere & effugere est triumphus.

135

The General's force, as kept alive by fight,
  Now, not oppos'd, no longer can persue:
Lasting till Heav'n had done his courage right,
  When he had conquer'd he his weakness knew.

136

He casts a frown on the departing foe,
  And sighs to see him quit the watry field:
His stern fix'd eyes no satisfaction show,
  For all the glories which the Fight did yield.

137

Though, as when Fiends did Miracles avow,
  He stands confess'd ev'n by the boastful *Dutch*,
He onely does his conquest disavow,
  And thinks too little what they found too much.

536 *note* opimus] opinius *67 68 88*

138

Return'd, he with the Fleet resolv'd to stay,
No tender thoughts of home his heart divide:
Domestick joys and cares he puts away,
For Realms are housholds which the Great must guide.

139

As those who unripe veins in Mines explore,
On the rich bed again the warm turf lay,
Till time digests the yet imperfect Ore,
And know it will be Gold another day:

140

So looks our Monarch on this early fight,
Th' essay, and rudiments of great success,
Which all-maturing time must bring to light,
While he, like Heav'n, does each days labour bless.

141

Heav'n ended not the first or second day,
Yet each was perfect to the work design'd:
God and Kings work, when they their work survey,
And passive aptness in all subjects find.

142

In burden'd Vessels, first, with speedy care,
His plenteous Stores do season'd timber send:
Thither the brawny Carpenters repair,
And as the Surgeons of maim'd ships attend.

His Majesty repairs the Fleet.

143

With Cord and Canvass from rich *Hamburgh* sent,
His Navies molted wings he imps once more:
Tall *Norway* Fir, their Masts in Battel spent,
And *English* Oak sprung leaks and planks restore.

556 day:] day. *67 68 88*   568 Surgeons *67* (*errata*): Chyrurg'ons *67* (*text*)

144

All hands employ'd, [r]the Royal work grows warm,
  Like labouring Bees on a long Summers day,
Some sound the Trumpet for the rest to swarm,
  And some on bells of tasted Lillies play:

(r) Fervet opus: *the same similitude in* Virgil.

145

With glewy wax some new foundation lay
  Of Virgin combs, which from the roof are hung:
Some arm'd within doors, upon duty stay,
  Or tend the sick, or educate the young.

146

So here, some pick out bullets from the sides,
  Some drive old Okum through each seam and rift:
Their left-hand does the Calking-iron guide,
  The ratling Mallet with the right they lift.

147

With boiling Pitch another near at hand
  (From friendly *Sweden* brought) the seams instops:
Which well paid o'r the salt-Sea waves withstand,
  And shakes them from the rising beak in drops.

148

Some the gall'd ropes with dawby Marling bind,
  Or sear-cloth Masts with strong Tarpawling coats:
To try new shrouds one mounts into the wind,
  And one, below, their ease or stifness notes.

149

Our careful Monarch stands in Person by,
  His new-cast Canons firmness to explore:
The strength of big-corn'd powder loves to try,
  And Ball and Cartrage sorts for every bore.

577 foundation] Foundations *88*

150

Each day brings fresh supplies of Arms and Men,
And Ships which all last Winter were abrode:
And such as fitted since the Fight had been,
Or new from Stocks were fall'n into the Road.

151

The goodly *London* in her gallant trim,
(The *Phœnix* daughter of the vanish'd old:)
Like a rich Bride does to the Ocean swim,
And on her shadow rides in floating gold.

Loyal London *describ'd.*

152

Her Flag aloft spread ruffling to the wind,
And sanguine Streamers seem the floud to fire:
The Weaver charm'd with what his Loom design'd,
Goes on to Sea, and knows not to retire.

153

With roomy decks, her Guns of mighty strength,
(Whose low-laid mouthes each mounting billow laves:)
Deep in her draught, and warlike in her length,
She seems a Sea-wasp flying on the waves.

154

This martial Present, piously design'd,
The Loyal City give their best-lov'd King:
And with a bounty ample as the wind,
Built, fitted and maintain'd to aid him bring.

155

By viewing Nature, Natures Hand-maid, Art,
Makes mighty things from small beginnings grow:
Thus fishes first to shipping did impart
Their tail the Rudder, and their head the Prow.

Digression concerning Shipping and Navigation.

600 the *om. 88*

156

Some Log, perhaps, upon the waters swam
  An useless drift, which, rudely cut within,
And hollow'd, first a floating trough became,
  And cross some Riv'let passage did begin.

157

In shipping such as this the *Irish Kern*,
  And untaught *Indian*, on the stream did glide:
Ere sharp-keel'd Boats to stem the floud did learn,
  Or fin-like Oars did spread from either side.

158

Adde but a Sail, and *Saturn* so appear'd,
  When, from lost Empire, he to Exile went,
And with the Golden age to *Tyber* steer'd,
  Where Coin and first Commerce he did invent.

159

Rude as their Ships was Navigation, then;
  No useful Compass or Meridian known:
Coasting, they kept the Land within their ken,
  And knew no North but when the Pole-star shone.

160

Of all who since have us'd the open Sea,
  Then the bold *English* none more fame have won:
[s]Beyond the Year, and out of Heav'ns high-way,
  They make discoveries where they see no Sun.

(s) Extra anni solisque vias. *Virg.*

161

But what so long in vain, and yet unknown,
  By poor man-kinds benighted wit is sought,
Shall in this Age to *Britain* first be shown,
  And hence be to admiring Nations taught.

639 *note* vias 67 (*errata*): vicis 67 (*text*)

162

The Ebbs of Tydes, and their mysterious flow,
  We, as Arts Elements shall understand:
And as by Line upon the Ocean go,
  Whose paths shall be familiar as the Land.

163

[t]Instructed ships shall sail to quick Commerce;
  By which remotest Regions are alli'd:
Which makes one City of the Universe,
  Where some may gain, and all may be suppli'd.

(t) *By a more exact measure of Longitude.*

164

Then, we upon our Globes last verge shall go,
  And view the Ocean leaning on the sky:
From thence our rolling Neighbours we shall know,
  And on the Lunar world securely pry.

165

This I fore-tel, from your auspicious care,
  Who great in search of God and Nature grow:
Who best your wise Creator's praise declare,
  Since best to praise his works is best to know.

Apostrophe to the Royal Society.

166

O truly Royal! who behold the Law,
  And rule of beings in your Makers mind,
And thence, like Limbecks, rich Idea's draw,
  To fit the levell'd use of humane kind.

649 note *measure of Longitude 88*: *knowledge of Longitudes 67 68 88*: know. *67*   655 know, *68*

167

But first the toils of war we must endure,
  And, from th' Injurious *Dutch* redeem the Seas.
War makes the valiant of his right secure,
  And gives up fraud to be chastis'd with ease.

168

Already were the *Belgians* on our coast,
  Whose Fleet more mighty every day became,
By late success, which they did falsly boast,
  And now, by first appearing seem'd to claim.

169

Designing, subtil, diligent, and close,
  They knew to manage War with wise delay:
Yet all those arts their vanity did cross,
  And, by their pride, their prudence did betray.

170

Nor staid the *English* long: but, well suppli'd,
  Appear as numerous as th' insulting foe.
The Combat now by courage must be tri'd,
  And the success the braver Nation show.

171

There was the *Plimouth* Squadron new come in,
  Which in the *Straights* last Winter was abroad:
Which twice on *Biscay*'s working Bay had been,
  And on the Mid-land Sea the *French* had aw'd.

172

Old expert *Allen*, loyal all along,
  Fam'd for his action on the *Smirna* Fleet,
And *Holmes*, whose name shal live in Epique Song,
  While Musick Numbers, or while Verse has Feet.

173

Holmes, the *Achates* of the Gen'rals fight,
Who first bewitch'd our eyes with *Guinny* Gold:
As once old *Cato* in the *Roman*'s sight
The tempting fruits of *Africk* did unfold.

174

With him went *Sprag*, as bountiful as brave,
Whom his high courage to command had brought:
Harman, who did the twice fir'd *Harry* save,
And in his burning ship undaunted fought.

175

Young Hollis, on a *Muse* by *Mars* begot
Born, *Cesar*-like, to write and act great deeds:
Impatient to revenge his fatal shot,
His right hand doubly to his left succeeds.

176

Thousands were there in darker fame that dwell,
Whose deeds some nobler Poem shall adorn:
And, though to me unknown, they, sure, fought well,
Whom *Rupert* led, and who were *British* born.

177

Of every size an hundred fighting Sail,
So vast the Navy now at Anchor rides,
That underneath it the press'd waters fail,
And, with its weight, it shoulders off the Tydes.

178

Now Anchors weigh'd, the Sea-men shout so shrill,
That Heav'n and Earth and the wide Ocean rings:
A breeze from Westward waits their sails to fill,
And rests, in those high beds, his downy wings.

179

The wary *Dutch* this gathering storm foresaw,
And durst not bide it on the *English* coast:
Behind their treach'rous shallows they withdraw,
And their lay snares to catch the *British* Hoast.

180

So the false Spider, when her Nets are spread,
Deep ambush'd in her silent den does lie:
And feels, far off, the trembling of her thread,
Whose filmy cord should bind the strugling Fly.

181

Then, if at last, she find him fast beset,
She issues forth, and runs along her Loom:
She joys to touch the Captive in her Net,
And drags the little wretch in triumph home.

182

The *Belgians* hop'd that, with disorder'd haste,
Our deep-cut keels upon the sands might run:
Or, if with caution leisurely were past,
Their numerous gross might charge us one by one

183

But, with a fore-wind pushing them above,
And swelling tyde that heav'd them from below,
O'r the blind flats our warlike Squadrons move,
And, with spread sails, to welcome Battel go.

184

It seem'd as there the *British Neptune* stood,
With all his host of waters at command,
Beneath them to submit th' officious floud:
[u]And, with his Trident, shov'd them off the sand.

(u) Levat ipse Tridenti, & vastas aperit Syrtes, &c. *Virg.*

731 flats *67* (*errata*): flots *67* (*text*) 734 host] hosts *88*

185

To the pale foes they suddenly draw near,
  And summon them to unexpected fight:
They start like Murderers when Ghosts appear,
  And draw their Curtains in the dead of night.

186

Now Van to Van the formost Squadrons meet,
  The midmost Battels hasting up behind,
Who view, far off, the storm of falling Sleet,
  And hear their thunder ratling in the wind.

Second Battel.

187

At length the adverse Admirals appear;
  (The two bold Champions of each Countries right)
Their eyes describe the lists as they come near,
  And draw the lines of death before they fight.

188

The distance judg'd for shot of every size,
  The Linstocks touch, the pond'rous ball expires:
The vig'rous Sea-man every port-hole plies,
  And adds his heart to every Gun he fires.

189

Fierce was the fight on the proud *Belgians* side,
  For honour, which they seldome sought before:
But now they by their own vain boasts were ti'd,
  And forc'd, at least in show, to prize it more.

190

But sharp remembrance on the *English* part,
  And shame of being match'd by such a foe,
Rouze conscious vertue up in every heart,
  [w]And seeming to be stronger makes them so.

(w) Possunt quia posse videntur. *Virg.*

742 hasting] hastning *88*   758 foe, *88*: foe: *67 68*

191

Nor long the *Belgians* could that Fleet sustain,
  Which did two Gen'rals fates, and *Cesar*'s bear.
Each several Ship a victory did gain,
  As *Rupert* or as *Albemarl* were there.

192

Their batter'd Admiral too soon withdrew,
  Unthank'd by ours for his unfinish'd fight:
But he the minds of his *Dutch* Masters knew,
  Who call'd that providence which we call'd flight.

193

Never did men more joyfully obey,
  Or sooner understood the sign to flie:
With such alacrity they bore away,
  As if to praise them all the States stood by.

194

O famous Leader of the *Belgian* Fleet,
  Thy Monument inscrib'd such praise shall wear
As *Varro*, timely flying, once did meet,
  Because he did not of his *Rome* despair.

195

Behold that Navy which a while before
  Provok'd the tardy *English* to the fight,
Now draw their beaten vessels close to shore,
  As Larks lie dar'd to shun the Hobbies flight.

196

Who ere would *English* Monuments survey,
  In other records may our courage know:
But let them hide the story of this day,
  Whose fame was blemish'd by too base a foe.

775 *Varro 67* (*errata*): *Verro 67* (*text*)   778 to the] close to *88*

197

Or if too busily they will enquire
Into a victory which we disdain:
Then let them know, the *Belgians* did retire
[x]Before the Patron Saint of injur'd *Spain.*

(x) *Patron Saint:* St. James, *on whose day this victory was gain'd.*

198

Repenting *England* this revengeful day
[y]To *Philip*'s Manes did an off'ring bring:
England, which first, by leading them astray,
Hatch'd up Rebellion to destroy her King.

(y) Philip'*s Manes:* Philip *the second, of* Spain, *against whom the* Hollanders *rebelling, were aided by Queen* Elizabeth.

199

Our Fathers bent their baneful industry
To check a Monarchy that slowly grew:
But did not *France* or *Holland*'s fate foresee,
Whose rising pow'r to swift Dominion flew.

200

In fortunes Empire blindly thus we go,
And wander after pathless destiny:
Whose dark resorts since prudence cannot know
In vain it would provide for what shall be.

201

But what ere *English* to the bless'd shall go,
And the fourth *Harry* or first *Orange* meet:
Find him disowning of a *Burbon* foe,
And him detesting a *Batavian* Fleet.

790 bring: *88*: bring. *67 68* 799 know, *68*: know. *67*: know; *88*

202

Now on their coasts our conquering Navy rides,
Way-lays their Merchants, and their Land besets:
Each day new wealth without their care provides,
They lie asleep with prizes in their nets.

203

So, close behind some Promontory lie
The huge Leviathans t' attend their prey:
And give no chace, but swallow in the frie,
Which through their gaping jaws mistake the way.

204

Nor was this all: in Ports and Roads remote,
Destructive Fires among whole Fleets we send:
Triumphant flames upon the water flote,
And out-bound ships at home their voyage end.

Burning of the Fleet in the Vly *by Sir* Robert Holmes.

205

Those various Squadrons, variously design'd,
Each vessel fraighted with a several load:
Each Squadron waiting for a several wind,
All find but one, to burn them in the Road.

206

Some bound for *Guinny*, golden sand to find,
Bore all the gawds the simple Natives wear:
Some for the pride of *Turkish* Courts design'd,
For folded *Turbans* finest *Holland* bear.

207

Some *English* Wool, vex'd in a *Belgian* Loom,
And into Cloth of spungy softness made:
Did into *France* or colder *Denmark* doom,
To ruine with worse ware our staple Trade.

824 *Turbans*] *Turbants 88*

208

Our greedy Sea-men rummage every hold,
  Smile on the booty of each wealthier Chest:
And, as the Priests who with their gods make bold,
  Take what they like, and sacrifice the rest.

209

But ah! how unsincere are all our joys!
  Which, sent from Heav'n, like Lightning make no stay:
Their palling taste the journeys length destroys,
  Or grief, sent post, o'r-takes them on the way.

Transitum *to the Fire of* London.

210

Swell'd with our late successes on the Foe,
  Which *France* and *Holland* wanted power to cross:
We urge an unseen Fate to lay us low,
  And feed their envious eyes with *English* loss.

211

Each Element his dread command obeys,
  Who makes or ruines with a smile or frown;
Who as by one he did our Nation raise,
  So now he with another pulls us down.

212

Yet, *London*, Empress of the Northern Clime,
  By an high fate thou greatly didst expire;
[z]Great as the worlds, which at the death of time
  Must fall, and rise a nobler frame by fire.

(z) Quum mare quum tellus correptaque regia Cœli, ardeat, &c. *Ovid*.

830 Smile *67* (*errata*): Smiles *67* (*text*)
835 palling *67* (*errata*): falling *67* (*text*)
833 *note* Transitum] Transit *88*

213

As when some dire Usurper Heav'n provides,
  To scourge his Country with a lawless sway:
His birth, perhaps, some petty Village hides,
  And sets his Cradle out of Fortune's way:

214

Till fully ripe his swelling fate breaks out,
  And hurries him to mighty mischiefs on:
His Prince surpriz'd at first, no ill could doubt,
  And wants the pow'r to meet it when 'tis known:

215

Such was the rise of this prodigious fire,
  Which in mean buildings first obscurely bred,
From thence did soon to open streets aspire,
  And straight to Palaces and Temples spread.

216

The diligence of Trades and noiseful gain,
  And luxury, more late, asleep were laid:
All was the nights, and in her silent reign,
  No sound the rest of Nature did invade.

217

In this deep quiet, from what source unknown,
  Those seeds of fire their fatal birth disclose:
And first, few scatt'ring sparks about were blown,
  Big with the flames that to our ruine rose.

218

Then, in some close-pent room it crept along,
  And, smouldring as it went, in silence fed:
Till th' infant monster, with devouring strong,
  Walk'd boldly upright with exalted head.

856 known: [known. *67 68 88*

219

Now, like some rich or mighty Murderer,
Too great for prison, which he breaks with gold:
Who fresher for new mischiefs does appear,
And dares the world to tax him with the old:

220

So scapes th' insulting fire his narrow Jail,
And makes small out-lets into open air:
There the fierce winds his tender force assail,
And beat him down-ward to his first repair.

221

[a]The winds, like crafty Courtezans, with-held
His flames from burning, but to blow them more:
And, every fresh attempt, he is repell'd
With faint denials, weaker then before.

(a) *Like crafty, &c.* Hæc arte tractabat cupidum virum, ut illius animum inopia accenderet.

222

And now, no longer letted of his prey,
He leaps up at it with inrag'd desire:
O'r-looks the neighbours with a wide survey,
And nods at every house his threatning fire.

223

The Ghosts of Traitors, from the *Bridge* descend,
With bold Fanatick Spectres to rejoyce:
About the fire into a Dance they bend,
And sing their Sabbath Notes with feeble voice.

874 Too *68 88*: To *67* 876 old:] old. *67 68 88* 879 tender *67* (*errata*): open *67* (*text*) 881 *note* accenderet *67* (*errata*): accruderet *67* (*text*)

224

Our Guardian Angel saw them where he sate
  Above the Palace of our slumbring King,
He sigh'd, abandoning his charge to Fate,
  And, drooping, oft lookt back upon the wing.

225

At length the crackling noise and dreadful blaze,
  Call'd up some waking Lover to the sight:
And long it was ere he the rest could raise,
  Whose heavy eye-lids yet were full of night.

226

The next to danger, hot pursu'd by fate,
  Half cloth'd, half naked, hastily retire:
And frighted Mothers strike their breasts, too late,
  For helpless Infants left amidst the fire.

227

Their cries soon waken all the dwellers near:
  Now murmuring noises rise in every street:
The more remote run stumbling with their fear,
  And, in the dark, men justle as they meet.

228

So weary Bees in little Cells repose:
  But if night-robbers lift the well-stor'd Hive,
An humming through their waxen City grows,
  And out upon each others wings they drive.

229

Now streets grow throng'd and busie as by day:
  Some run for Buckets to the hallow'd Quire:
Some cut the Pipes, and some the Engines play,
  And some more bold mount Ladders to the fire.

896 lookt *88*: look *67 68*   903 Mothers *88*: Mother *67 68*

230

In vain: for, from the East, a *Belgian* wind,
His hostile breath through the dry rafters sent:
The flames impell'd, soon left their foes behind,
And forward, with a wanton fury went.

231

A Key of fire ran all along the shore,
[b]And lighten'd all the River with the blaze:
The waken'd Tydes began again to roar,
And wond'ring Fish in shining waters gaze.

(b) Sigæa igni freta lata relucent. *Virg.*

232

Old Father *Thames* rais'd up his reverend head,
But fear'd the fate of *Simoeis* would return:
Deep in his *Ooze* he sought his sedgy bed,
And shrunk his waters back into his Urn.

233

The fire, mean time, walks in a broader gross,
To either hand his wings he opens wide:
He wades the streets, and straight he reaches cross,
And plays his longing flames on th' other side.

234

At first they warm, then scorch, and then they take:
Now with long necks from side to side they feed:
At length, grown strong, their Mother fire forsake,
And a new Collony of flames succeed.

235

To every nobler portion of the Town,
The curling billows roul their restless Tyde:
In parties now they straggle up and down,
As Armies, unoppos'd, for prey divide.

922 with the blaze] with a blaze *88* 923 waken'd] weaken'd *68*
939 straggle] struggle *88*

236

One mighty Squadron, with a side wind sped,
  Through narrow lanes his cumber'd fire does haste:
By pow'rful charms of gold and silver led,
  The *Lombard* Banquers and the *Change* to waste.

237

Another backward to the *Tow'r* would go,
  And slowly eats his way against the wind:
But the main body of the marching foe
  Against th' Imperial Palace is design'd.

238

Now day appears, and with the day the King,
  Whose early care had robb'd him of his rest:
Far off the cracks of falling houses ring,
  And shrieks of subjects pierce his tender breast.

239

Near as he draws, thick harbingers of smoke,
  With gloomy pillars, cover all the place:
Whose little intervals of night are broke
  By sparks that drive against his Sacred Face.

240

More then his Guards his sorrows made him known,
  And pious tears which down his cheeks did show'r:
The wretched in his grief forgot their own:
  (So much the pity of a King has pow'r.)

241

He wept the flames of what he lov'd so well,
  And what so well had merited his love.
For never Prince in grace did more excel,
  Or Royal City more in duty strove.

242

Nor with an idle care did he behold:
  (Subjects may grieve, but Monarchs must redress.)
He chears the fearful, and commends the bold,
  And makes despairers hope for good success.

243

Himself directs what first is to be done,
  And orders all the succours which they bring.
The helpful and the good about him run,
  And form an Army worthy such a King.

244

He sees the dire contagion spread so fast,
  That where it seizes, all relief is vain:
And therefore must unwillingly lay waste
  That Country which would, else, the foe maintain.

245

The powder blows up all before the fire:
  Th' amazed flames stand gather'd on a heap;
And from the precipices brinck retire,
  Afraid to venture on so large a leap.

246

Thus fighting fires a while themselves consume,
  But straight, like *Turks*, forc'd on to win or die,
They first lay tender bridges of their fume,
  And o'r the breach in unctuous vapours flie.

247

Part stays for passage till a gust of wind
  Ships o'r their forces in a shining sheet:
Part, creeping under ground, their journey blind,
  And, climbing from below, their fellows meet.

248

Thus, to some desart plain, or old wood side,
  Dire night-hags come from far to dance their round:
And o'r brode Rivers on their fiends they ride,
  Or sweep in clowds above the blasted ground.

249

No help avails: for, *Hydra*-like, the fire,
  Lifts up his hundred heads to aim his way.
And scarce the wealthy can one half retire,
  Before he rushes in to share the prey.

250

The rich grow suppliant, and the poor grow proud:
  Those offer mighty gain, and these ask more.
So void of pity is th' ignoble crowd,
  When others ruine may increase their store.

251

As those who live by shores with joy behold
  Some wealthy vessel split or stranded nigh;
And, from the Rocks, leap down for shipwrack'd Gold,
  And seek the Tempest which the others flie:

252

So these but wait the Owners last despair,
  And what's permitted to the flames invade:
Ev'n from their jaws they hungry morsels tear,
  And, on their backs, the spoils of *Vulcan* lade.

253

The days were all in this lost labour spent;
  And when the weary King gave place to night,
His Beams he to his Royal Brother lent,
  And so shone still in his reflective light.

990 night-hags *67* (*errata*): night has *67* (*text*) 1004 Tempest] Tempests *88* flie:] flie. *67 68 88*

254

Night came, but without darkness or repose,
  A dismal picture of the gen'ral doom:
Where Souls distracted when the Trumpet blows,
  And half unready with their bodies come.

255

Those who have homes, when home they do repair
  To a last lodging call their wand'ring friends.
Their short uneasie sleeps are broke with care,
  To look how near their own destruction tends.

256

Those who have none sit round where once it was,
  And with full eyes each wonted room require:
Haunting the yet warm ashes of the place,
  As murder'd men walk where they did expire.

257

Some stir up coals and watch the Vestal fire,
  Others in vain from sight of ruine run:
And, while through burning Lab'rinths they retire,
  With loathing eyes repeat what they would shun.

258

The most, in fields, like herded beasts lie down;
  To dews obnoxious on the grassie floor:
And while their Babes in sleep their sorrows drown,
  Sad Parents watch the remnants of their store.

259

While by the motion of the flames they ghess
  What streets are burning now, and what are near:
An Infant, waking, to the paps would press,
  And meets, instead of milk, a falling tear.

1015 blows, *68 88*: blows. *67*

260

No thought can ease them but their Sovereign's care,
  Whose praise th' afflicted as their comfort sing:
Ev'n those whom want might drive to just despair,
  Think life a blessing under such a King.

261

Mean time he sadly suffers in their grief,
  Out-weeps an Hermite, and out-prays a Saint:
All the long night he studies their relief,
  How they may be suppli'd, and he may want.

262

O God, said he, thou Patron of my days,
  Guide of my youth in exile and distress!
Who me unfriended, brought'st by wondrous ways
  The Kingdom of my Fathers to possess:

King's Prayer.

263

Be thou my Judge, with what unwearied care
  I since have labour'd for my People's good:
To bind the bruises of a Civil War,
  And stop the issues of their wasting bloud.

264

Thou, who hast taught me to forgive the ill,
  And recompense, as friends, the good misled;
If mercy be a Precept of thy will,
  Return that mercy on thy Servant's head.

265

Or, if my heedless Youth has stept astray,
  Too soon forgetful of thy gracious hand:
On me alone thy just displeasure lay,
  But take thy judgments from this mourning Land.

1048 possess:] possess. *67 68 88*   1054 friends, the good *88*: friends the good, *67 68*

266

We all have sinn'd, and thou hast laid us low,
  As humble Earth from whence at first we came:
Like flying shades before the clowds we show,
  And shrink like Parchment in consuming flame.

267

O let it be enough what thou hast done,
  When spotted deaths ran arm'd through every street,
With poison'd darts, which not the good could shun,
  The speedy could out-fly, or valiant meet.

268

The living few, and frequent funerals then,
  Proclam'd thy wrath on this forsaken place:
And now those few who are return'd agen
  Thy searching judgments to their dwellings trace.

269

O pass not, Lord, an absolute decree,
  Or bind thy sentence unconditional:
But in thy sentence our remorce foresee,
  And, in that foresight, this thy doom recall.

270

Thy threatnings, Lord, as thine, thou maist revoke:
  But, if immutable and fix'd they stand,
Continue still thy self to give the stroke,
  And let not foreign foes oppress thy Land.

271

Th' Eternal heard, and from the Heav'nly Quire,
  Chose out the Cherub with the flaming sword:
And bad him swiftly drive th' approaching fire
  From where our Naval Magazins were stor'd.

1067 shun, *88*: shun. *67 68* 1077 threatnings] Threatings *88*

272

The blessed Minister his wings displai'd,
  And like a shooting Star he cleft the night:
He charg'd the flames, and those that disobey'd,
  He lash'd to duty with his sword of light.

273

The fugitive flames, chastis'd, went forth to prey
  On pious Structures, by our Fathers rear'd:
By which to Heav'n they did affect the way,
  Ere Faith in Church-men without Works was heard.

274

The wanting Orphans saw, with watry eyes,
  Their Founders charity in dust laid low:
And sent to God their ever-answer'd cries,
  (For he protects the poor who made them so.)

275

Nor could thy Fabrick, *Paul*'s, defend thee long,
  Though thou wert Sacred to thy Makers praise:
Though made immortal by a Poet's Song;
  And Poets Songs the *Theban* walls could raise.

276

The dareing flames peep't in and saw from far,
  The awful beauties of the Sacred Quire:
But, since it was prophan'd by Civil War,
  Heav'n thought it fit to have it purg'd by fire.

277

Now down the narrow streets it swiftly came,
  And, widely opening, did on both sides prey.
This benefit we sadly owe the flame,
  If onely ruine must enlarge our way.

1094 in dust] in the Dust *88*

278

And now four days the Sun had seen our woes,
Four nights the Moon beheld th' incessant fire:
It seem'd as if the Stars more sickly rose,
And farther from the feav'rish North retire.

279

In th' Empyrean Heaven, (the bless'd abode)
The Thrones and the Dominions prostrate lie,
Not daring to behold their angry God:
And an hush'd silence damps the tuneful sky.

280

At length th' Almighty cast a pitying eye,
And mercy softly touch'd his melting breast:
He saw the Town's one half in rubbish lie,
And eager flames give on to storm the rest.

281

An hollow chrystal Pyramid he takes,
In firmamental waters dipt above;
Of it a brode Extinguisher he makes,
And hoods the flames that to their quarry strove.

282

The vanquish'd fires withdraw from every place,
Or full with feeding, sink into a sleep:
Each houshold Genius shows again his face,
And, from the hearths, the little Lares creep.

283

Our King this more then natural change beholds;
With sober joy his heart and eyes abound:
To the All-good his lifted hands he folds,
And thanks him low on his redeemed ground.

1120 give] drive *88*

284

As when sharp frosts had long constrain'd the earth,
  A kindly thaw unlocks it with mild rain:
And first the tender blade peeps up to birth,
  And straight the green fields laugh with promis'd grain:

285

By such degrees, the spreading gladness grew
  In every heart, which fear had froze before:
The standing streets with so much joy they view,
  That with less grief the perish'd they deplore.

286

The Father of the people open'd wide
  His stores, and all the poor with plenty fed:
Thus God's Annointed God's own place suppli'd,
  And fill'd the empty with his daily bread.

287

This Royal bounty brought its own reward,
  And, in their minds, so deep did print the sense:
That if their ruines sadly they regard,
  'Tis but with fear the sight might drive him thence.

288

But so may he live long, that Town to sway,
  Which by his Auspice they will nobler make,
As he will hatch their ashes by his stay,
  And not their humble ruines now forsake.

Cities request to the King not to leave them.

289

They have not lost their Loyalty by fire;
  Nor is their courage or their wealth so low,
That from his Wars they poorly would retire,
  Or beg the pity of a vanquish'd foe.

290

Not with more constancy the *Jews* of old,
By *Cyrus* from rewarded Exile sent:
Their Royal City did in dust behold,
Or with more vigour to rebuild it went.

291

The utmost malice of their Stars is past,
And two dire Comets which have scourg'd the Town,
In their own Plague and Fire have breath'd their last,
Or, dimly, in their sinking sockets frown.

292

Now frequent Trines the happier lights among,
And high-rais'd *Jove* from his dark prison freed:
(Those weights took off that on his Planet hung)
Will gloriously the new laid work succeed.

293

Me-thinks already, from this Chymick flame,
I see a City of more precious mold:
Rich as the Town which gives the [c]*Indies* name,
With Silver pav'd, and all divine with Gold.

(c) *Mexico.*

294

Already, Labouring with a mighty fate,
She shakes the rubbish from her mounting brow,
And seems to have renew'd her Charters date,
Which Heav'n will to the death of time allow.

295

More great then humane, now, and more [d]*August*,
New deifi'd she from her fires does rise:
Her widening streets on new foundations trust,
And, opening, into larger parts she flies.

(d) Augusta, *the old name of* London.

1168 work] Works *88*

296

Before, she like some Shepherdess did show,
  Who sate to bathe her by a River's side:
Not answering to her fame, but rude and low,
  Nor taught the beauteous Arts of Modern pride.

297

Now, like a Maiden Queen, she will behold,
  From her high Turrets, hourly Sutors come:
The East with Incense, and the West with Gold,
  Will stand, like Suppliants, to receive her doom.

298

The silver *Thames*, her own domestick Floud,
  Shall bear her Vessels, like a sweeping Train;
And often wind (as of his Mistress proud)
  With longing eyes to meet her face again.

299

The wealthy *Tagus*, and the wealthier *Rhine*,
  The glory of their Towns no more shall boast:
And *Sein*, That would with *Belgian* Rivers joyn,
  Shall find her lustre stain'd, and Traffick lost.

300

The vent'rous Merchant, who design'd more far,
  And touches on our hospitable shore:
Charm'd with the splendour of this Northern Star,
  Shall here unlade him, and depart no more.

301

Our pow'rful Navy shall no longer meet,
  The wealth of *France* or *Holland* to invade:
The beauty of this Town, without a Fleet,
  From all the world shall vindicate her Trade.

302

And, while this fam'd Emporium we prepare,
The *British* Ocean shall such triumphs boast,
That those who now disdain our Trade to share,
Shall rob like Pyrats on our wealthy Coast.

303

Already we have conquer'd half the War,
And the less dang'rous part is left behind:
Our trouble now is but to make them dare,
And not so great to vanquish as to find.

304

Thus to the Eastern wealth through storms we go;
But now, the Cape once doubled, fear no more:
A constant Trade-wind will securely blow,
And gently lay us on the Spicy shore.

PROLOGUE and SONG from *SECRET-LOVE*

PROLOGUE

I

He who writ this, not without pains and thought
From *French* and *English* Theaters has brought
Th' exactest Rules by which a Play is wrought.

II

The Unities of Action, Place, and Time;
The Scenes unbroken; and a mingled chime
Of *Johnsons* humour, with *Corneilles* rhyme.

III

But while dead colours he with care did lay,
He fears his Wit, or Plot he did not weigh,
Which are the living Beauties of a Play.

IV

Plays are like Towns, which howe're fortifi'd
By Engineers, have still some weaker side
By the o'reseen Defendant unespy'd.

V

And with that Art you make approaches now;
Such skilful fury in Assaults you show,
That every Poet without shame may bow.

Prologue and Song. Text from Secret-Love, or The Maiden-Queen, *1668, collated with the editions of 1669, 1679, 1691, 1698*
Prologue. 1 thought] thought, *79 91 98*

VI

Ours therefore humbly would attend your doom,
If Souldier-like, he may have termes to come
With flying colours, and with beat of Drum.

The Prologue goes out, and stayes while a Tune is play'd, after which he returnes again.

Second PROLOGUE

I HAD forgot one half I do protest,
And now am sent again to speak the rest.
He bowes to every great and noble Wit,
But to the little Hectors of the Pit
Our Poet 's sturdy, and will not submit.
He'll be before-hand with 'em, and not stay
To see each peevish Critick stab his Play:
Each Puny Censor, who his skill to boast,
Is cheaply witty on the Poets cost.
No Criticks verdict, should, of right, stand good,
They are excepted all as men of blood:
And the same Law should shield him from their fury
Which has excluded Butchers from a Jury.
You'd all be Wits—
But writing's tedious, and that way may fail;
The most compendious method is to rail:
Which you so like, you think your selves ill us'd
When in smart Prologues you are not abus'd.
A civil Prologue is approv'd by no man;
You hate it as you do a Civil woman:
Your Fancy's pall'd, and liberally you pay
To have it quicken'd, e're you see a Play.
Just as old Sinners worn from their delight,
Give money to be whip'd to appetite.
But what a Pox keep I so much ado
To save our Poet? he is one of you;
A Brother Judgment, and as I hear say,

30 should shield him] should shield them *69 (some copies) 98*: shall shield them *69 (some copies) 79 91*

A cursed Critick as e're damn'd a Play.
Good salvage Gentlemen your own kind spare,
He is, like you, a very Wolf, or Bear;
Yet think not he'll your ancient rights invade,
Or stop the course of your free damning trade:
For he, (he vows) at no friends Play can sit
But he must needs find fault to shew his Wit:
Then, for his sake, ne're stint your own delight;
Throw boldly, for he sets to all that write;
With such he ventures on an even lay,
For they bring ready money into Play.
Those who write not, and yet all Writers nick,
Are Bankrupt Gamesters, for they damn on Tick.

SONG

I FEED a flame within which so torments me
That it both pains my heart, and yet contents me:
'Tis such a pleasing smart, and I so love it,
That I had rather die, then once remove it.

Yet he for whom I grieve shall never know it,
My tongue does not betray, nor my eyes show it:
Not a sigh nor a tear my pain discloses,
But they fall silently like dew on Roses.

Thus to prevent my love from being cruel,
My heart's the sacrifice as 'tis the fuel:
And while I suffer this to give him quiet,
My faith rewards my love, though he deny it.

On his eyes will I gaze, and there delight me;
While I conceal my love, no frown can fright me:
To be more happy I dare not aspire;
Nor can I fall more low, mounting no higher.

PROLOGUE, EPILOGUE and SONGS from *SIR MARTIN MAR-ALL*

PROLOGUE

FOOLS, which each man meets in his Dish each day,
Are yet the great Regalios of a Play;
In which to Poets you but just appear,
To prize that highest which cost them so dear:
Fops in the Town more easily will pass;
One story makes a statutable Ass:
But such in Plays must be much thicker sown,
Like yolks of Eggs, a dozen beat to one.
Observing Poets all their walks invade,
As men watch Woodcocks gliding through a Glade:
And when they have enough for Comedy,
They stow their several Bodies in a Pye:
The Poet 's but the Cook to fashion it,
For, Gallants, you your selves have found the wit.
To bid you welcome would your bounty wrong,
None welcome those who bring their chear along.

EPILOGUE

AS Country Vicars, when the Sermon's done,
Run hudling to the Benediction;
Well knowing, though the better sort may stay,
The Vulgar Rout will run unblest away:
So we, when once our Play is done, make haste
With a short Epilogue to close your taste.
In thus withdrawing we seem mannerly,
But when the Curtain's down we peep, and see
A Jury of the Wits who still stay late,
And in their Club decree the poor Plays fate;

Prologue, Epilogue and Songs. Text from S[r] Martin Mar-all, or The Feign'd Innocence: A Comedy, *1668 (a), collated with the second edition, 1668 (b) and the editions of 1678, 1691, 1697. See Commentary*

Prologue. 4 cost *68b–97*: costs *68a*   6 Ass:] Ass, *68b*: Ass; *78–97*   8 yolks] Yelks *78 91 97*

Epilogue. 8 peep,] peep *68b–97*

Their Verdict back is to the Boxes brought,
Thence all the Town pronounces it their thought.
Thus, Gallants, we like *Lilly* can foresee,
But if you ask us what our doom will be,
We by to morrow will our Fortune cast,
As he tells all things when the Year is past.

SONGS

I

[WARNER] *SINGS*

MAKE ready fair Lady to night,
  And stand at the Door below,
For I will be there
To receive you with care,
  And to your true Love you shall go.

[MILLISENT] *SINGS*

And when the Stars twinckle so bright,
Then down to the Door will I creep,
    To my Love will I flye,
    E're the jealous can spye,
And leave my old daddy asleep.

II

The SONG

BLIND Love to this hour
Had never like me, a Slave under his power.
Then blest be the Dart
That he threw at my heart,
For nothing can prove
A joy so great as to be wounded with love.

My Days and my Nights
Are fill'd to the purpose with sorrows and frights;
    From my heart still I sigh
    And my Eyes are ne're dry,

So that *Cupid* be prais'd,
I am to the top of Love's happiness rais'd.

My Soul's all on fire,
So that I have the pleasure to doat and desire,
Such a pretty soft pain
That it tickles each vein;
'Tis the dream of a smart,
Which makes me breathe short when it beats at my heart.

Sometimes in a Pet,
When I am despis'd, I my freedom would get;
But streight a sweet smile
Does my anger beguile,
And my heart does recall,
Then the more I do struggle, the lower I fall.

Heaven does not impart
Such a grace as to love unto ev'ry ones heart;
For many may wish
To be wounded and miss:
Then blest be loves Fire,
And more blest her Eyes that first taught me desire.

PROLOGUES and EPILOGUES to *THE WILD GALLANT*

PROLOGUE to the WILD GALLANT as it was first Acted

Is it not strange, to hear a Poet say,
He comes to ask you, how you like the Play?
You have not seen it yet! alas 'tis true,
But now your Love and Hatred judge, not You.
And cruel Factions (brib'd by Interest) come,
Not to weigh Merit, but to give their Doome:

Prologues and Epilogues. Text from The Wild Gallant: A Comedy, *1669 (a) collated with the second edition, 1669 (b) and the editions of 1684 and 1694. See Commentary.*

Our Poet therefore, jealous of th' Event,
And (though much boldness takes) not confident,
Has sent me, whither you, fair Ladies, too
Sometimes upon as small occasions goe,
And from this Scheme, drawn for the hour and day,
Bid me inquire the fortune of his Play.

The Curtain drawn discovers two Astrologers; The Prologue is presented to them.

First Astrol. reads. A Figure of the heavenly Bodies in their several Apartments, *Feb.* the *5th.* half an hour after three after Noon, from whence you are to judge the success of a new Play called the *Wild Gallant.*

2. *Astrol.* Who must Judge of it, we, or these Gentlemen? We'l not meddle with it, so tell your Poet. Here are in this House the ablest Mathematicians in *Europe* for his purpose.
They will resolve the question e'r they part.

1. *Ast.* Yet let us judge it by the rules of Art.
First *Jupiter*, the Ascendants Lord disgrac'd,
In the twelfth House, and near grim *Saturn* plac'd,
Denote short life unto the Play:—

2. *Ast.* *Jove* yet,
In his Apartment *Sagitary*, set
Under his own Roof, canot take much wrong;

1. *Ast.* Why then the Lifes not very short, nor long;

2. *Ast.* The Luck not very good, nor very ill,

Prolo. That is to say, 'tis as 'tis taken still.

1. *Ast.* But, Brother, *Ptolomy* the Learned says,
'Tis the fifth house from whence we judge of Plays.
Venus the Lady of that House I find
Is *Peregrine*, your Play is ill design'd,
It should have been but one continued Song,
Or at the least a Dance of 3 hours long.

2. *Ast.* But yet the greatest Mischief does remain,
The twelfth apartment bears the Lord of *Spain*;
Whence I conclude it is your Authors lot,
To be indanger'd by a *Spanish* Plot.

Prolo. Our Poet yet protection hopes from you,
But bribes you not with any thing that's new.
Nature is old, which Poets imitate,
And for Wit, those that boast their own estate,
Forget *Fletcher* and *Ben* before them went,
Their Elder Brothers, and that vastly spent:
So much 'twill hardly be repair'd again,
Not, though supply'd with all the wealth of *Spain*:
This Play is *English*, and the growth your own;
As such it yields to *English* Plays alone.
He could have wish'd it better for your sakes;
But that in Plays he finds you love mistakes:
Besides he thought it was in vain to mend
What you are bound in honour to defend,
That *English* Wit (how e'r despis'd by some)
Like *English* Valour still may overcome.

EPILOGUE *to the WILD GALLANT, as it was first Acted*

THE *Wild Gallant* has quite playd out his game;
He's marry'd now, and that will make him tame;
Or if you think Marriage will not reclaim him,
The Critiques swear they'll damn him, but they'll tame him.
Yet though our Poet 's threatned most by these,
They are the only People he can please:
For he to humour them, has shown to day,
That which they only like, a wretched Play:
But though his Play be ill, here have been shown
The greatest Wits and Beauties of the Town.
And his Occasion having brought you here
You are too grateful to become severe.
There is not any Person here so mean,
But he may freely judge each Act and Scene:
But if you bid him choose his Judges then,
He boldly names true English Gentlemen:
For he ne'r thought a handsome Garb or Dress,
So great a Crime to make their Judgement less:

And with these Gallants he these Ladies joyns,
To judge that Language their Converse refines.
But if their Censures should condemn his Play,
Far from Disputing, he does only pray
He may *Leanders* Destiny obtain:
Now spare him, drown him when he comes again.

PROLOGUE to the WILD-GALLANT *Reviv'd*

As some raw Squire, by tender Mother bred,
Till one and Twenty keeps his Maidenhead,
(Pleas'd with some Sport which he alone does find,
And thinks a secret to all Humane kind;)
Till mightily in love, yet halfe afraid,
He first attempts the gentle Dairymaid:
Succeeding there, and led by the renown
Of *Whetstones Park*, he comes at length to Town,
Where enter'd, by some School-fellow, or Friend,
He grows to break Glass-Windows in the end:
His valour too, which with the Watch began,
Proceeds to duell, and he kills his Man.
By such degrees, while knowledge he did want,
Our unfletch'd Author, writ a *Wild Gallant*.
He thought him monstrous leud (I'l lay my life)
Because suspected with his Landlords Wife:
But since his knowledge of the Town began,
He thinks him now a very civil man:
And, much asham'd of what he was before,
Has fairly play'd him at three Wenches more.
'Tis some amends his frailties to confess;
Pray pardon him his want of wickedness:
He's towardly, and will come on apace;
His frank confession shows he has some grace.
You balk'd him when he was a young beginner,
And almost spoyl'd a very hopeful sinner:
But, if once more you slight his weak indeavour;
For ought I know, he may turn taile for ever.

EPILOGUE *to the* WILD GALLANT *reviv'd*

OF all Dramatique Writing, Comick Wit,
As 'tis the best, so 'tis most hard to hit.
For it lies all in level to the eye,
Where all may judge, and each defect may spye.
Humour is that which every day we meet,
And therefore known as every publick street;
In which, if e'r the Poet go astray
You all can point, 'twas there he lost his way.
But, What's so common, to make pleasant too,
Is more than any wit can alwayes do.
For 'tis, like *Turkes*, with Hen and Rice to treat;
To make regallio's out of common meat.
But, in your Diet you grow Salvages:
Nothing but Humane flesh your taste can please:
And, as their Feasts with slaughter'd slaves began,
So you, at each new Play, must have a Man.
Hither you come, as to see Prizes fought;
If no Blood's drawn, you cry the Prize is naught.
But fooles grow wary now; and when they see
A Poet eyeing round the Company,
Straight each man for himself begins to doubt;
They shrink like Seamen when a Press comes out.
Few of 'em will be found for Publick use,
Except you charge an Oph upon each house,
Like the Traind-Bands, and every man ingage
For a sufficient Foole to serve the Stage.
And, when with much adoe you get him there,
Where he in all his glory shou'd appear,
Your Poets make him such rare things to say,
That he's more wit than any Man ith' Play.
But of so ill a mingle with the rest,
As when a Parrat 's taught to break a jeast.
Thus aiming to be fine, they make a show
As tawdry Squires in Country Churches do.
Things well consider'd, 'tis so hard to make
A Comedy, which should the knowing take:

Epilogue. 11 Hen] *Hen 69a–94* 23 'em] them *84 94* 25 Traind-Bands] Train-Bands *69b 84 94* 28 in] and *84 94*

That our dull Poet, in despair to please,
Does humbly beg by me his writ of ease.
'Tis a Land-tax which he's too poor to pay;
You, therefore, must some other impost lay.
Would you but change for serious Plot and Verse
This mottley garniture of Fool and Farce,
Nor scorn a Mode, because 'tis taught at home,
Which does, like Vests, our Gravity become;
Our Poet yields you should this Play refuse,
As Tradesmen, by the change of fashions, lose
With some content their fripperies of *France*,
In hope it may their staple Trade advance.

PROLOGUE and EPILOGUE to *THE TEMPEST*

PROLOGUE to the Tempest, *or the* Enchanted Island

As when a Tree's cut down the secret root
Lives under ground, and thence new Branches shoot;
So, from old *Shakespear*'s honour'd dust, this day
Springs up and buds a new reviving Play.
Shakespear, who (taught by none) did first impart
To *Fletcher* Wit, to labouring *Johnson* Art.
He Monarch-like gave those his subjects law,
And is that Nature which they paint and draw.
Fletcher reach'd that which on his heights did grow,
Whilst *Johnson* crept and gather'd all below.
This did his Love, and this his Mirth digest:
One imitates him most, the other best.
If they have since out-writ all other men,
'Tis with the drops which fell from *Shakespear*'s Pen.
The Storm which vanish'd on the Neighb'ring shore,
Was taught by *Shakespear*'s Tempest first to roar.

Prologue and Epilogue. Text from The Tempest, or The Enchanted Island. A Comedy, *1670, collated with the editions of 1674, 1676, 1690, c. 1692, 1695. See Commentary*

Prologue. Heading. Island] Isle *76 (92)* shoot; *74 76 90*: shoot *70*

That innocence and beauty which did smile
In *Fletcher*, grew on this *Enchanted Isle.*
But *Shakespear*'s Magick could not copy'd be,
Within that Circle none durst walk but he.
I must confess 'twas bold, nor would you now,
That liberty to vulgar Wits allow,
Which works by Magick supernatural things:
But *Shakespear*'s pow'r is sacred as a King's.
Those Legends from old Priest-hood were receiv'd,
And he then writ, as people then believ'd.
But, if for *Shakespear* we your grace implore,
We for our Theatre shall want it more:
Who by our dearth of Youths are forc'd t' employ
One of our Women to present a Boy.
And that's a transformation you will say
Exceeding all the Magick in the Play.
Let none expect in the last Act to find,
Her Sex transform'd from man to Woman-kind.
What e're she was before the Play began,
All you shall see of her is perfect man.
Or if your fancy will be farther led,
To find her Woman, it must be abed.

EPILOGUE

GALLANTS, by all good signs it does appear,
That Sixty Seven's a very damning year,
For Knaves abroad, and for ill Poets here.

Among the Muses there's a gen'ral rot,
The Rhyming Mounsieur and the Spanish Plot:
Defie or Court, all's one, they go to Pot.

The Ghosts of Poets walk within this place,
And haunt us Actors wheresoe're we pass,
In Visions bloodier than King *Richard*'s was.

For this poor wretch he has not much to say,
But quietly brings in his part o'th' Play,
And begs the favour to be damn'd to day.

Epilogue. 3 abroad] aboard *76* [*92*]

He sends me only like a Sh'riffs man here
To let you know the Malefactor's neer;
And that he means to dye, *en Cavalier*.

For if you shou'd be gracious to his Pen,
Th' Example will prove ill to other men,
And you'll be troubled with 'em all agen.

PROLOGUE, EPILOGUE and SONGS from *TYRANNICK LOVE*

PROLOGUE

SELF-LOVE (which never rightly understood)
Makes Poets still conclude their Plays are good:
And malice in all Criticks raigns so high,
That for small Errors, they whole Plays decry;
So that to see this fondness, and that spite,
You'd think that none but Mad-men judge or write.
Therefore our Poet, as he thinks not fit
T' impose upon you, what he writes for Wit,
So hopes that leaving you your censures free,
You equal Judges of the whole will be:
They judge but half who only faults will see.
Poets like Lovers should be bold and dare,
They spoil their business with an over-care.
And he who servilely creeps after sence,
Is safe, but ne're will reach an Excellence.
Hence 'tis our Poet in his conjuring,
Allow'd his Fancy the full scope and swing.
But when a Tyrant for his Theme he had,
He loos'd the Reins, and bid his Muse run mad:
And though he stumbles in a full career;
Yet rashness is a better fault than fear.
He saw his way; but in so swift a pace,
To chuse the ground, might be to lose the race.
They then who of each trip th' advantage take,
Find but those Faults which they want Wit to make.

Prologue, Epilogue and Songs. Text from Tyrannick Love, or The Royal Martyr. A Tragedy, *1670, collated with the editions of 1672, 1677, 1686, 1695*

EPILOGUE

Spoked by Mrs. Ellen, *when she was to be carried off dead by the Bearers*

To the Bearer. HOLD, are you mad? you damn'd confounded Dog,
I am to rise, and speak the Epilogue.
To the Audience. I come, kind Gentlemen, strange news to tell ye,
I am the Ghost of poor departed *Nelly.*
Sweet Ladies, be not frighted, I'le be civil,
I'm what I was, a little harmless Devil.
For after death, we Sprights, have just such Natures,
We had for all the World, when humane Creatures;
And therefore I that was an Actress here,
Play all my Tricks in Hell, a Goblin there.
Gallants, look to't, you say there are no Sprights;
But I'le come dance about your Beds at nights.
And faith you'l be in a sweet kind of taking,
When I surprise you between sleep and waking.
To tell you true, I walk because I dye
Out of my Calling in a Tragedy.
O Poet, damn'd dull Poet, who could prove
So sensless! to make *Nelly* dye for Love,
Nay, what's yet worse, to kill me in the prime
Of *Easter*-Term, in Tart and Cheese-cake time!
I'le fit the Fopp; for I'le not one word say
T'excuse his godly out of fashion Play.
A Play which if you dare but twice sit out,
You'l all be slander'd, and be thought devout.
But, farewel Gentlemen, make haste to me,
I'm sure e're long to have your company.
As for my Epitaph when I am gone,
I'le trust no Poet, but will write my own.

Here Nelly *lies, who, though she liv'd a Slater'n,*
Yet dy'd a Princess, acting in S. Cathar'n.

SONGS

I

Nakar and *Damilcar* descend in Clouds, and sing

Nakar. HARK, my *Damilcar*, we are call'd below!
Dam. Let us go, let us go!
Go to relieve the care
Of longing Lovers in despair!
Nakar. Merry, merry, merry, we sail from the East
Half tippled at a Rain-bow Feast.
Dam. In the bright Moon-shine while winds whistle loud,
Tivy, tivy, tivy, we mount and we fly,
All racking along in a downy white Cloud:
And lest our leap from the Skie should prove too far,
We slide on the back of a new-falling Star.
Nakar. And drop from above,
In a Gelly of Love!
Dam. But now the Sun's down, and the Element's red,
The Spirits of Fire against us make head!
Nakar. They muster, they muster, like Gnats in the Air:
Alas! I must leave thee, my Fair;
And to my light Horse-men repair.
Dam. O stay, for you need not to fear 'em to night;
The wind is for us, and blows full in their sight:
And o're the wide Ocean we fight!
Like leaves in the Autumn our Foes will fall down;
And hiss in the Water—
Both. And hiss in the Water and drown!
Nakar. But their men lye securely intrench'd in a Cloud:
And a Trumpeter-Hornet to battel sounds loud.
Dam. Now Mortals that spie
How we tilt in the Skie
With wonder will gaze;
And fear such events as will ne're come to pass!
Nakar. Stay you to perform what the man will have done.
Dam. Then call me again when the Battel is won.
Both. So ready and quick is a Spirit of Air
To pity the Lover, and succour the fair,

That, silent and swift, the little soft God
Is here with a wish, and is gone with a nod.

The Clouds part, *Nakar* flies up, and *Damilcar* down.

II

Damilcar stamps, and the Bed arises with S. *Catharine* in it

Dam. singing. YOU pleasing dreams of Love and sweet delight,
Appear before this slumbring Virgins sight:
Soft visions set her free
From mournful piety.
Let her sad thoughts from Heav'n retire;
And let the Melancholy Love
Of those remoter joys above
Give place to your more sprightly fire.
Let purling streams be in her fancy seen;
And flowry Meads, and Vales of chearful green:
And in the midst of deathless Groves
Soft sighing wishes ly,
And smiling hopes fast by,
And just beyond 'em ever laughing Loves.

A Scene of a *Paradise* is discovered.

III

SONG

Dam. AH how sweet it is to love,
Ah how gay is young desire!
And what pleasing pains we prove
When we first approach Loves fire!
Pains of Love be sweeter far
Than all other pleasures are.

Sighs which are from Lovers blown,
Do but gently heave the Heart:
Ev'n the tears they shed alone
Cure, like trickling Balm their smart.
Lovers when they lose their breath,
Bleed away in easie death.

Songs. I. 35 the] that *77 86 95*

Love and Time with reverence use,
Treat 'em like a parting friend:
Nor the golden gifts refuse
Which in youth sincere they send:
For each year their price is more,
And they less simple than before.

Love, like Spring-tides full and high,
Swells in every youthful vein:
But each Tide does less supply,
Till they quite shrink in again:
If a flow in Age appear,
'Tis but rain, and runs not clear.

At the end of the Song a Dance of Spirits. . . .

PROLOGUE, EPILOGUE and SONGS from *AN EVENING'S LOVE*

PROLOGUE

WHEN first our Poet set himself to write,
Like a young Bridegroom on his Wedding-night
He layd about him, and did so bestir him,
His Muse could never lye in quiet for him:
But now his Honey-moon is gone and past,
Yet the ungrateful drudgery must last:
And he is bound, as civil Husbands do,
To strain himself, in complaisance to you:
To write in pain, and counterfeit a bliss,
Like the faint smackings of an after kiss.
But you, like Wives ill pleas'd, supply his want;
Each writing Monsieur is a fresh Gallant:
And though, perhaps, 'twas done as well before,
Yet still there's something in a new amour.
Your several Poets work with several tools,
One gets you wits, another gets you fools:

Prologue, Epilogue and Songs. Text from An Evening's Love, or The Mock-Astrologer, 1671 (*a*), *collated with the second edition*, 1671 (*b*), *and the edition of* 1691. *See Commentary*
Prologue. 10 smackings] smacking *91*

This pleases you with some by-stroke of wit,
This finds some cranny, that was never hit.
But should these janty Lovers daily come
To do your work, like your good man at home,
Their fine small timber'd wits would soon decay;
These are Gallants but for a Holiday.
Others you had who oftner have appear'd,
Whom, for meer impotence you have cashier'd:
Such as at first came on with pomp and glory,
But, overstraining, soon fell flat before yee.
Their useless weight with patience long was born,
But at the last you threw 'em off with scorn.
As for the Poet of this present night,
Though now he claims in you an Husbands right,
He will not hinder you of fresh delight.
He, like a Seaman, seldom will appear;
And means to trouble home but thrice a year:
That only time from your Gallants he'll borrow;
Be kind to day, and Cuckold him to morrow.

EPILOGUE

MY part being small, I have had time to day,
To mark your various censures of our Play:
First, looking for a Judgement or a Wit,
Like *Jews* I saw 'em scatter'd through the Pit:
And where a knot of Smilers lent an eare
To one that talk'd, I knew the foe was there.
The Club of jests went round; he who had none
Borrow'd oth' next, and told it for his own:
Among the rest they kept a fearfull stir,
In whisp'ring that he stole th' *Astrologer*;
And said, betwixt a *French* and *English* Plot
He eas'd his half-tir'd Muse, on pace and trot.
Up starts a Monsieur new come o're; and warm
In the *French* stoop; and the pull-back oth' arm;
Morbleu dit il, and cocks, I am a rogue
But he has quite spoil'd the feint *Astrologue.*
Pox, sayes another; here's so great a stir
With a son of a whore Farce that's regular,

A rule where nothing must decorum shock!
Dam'me 'ts as dull as dining by the clock.
An Evening! why the devil should we be vext
Whither he gets the Wench this night or next?
When I heard this, I to the Poet went,
Told him the house was full of discontent,
And ask'd him what excuse he could invent.
He neither swore nor storm'd as Poets do,
But, most unlike an Author, vow'd 'twas true.
Yet said, he us'd the *French* like Enemies,
And did not steal their Plots, but made 'em prize.
But should he all the pains and charges count
Of taking 'em, the bill so high wou'd mount,
That, like Prize-goods, which through the Office come,
He could have had 'em much more cheap at home.
He still must write; and Banquier-like, each day
Accept new Bills, and he must break, or pay.
When through his hands such sums must yearly run,
You cannot think the Stock is all his own.
His haste his other errors might excuse;
But there's no mercy for a guilty Muse:
For like a Mistress, she must stand or fall,
And please you to a height, or not at all.

SONGS

I

SONG

YOU charm'd me not with that fair face
  Though it was all divine:
To be anothers is the Grace,
  That makes me wish you mine.
The Gods and Fortune take their part
  Who like young Monarchs fight;
And boldly dare invade that heart
  Which is anothers right.
First mad with hope we undertake
  To pull up every barr;

But once possess'd, we faintly make
  A dull defensive warr.
Now every friend is turn'd a foe
  In hope to get our store:
And passion makes us Cowards grow,
  Which made us brave before.

II

SONG

AFTER the pangs of a desperate Lover,
When day and night I have sigh'd all in vain,
Ah what a pleasure it is to discover
In her eyes pity, who causes my pain!

2

When with unkindness our love at a stand is,
And both have punish'd our selves with the pain,
Ah what a pleasure the touch of her hand is,
Ah what a pleasure to press it again!

3

When the denyal comes fainter and fainter,
And her eyes give what her tongue does deny,
Ah what a trembling I feel when I venture,
Ah what a trembling does usher my joy!

4

When, with a Sigh, she accords me the blessing,
And her eyes twinkle 'twixt pleasure and pain;
Ah what a joy 'tis beyond all expressing,
Ah what a joy to hear, shall we again!

III

SONG

CALM was the Even, and cleer was the Skie,
  And the new budding flowers did spring,
When all alone went *Amyntas* and I
  To hear the sweet Nightingale sing;
I sate, and he laid him down by me;
  But scarcely his breath he could draw;
For when with a fear he began to draw near,
  He was dash'd with A ha ha ha ha!

2

He blush'd to himself, and lay still for a while,
  And his modesty curb'd his desire;
But streight I convinc'd all his fear with a smile,
  Which added new flames to his fire.
O *Sylvia*, said he, you are cruel,
  To keep your poor Lover in awe;
Then once more he prest with his hand to my brest,
  But was dash'd with A ha ha ha ha.

3

I knew 'twas his passion that caus'd all his fear;
  And therefore I pity'd his case:
I whisper'd him softly there's no body near,
  And layd my cheek close to his face:
But as he grew bolder and bolder,
  A Shepherd came by us and saw;
And just as our bliss we began with a kiss,
  He laughd out with A ha ha ha ha.

IV

SONG

Damon. CELIMENA, of my heart,
  None shall e're bereave you:
  If, with your good leave, I may
  Quarrel with you once a day,
  I will never leave you.

2

Celimena. Passion's but an empty name
Where respect is wanting:
Damon you mistake your ayme;
Hang your heart, and burn your flame,
If you must be ranting.

3

Damon. Love as dull and muddy is,
As decaying liquor:
Anger sets it on the lees,
And refines it by degrees,
Till it workes it quicker.

4

Celimena. Love by quarrels to beget
Wisely you endeavour;
With a grave Physician's wit
Who to cure an Ague fit
Put me in a Feavor.

5

Damon. Anger rouzes love to fight,
And his only bayt is,
'Tis the spurre to dull delight,
And is but an eager bite,
When desire at height is.

6

Celimena. If such drops of heat can fall
In our wooing weather;
If such drops of heat can fall,
We shall have the Devil and all
When we come together.

PROLOGUES, EPILOGUES and SONGS from *THE CONQUEST OF GRANADA*

PROLOGUE to the First Part

Spoken by Mris. Ellen Guyn *in a broad-brim'd hat, and wast-belt*

THIS jeast was first of t'other houses making,
And, five times try'd, has never fail'd of taking.
For 'twere a shame a Poet shoud be kill'd
Under the shelter of so broad a shield.
This is that hat whose very sight did win yee
To laugh and clap, as though the Devil were in yee.
As then, for *Nokes*, so now, I hope, you'l be
So dull, to laugh, once more, for love of me.
I'll write a Play, sayes one, for I have got
A broad-brim'd hat, and wastbelt tow'rds a Plot.
Sayes t'other, I have one more large than that:
Thus they out-write each other with a hat.
The brims still grew with every Play they writ;
And grew so large, they cover'd all the wit.
Hat was the Play: 'twas language, wit and tale:
Like them that find, Meat, drink, and cloth, in Ale.
What dulness do these Mungrill-wits confess
When all their hope is acting of a dress!
Thus two, the best Comedians of the Age
Must be worn out, with being blocks o'th' Stage.
Like a young Girl, who better things has known,
Beneath their Poets Impotence they groan.
See now, what Charity it was to save!
They thought you lik'd, what onely you forgave:
And brought you more dull sence.—dull sence, much worse
Than brisk, gay Non-sence; and the heavyer Curse.
They bring old Ir'n, and glass upon the Stage,
To barter with the Indians of our Age.

Prologues, Epilogues and Songs. Text from The Conquest of Granada by the Spaniards: In Two Parts, *1672, collated with the editions of 1673, 1678, 1687, 1695,* Westminster-Drollery, *1672, and Bodl. MS. Don. B. 8, pp. 248–9. See Commentary*

Prologue to the First Part. 1, 11 t'other] th'other *73–95*

Still they write on; and like great Authors show:
But 'tis as Rowlers in wet gardens grow;
Heavy with dirt, and gath'ring as they goe.
May none who have so little understood
To like such trash, presume to praise what's good!
And may those drudges of the Stage, whose fate
Is, damn'd dull farce more dully to translate,
Fall under that excise the State thinks fit
To set on all French wares, whose worst, is wit.
French farce worn out at home, is sent abroad;
And, patch'd up here, is made our English mode.
Hence forth, let Poets, 'ere allow'd to write,
Be search'd, like Duellists, before they fight,
For wheel-broad hats, dull humour, all that chaffe,
Which makes you mourn, and makes the Vulgar laugh.
For these, in Playes, are as unlawful Arms,
As, in a Combat, Coats of Mayle, and Charms.

EPILOGUE

SUCCESS, which can no more than beauty last,
Makes our sad Poet mourn your favours past:
For, since without desert he got a name,
He fears to loose it now with greater shame.
Fame, like a little Mistriss of the town,
Is gaind with ease; but then she's lost as soon.
For, as those taudry Misses, soon or late
Jilt such as keep 'em at the highest rate:
(And oft the Lacquey, or the Brawny Clown,
Gets what is hid in the loose body'd gown;)
So, Fame is false to all that keep her long;
And turns up to the Fop that's brisk and young.
Some wiser Poet now would leave Fame first:
But elder wits are like old Lovers, curst;
Who, when the vigor of their youth is spent,
Still grow more fond as they grow impotent.

Epilogue. Heading in MS: Epilogue to the second part of the Seige of Granada. spoken by Hart. 2 favours] Favour's *73 78* 14 Lovers, *73–95*: Lovers *72*

This, some years hence, our Poets case may prove;
But, yet, he hopes, he's young enough to love.
When forty comes, if 'ere he live to see
That wretched, fumbling age of poetry;
T'will be high time to bid his Muse adieu:
Well he may please him self, but never you.
Till then he'l do as well as he began;
And hopes you will not finde him less a man.
Think him not duller for this years delay;
He was prepar'd, the women were away;
And men, without their parts, can hardly play.
If they, through sickness, seldome did appear,
Pity the virgins of each Theatre!
For, at both houses, 'twas a sickly year!
And pity us, your servants, to whose cost,
In one such sickness, nine whole Mon'ths are lost.
Their stay, he fears, has ruin'd what he writ:
Long waiting both disables love and wit.
They thought they gave him leisure to do well:
But when they forc'd him to attend, he fell!
Yet though he much has faild, he begs to day
You will excuse his unperforming Play:
Weakness sometimes great passion does express;
He had pleas'd better, had he lov'd you less.

SONGS

I

SONG

I

BENEATH a Myrtle shade
Which Love for none but happy Lovers made,
I slept, and straight my Love before me brought
Phillis the object of my waking thought;
Undress'd she came my flames to meet,

22 Well he may] Well, he may *73 78*: Well may hee *MS* 23–24, 31–32, 35–36 *MS has* not spoke *in margin* 32 are] were *MS* 37 much has] has much *MS* 39 does] may *MS*
Songs. I. *Two versions are printed in* Westminster-Drollery *I, 1671:* (*a*) A Song at the Kings house, (*b*) A Vision 2 Love] *Jove WDb*

While Love strow'd flow'rs beneath her feet;
Flow'rs, which so press'd by her, became more sweet.

2

From the bright Visions head
A careless vail of Lawn was loosely spread:
From her white temples fell her shaded hair,
Like cloudy sunshine not too brown nor fair:
Her hands, her lips did love inspire;
Her every grace my heart did fire:
But most her eyes which languish'd with desire.

3

Ah, Charming fair, said I,
How long can you my bliss and yours deny?
By Nature and by love this lonely shade
Was for revenge of suffring Lovers made:
Silence and shades with love agree:
Both shelter you and favour me;
You cannot blush because I cannot see.

4

No, let me dye, she said,
Rather than loose the spotless name of Maid:
Faintly me thought she spoke, for all the while
She bid me not believe her, with a smile.
Then dye, said I, she still deny'd:
And, is it thus, thus, thus she cry'd
You use a harmless Maid, and so she dy'd!

5

I wak'd, and straight I knew
I lov'd so well it made my dream prove true:

6 While] Whilst *WDab* 7 which] that *WDab* 8 Visions] Virgins *WDa* 10 temples] Temple *WDa*: shoulders *WDb* 14 which] that *WDb* languish'd] languish *WDa* 16 and yours *om. WDa* 17 lonely] lovely *WDa*: lonesome *WDb* 24 me thought she spoke] she spoke methought *WDb* 26 she] she's *87 95* 27 is it thus, thus, thus] yet, *Thus*, thus *WDa*

Fancy, the kinder Mistress of the two,
Fancy had done what *Phillis* wou'd not do!
Ah, Cruel Nymph, cease your disdain,
While I can dream you scorn in vain;
Asleep or waking you must ease my pain.

II

SONG

1

WHEREVER I am, and whatever I doe;
My *Phillis* is still in my mind:
When angry I mean not to *Phillis* to goe,
My Feet of themselves the way find:
Unknown to my self I am just at her door,
And when I would raile, I can bring out no more,
Than *Phillis* too fair and unkind!

2

When *Phillis* I see, my Heart bounds in my Breast,
And the Love I would stifle is shown:
But asleep, or awake, I am never at rest
When from my Eyes *Phillis* is gone!
Sometimes a sweet Dream does delude my sad mind,
But, alas, when I wake and no *Phillis* I find
How I sigh to my self all alone.

3

Should a King be my Rival in her I adore
He should offer his Treasure in vain:
O let me alone to be happy and poor,
And give me my *Phillis* again:
Let *Phillis* be mine, and for ever be kind
I could to a Desart with her be confin'd,
And envy no Monarch his Raign.

34 While[Whilst *WDa* 35 you] I *WDa*
Songs. II. *A version is printed in* Westminster-Drollery *I, 1672* 8 bounds] burns *WD* 11 my] mine *WD* 12 sweet *WD*: sad *72–95* 14 How] Then *WD* 19 for *73 78*: but *72 87 95*

4

Alas, I discover too much of my Love,
And she too well knows her own power!
She makes me each day a new Martyrdom prove,
And makes me grow jealous each hour:
But let her each minute torment my poor mind
I had rather love *Phillis* both False and Unkind,
Then ever be freed from her Pow'r.

PROLOGUE To the Second Part, of The CONQUEST OF GRANADA

THEY who write Ill, and they who ne'r durst write,
Turn Critiques, out of meer Revenge and Spight:
A *Play-house* gives 'em Fame; and up there starts,
From a mean Fifth-rate Wit, a Man of Parts.
(So Common Faces on the Stage appear:
We take 'em in; and they turn Beauties here.)
Our Authour fears those Critiques as his Fate:
And those he Fears, by consequence, must Hate.
For they the Trafficque of all Wit, invade;
As Scriv'ners draw away the Bankers Trade.
Howe're, the Poet's safe enough to day:
They cannot censure an unfinish'd Play.
But, as when Vizard Masque appears in Pit,
Straight, every man who thinks himself a Wit,
Perks up; and, managing his Comb, with grace,
With his white Wigg sets off his Nut-brown Face:
That done, bears up to th' prize, and views each Limb,
To know her by her Rigging and her Trimm:

26 her] me *73 78*
Prologue To the Second Part. Heading in MS: Prologue to the first part of ye Conquest of Granada. spoken by Mohun. 1 They . . . they] those, . . . those, *MS* 2 Critiques, out] Criticks now out *MS* 4 mean] meere *MS* 10 *Additional lines follow in MS*:

Some of them seeme indeede ye Poetts freinds;
But 'tis, as France courts England, for her ends.
They build up this Lampoone, & th' other Songe,
And Court him, to lye still, while they grow stronge.

13 Vizard . . . Pit] Vizor-Maskes appeare ith' pitt *MS* 14 who] that *MS* 15 Perks] Ierkes *MS* his] the *MS* 16 off his Nut-brown] off Nut-browne *MS* 17 bears] bares *MS*

Then, the whole noise of Fopps to wagers go,
Pox on her, 't must be she; and *Damm'ee* no:
Just so I Prophecy, these Wits to day,
Will blindly guess at our imperfect Play:
With what new Plots our Second Part is fill'd;
Who must be kept alive, and who be kill'd.
And as those Vizard Masques maintain that Fashion,
To sooth and tickle sweet Imagination:
So, our dull Poet keeps you on with Masquing;
To make you think there's something worth your asking:
But when 'tis shown, that which does now delight you,
Will prove a Dowdy, with a Face to fright you.

EPILOGUE to the Second Part of GRANADA

THEY, who have best succeeded on the Stage,
Have still conform'd their Genius to their Age.
Thus *Jonson* did Mechanique humour show,
When men were dull, and conversation low.
Then, Comedy was faultless, but 'twas course:
Cobbs Tankard was a jest, and *Otter*'s horse.
And as their Comedy, their love was mean:
Except, by chance, in some one labour'd Scene,
Which must attone for an ill-written Play.
They rose; but at their height could seldome stay.
Fame then was cheap, and the first commer sped;
And they have kept it since, by being dead.
But were they now to write when Critiques weigh
Each Line, and ev'ry word, throughout a Play,
None of 'em, no not *Jonson*, in his height
Could pass, without allowing grains for weight.
Think it not envy that these truths are told,
Our Poet's not malicious, though he's bold.
'Tis not to brand 'em that their faults are shown,
But, by their errours, to excuse his own.

20 *Damm'ee*] damme mee *MS*: *Damm'ye 73 78* 21 these] the *MS* 25 And] But *MS* that] y^e^ *MS*
Epilogue to the Second Part. 12 dead. *73–95*: dead, *72*

If Love and Honour now are higher rais'd,
'Tis not the Poet, but the Age is prais'd.
Wit's now arriv'd to a more high degree;
Our native Language more refin'd and free.
Our Ladies and our men now speak more wit
In conversation, than those Poets writ.
Then, one of these is, consequently, true;
That what this Poet writes comes short of you,
And imitates you ill, (which most he fears)
Or else his writing is not worse than theirs.
Yet, though you judge, (as sure the Critiques will)
That some before him writ with greater skill,
In this one praise he has their fame surpast,
To please an Age more Gallant than the last.

SONGS

SONG, In two Parts

He. HOW unhappy a Lover am I
While I sigh for my *Phillis* in vain;
All my hopes of Delight
Are another man's Right,
Who is happy while I am in pain!

2

She. Since her Honour allows no Relief,
But to pity the pains which you bear,
'Tis the best of your Fate,
(In a hopeless Estate,)
To give o're, and betimes to despair.

3

He. I have try'd the false Med'cine in vain;
For I wish what I hope not to win:
From without, my desire
Has no Food to its Fire,
But it burns and consumes me within.

Epilogue to the Second Part. 33 has] hath *73 78*

4

She. Yet at least 'tis a pleasure to know
That you are not unhappy alone:
For the Nymph you adore
Is as wretched and more,
And accounts all your suff'rings her own.

5

He. O ye Gods, let me suffer for both;
At the feet of my *Phillis* I'le lye:
I'le resign up my Breath,
And take pleasure in Death,
To be pity'd by her when I dye.

6

She. What her Honour deny'd you in Life
In her Death she will give to your Love.
Such a Flame as is true
After Fate will renew,
For the Souls to meet closer above.

A SONG

I

FAREWEL, fair *Armeda*, my Joy and my Grief;
In vain I have Lov'd you, and find no Relief:
Undone by your Vertue, too strict and severe,
Your Eyes gave me Love, and you gave me Despair.
Now, call'd by my Honour, I seek, with Content,
A Fate which in pity you wou'd not prevent:

Song, In two Parts. 19 wretched *73 78*: wretch'd *72*
A Song. Text from New Court-Songs, and Poems. By *R. V.* Gent., *1672*, *collated with* Covent Garden Drolery . . . Collected by R.B. (*CGD*), *1672*, Westminster-Drollery (*WMD*) *1672*, Windsor-Drollery (*WD*), *1672*, *and* Choice Songs and Ayres for One Voyce (*CSA*), *1673*. *See Commentary*
1 fair *Armeda*] fair *Arminda CGD*: my *Almeda WD* 2 I have] have I *WMD* find] hope *CGD WMD CSA*: found *WD* 3 Vertue] Honour *WD* 5 my *om. WD* 6 A Fate] The Fate *CGD WMD CSA*: My fall *WD*

To languish in Love, were to find by delay
A Death, that's more welcom the speediest way.

2

On Seas, and in Battels, in Bullets and Fire,
The Danger is less than in Hopeless Desire.
My Deaths Wound you gave me, though far off I bear
My Fate from your sight, not to cost you a Tear.
But if the kind Flood on a Wave should convey,
And under your Window my Body should lay,
The Wound on my Breast when you happen to see,
You'll say with a Sigh,—*It was given by me.*

7 were to find] or to pine *WD* 8 speediest] speedier *WMD CSA* 9 On] Or *CGD* in Bullets] through bullets *WD* 11 me *om. CGD* 12 Fate] fall *CGD WD* 13 Flood] Floods *CSA* should] would *WMD WD CSA* 14 should] would *CGD WMD WD CSA* 15 The Wound . . . when you] When the wound . . . you *WD* 16 You'll] You'd *WD*: You will *WMD*

POEMS FROM *COVENT GARDEN DROLERY*

PROLOGUE and EPILOGUE to *SECRET-LOVE* Spoken by the Women

PROLOGUE

Spoken by Mrs. Boutell *to the Maiden Queen, in mans Cloathes*

WOMEN like us (passing for men) you'l cry,
Presume too much upon your Secresie.
There's not a fop in town but will pretend,
To know the cheat himself, or by his friend;
Then make no words on 't, Gallants, tis e'ne true,
We are condemn'd to look, and strut, like you.
Since we thus freely, our hard fate confess,
Accept us these bad times in any dress.
You'l find the sweet on 't, now old Pantaloons,
Will go as far, as formerly new Gowns,
And from your own cast Wigs, expect no frowns.
The Ladies we shall not so easily please.
They'l say what impudent bold things are these,
That dare provoke, yet cannot do us right,
Like men with huffing looks, that dare not fight.
But this reproach, our courage must not daunt,
The Bravest Souldier may a Weapon want,
Let Her that doubts us still, send her Gallant.
Ladies in us, you'l Youth and Beauty find,
All things but one, according to your mind.
And when your Eyes and Ears, are feasted here,
Rise up and make out the short Meal, elsewhere.

Poems. Text from Covent Garden Drolery, *1672* (*CGDa*), *collated with* The Second Impression *1672(b)*, *BM. Eg. MS. 2623, ff. 43–44,* Westminster Drollery. The Second Part, *1672* (*WD*), *and* Miscellany Poems, *1684 and 1692. See Commentary*
Prologue. Heading: '*in mans Cloathes*' added in *CGDb* 4 friend;] friend, *CGDab* 5 Gallants, *CGDb*: Gallants *CGDa* 21 Ears, *CGDb*: Ears *CGDa* 22 Meal, *CGDb*: Meal *CGDa*

EPILOGUE

Spoken by Mrs. Reeves *to the Maiden Queen, in mans Cloathes*

WHAT think you Sirs, was't not all well enough,
Will you not grant that we can strut, and huff.
Men may be proud, but faith for ought I see,
They neither walk, nor cock, so well as we.
And for the fighting Part we may in time,
Grow up to swagger in heroick Rhime.
For though we cannot boast of equal force,
Yet at some Weapon's men have still the worse.
Why should not then we Women act alone,
Or whence are men so necessary grown,
Our's are so old, they are as good as none.
Some who have tri'd 'em, if you'l take their Oaths,
Swear they're as arrant tinsell as their Cloaths.
Imagine us but what we represent,
And we could e'ne give you as good content.
Our faces, shapes, all's better that you see,
And for the rest they want as much as we.
Oh would the higher Powers be kind to us,
And grant us to set up a female house;
We'l make our selves to please both Sexes then,
To the Men Women, to the Women Men.
Here we presume, our Legs are no ill sight,
And they will give you no ill Dreams at night.
In Dream's both Sexes may their passions ease,
You make us then as civil as you please.
This would prevent the houses joyning too,
At which we are as much displeas'd as you.
For all our Women most devoutly swear,
Each would be rather a poor Actress here,
Then to be made a *Mamamouchi* there.

Epilogue. Heading: '*in mans Cloathes*' added in *CGDb* 11 so] too *MS* 12 'em, *CGDb*: 'em *CGDa* 15 e'ne *CGDb*: e'ne, *CGDa* 16 that *MS*: than *CGDa CGDb* 19 house; *CGDb*: house. *CGDa* 23 will *CGDb MS*: would *CGDa* 26 too *CGDb MS*: two *CGDa*

The Prologue to Witt without Money being the first Play acted after the Fire

So shipwrack't Passengers escape to Land,
So look they, when on the bare Beach they stand,
Dropping and cold; and their first fear scarce o're,
Expecting Famine on a Desart Shore;
From that hard Climate, we must wait for Bread,
Whence even the Natives forc't by hunger fled.
Our Stage does humane chance present to view,
But ne're before was seen so sadly true,
You are chang'd too, and your pretence to see
Is but a nobler name for charity.
Your own provisions furnish out our Feasts
While you the Founders make your selves the guests.
Of all mankind beside Fate had some care,
But for poor Wit no portion did prepare,
'Tis left a rent-charge to the brave and fair.
You cherish'd it, and now its fall you mourn,
Which blind unmanner'd *Zealots* make their scorn,
Who think that Fire a judgement on the Stage,
Which spar'd not *Temples* in its furious rage.
But as our new-built City rises higher,
So from old Theaters *may new aspire,*
Since Fate contrives magnificence by fire.
Our great *Metropolis*, does far surpass
What e're is now, and equals all that was:
Our wit as far, does Forreign wit excell;
And, like a King, should in a Palace dwell,
But we with golden hopes, are vainly fed,
Talk high, and entertain you in a Shed.
Your presence here (for which we humbly sue)
Will grace old Theatres, and build up new.

The Prologue to Witt without Money. Heading in 84 92: Prologue Spoken the first day of the King's House Acting after the Fire. Writ by Mr. *Dryden*. 2 the *84 92*: *om. CGD WD* 4 on *84 92*: from *CGD WD* 9 too] to *CGDa* 10 for *84 92*: of *CGD WD* 12 While *84 92*: Whilst *CGD WD* the guests *84 92*: our guests *CGD WD* 13 *beside 84 92*: *besides CGD WD* 16 cherish'd *84 92 WD*: cherish *CGD* 18 that] the *CGDa WD* 23–30 *added in CGDb WD 84 92* 23 does far *84 92*: does so far *CGDb*: doth farr *WD* 24 equals] equald *WD* 25 does] doth *WD*

Prologue to Albumazar

To say this Commedy pleas'd long ago,
Is not enough, to make it pass you now:
Yet gentlemen, your Ancestors had witt,
When few men censurd, and when fewer writ.
And *Johnson* (of those few the best) chose this,
As the best modell of his master piece;
Subtle was got by our *Albumazar*,
That *Alchamist* by this Astrologer.
Here he was fashion'd, and we may suppose,
He lik'd the Fashion well, who wore the Cloaths.
But *Ben* made nobly his, what he did mould,
What was another's Lead, becomes his Gold;
Like an unrighteous Conquerer he raigns,
Yet rules that well, which he unjustly gains.
But this our age such Authors does afford,
As make whole Playes, and yet scarce write one word:
Who in this Anarchy of witt, rob all,
And what's their Plunder, their Possession call.
Who like bold Padders scorn by night to prey,
But Rob by Sun-shine, in the face of day;
Nay scarce the common Ceremony use,
Of stand, Sir, and deliver up your Muse;
But knock the Poet down; and, with a grace,
Mount *Pegasus* before the owners Face.
Faith if you have such Country *Toms*, abroad,
Tis time for all true men to leave that Road.
Yet it were modest, could it but be sed,
They strip the living, but these rob the dead:
Dare with the Mummyes of the Muses Play,
And make love to 'em, the *Ægyptian*, way.
Or as a Rhyming Authour would have sed,
Joyn the dead living, to the living dead.

Prologue to Albumazar. *Heading in 84 92*: The Prologue to Albumazar: Written by *Mr. Dryden.* 4 when *84 92*: *om. CGD* 5 (of those few the best) *84 92*: of those few, the best *CGD* 6 As *84 92*: And *CGD* 9 we may *84 92*: I should *CGD* 10 He . . . Cloaths *84 92*: He likes my fashion well, that wears my Cloaths *CGD* 12 becomes *84 92*: became *CGD* 16 one *84 92*: a *CGD* 21 Nay *84 92*: Who *CGD* 22 Muse; *84 92*: Muse. *CGD* 28 strip *84 92*: stript *CGD* these *84 92*: they *CGD* 29 Dare *84 92*: 'Twill *CGD* Mummyes *84 92*: mummey *CGD*

Such Men in Poetry may claim some part,
They have the Licence, though they want the Art,
And might, where Theft was prais'd, for Lawreats stand
Poets, not of the head, but of the hand;
They make the benefits of others studying,
Much like the meales of Politick *Jack Pudding*:
Whose dish to challenge, no Man has the courage,
'Tis all his own, when once h' has spit i'th' Porredge.
But Gentlemen, y'are all concernd in this,
You are in fault for what they do amiss:
For they their thefts still undiscover'd think,
And durst not steal unless you please to winck.
Perhaps, You may award by Your Decree,
They shou'd refund, but that can never be.
For should You Letters of reprizall seal,
These men write that, which no man else would steale.

Prologue to Iulius Cæsar

In Country Beauties as we often see,
Something that takes in their simplicity;
Yet while they charm, they know not they are fair,
And take without the spreading of the snare;
Such Artless beauty lies in *Shakespears* wit,
'Twas well in spight of him what ere he writ.
His Excellencies came and were not sought,
His words like casual Atoms made a thought:
Drew up themselves in Rank and File, and writ,
He wondring how the Devil it was such wit.
Thus like the drunken Tinker, in his Play,
He grew a Prince, and never knew which way.
He did not know what trope or Figure meant,
But to perswade is to be eloquent,

33 Such Men *84 92*: Yet such *CGD* 34 Art,] Art. *CGD 84 92* 35 And . . . stand *84 92*: Such as in *Sparta* weight for Laurels stand, *CGDa*: Such . . . might . . . stand *CGDb* 37 the benefits *84 92*: their benefit *CGD* 38 Politick *84 92*: Politick, *CGD* 39 Whose . . . Man *84 92*: Where Broth to claim, there's no one *CGD* 40 when once h'has *84 92*: after he has *CGD* 42 amiss *84 92*: a miss *CGD* 43 still *84 92*: will *CGD* 45–46 *added in 84 92* 47 For should You *84 92*: Now should we *CGD*

Prologue. 2 simplicity;] simplicity. *CGD* 4 the *CGDb*: their *CGDa* 10 was *CGDb*: were *CGDa*

So in this *Cæsar* which to day you see,
Tully ne'r spoke as he makes *Anthony*.
Those then that tax his Learning are to blame,
He knew the thing, but did not know the Name:
Great *Iohnson* did that Ignorance adore,
And though he envi'd much, admir'd him more;
The faultless *Iohnson* equally writ well,
Shakespear made faults; but then did more excel.
One close at Guard like some old Fencer lay,
T'other more open, but he shew'd more play.
In Imitation *Iohnsons* wit was shown,
Heaven made his men; but *Shakespear* made his own.
Wise *Iohnson*'s talent in observing lay,
But others follies still made up his play.
He drew the life in each elaborate line,
But *Shakespear* like a Master did design.
Iohnson with skill dissected humane kind,
And show'd their faults that they their faults might find:
But then as all Anatomists must do,
He to the meanest of mankind did go,
And took from Gibbets such as he would show.
Both are so great that he must boldly dare,
Who both of 'em does judge and both compare.
If amongst Poets one more bold there be,
The man that dare attempt in either way, is he.

15 to *CGDb*: this *CGDa* 17 to] too *CGD* 20 more;] more, *CGDa*: more. *CGDb* 26 men; *CGDb*: men *CGDa* 29 life] like *CGD* 32 find: *CGDb*: find. *CGDa* 34 go, *CGDb*: go. *CGDa*

PROLOGUE, EPILOGUE and SONGS from *MARRIAGE A-LA-MODE*

PROLOGUE

LORD, how reform'd and quiet we are grown,
Since all our Braves and all our Wits are gone:
Fop-corner now is free from Civil War:
White-Wig and Vizard make no longer jar.
France, and the Fleet, have swept the Town so clear,
That we can Act in peace, and you can hear.
'Twas a sad sight, before they march'd from home,
To see our Warriours, in Red Wastecoats, come,
With hair tuck'd up, into our Tireing-room.
But 'twas more sad to hear their last Adieu,
The Women sob'd, and swore they would be true;
And so they were, as long as e're they cou'd:
But powerful *Guinnee* cannot be withstood,
And they were made of Play house flesh and bloud.
Fate did their Friends for double use ordain,
In Wars abroad, they grinning Honour gain,
And Mistresses, for all that stay, maintain.
Now they are gone, 'tis dead Vacation here,
For neither Friends nor Enemies appear.
Poor pensive Punk now peeps ere Plays begin,
Sees the bare Bench, and dares not venture in:
But manages her last Half-crown with care,
And trudges to the *Mall*, on foot, for Air.
Our City Friends so far will hardly come,

Prologue, Epilogue and Songs. Text from Marriage a-la-Mode. A Comedy, *1673, collated with the editions of 1684, 1691, 1698, Covent Garden* Drolery, *1672, (a), and Covent Garden* Drolery . . . The Second Impression, *1672 (b). See Commentary*

Prologue. Heading in CGD: A Prologue to Marriage Al la mode, *By Mr.* Heart
1 we are] are we *CGD* 3–6 *om. CGDb* 4 White] While *CGDa* make] Masks, *CGDa* 5 have] hath *CGDa* 6 *additional two lines follow in CGD:*

Those that durst fight are gone to get renown,
And those that durst not, blush to stand in Town.

7 march'd] went *CGD* 16 they] the *CGD* 22 last *om. CGD* 24 come] roame *CGD*

They can take up with Pleasures nearer home;
And see gay Shows, and gawdy Scenes elsewhere:
For we presume they seldom come to hear.
But they have now ta'n up a glorious Trade,
And cutting *Moorcraft*, struts in Masquerade.
There's all our hope, for we shall show to day,
A Masquing Ball, to recommend our Play:
Nay, to endear 'em more, and let 'em see,
We scorn to come behind in Courtesie,
We'll follow the new Mode which they begin,
And treat 'em with a Room, and Couch within:
For that's one way, how e're the Play fall short,
T' oblige the Town, the City, and the Court.

EPILOGUE

THUS have my Spouse and I inform'd the Nation,
And led you all the way to Reformation.
Not with dull Morals, gravely writ, like those,
Which men of easie Phlegme, with care compose.
Your Poet's of stiff words, and limber sense,
Born on the confines of indifference.
But by examples drawn, I dare to say,
From most of you, who hear, and see the Play.
There are more *Rhodophils* in this Theatre,
More *Palamedes*, and some few Wives, I fear.
But yet too far our Poet would not run,
Though 'twas well offer'd, there was nothing done.
He would not quite the Woman's frailty bare,
But stript 'em to the waste, and left 'em there.
And the men's faults are less severely shown,
For he considers that himself is one.
Some stabbing Wits, to bloudy Satyr bent,
Would treat both Sexes with less complement:

26 and] with *CGD* 27 we presume] 'tis presumed, *CGD* 29 cutting] cunning *CGDa* struts] strut *CGDa* 30 There's] Here's *CGD* 36 fall] falls *CGD*
Epilogue. Heading *Epilogue by Mr.* Moon *CGDa*: *Epilogue . . .* Mohun *CGDb* 7 examples] example *CGD* 8 hear, and see] see and hear *CGD* 13 Woman's frailty] Women faulty *CGD* 15 are] were *CGD* 17 bent] lent *CGDa* 18 treat] fret *CGD*

Would lay the Scene at home, of Husbands tell,
For Wenches, taking up their Wives i'th' *Mell*,
And a brisk bout which each of them did want,
Made by mistake of Mistris and Gallant.
Our modest Authour, thought it was enough
To cut you off a Sample of the stuff:
He spar'd my shame, which you, I'm sure, would not,
For you were all for driving on the Plot:
You sigh'd when I came in to break the sport,
And set your teeth when each design fell short.
To Wives, and Servants all good wishes lend,
But the poor Cuckold seldom finds a friend.
Since therefore Court and Town will take no pity,
I humbly cast my self upon the City.

SONGS

I

1

WHY should a foolish Marriage Vow
  Which long ago was made,
Oblige us to each other now
  When Passion is decay'd?
We lov'd, and we lov'd, as long as we cou'd,
  Till our love was lov'd out in us both:
But our Marriage is dead, when the Pleasure is fled:
  'Twas Pleasure first made it an Oath.

2

If I have Pleasures for a Friend,
  And farther love in store,
What wrong has he whose joys did end,
  And who cou'd give no more?

'Tis a madness that he
Should be jealous of me,

19 Husbands] Husband *CGD* 21 each *om.* *CGD* 26 were] are *CGD*
31 Court and Town] Town, nor Court *CGD* 32 I] O *CGDa*

Or that I shou'd bar him of another:
For all we can gain,
Is to give our selves pain,
When neither can hinder the other.

II

SONG

I

WHIL'ST *Alexis* lay prest
In her Arms he lov'd best,
With his hands round her neck,
And his head on her breast,
He found the fierce pleasure too hasty to stay,
And his soul in the tempest just flying away.

2

When *Cælia* saw this,
With a sigh, and a kiss,
She cry'd, Oh my dear, I am robb'd of my bliss;
'Tis unkind to your Love, and unfaithfully done,
To leave me behind you, and die all alone.

3

The Youth, though in haste,
And breathing his last,
In pity dy'd slowly, while she dy'd more fast;
Till at length she cry'd, Now, my dear, now let us go,
Now die, my *Alexis*, and I will die too.

4

Thus intranc'd they did lie,
Till *Alexis* did try
To recover new breath, that again he might die:
Then often they di'd; but the more they did so,
The Nymph di'd more quick, and the Shepherd more slow.

Songs. II. 8 and a kiss] and kiss *84*

PROLOGUE, EPILOGUE and SONG from *THE ASSIGNATION*

PROLOGUE

PROLOGUES, like Bells to Churches, toul you in
With Chimeing Verse; till the dull Playes begin:
With this sad difference though, of Pit and Pue;
You damn the *Poet*, but the *Priest* damns you.
But Priests can treat you at your own expence:
And, gravely, call you Fooles, without offence.
Poets, poor Devils, have ne'r your Folly shown
But, to their cost, you prov'd it was their own.
For, when a Fop's presented on the Stage,
Straight all the Coxcombs in the Town ingage:
For his deliverance, and revenge they joyn:
And grunt, like Hogs, about their Captive Swine.
Your Poets daily split upon this shelfe:
You must have Fooles, yet none will have himself.
Or, if in kindness, you that leave would give,
No man could write you at that rate you live:
For some of you grow Fops with so much haste,
Riot in nonsence, and commit such waste,
'Twould Ruine Poets should they spend so fast.
He who made this, observ'd what Farces hit,
And durst not disoblige you now with wit.
But, Gentlemen, you overdo the Mode:
You must have Fooles out of the common Rode.
Th' unnatural strain'd Buffoon is onely taking:
No Fop can please you now of Gods own making.
Pardon our Poet if he speaks his Mind,
You come to Plays with your own Follies lin'd:
Small Fooles fall on you, like small showers, in vain:
Your own oyl'd Coates keep out all common raine.
You must have Mamamouchi, such a Fop
As would appear a Monster in a Shop:

Prologue, Epilogue and Song. Text from The Assignation: or, Love in a Nunnery, *1673, collated with the editions of 1678 and 1692*
Prologue. 26 Poet] Poets, *92*

Hee'l fill your Pit and Boxes to the brim,
Where, Ram'd in Crowds, you see your selves in him.
Sure there's some spell our Poet never knew,
In hullibabilah da, and Chu, chu, chu.
But Marabarah sahem most did touch you,
That is: Oh how we love the Mamamouchi!
Grimace and habit sent you pleas'd away:
You damn'd the Poet, and cry'd up the Play.
  This thought had made our Author more uneasie,
But that he hopes I'm Fool enough to please ye:
But here's my griefe; though Nature joyn'd with art,
Have cut me out to act a Fooling Part;
Yet, to your praise, the few wits here will say,
'Twas imitating you taught *Haynes* to Play.

EPILOGUE

SOME have expected from our Bills to day
To find a *Satyre* in our *Poet*'s *Play*.
The *Zealous Rout* from *Coleman-street* did run,
To see the Story of the *Fryer* and *Nun*.
Or Tales, yet more Ridiculous to hear,
Vouch'd by their Vicar of Ten pounds a year;
Of Nuns, who did against Temptation Pray,
And Discipline laid on the Pleasant way:
Or that to please the Malice of the Town,
Our *Poet* should in some close Cell have shown
Some Sister, Playing at Content alone:
This they did hope; the other side did fear,
And both you see alike are Couzen'd here.
Some thought the Title of our Play to blame,
They lik'd the thing, but yet abhor'd the Name:
Like Modest *Puncks*, who all you ask afford,
But, for the *World*, they would not name that word.
Yet, if you'll credit what I heard him say,
Our *Poet* meant no Scandal in his *Play*;
His Nuns are good which on the Stage are shown,
And, sure, behind our *Scenes* you'll look for none.

35 da] de *78*

SONG and DANCE

LONG betwixt Love and fear *Phillis* tormented,
Shun'd her own wish yet at last she consented:
But loath that day shou'd her blushes discover,
    Come gentle Night She said,
    Come quickly to my aid,
    And a poor Shamefac'd Maid
    Hide from her Lover.

Now cold as Ice I am, now hot as Fire,
I dare not tell my self my own desire;
But let Day fly away, and let Night hast her:
    Grant yee kind Powers above,
    Slow houres to parting Love,
    But when to Bliss we move,
    Bid 'em fly faster.

How sweet it is to Love when I discover,
That Fire which burns my Heart, warming my Lover;
'Tis pitty Love so true should be mistaken:
    But if this Night he be
    False or unkinde to me,
    Let me dye ere I see
    That I'me forsaken.

PROLOGUE, EPILOGUE and SONGS from *AMBOYNA*

PROLOGUE To AMBOYNA

As needy Gallants in the Scriv'ners hands,
Court the rich Knave that gripes their Mortgag'd Lands,
The first fat Buck of all the Season's sent
And Keeper takes no Fee in Complement:

Prologue, Epilogue and Songs. Text from Amboyna: A Tragedy, *1673, collated with the edition of 1691 and Bodl. MS. Don. B. 8, pp. 463–4. See Commentary*

Prologue. Heading in MS: Prologue to ye Play of Amboyna.   2 Knave that] Rogue, who *MS*   their] his *MS*

The doteage of some *Englishmen* is such
To fawn on those who ruine them; the *Dutch*.
They shall have all rather then make a War
With those who of the same Religion are.
The *Streights*, the *Guiney* Trade, the Herrings too,
Nay, to keep friendship, they shall pickle you:
Some are resolv'd not to find out the Cheat,
But Cuckold like, love him who does the Feat:
What injuries soe'r upon us fall,
Yet still the same Religion answers all:
Religion wheedled you to Civil War,
Drew *English* Blood, and *Dutchmens* now wou'd spare:
Be gull'd no longer, for you'l find it true,
They have no more Religion, faith—then you;
Interest's the God they worship in their State,
And you, I take it, have not much of that.
Well Monarchys may own Religions name,
But States are Atheists in their very frame.
They share a sin, and such proportions fall
That like a stink, 'tis nothing to 'em all.
How they love *England*, you shall see this day:
No Map shews *Holland* truer then our Play:
Their Pictures and Inscriptions well we know;
We may be bold one Medal sure to show.
View then their Falshoods, Rapine, Cruelty;
And think what once they were, they still would be:
But hope not either Language, Plot, or Art,
'Twas writ in haste, but with an *English* Heart:
And lest Hope, Wit; in *Dutchmen* that would be
As much improper as would Honesty.

6 who] that *MS* 9 The . . . the . . . the] Your . . . your . . . your *MS* 12 love *MS*: loves *73 91* him who does] them, that did *MS* 13 us] you *MS* 14 still . . . answers] shall . . . answer *MS* 16 *Additional couplet follows in MS*:
One would haue thought, you should haue growne more wise,
Then to be caught with ye same bargaine twice.
17 Be gull'd] Beguil'd *MS* 18 Religion, *91*: Religion *73* 19–20 *om. in MS* 21 own Religions] one Religion *MS* 25 love] Lou'd *MS* 26 our] this *MS* 29 Falshoods] falsehood *MS* 31 Plot] Witt *MS* 33 And lest Hope, Wit; in *Dutchmen*] And lest Hope, Wit, in *Dutchmen 73 91*: Nor hope for Witt in Dutch men, *MS*

EPILOGUE

A POET once the *Spartans* led to fight,
And made 'em Conquer in the Muses right:
So wou'd our Poet lead you on this day:
Showing your tortur'd Fathers in his Play.
To one well born, th' affront is worse and more,
When he's abus'd, and baffled by a Bore:
With an ill Grace the *Dutch* their mischiefs do,
They've both ill Nature and ill Manners too.
Well may they boast themselves an antient Nation,
For they were bred e're Manners, were in fashion:
And their new Common-wealth has set 'em free,
Onely from Honour and Civility.
Venetians do not more uncouthly ride,
Than did their Lubber-State Mankind bestride.
Their sway became 'em with as ill a Meen,
As their own Paunches swell above their Chin:
Yet is their Empire no true Growth but Humour,
And onely two Kings Touch can cure the Tumor.
As *Cato* did his *Affricque* Fruits display:
So we before your Eies their *Indies* lay:
All Loyal *English* will like him conclude,
Let *Cæsar* Live, and *Carthage* be subdu'd.

SONGS

I

Epithalamium

THE day is come, I see it rise,
Betwixt the Bride's and Bridegroom's Eyes,
That Golden day they wish'd so long,
Love pick'd it out amidst the throng;

Epilogue. Heading in MS: The Epilogue 1 *Spartans 91*: *Spartan's 73* 2 right] sight *MS* 4 your . . . his] y^e^ . . . y^e^ *MS* 5 and] nay *MS* 7 mischiefs] mischeife *MS* 8 They've . . . Manners] They're boeit ill-natur'd, & ill-manner'd *MS* 11 has] hath *MS* 14 Lubber-State] Lubber States *MS* 18 Kings *91*: King's *73* the] their *MS* 19 Fruits] Prince *MS* 20 your] our *MS* 21 Loyal *English*] English Catoes *MS* like] with *MS*

He destin'd to himself this Sun,
And took the Reins and drove him on;
In his own Beams he drest him bright,
Yet bid him bring a better night.

The day you wish'd arriv'd at last,
You wish as much that it were past,
One Minute more and night will hide,
The Bridegroom and the blushing Bride.
The Virgin now to Bed do's goe:
Take care oh Youth, she rise not soe;
She pants and trembles at her doom,
And fears and wishes thou wou'dst come.

The Bridegroom comes, He comes apace
With Love and Fury in his Face;
She shrinks away, He close pursues,
And Prayers and Threats, at once do's use,
She softly sighing begs delay,
And with her hand puts his away,
Now out a loud for help she cryes,
And now despairing shuts her Eyes.

II

The Sea Fight

WHO ever saw a noble sight,
That never view'd a brave Sea Fight:
Hang up your bloody Colours in the Aire,
Up with your Fights and your Nettings prepare,
Your Merry Mates chear, with a lusty bold spright,
Now each Man his brindice, and then to the Fight,
St. George, St. George we cry,
The shouting *Turks* reply.
Oh now it begins, and the Gunroom grows hot,
Plie it with Culverin and with small shot;
Heark do's it not Thunder, no 'tis the Guns roar,
The Neighbouring Billows are turn'd into Gore,
Now each man must resolve to dye,
For here the Coward cannot flye.

Epithalamium. 22 puts *91*: put *73*

Drums and Trumpets toll the Knell,
And Culverins the Passing Bell.
Now now they Grapple, and now board a Main,
Blow up the Hatches, they're off all again:
Give 'em a broadside, the Dice run at all,
Down comes the Mast and Yard, and tacklings fall,
She grows giddy now like blind fortunes wheel,
She sinks there, she sinks, she turns up her Keel.
Who ever beheld so noble a sight
As this so brave, so bloody Sea Fight.

TO THE Lady *CASTLEMAIN*, UPON *Her incouraging his first Play*

As Sea-men shipwrackt on some happy shore,
Discover Wealth in Lands unknown before;
And what their Art had labour'd long in vain,
By their misfortunes happily obtain:
So my much-envy'd Muse by Storms long tost,
Is thrown upon your Hospitable Coast;
And finds more favour by her ill success,
Than she could hope for by her happiness.
Once *Cato*'s Vertue did the Gods oppose,
While they the Victor, he the Vanquish'd chose:
But you have done what *Cato* could not do,
To chuse the Vanquish'd, and restore him too.
Let others still triumph, and gain their cause
By their deserts, or by the Worlds applause;
Let Merit Crowns, and Justice Laurels give,
But let me Happy by your Pity live.
True Poets empty Fame, and Praise despise;
Fame is the Trumpet, but your Smile the Prize.
You sit above, and see vain men below

The Sea Fight. 22 Keel. *91*: Keel, *73*
To the Lady Castlemain. Text from A New Collection of Poems and Songs. . . . Collected by John Bulteel, *1674*, *collated with* Examen Poeticum, *1693*, *and MS. Bodl. Eng. Poet. e. 4, pp. 173–4. See Commentary*
Heading To the Lady Castlemain . . . *93*: To the Dutchess of *Cleaveland* *74*: To the Countess of Castlemaine, for procuring a Play of his might be printed *MS* 3 And] For *MS* long *93 MS*: for *74* 4 By their misfortunes] They by misfortune *MS* 5 So my much-envy'd] Just so my envyed *MS* 6 thrown *93*: cast *74 MS* 9 Vertue *93 MS*: Virtues *74* 10 While *93*: When *74 MS* 17 Fame, and Praise *93 MS*: Praise and Fame *74* 18 Smile *93 MS*: Smiles *74*

Contend for what you only can bestow:
But those great Actions others do by chance,
Are, like your Beauty, your Inheritance.
So great a Soul, such sweetness joyn'd in One,
Could only spring from Noble *Grandison*;
You, like the Stars, not by reflexion bright,
Are born to your own Heav'n, and your own Light:
Like them are good, but from a Nobler Cause,
From your own Knowledg, not from Natures Laws.
Your pow'r you never use, but for Defence,
To guard your own, or others Innocence.
Your Foes are such as they, not you, have made;
And Virtue may repel, though not invade.
Such courage did the Ancient *Hero's* show,
Who, when they might prevent, wou'd wait the blow:
With such assurance, as they meant to say,
We will o'recome, but scorn the safest way.
  Well may I rest secure in your great Fate,
And dare my Stars to be unfortunate.
What further fear of danger can there be?
Beauty, which captives all things, sets me free.
Posterity will judge by my success,
I had the *Grecian* Poets happiness,
Who waving Plots, found out a better way;
Some God descended and preserv'd the Play.
  When first the Triumphs of your Sex were sung
By those old Poets, Beauty was but young;
And few admir'd the native red and white,
Till Poets drest them up to charm the sight.
So Beauty took on trust, and did engage
For sums of praises, till she came to age:
But this long growing Debt to Poesie,
You justly (Madam) have discharg'd to me,

26 born] sun *MS* and *om. MS* 29 never use, but for *93 MS*: use but for your own *74* 32 though] but *MS* 34 wou'd wait *93*: did wait *74*: would ward *MS* 35 such *93*: that *74 MS* 37–38 Well . . . unfortunate. *om. 93* 40 which *93*: that *74 MS* captives *93 MS*: castives *74* 41 will *93 MS*: would *74* 43 Who] Which *MS* 47 the *93*: her *74*: their *MS* 48 them *93 MS*: her *74* 50 to *93 MS*: of *74*. *Cf.* Astræa Redux, *l. 28* 51 this long growing *93*: this vast growing *74*: your vast wondrous *MS* to *93 MS*: of *74* Poesie] Poetry *93 MS* 52 You justly (Madam) *93*: You, Madam, justly *74 MS*

When your applause and favour did infuse
New life to my condemn'd and dying Muse;
Which, that the World as well as you may see,
Let these rude Verses your Acquittance be.
  Receiv'd in full this present day and year,
  One soveraign smile from Beauties general Heir.

PROLOGUE and EPILOGUE to *AURENG-ZEBE*

PROLOGUE

OUR Author by experience finds it true,
'Tis much more hard to please himself than you:
And out of no feign'd modesty, this day,
Damns his laborious Trifle of a Play:
Not that its worse than what before he writ,
But he has now another taste of Wit;
And to confess a truth, (though out of time)
Grows weary of his long-lov'd Mistris, Rhyme.
Passion's too fierce to be in Fetters bound,
And Nature flies him like Enchanted Ground.
What Verse can do, he has perform'd in this,
Which he presumes the most correct of his:
But spite of all his pride a secret shame,
Invades his breast at *Shakespear*'s sacred name:
Aw'd when he hears his Godlike *Romans* rage,
He, in a just despair, would quit the Stage.
And to an Age less polish'd, more unskill'd,
Does, with disdain the foremost Honours yield.
As with the greater Dead he dares not strive,
He wou'd not match his Verse with those who live:
Let him retire, betwixt two Ages cast,
The first of this, and hindmost of the last.

55–58 *om.* 93 56 your] their *MS* 57 this] the *MS* 58 One soveraign] I had a *MS*

Prologue and Epilogue. Text from Aureng-Zebe: A Tragedy, *1676, collated with the editions of 1685, 1690, 1692, 1694, 1699.*

A losing Gamester, let him sneak away;
He bears no ready Money from the Play.
The Fate which governs Poets, thought it fit,
He shou'd not raise his Fortunes by his Wit.
The Clergy thrive, and the litigious Bar;
Dull Heroes fatten with the spoils of War:
All Southern Vices, Heav'n be prais'd, are here;
But Wit's a luxury you think too dear.
When you to cultivate the Plant are loath,
'Tis a shrewd sign 'twas never of your growth:
And Wit in Northern Climates will not blow,
Except, like *Orange-trees*, 'tis hous'd from Snow.
There needs no care to put a Play-house down,
'Tis the most desart place of all the Town.
We and our Neighbours, to speak proudly, are
Like Monarchs, ruin'd with expensive War.
While, like wise *English*, unconcern'd, you sit,
And see us play the Tragedy of Wit.

EPILOGUE

A PRETTY task! and so I told the Fool,
Who needs would undertake to please by Rule:
He thought that, if his Characters were good,
The Scenes entire, and freed from noise and bloud;
The Action great, yet circumscrib'd by Time,
The Words not forc'd, but sliding into Rhime,
The Passions rais'd and calm'd by just Degrees,
As Tides are swell'd, and then retire to Seas;
He thought, in hitting these, his bus'ness done,
Though he, perhaps, has fail'd in ev'ry one:
But, after all, a Poet must confess,
His Art's like Physick, but a happy ghess.
Your Pleasure on your Fancy must depend:
The Lady's pleas'd, just as she likes her Friend.
No Song! no Dance! no Show! he fears you'l say,
You love all naked Beauties, but a Play.

Epilogue. 12 Art's] Art *90*

He much mistakes your methods to delight;
And, like the French, abhors our Target-fight:
But those damn'd Dogs can never be i'th' right.
True English hate your Monsieur's paltry Arts;
For you are all Silk-weavers, in your hearts.
Bold Brittons, at a brave Bear-garden Fray,
Are rouz'd: and, clatt'ring Sticks, cry, *Play, play, play*.
Mean time, your filthy Forreigner will stare,
And mutter to himself, *Ha gens Barbare!*
And, Gad, 'tis well he mutters; well for him;
Our Butchers else would tear him limb from limb.
'Tis true, the time may come, your Sons may be
Infected with this French civility;
But this in After-ages will be done:
Our Poet writes a hundred years too soon.
This Age comes on too slow, or he too fast:
And early Springs are subject to a blast!
Who would excel, when few can make a Test
Betwixt indiff'rent Writing and the best?
For Favours cheap and common, who wou'd strive,
Which, like abandon'd Prostitutes, you give?
Yet scatter'd here and there I some behold,
Who can discern the Tinsel from the Gold:
To these he writes; and, if by them allow'd,
'Tis their Prerogative to rule the Crowd.
For he more fears (like a presuming Man)
Their Votes who cannot judge, than theirs who can.

EPILOGUE to *THE MAN OF MODE*

Most Modern Wits, such monstrous Fools have shown,
They seem'd not of heav'ns making but their own.
Those Nauseous Harlequins in Farce may pass,
But there goes more to a substantial Ass!
Something of man must be expos'd to View,
That, Gallants, it may more resemble you:

Epilogue. Text from Etherege's The Man of Mode, or, Sr Fopling Flutter. A Comedy, *1676, collated with the editions of 1684 and 1693 and Bodl. MS. Don. B. 8, pp. 558–9. See Commentary*

3 Those] These *MS* 6 it *MS*: they *76 84 93*

Sir *Fopling* is a Fool so nicely writ,
The Ladies wou'd mistake him for a Wit,
And when he sings, talks lowd, and cocks; wou'd cry,
I now methinks he's pretty Company,
So brisk, so gay, so travail'd, so refin'd!
As he took pains to graff upon his kind.
True Fops help Natures work, and go to school,
To file and finish god-a'mighty's fool.
Yet none Sir *Fopling* him, or him can call;
He's Knight o'th' Shire, and represents ye all.
From each he meets, he culls what e're he can,
Legion's his name, a people in a Man.
His bulky folly gathers as it goes,
And, rolling o're you, like a Snow-ball growes.
His various modes from various Fathers follow,
One taught the Toss, and one the new *French* Wallow.
His Sword-knot, this; his Crevat, this design'd,
And this, the yard long Snake he twirls behind.
From one the sacred Perriwig he gain'd,
Which Wind ne're blew, nor touch of Hat prophan'd.
Anothers diving Bow he did adore,
Which with a shog casts all the hair before:
Till he with full Decorum brings it back,
And rises with a Water Spaniel shake.
As for his Songs (the Ladies dear delight)
Those sure he took from most of you who Write.
Yet every man is safe from what he fear'd,
For no one fool is hunted from the herd.

8 Wit,] Wit. *76 84 93* 10 I now] I vow *76 84 93*: I, now *MS*. *See Commentary*
14 fool] Toole *MS* *Additional lines follow in MS*:
Labour, to put in more, as Master Bayes
Thrumms in Additions to his ten-yeares playes. *See Commentary*
26 touch of *om. MS* 28 a] one *MS* 30 a] his *MS* 32 took] takes *MS*
who] that *MS*

PROLOGUE *to* CIRCE, *A Tragedy*

(A) THE PROLOGUE

WERE you but half so wise as you're severe,
Our youthful Poet shou'd not need to fear;
To his green years your Censures you wou'd suit,
Not blast the Blossom, but expect the Fruit.
The Sex that best does pleasure understand,
Will always chuse to err on t'other hand.
They check not him that's Aukward in delight,
But clap the young Rogues Cheek, and set him right.
Thus heartn'd well, and flesh't upon his Prey,
The youth may prove a man another day;
For your own sakes, instruct him when he's out,
You'l find him mend his work at every bout.
When some young lusty Thief is passing by,
How many of your tender Kind will cry,
A proper Fellow, pity he shou'd dye.
He might be sav'd, and thank us for our pains,
There's such a stock of Love within his Veins.
These Arguments the Women may perswade,
But move not you, the Brothers of the Trade,
Who scattering your Infection through the Pit,
With aking hearts and empty Purses sit,
To take your dear Five Shillings worth of Wit.
The praise you give him in your kindest mood,
Comes dribling from you, just like drops of blood;
And then you clap so civilly, for fear
The loudness might offend your Neighbours ear;
That we suspect your Gloves are lin'd within,
For silence sake, and Cotten'd next the skin.
From these Usurpers we appeal to you,
The only knowing, only judging few;
You who in private have this Play allow'd,
Ought to maintain your Suffrage to the Crowd.
The Captive once submitted to your Bands,
You shou'd protect from Death by Vulgar hands.

Prologue. Version (A): text from Charles D'Avenant's Circe, A Tragedy, *1677, collated with the second edition, 1685. Version (B): text from* Miscellany Poems, *1684, reprinted 1692. See Commentary*

(B) An EPILOGUE

WERE you but half so Wise as y'are Severe,
Our youthful Poet shou'd not need to fear:
To his green Years your Censures you would suit,
Not blast the Blossom, but expect the Fruit.
The Sex that best does pleasure understand,
Will always chuse to err on t'other hand.
They check not him that 's awkard in delight,
But Clap the young Rogues Cheek, and set him right.
Thus heart'nd well and flesh'd upon his prey,
The Youth may prove a Man another day.
Your *Ben* and *Fletcher* in their first young flight
Did no *Volpone*, no *Arbaces* write.
But hopp'd about, and short excursions made
From Bough to Bough, as if they were afraid,
And each were guilty of some *slighted Maid*.
Shakespear's own Muse her *Pericles* first bore,
The Prince of *Tyre* was elder than the *Moore*:
'Tis miracle to see a first good Play,
All Hawthorns do not bloom on *Christmas-day*.
A slender Poet must have time to grow,
And spread and burnish as his Brothers do.
Who still looks lean, sure with some Pox is curst,
But no Man can be *Falstaff* fat at first.
Then damn not, but indulge his stew'd essays,
Encourage him, and bloat him up with praise,
That he may get more bulk before he dyes;
He 's not yet fed enough for Sacrifice.
Perhaps if now your Grace you will not grudge,
He may grow up to Write, and you to Judge.

To Mr. *Lee*, on his *Alexander*

THE Blast of common Censure cou'd I fear,
Before your Play my Name shou'd not appear;
For 'twill be thought, and with some colour too,
I pay the Bribe I first receiv'd from You:

25 praise,] praise. *84 92* 26 dyes;] dyes, *84 92*
To Mr. Lee. Text from The Rival Queens, or The Death of Alexander the Great, *1677, collated with the editions of 1684, 1694, 1699* 4 Bribe] Bride *94*

That mutual Vouchers for our Fame we stand,
To play the Game into each others Hand;
And as cheap Pen'orths to our selves afford
As *Bessus*, and the Brothers of the Sword.
Such Libels private Men may well endure,
When States, and Kings themselves are not secure:
For ill Men, conscious of their inward guilt,
Think the best Actions on By-ends are built.
And yet my silence had not scap'd their spight,
Then envy had not suffer'd me to write:
For, since I cou'd not Ignorance pretend,
Such worth I must or envy or commend.
So many Candidates there stand for Wit,
A place in Court is scarce so hard to get;
In vain they croud each other at the Door;
For ev'n Reversions are all beg'd before:
Desert, how known so e're, is long delay'd;
And, then too, Fools and Knaves are better pay'd.
Yet, as some Actions bear so great a Name,
That Courts themselves are just, for fear of shame:
So has the mighty Merit of your Play
Extorted praise, and forc'd it self a Way.
'Tis here, as 'tis at Sea; who farthest goes,
Or dares the most, makes all the rest his Foes;
Yet, when some Virtue much out-grows the rest,
It shoots too fast, and high, to be opprest;
As his Heroic worth struck Envy dumb
Who took the *Dutchman*, and who cut the Boom:
Such praise is yours, while you the Passions move,
That 'tis no longer feign'd; 'tis real Love:
Where Nature Triumphs over wretched Art;
We only warm the Head, but you the Heart.
Alwayes you warm! and if the rising Year,
As in hot Regions, bring the Sun too near,
Tis but to make your Fragrant Spices blow,
Which in our colder Climates will not grow.
They only think you animate your Theme
With too much Fire, who are themselves all Phle'me:
Prizes wou'd be for Lags of slowest pace,

30 opprest] exprest *84 94 99*

Were Cripples made the Judges of the Race.
Despise those Drones, who praise while they accuse
The too much vigour of your youthful Muse:
That humble Stile which they their Virtue make
Is in your pow'r; you need but stoop and take.
Your beauteous Images must be allow'd
By all, but some vile Poets of the Crowd;
But how shou'd any Sign-post-dawber know
The worth of *Titian*, or of *Angelo*?
Hard Features every Bungler can command;
To draw true Beauty shews a Masters Hand.

EPILOGUE to
MITHRIDATES KING OF PONTUS

YO'VE seen a Pair of faithful Lovers die:
And much you care; for, most of you will cry,
'Twas a just Judgment on their Constancy.
For, Heav'n be thank'd, we live in such an Age
When no man dies for Love, but on the Stage:
And ev'n those Martyrs are but rare in Plays;
A cursed sign how much true Faith decays.
Love is no more a violent desire;
'Tis a meer Metaphor, a painted Fire.
In all our Sex, the name examin'd well,
Is Pride, to gain; and Vanity to tell:
In Woman, 'tis of subtil int'rest made,
Curse on the Punk that made it first a Trade!
She first did Wits Prerogative remove,
And made a Fool presume to prate of Love.
Let Honour and Preferment go for Gold;
But glorious Beauty is not to be sold:
Or, if it be, 'tis at a rate so high,
That nothing but adoring it shou'd buy.
Yet the rich Cullies may their boasting spare;
They purchase but sophisticated Ware.

46 your] you *84*
Epilogue. Text from Mithridates King of Pontus, A Tragedy, *1678, collated with the editions of 1685 and 1693*
11 Is] 'Tis *85 93*

'Tis Prodigality that buys deceit;
Where both the Giver, and the Taker cheat.
Men but refine on the old Half-Crown way:
And Women fight, like *Swizzers*, for their Pay.

PROLOGUE and EPILOGUE to *ALL FOR LOVE*

PROLOGUE to Anthony *and* Cleopatra

WHAT Flocks of Critiques hover here to day,
As Vultures wait on Armies for their Prey,
All gaping for the Carcass of a Play!
With Croaking Notes they bode some dire event;
And follow dying Poets by the scent.
Ours gives himself for gone; y'have watch'd your time!
He fights this day unarm'd; without his Rhyme.
And brings a Tale which often has been told;
As sad as *Dido*'s; and almost as old.
His Heroe, whom you Wits his Bully call,
Bates of his mettle; and scarce rants at all:
He's somewhat lewd; but a well-meaning mind;
Weeps much; fights little; but is wond'rous kind.
In short, a Pattern, and Companion fit,
For all the keeping Tonyes of the Pit.
I cou'd name more: A Wife, and Mistress too;
Both (to be plain) too good for most of you:
The Wife well-natur'd, and the Mistress true.
Now, Poets, if your fame has been his care;
Allow him all the candour you can spare.
A brave Man scorns to quarrel once a day;
Like Hectors, in at every petty fray.
Let those find fault whose Wit's so very small,
They've need to show that they can think at all:
Errours like Straws upon the surface flow;
He who would search for Pearls must dive below.
Fops may have leave to level all they can;

Prologue and Epilogue. Text from All for Love: or, The World well Lost. A Tragedy, *1678, collated with the editions of 1692 and 1696*

As Pigmies wou'd be glad to lopp a Man.
Half-Wits are Fleas; so little and so light;
We scarce cou'd know they live, but that they bite.
But, as the Rich, when tir'd with daily Feasts,
For change, become their next poor Tenants Ghests;
Drink hearty Draughts of Ale, from plain brown Bowls,
And snatch the homely Rasher from the Coals:
So you, retiring from much better Cheer,
For once, may venture to do penance here.
And since that plenteous Autumn now is past,
Whose Grapes and Peaches have Indulg'd your taste,
Take in good part from our poor Poets boord,
Such rivell'd Fruits as Winter can afford.

EPILOGUE

POETS, like Disputants, when Reasons fail,
Have one sure Refuge left; and that's to rail.
Fop, Coxcomb, Fool, are thunder'd through the Pit;
And this is all their Equipage of Wit.
We wonder how the Devil this diff'rence grows,
Betwixt our Fools in Verse, and yours in Prose:
For, 'Faith, the quarrel rightly understood,
'Tis *Civil War* with their own Flesh and Blood.
The thread-bare Author hates the gawdy Coat;
And swears at the Guilt Coach, but swears a foot:
For 'tis observ'd of every Scribling Man,
He grows a Fop as fast as e'er he can;
Prunes up, and asks his Oracle the Glass,
If Pink or Purple best become his face.
For our poor Wretch, he neither rails nor prays;
Nor likes your Wit just as you like his Plays;
He has not yet so much of Mr. *Bays*.
He does his best; and, if he cannot please,
Wou'd quietly sue out his *Writ of Ease*.
Yet, if he might his own Grand Jury call,
By the Fair Sex he begs to stand or fall.
Let *Cæsar*'s Pow'r the Mens ambition move,
But grace You him who lost the World for Love.

Yet if some antiquated Lady say,
The last Age is not Copy'd in his Play;
Heav'n help the Man who for that face must drudge,
Which only has the wrinkles of a Judge.
Let not the Young and Beauteous join with those;
For shou'd you raise such numerous Hosts of Foes,
Young Wits and Sparks he to his aid must call;
'Tis more than one Man's work to please you all.

PROLOGUE to *A TRUE WIDOW*

HEAV'N save ye Gallants, and this hopeful Age,
Y'are welcome to the downfal of the Stage:
The Fools have labour'd long in their Vocation;
And Vice, (the Manufacture of the Nation)
O're-stocks the Town so much, and thrives so well,
That Fopps and Knaves grow Druggs, and will not sell.
In vain our Wares on Theaters are shown,
When each has a Plantation of his own.
His Cruse ne'r fails; for whatsoe're he spends,
There's still God's plenty for himself and friends.
Shou'd Men be rated by Poetick Rules,
Lord what a Poll would there be rais'd from Fools!
Mean time poor Wit prohibited must lye,
As if 'twere made some *French* Commodity.
Fools you will have, and rais'd at vast expence,
And yet as soon as seen, they give offence.
Time was, when none would cry, that Oaf was mee,
But now you strive about your Pedigree:
Bawble and Cap no sooner are thrown down,
But there's a Muss of more than half the Town.
Each one will challenge a Child's part at least,
A sign the Family is well increas'd.
Of Forreign Cattle! there's no longer need,
When w' are supply'd so fast with *English* Breed.

Prologue. Text from Shadwell's A True Widow. A Comedy, *1679, collated with Aphra Behn's* The Widdow Ranter or, The History of Bacon in Virginia. A Tragi-Comedy, *1690. See Commentary*
9 Cruse] Cause *90*   22 increas'd.] increas'd *79 90*

Well! Flourish, Countrymen: drink swear and roar,
Let every free-born Subject keep his Whore;
And wandring in the Wilderness about,
At end of 40 years not wear her out.
But when you see these Pictures, let none dare
To own beyond a Limb, or single share:
For where the Punk is common! he's a Sot,
Who needs will Father what the Parish got.

PROLOGUE, EPILOGUE and SONGS from *OEDIPUS*

PROLOGUE

WHEN *Athens* all the *Græcian* State did guide,
And *Greece* gave Laws to all the World beside,
Then *Sophocles* with *Socrates* did sit,
Supreme in Wisdom one, and one in Wit:
And Wit from Wisdom differ'd not in those,
But as 'twas Sung in Verse, or said in Prose.
Then, *Oedipus*, on Crowded Theaters,
Drew all admiring Eyes and listning Ears;
The pleas'd Spectator shouted every Line,
The noblest, manliest, and the best Design!
And every Critick of each learned Age
By this just Model has reform'd the Stage.
Now, should it fail, (as Heav'n avert our fear!)
Damn it in silence, lest the World should hear.
For were it known this Poem did not please,
You might set up for perfect Salvages:
Your Neighbours would not look on you as men:
But think the Nation all turn'd *Picts* agen.
Faith, as you manage matters, 'tis not fit
You should suspect your selves of too much Wit.

Prologue, Epilogue and Songs. Text from Oedipus: A Tragedy, *1679, collated with the editions of 1682, 1687, 1692, [1696]*
Prologue. 7 Crowded] Crowned *92* [*96*]

Drive not the jeast too far, but spare this piece;
And, for this once, be not more Wise than *Greece*.
See twice! Do not pell-mell to Damning fall,
Like true born *Brittains*, who ne're think at all:
Pray be advis'd; and though at *Mons* you won,
On pointed Cannon do not always run.
With some respect to antient Wit proceed;
You take the four first Councils for your Creed.
But, when you lay Tradition wholly by,
And on the private Spirit alone relye,
You turn Fanaticks in your Poetry.
If, notwithstanding all that we can say,
You needs will have your pen'worths of the Play:
And come resolv'd to Damn, because you pay,
Record it, in memorial of the Fact,
The first Play bury'd since the Wollen Act.

EPILOGUE

WHAT *Sophocles* could undertake alone,
Our Poets found a Work for more than one;
And therefore Two lay tugging at the piece,
With all their force, to draw the pondrous Mass from *Greece*.
A weight that bent ev'n *Seneca*'s strong Muse,
And which *Corneille*'s Shoulders did refuse.
So hard it is th' *Athenian* Harp to string!
So much two Consuls yield to one just King.
Terrour and pity this whole Poem sway;
The mightiest Machines that can mount a Play;
How heavy will those Vulgar Souls be found,
Whom two such Engines cannot move from ground?
When *Greece* and *Rome* have smil'd upon this Birth,
You can but Damn for one poor spot of Earth;
And when your Children find your judgment such,
They'll scorn their Sires, and wish themselves born *Dutch*;
Each haughty Poet will infer with ease,
How much his Wit must under-write to please.
As some strong Churle would brandishing advance
The monumental Sword that conquer'd *France*;

So you, by judging this, your judgments teach
Thus far you like, that is, thus far you reach.
Since then the Vote of full two Thousand years
Has Crown'd this Plot, and all the Dead are theirs;
Think it a Debt you pay, not Alms you give,
And in your own defence, let this Play live.
Think 'em not vain, when *Sophocles* is shown,
To praise his worth, they humbly doubt their own.
Yet as weak States each others pow'r assure,
Weak Poets by Conjunction are secure.
Their Treat is what your Pallats rellish most,
Charm! Song! and Show! a Murder and a Ghost!
We know not what you can desire or hope,
To please you more, but burning of a *Pope*.

SONGS

I

SONG to Apollo

PHŒBUS, God belov'd by men;
At thy dawn, every Beast is rouz'd in his Den;
At thy setting, all the Birds of thy absence complain,
And we dye, all dye till the morning comes again,
        Phœbus, God belov'd by men!
        Idol of the Eastern Kings,
        Awful as the God who flings
        His Thunder round, and the Lightning wings;
        God of Songs, and *Orphean* strings,
        Who to this mortal bosom brings,
        All harmonious heav'nly things!
        Thy drouzie Prophet to revive,
Ten thousand thousand forms before him drive;
With Chariots and Horses all o' fire awake him,
Convulsions, and Furies, and Prophesies shake him:
Let him tell it in groans, tho' he bend with the load,
Tho' he burst with the weight of the terrible God.

Epilogue. 24 theirs; *82*–[*96*]: theirs. *79*

II

Tir. Chuse the darkest part o' th' Grove;
Such as Ghosts at noon-day love.
Dig a Trench, and dig it nigh
Where the bones of *Lajus* lye.
Altars rais'd of Turf or Stone,
Will th' Infernal Pow'rs have none.
Answer me, if this be done?
All Pr. 'Tis done.

Tir. Is the Sacrifice made fit?
Draw her backward to the pit:
Draw the barren Heyfer back;
Barren let her be and black.
Cut the curled hair that grows
Full betwixt her horns and brows:
And turn your faces from the Sun:
Answer me, if this be done?
All Pr. 'Tis done.

Tir. Pour in blood, and blood like wine,
To Mother Earth and *Proserpine*:
Mingle Milk into the stream;
Feast the Ghosts that love the steam;
Snatch a brand from funeral pile;
Toss it in to make 'em boil;
And turn your faces from the Sun;
Answer me, if all be done?
All Pr. All is done.

III

1. Hear, ye sullen Pow'rs below:
   Hear, ye taskers of the dead.
2. You that boiling Cauldrons blow,
   You that scum the molten Lead.
3. You that pinch with Red-hot Tongs;
1. You that drive the trembling hosts
   Of poor, poor Ghosts,
With your Sharpen'd Prongs;

2. You that thrust 'em off the Brim.
3. You that plunge 'em when they Swim:
1. Till they drown;
   Till they go
   On a row
Down, down, down
Ten thousand thousand, thousand fadoms low.
Chorus. Till they drown, *&c.*

1. Musick for a while
Shall your cares beguile:
Wondring how your pains were eas'd.
2. And disdaining to be pleas'd;
3. Till *Alecto* free the dead
   From their eternal bands;
Till the snakes drop from her head,
   And whip from out her hands.
1. Come away
Do not stay,
But obey
While we play,
For Hell 's broke up, and Ghosts have holy-day.
Chorus. Come away, *&c.*

[*A flash of Lightning: the Stage is made bright; and the Ghosts are seen passing betwixt the Trees.*

1 Lajus! 2 Lajus! 3 Lajus!
1 Hear! 2 Hear! 3 Hear!
Tir. Hear and appear:
By the Fates that spun thy thread;
Cho. Which are three,
Tir. By the Furies fierce, and dread!
Cho. Which are three,
Tir. By the Judges of the dead!
Cho. Which are three,
Three times three!
Tir. By Hells blew flame:
   By the *Stygian* Lake:
And by *Demogorgon*'s name,
   At which Ghosts quake,
Hear and appear.

PROLOGUE, EPILOGUE and SONG from *TROILUS and CRESSIDA*

THE PROLOGUE

Spoken by Mr. Betterton, *Representing the Ghost of* Shakespear

SEE, my lov'd *Britons*, see your *Shakespeare* rise,
An awfull ghost confess'd to human eyes!
Unnam'd, methinks, distinguish'd I had been
From other shades, by this eternal green,
About whose wreaths the vulgar Poets strive,
And with a touch, their wither'd Bays revive.
Untaught, unpractis'd, in a barbarous Age,
I found not, but created first the Stage.
And, if I drain'd no *Greek* or *Latin* store,
'Twas, that my own abundance gave me more.
On foreign trade I needed not rely
Like fruitfull *Britain*, rich without supply.
In this my rough-drawn Play, you shall behold
Some Master-strokes, so manly and so bold
That he, who meant to alter, found 'em such
He shook; and thought it Sacrilege to touch.
Now, where are the Successours to my name?
What bring they to fill out a Poets fame?
Weak, short-liv'd issues of a feeble Age;
Scarce living to be Christen'd on the Stage!
For Humour farce, for love they rhyme dispence,
That tolls the knell, for their departed sence.
Dulness might thrive in any trade but this:
'T wou'd recommend to some fat Benefice.
Dulness, that in a Playhouse meets disgrace
Might meet with Reverence, in its proper place.
The fulsome clench that nauseats the Town
Wou'd from a Judge or Alderman go down!
Such virtue is there in a Robe and gown!

Prologue, Epilogue and Song. Text from Troilus and Cressida, or, Truth Found too Late. A Tragedy, *1679, collated with the editions of* c. *1692 and 1695*

And that insipid stuff which here you hate
Might somewhere else be call'd a grave debate:
Dulness is decent in the Church and State.
But I forget that still 'tis understood
Bad Plays are best decry'd by showing good:
Sit silent then, that my pleas'd Soul may see
A Judging Audience once, and worthy me:
My faithfull Scene from true Records shall tell
How *Trojan* valour did the *Greek* excell;
Your great forefathers shall their fame regain,
And *Homers* angry Ghost repine in vain.

THE EPILOGUE

Spoken by *Thersites*

THESE cruel Critiques put me into passion;
For in their lowring looks I reade damnation:
Ye expect a Satyr, and I seldom fail,
When I'm first beaten, 'tis my part to rail.
You *British* fools, of the Old *Trojan* stock,
That stand so thick one cannot miss the flock,
Poets have cause to dread a keeping Pit,
When Womens Cullyes come to judge of Wit.
As we strow Rats-bane when we vermine fear,
'Twere worth our cost to scatter fool-bane here.
And after all our judging Fops were serv'd,
Dull Poets too shou'd have a dose reserv'd,
Such Reprobates, as past all sence of shaming
Write on, and nere are satisfy'd with damming,
Next, those, to whom the Stage does not belong,
Such whose Vocation onely is to Song;
At most to Prologue, when for want of time
Poets take in for Journywork in Rhime.
But I want curses for those mighty shoales,
Of scribling *Chlorisses*, and *Phillis* fools,
Those Ophs shou'd be restraind, during their lives,
From Pen and Ink, as Madmen are from knives:

The Epilogue. 15 belong,] belong *79* [*92*] *95*

I cou'd rayl on, but 'twere a task as vain
As Preaching truth at *Rome*, or wit in *Spain*,
Yet to huff out our Play was worth my trying,
John Lilbourn scap'd his Judges by defying:
If guilty, yet I'm sure oth' Churches blessing,
By suffering for the Plot, without confessing.

SONG

CAN life be a blessing,
Or worth the possessing,
Can life be a blessing if love were away?
Ah no! though our love all night keep us waking,
And though he torment us with cares all the day,
Yet he sweetens he sweetens our pains in the taking,
There's an hour at the last, there's an hour to repay.

2

In every possessing,
The ravishing blessing,
In every possessing the fruit of our pain,
Poor lovers forget long ages of anguish,
Whate're they have suffer'd and done to obtain;
'Tis a pleasure, a pleasure to sigh and to languish,
When we hope, when we hope to be happy again.

PROLOGUE, EPILOGUE and SONGS from *THE KIND KEEPER*

PROLOGUE

TRUE Wit has seen its best days long ago,
It ne're look'd up, since we were dipt in Show:
When Sense in Dogrel Rhimes and Clouds was lost,
And Dulness flourish'd at the Actors cost.

Prologue, Epilogue and Songs. Text from The Kind Keeper; or, Mr. Limberham: A Comedy, *1680, collated with the edition of 1690*

Nor stopt it here, when Tragedy was done,
Satyre and Humour the same Fate have run;
And Comedy is sunk to Trick and Pun.
Now our Machining Lumber will not sell,
And you no longer care for Heav'n or Hell;
What Stuff will please you next, the Lord can tell.
Let them, who the Rebellion first began,
To wit, restore the Monarch if they can;
Our Author dares not be the first bold Man.
He, like the prudent Citizen, takes care,
To keep for better Marts his Staple Ware,
His Toys are good enough for *Sturbridge* Fair.
Tricks were the Fashion; if it now be spent,
'Tis time enough at *Easter* to invent;
No Man will make up a new Suit for *Lent*:
If now and then he takes a small pretence
To forrage for a little Wit and Sense,
Pray pardon him, he meant you no offence.
Next Summer *Nostradamus* tells, they say,
That all the *Criticks* shall be shipt away,
And not enow be left to damn a Play.
To every Sayl beside, good Heav'n be kind;
But drive away that Swarm with such a Wind,
That not one *Locust* may be left behind.

EPILOGUE

Spoken by LIMBERHAM

I BEG a Boon, that e're you all disband,
Some one would take my Bargain off my hand;
To keep a Punk is but a common evil,
To find her false, and Marry, that's the Devil.
Well, I ne're Acted Part in all my life,
But still I was fobb'd off with some such Wife:
I find the Trick; these Poets take no pity
Of one that is a Member of the City.
We Cheat you lawfully, and in our Trades,
You Cheat us basely with your Common Jades.

Now I am Married, I must sit down by it;
But let me keep my Dear-bought Spouse in quiet:
Let none of you Damn'd *Woodalls* of the Pit,
Put in for Shares to mend our breed, in Wit;
We know your Bastards from our Flesh and Blood,
Not one in ten of yours e're comes to good.
In all the Boys their Fathers Vertues shine,
But all the Female Fry turn *Pugs* like mine.
When these grow up, Lord with what Rampant Gadders
Our Counters will be throng'd, and Roads with Padders.
This Town two Bargains has, not worth one farthing,
A *Smithfield* Horse, and Wife of *Covent-Garden.*

SONGS

I

A SONG

1

'GAINST Keepers we petition,
Who wou'd inclose the Common:
'Tis enough to raise Sedition
In the free-born subject Woman.
Because for his gold
I my body have sold,
He thinks I'm a Slave for my life;
He rants, domineers,
He swaggers and swears,
And wou'd keep me as bare as his Wife.

2

'Gainst Keepers we petition, *&c.*
'Tis honest and fair,
That a Feast I prepare;
But when his dull appetite's o're,
I'le treat with the rest
Some welcomer Ghest,
For the Reck'ning was paid me before.

II

A SONG from the ITALIAN

BY a dismal Cypress lying,
Damon cry'd, all pale and dying,
Kind is Death that ends my pain,
But cruel She I lov'd in vain.
The Mossy Fountains
Murmure my trouble,
And hollow Mountains
My groans redouble:
Every Nymph mourns me,
Thus while I languish;
She only scorns me,
Who caus'd my anguish.
No Love returning me, but all hope denying;
By a dismal Cypress lying,
Like a *Swan*, so sung he dying:
Kind is Death that ends my pain,
But cruel She I lov'd in vain.

OVID'S EPISTLES

Translated by *Several Hands*

THE PREFACE TO OVID'S EPISTLES

THE Life of Ovid *being already writen in our Language before the Translation of his* Metamorphoses, *I will not presume so far upon my self, to think I can add any thing to Mr.* Sandys *his undertaking. The* English *Reader may there be satisfied, that he flourish'd in the Reign of* Augustus Cæsar, *that he was Extracted from an Antient Family of* Roman *Knights; that he was born to the Inheritance of a Splendid Fortune, that he was design'd to the Study of the Law; and had made considerable progress in it, before he quitted that Profession, for this of* Poetry, *to which he was more naturally form'd. The Cause of his Banishment is unknown; because he was himself unwilling further to provoke the Emperour, by ascribing it to any other reason, than what was pretended by* Augustus, *which was the Lasciviousness of his Elegies, and his Art of Love. 'Tis true they are not to be Excus'd in the severity of Manners, as being able to Corrupt a larger Empire, if there were any, than that of* Rome*; yet this may be said in behalf of* Ovid, *that no man has ever treated the Passion of Love with so much Delicacy of Thought, and of Expression, or search'd into the nature of it more Philosophically than he. And the Emperour who Condemn'd him, had as little reason as another man to punish that fault with so much severity, if at least he were the Authour of a certain* Epigram, *which is ascrib'd to him, relating to the Cause of the first Civil War betwixt himself and* Mark Anthony *the Triumvir, which is more fulsome than any passage I have met with in our Poet. To pass by the naked Familiarity of his Expressions to* Horace, *which are cited in that Authours Life, I need only mention one notorious Act of his in taking* Livia *to his Bed, when she was not only Married, but with Child by her Husband, then living. But Deeds, it seems, may be Justified by Arbitrary Power, when words are question'd in a Poet. There is another ghess of the* Grammarians, *as far from truth as the first from Reason; they will have him Banish'd for some favours, which they say he receiv'd from* Julia, *the Daughter of* Augustus, *whom they think he Celebrates under the Name of* Corinna *in his* Elegies*: but he who will observe the Verses which are made to that Mistress, may gather from the whole Contexture of them, that* Corinna *was not a Woman of the highest Quality: If* Julia *were then Married to* Agrippa, *why should our Poet make his*

Ovid's Epistles. Text from the first edition, 1680, collated with the editions of 1681, 1683, 1688, and 1693

Petition to Isis, *for her safe Delivery, and afterwards, Condole her Miscarriage; which for ought he knew might be by her own Husband? Or indeed how durst he be so bold to make the least discovery of such a Crime, which was no less than Capital, especially Committed against a Person of* Agrippa's *Rank? Or if it were before her Marriage, he would surely have been more discreet, than to have publish'd an Accident, which must have been fatal to them both. But what most Confirms me against this Opinion is, that* Ovid *himself complains that the true Person of* Corinna *was found out by the Fame of his Verses to her: which if it had been* Julia, *he durst not have own'd; and besides, an immediate punishment must have follow'd. He seems himself more truly to have touch'd at the Cause of his Exile in those obscure Verses,*

Cur aliquid vidi, cur noxia Lumina feci? *&c.*

Namely, that he had either seen, or was Conscious to somewhat, which had procur'd him his disgrace. But neither am I satisfyed that this was the Incest of the Emperour with his own Daughter: For Augustus *was of a Nature too vindicative to have contented himself with so small a Revenge, or so unsafe to himself, as that of simple Banishment, and would certainly have secur'd his Crimes from publick notice by the death of him who was witness to them. Neither have Histories given us any sight into such an Action of this Emperour: nor would he (the greatest Polititian of his time,) in all probability, have manag'd his Crimes with so little secresie, as not to shun the Observation of any man. It seems more probable that* Ovid *was either the Confident of some other passion, or that he had stumbled by some inadvertency upon the privacies of* Livia, *and seen her in a Bath: For the words*

Sine veste Dianam,

agree better with Livia, *who had the Fame of Chastity, than with either of the* Julias, *who were both noted of Incontinency. The first Verses which were made by him in his Youth, and recited publickly, according to the Custom were, as he himself assures us to* Corinna*: his Banishment happen'd not till the Age of fifty; from which it may be deduc'd, with probability enough, that the love of* Corinna, *did not occasion it: Nay he tells us plainly, that his offence was that of Errour only, not of wickedness: and in the same paper of Verses also, that the cause was notoriously known at* Rome, *though it be left so obscure to after Ages.*

But to leave Conjectures on a Subject so incertain, and to write somewhat more Authentick of this Poet: That he frequented the Court of Augustus, *and was well receiv'd in it, is most undoubted: all his Poems bear the Character of a Court, and appear to be written as the* French *call it* Cavalierement*: Add to this, that the Titles of many of his Elegies, and more of his Letters in his Banishment, are*

56 Sine . . . Dianam *81–93*: Nudam sine . . . Dianam *80*

address'd to persons well known to us, even at this distance, to have been considerable in that Court.

Nor was his acquaintance less with the famous Poets of his Age, than with the Noblemen and Ladies; he tells you himself, in a particular Account of his own Life, that Macer, Horace, Tibullus, Propertius, *and many others of them were his familiar Friends, and that some of them communicated their Writings to him: but that he had only seen* Virgil.

If the Imitation of Nature be the business of a Poet, I know no Authour who can justly be compar'd with ours, especially in the Description of the Passions. And to prove this, I shall need no other Judges than the generality of his Readers: for all Passions being inborn with us, we are almost equally Judges when we are concern'd in the representation of them: Now I will appeal to any man who has read this Poet, whether he find not the natural Emotion of the same Passion in himself, which the Poet describes in his feign'd Persons? His thoughts which are the Pictures and results of those Passions, are generally such as naturally arise from those disorderly Motions of our Spirits. Yet, not to speak too partially in his behalf, I will confess that the Copiousness of his Wit was such, that he often writ too pointedly for his Subject, and made his persons speak more Eloquently than the violence of their Passion would admit: so that he is frequently witty out of season: leaving the Imitation of Nature, and the cooler dictates of his Judgment, for the false applause of Fancy. Yet he seems to have found out this Imperfection in his riper age: for why else should he complain that his Metamorphosis *was left unfinish'd? Nothing sure can be added to the Wit of that Poem, or of the rest: but many things ought to have been retrench'd; which I suppose would have been the business of his Age, if his Misfortunes had not come too fast upon him. But take him uncorrected as he is transmitted to us, and it must be acknowledg'd in spight of his* Dutch *Friends, the Commentators, even of* Julius Scaliger *himself, that* Seneca's *Censure will stand good against him;*

Nescivit quod bene cessit relinquere:

he never knew how to give over, when he had done well: but continually varying the same sence an hundred waies, and taking up in another place, what he had more than enough inculcated before, he sometimes cloys his Readers instead of satisfying them: and gives occasion to his Translators, who dare not Cover him, to blush at the nakedness of their Father. This then is the Allay of Ovids *writing, which is sufficiently recompenc'd by his other Excellencys; nay this very fault is not without it's Beauties: for the most severe Censor cannot but be pleas'd with the prodigality of his Wit, though at the same time he could have wish'd, that the Master of it had been a better Menager. Every thing which he does, becomes him, and if sometimes he appear too gay, yet there is a secret gracefulness of youth, which accompanies his Writings, though the staydness and sobriety of Age be wanting. In the most material part, which is the Conduct, 'tis certain that he seldom has miscarried: for if his Elegies be compar'd with those of* Tibullus, *and* Propertius *his Contemporaries, it will be found that those Poets seldom design'd before they writ; And though the Language of* Tibullus *be more polish'd, and the Learning of* Propertius, *especially in his Fourth Book, more set out to ostentation: Yet their common practice, was to look no further before them than the next Line: whence it will inevitably follow, that they can drive to no certain point, but ramble from one Subject to another, and conclude with somewhat which is not of a piece with their beginning:*

> Purpureus late qui splendeat, unus & alter
> Assuitur pannus:

As Horace *says, though the Verses are golden, they are but patch'd into the Garment. But our Poet has always the Goal in his Eye, which directs him in his Race; some Beautiful design, which he first establishes, and then contrives the means, which will naturally conduct it to his end. This will be Evident to Judicious Readers in this work of his Epistles, of which somewhat, at least in general, will be expected.*

The Title of them in our late Editions is Epistolæ Heroidum, *The Letters of the* Heroines. *But* Heinsius *has Judg'd more truly, that the* Inscription *of our Authour was barely,* Epistles*; which he concludes from his cited Verses, where* Ovid *asserts this work as his own Invention, and not borrow'd from the* Greeks, *whom (as the Masters of their Learning,) the* Romans *usually did imitate. But it appears not from their writers, that any of the* Grecians *ever touch'd upon this way, which our Poet therefore justly has vindicated to himself. I quarrel not at the word* Heroidum, *because 'tis us'd by* Ovid *in his Art of Love:*

> Jupiter ad veteres supplex *Heroidas* ibat.

But sure he cou'd not be guilty of such an Oversight, to call his Work by the Name of Heroines, *when there are divers men or* Heroes, *as Namely* Paris, Leander, *and* Acontius, *joyn'd in it. Except* Sabinus, *who writ some Answers to* Ovids *Letters,*

> (Quam celer è toto rediit meus orbe Sabinus,)

I remember not any of the Romans *who have treated this Subject, save only* Propertius, *and that but once, in his Epistle of* Arethusa *to* Lycotas, *which is written so near the Style of* Ovid, *that it seems to be but an Imitation, and therefore ought not to defraud our Poet of the Glory of his Invention.*

Concerning this work of the Epistles, I shall content my self to observe these few particulars. First, that they are generally granted to be the most perfect piece of

Ovid, *and that the Style of them is tenderly passionate and Courtly; two properties well agreeing with the Persons which were* Heroines, *and* Lovers. *Yet where the Characters were lower, as in* Oenone, *and* Hero, *he has kept close to Nature in drawing his Images after a Country Life, though perhaps he has Romaniz'd his* Grecian *Dames too much, and made them speak sometimes as if they had been born in the City of* Rome, *and under the Empire of* Augustus. *There seems to be no great variety in the particular Subjects which he has chosen: most of the Epistles being written from Ladies who were forsaken by their Lovers: which is the reason that many of the same thoughts come back upon us in divers Letters: But of the general Character of Women which is Modesty, he has taken a most becoming care; for his amorous Expressions go no further than virtue may allow, and therefore may be read, as he intended them, by Matrons without a blush.*

Thus much concerning the Poet: whom you find translated by divers hands, that you may at least have that variety in the English, *which the Subject denyed to the Authour of the* Latine. *It remains that I should say somewhat of Poetical Translations in general, and give my Opinion (with submission to better Judgments) which way of Version seems to me most proper.*

All Translation I suppose may be reduced to these three heads.

First, that of Metaphrase, or turning an Authour word by word, and Line by Line, from one Language into another. Thus, or near this manner, was Horace *his Art of Poetry translated by* Ben. Johnson. *The second way is that of Paraphrase, or Translation with Latitude, where the Authour is kept in view by the Translator, so as never to be lost, but his words are not so strictly follow'd as his sense, and that too is admitted to be amplyfied, but not alter'd. Such is Mr.* Wallers *Translation of* Virgils *Fourth* Æneid. *The Third way is that of Imitation, where the Translator (if now he has not lost that Name) assumes the liberty not only to vary from the words and sence, but to forsake them both as he sees occasion: and taking only some general hints from the Original, to run division on the ground-work, as he pleases. Such is Mr.* Cowleys *practice in turning two Odes of* Pindar, *and one of* Horace *into* English.

Concerning the first of these Methods, our Master Horace *has given us this Caution,*

> Nec verbum verbo curabis reddere, fidus
> Interpres—

Nor word for word too faithfully translate. *As the* Earl *of* Roscommon *has excellently render'd it. Too faithfully is indeed pedantically: 'tis a faith like that which proceeds from Superstition, blind and zealous: Take it in the Expression of Sir* John Denham, *to Sir* Rich. Fanshaw, *on his Version of the* Pastor Fido.

That servile path, thou nobly do'st decline,
Of tracing word by word and Line by Line;
A new and nobler way thou do'st pursue,
To make Translations, and Translators too:
They but preserve the Ashes, thou the Flame,
True to his Sence, but truer to his Fame.

'Tis almost impossible to Translate verbally, and well, at the same time; For the Latin, (*a most severe and Compendious Language*) *often expresses that in one word, which either the Barbarity, or the narrowness of modern Tongues cannot supply in more. 'Tis frequent also that the Conceit is couch'd in some Expression, which will be lost in* English.

Atque ijdem Venti vela fidemq; ferent.

What Poet of our Nation is so happy as to express this thought Literally in English, *and to strike Wit or almost Sense out of it?*

In short the Verbal Copyer is incumber'd with so many difficulties at once, that he can never disintangle himself from all. He is to consider at the same time the thought of his Authour, and his words, and to find out the Counterpart to each in another Language: and besides this he is to confine himself to the compass of Numbers, and the Slavery of Rhime. 'Tis much like dancing on Ropes with fetter'd Leggs: A man may shun a fall by using Caution, but the gracefulness of Motion is not to be expected: and when we have said the best of it, 'tis but a foolish Task; for no sober man would put himself into a danger for the Applause of scaping without breaking his Neck. We see Ben. Johnson *could not avoid obscurity in his literal Translation of* Horace, *attempted in the same compass of Lines: nay* Horace *himself could scarce have done it to a* Greek *Poet.*

Brevis esse laboro, obscurus fio.

Either perspicuity or gracefulness will frequently be wanting. Horace *has indeed avoided both these Rocks in his Translation of the three first Lines of* Homers Odysses, *which he has Contracted into two.*

Dic mihi Musa Virum captæ post tempora Trojæ
Qui mores hominum multorum vidit & urbes.

Muse, speak the man, who since the Siege of Troy, } Earl of
So many Towns, such Change of Manners saw. } *Rosc.*

But then the sufferings of Ulysses, *which are a Considerable part of that Sentence are omitted.*

Ὅς μάλα πολλὰ πλάγχθη.

195 *in more 81–93*: *it more 80*

The Consideration of these difficulties, in a servile, literal Translation, not long since made two of our famous Wits, Sir John Denham, *and Mr.* Cowley *to contrive another way of turning Authours into our Tongue, call'd by the latter of them, Imitation. As they were Friends, I suppose they Communicated their thoughts on this Subject to each other, and therefore their reasons for it are little different: though the practice of one is much more moderate. I take Imitation of an Authour in their sense to be an Endeavour of a later Poet to write like one who has written before him on the same Subject: that is, not to Translate his words, or to be Confin'd to his Sense, but only to set him as a Patern, and to write, as he supposes, that Authour would have done, had he liv'd in our Age, and in our Country. Yet I dare not say that either of them have carried this libertine way of rendring Authours (as Mr.* Cowley *calls it) so far as my Definition reaches. For in the* Pindarick Odes, *the Customs and Ceremonies of Ancient* Greece *are still preserv'd: but I know not what mischief may arise hereafter from the Example of such an Innovation, when writers of unequal parts to him, shall imitate so bold an undertaking; to add and to diminish what we please, which is the way avow'd by him, ought only to be granted to Mr.* Cowley, *and that too only in his Translation of* Pindar, *because he alone was able to make him amends, by giving him better of his own, when ever he refus'd his Authours thoughts.* Pindar *is generally known to be a dark writer, to want Connexion, (I mean as to our understanding) to soar out of sight, and leave his Reader at a Gaze: So wild and ungovernable a Poet cannot be Translated litterally, his Genius is too strong to bear a Chain, and* Sampson *like he shakes it off: A Genius so Elevated and unconfin'd as Mr.* Cowley's, *was but necessary to make* Pindar *speak* English, *and that was to be perform'd by no other way than Imitation. But if* Virgil *or* Ovid, *or any regular intelligible Authours be thus us'd, 'tis no longer to be call'd their work, when neither the thoughts nor words are drawn from the Original: but instead of them there is something new produc'd, which is almost the creation of another hand. By this way 'tis true, somewhat that is Excellent may be invented perhaps more Excellent than the first design, though* Virgil *must be still excepted, when that perhaps takes place: Yet he who is inquisitive to know an Authours thoughts will be disapointed in his expectation. And 'tis not always that a man will be contented to have a Present made him, when he expects the payment of a Debt. To state it fairly, Imitation of an Authour is the most advantagious way for a Translator to shew himself, but the greatest wrong which can be done to the Memory and Reputation of the dead. Sir* John Denham *(who advis'd more Liberty than he took himself,) gives this Reason for his Innovation, in his admirable Preface before the Translation of the second* Æneid: *"Poetry is of so subtil a Spirit, that in pouring out of one Language into another, it will all*

237 *undertaking;* 83–93: *undertaking,* 80: *undertaking.* 81

Evaporate; and if a new Spirit be not added in the transfusion, there will remain nothing but a Caput Mortuum". *I confess this Argument holds good against a litteral Translation, but who defends it? Imitation and verbal Version are in my Opinion the two Extreams, which ought to be avoided: and therefore when I have propos'd the mean betwixt them, it will be seen how far his Argument will reach.*

No man is capable of Translating Poetry, who besides a Genius to that Art, is not a Master both of his Authours Language, and of his own: Nor must we understand the Language only of the Poet, but his particular turn of Thoughts, and of Expression, which are the Characters that distinguish, and as it were individuate him from all other writers. When we are come thus far, 'tis time to look into our selves, to conform our Genius to his, to give his thought either the same turn if our tongue will bear it, or if not, to vary but the dress, not to alter or destroy the substance. The like Care must be taken of the more outward Ornaments, the Words: when they appear (which is but seldom) litterally graceful, it were an injury to the Authour that they should be chang'd: But since every Language is so full of its own proprieties, that what is Beautiful in one, is often Barbarous, nay sometimes Nonsence in another, it would be unreasonable to limit a Translator to the narrow compass of his Authours words: 'tis enough if he choose out some Expression which does not vitiate the Sense. I suppose he may stretch his Chain to such a Latitude, but by innovation of thoughts, methinks he breaks it. By this means the Spirit of an Authour may be transfus'd, and yet not lost: and thus 'tis plain that the reason alledg'd by Sir John Denham, *has no farther force than to Expression: for thought, if it be Translated truly, cannot be lost in another Language, but the words that convey it to our apprehension (which are the Image and Ornament of that thought) may be so ill chosen as to make it appear in an unhandsome dress, and rob it of its native Lustre. There is therefore a Liberty to be allow'd for the Expression, neither is it necessary that Words and Lines should be confin'd to the measure of their Original. The sence of an Authour, generally speaking, is to be Sacred and inviolable. If the Fancy of* Ovid *be luxuriant, 'tis his Character to be so, and if I retrench it, he is no longer* Ovid. *It will be replyed that he receives advantage by this lopping of his superfluous branches, but I rejoyn that a Translator has no such Right: when a* Painter *Copies from the life, I suppose he has no priviledge to alter Features, and Lineaments, under pretence that his Picture will look better: perhaps the Face which he has drawn would be more Exact, if the Eyes, or Nose were alter'd, but 'tis his business to make it resemble the Original. In two Cases only there may a seeming difficulty arise, that is, if the thought be notoriously trivial or dishonest; But the same Answer will serve for both, that then they ought not to be Translated.*

289 *Original. 81–93: Original, 80*

—Et quae
Desperes tractata nitescere posse, relinquas.

Thus I have ventur'd to give my Opinion on this Subject against the Authority of two great men, but I hope without offence to either of their Memories, for I both lov'd them living, and reverence them now they are dead. But if after what I have urg'd, it be thought by better Judges that the praise of a Translation Consists in adding new Beauties to the piece, thereby to recompence the loss which it sustains by change of Language, I shall be willing to be taught better, and to recant. In the mean time it seems to me, that the true reason why we have so few Versions which are tolerable, is not from the too close persuing of the Authours Sence: but because there are so few who have all the Talents which are requisite for Translation: and that there is so little praise and so small Encouragement for so considerable a part of Learning.

To apply in short, what has been said, to this present work, the Reader will here find most of the Translations, with some little Latitude or variation from the Authours Sence: That of Oenone *to* Paris, *is in Mr.* Cowleys *way of Imitation only. I was desir'd to say that the Authour who is of the* Fair Sex, *understood not* Latine. *But if she does not, I am afraid she has given us occasion to be asham'd who do.*

For my own part I am ready to acknowledge that I have transgress'd the Rules which I have given; and taken more liberty than a just Translation will allow. But so many Gentlemen whose Wit and Learning are well known, being Joyn'd in it, I doubt not but that their Excellencies will make you ample Satisfaction for my Errours.

J. Dryden.

CANACE to MACAREUS

The ARGUMENT

Macareus *and* Canace *Son and Daughter to* Æolus, *God of the Winds, lov'd each other Incestuously:* Canace *was delivered of a Son, and committed him to her Nurse, to be secretly convey'd away. The Infant crying out, by that means was discover'd to* Æolus, *who inrag'd at the wickedness of his Children, commanded the Babe to be expos'd to Wild Beasts on the Mountains: and, withal, sent a Sword to* Canace, *with this Message, That her Crimes would instruct her how to use it. With this Sword she slew her self: but before she died, she writ the following Letter to her Brother* Macareus, *who had taken Sanctuary in the Temple of* Apollo.

Canace to Macareus. Editor's paragraphs

IF streaming blood my fatal Letter stain,
Imagine, e're you read, the Writer slain:
One hand the Sword, and one the Pen employs,
And in my lap the ready paper lyes.
Think in this posture thou behold'st me Write:
In this my cruel Father wou'd delight.
O were he present, that his eyes and hands
Might see and urge the death which he commands,
Than all his raging Winds more dreadful, he
Unmov'd, without a tear, my wounds wou'd see.
Jove justly plac'd him on a stormy Throne,
His Peoples temper is so like his own.
The *North* and *South*, and each contending blast
Are underneath his wide Dominion cast:
Those he can rule; but his tempestuous mind
Is, like his airy Kingdom, unconfin'd.
Ah! what avail my Kindred Gods above,
That in their number I can reckon *Jove*!
What help will all my heav'nly friends afford,
When to my breast I lift the pointed Sword?
That hour which joyn'd us came before its time,
In death we had been one without a crime:
Why did thy flames beyond a *Brothers* move?
Why lov'd I thee with more than *Sisters* love?
For I lov'd too; and knowing not my wound,
A secret pleasure in thy Kisses found:
My Cheeks no longer did their colour boast,
My Food grew loathsom, and my strength I lost:
Still e're I spoke, a sigh wou'd stop my tongue;
Short were my slumbers, and my nights were long.
I knew not from my love these griefs did grow,
Yet was, alas, the thing I did not know.
My wily Nurse by long experience found,
And first discover'd to my Soul its wound.
'Tis Love, said she; and then my down-cast eyes,
And guilty dumbness, witness'd my surprize.
Forc'd at the last, my shameful pain I tell:
And, oh, what follow'd we both know too well!
'When half denying, more than half content,

9 his] the *83–93*

'Embraces warm'd me to a full consent:
'Then with Tumultuous Joyes my Heart did beat,
'And guilt that made them anxious, made them great.
  But now my swelling womb heav'd up my breast,
And rising weight my sinking Limbs opprest.
What Herbs, what Plants, did not my Nurse produce
To make Abortion by their pow'rful Juice?
What Medicines try'd we not, to thee unknown?
Our first crime common; this was mine alone.
But the strong Child, secure in his dark Cell,
With Natures vigour did our arts repell.
And now the pale-fac'd Empress of the Night
Nine times had fill'd her Orb with borrow'd light:
Not knowing 'twas my Labour, I complain
Of sudden shootings, and of grinding pain:
My throws came thicker, and my cryes increast,
Which with her hand the conscious Nurse supprest:
To that unhappy fortune was I come,
Pain urg'd my clamours; but fear kept me dumb.
With inward struggling I restrain'd my cries;
And drunk the tears that trickled from my eyes.
Death was in sight, *Lucina* gave no aid;
And ev'n my dying had my guilt betray'd.
Thou cam'st; and in thy Count'nance sate Despair:
Rent were thy Garments all, and torn thy Hair:
Yet, feigning comfort which thou cou'dst not give,
(Prest in thy Arms, and whisp'ring me to live)
For both our sakes, (said'st thou) preserve thy life;
Live, my dear Sister, and my dearer Wife.
Rais'd by that name, with my last pangs I strove:
Such pow'r have words, when spoke by those we love.
The *Babe*, as if he heard what thou hadst sworn,
With hasty joy sprung forward to be born.
What helps it to have weather'd out one Storm?
Fear of our *Father* does another form.
High in his Hall, rock'd in a Chair of State,
The King with his tempestuous Council sate:
Through this large Room our only passage lay,
By which we cou'd the new-born *Babe* convey.

47 not, *83–93*: not *80 81*

Swath'd, in her lap, the bold Nurse bore him out;
With Olive branches cover'd round about:
And, mutt'ring pray'rs, as holy Rites she meant,
Through the divided Crowd, unquestion'd, went.
Just at the door th' unhappy Infant cry'd:
The Grandsire heard him, and the theft he spy'd.
Swift as a Whirl-wind to the Nurse he flyes;
And deafs his stormy Subjects with his cries.
With one fierce puff, he blows the leaves away:
Expos'd the self-discover'd Infant lay.
The noise reach'd me, and my presaging mind
Too soon its own approaching woes divin'd.
Not Ships at Sea with winds are shaken more,
Nor Seas themselves, when angry Tempests roar,
Than I, when my loud Fathers voice I hear:
The *Bed* beneath me trembled with my fear.
He rush'd upon me, and divulg'd my stain;
Scarce from my Murther cou'd his hands refrain.
I only answer'd him with silent tears;
They flow'd; my tongue was frozen up with fears.
His little Grandchild he commands away,
To Mountain Wolves, and every Bird of prey.
The Babe cry'd out, as if he understood,
And beg'd his pardon with what voice he cou'd.
By what expressions can my grief be shown?
(Yet you may guess my anguish by your own)
To see my bowels, and what yet was worse,
Your bowels too, condemn'd to such a Curse!
Out went the King; my voice its freedom found,
My breasts I beat, my blubber'd Cheeks I wound.
  And now appear'd the Messenger of death,
Sad were his Looks, and scarce he drew his Breath,
To say, *Your Father sends you*—(with that word
His trembling hands presented me a Sword:)
Your Father sends you this: and lets you know
That your own Crimes the use of it will show.
Too well I know the sence those words impart:
His *Present* shall be treasur'd in my heart.
Are these the Nuptial Gifts a Bride receives?

85 as a] as the *93*

And this the fatal Dow'r a Father gives?
Thou God of Marriage shun thy own disgrace;
And take thy Torch from this detested place:
Instead of that, let Furies light their brands;
And Fire my pile with their infernal hands.
With happier fortune may my Sisters wed;
Warn'd by the dire Example of the dead.
For thee, poor Babe, what Crime cou'd they pretend?
How cou'd thy Infant innocence offend?
A guilt there was; but oh that guilt was mine!
Thou suffer'st for a sin that was not thine.
Thy Mothers grief and Crime! but just enjoy'd,
Shown to my sight, and born to be destroy'd!
Unhappy Off-spring of my teeming Womb!
Drag'd head-long from thy Cradle to thy Tomb!
Thy unoffending life I could not save,
Nor weeping cou'd I follow to thy Grave!
Nor on thy Tomb cou'd offer my shorn Hair;
Nor show the grief which tender Mothers bear.
Yet long thou shalt not from my Arms be lost,
For soon I will o're-take thy Infant Ghost.
But thou, my Love, and now my Love's Despair,
Perform his Funerals with paternal care.
His scatter'd Limbs with my dead body burn;
And once more joyn us in the pious Urn.
If on my wounded breast thou drop'st a tear,
Think for whose sake my breast that wound did bear;
And faithfully my last desires fulfill,
As I perform my cruel Fathers will.

HELEN TO PARIS

By the Right Honourable the Earl of MULGRAVE AND Mr. *DRYDEN*

The ARGUMENT

Helen, *having received the foregoing Epistle from* Paris, *returns the following Answer: wherein she seems at first to chide him for his Presumption in Writing, as he had done, which could only proceed from his low Opinion of her Vertue; then owns her self to be sensible of the Passion, which he had expressed for her, tho she much suspect his Constancy; and at last discovers her Inclinations to be favourable to him. The whole Letter shewing the extream artifice of Woman-kind.*

WHEN loose Epistles violate Chast Eyes,
She half Consents, who silently denies:
How dares a Stranger with designs so vain,
Marriage and Hospitable Rights Prophane?
Was it for this, your Fate did shelter find
From swelling Seas and every faithless wind?
(For tho a distant Country brought you forth,
Your usage here was equal to your worth.)
Does this deserve to be rewarded so?
Did you come here a Stranger, or a Foe?
Your partial Judgment may perhaps complain;
And think me barbarous for my just disdain;
Ill-bred then let me be, but not unchast,
Nor my clear fame with any spot defac'd:
Tho in my face there's no affected Frown,
Nor in my Carriage a feign'd niceness shown,
I keep my Honor still without a stain,
Nor has my Love made any Coxcomb vain.
Your Boldness I with admiration see;
What hope had you to gain a Queen like me?
Because a Hero forc'd me once away,
Am I thought fit to be a second prey?
Had I been won, I had deserv'd your blame,
But sure my part was nothing but the shame:
Yet the base theft to him no fruit did bear,
I scap'd unhurt by any thing but fear.
Rude force might some unwilling Kisses gain,
But that was all he ever cou'd obtain.
You on such terms would nere have let me go,
Were he like you, we had not parted so.
Untouch'd the Youth restor'd me to my Friends,
And modest usage made me some amends;
'Tis vertue to repent a vicious deed;
Did he repent that *Paris* might succeed?

Sure 'tis some Fate that sets me above wrongs,
Yet still exposes me to busie tongues.
  I'le not complain, for who's displeas'd with Love,
If it sincere, discreet, and Constant prove?
But that I fear; not that I think you base,
Or doubt the blooming beauties of my face,
But all your Sex is subject to deceive,
And ours alas, too willing to believe.
Yet others yield: and Love o'recomes the best,
But why should I not shine above the rest?
Fair *Leda*'s Story seems at first to be
A fit example ready found for me;
But she was Cousen'd by a borrow'd shape,
And under harmless Feathers felt a Rape:
If I should yield, what Reason could I use?
By what mistake the Loving Crime excuse?
Her fault was in her pow'rful Lover lost,
But of what *Jupiter* have I to boast?
Tho you to Heroes, and to Kings succeed,
Our Famous Race does no addition need,
And great Alliances but useless prove
To one that's come her self from mighty *Jove*.
Go then and boast in some less haughty place,
Your *Phrygian* Blood, and *Priam*'s Ancient race,
Which I wou'd shew I valu'd, if I durst;
You are the fifth from *Jove*, but I the first.
The Crown of *Troy* is pow'rful I confess,
But I have reason to think ours no less.
Your Letter fill'd with promises of all,
That Men can good, or Women pleasant call,
Gives expectation such an ample field,
As wou'd move Goddesses themselves to yield.
But if I e're offend great *Juno*'s Laws,
Your self shall be the Dear, the only Cause;
Either my Honour I'll to death maintain,
Or follow you, without mean thoughts of Gain.
Not that so fair a Present I despise,
We like the Gift, when we the giver prize.
But 'tis your Love moves me, which made you take

37 who's *81–93*: whose's *80* 40 face, *81–93*: face? *80*

Such pains, and run such hazards for my sake;
I have perceiv'd (though I dissembled too)
A Thousand things that Love has made you do;
Your eager Eyes would almost dazle mine,
In which (wild man) your wanton thoughts wou'd shine.
Sometimes you'd sigh, sometimes disorder'd stand,
And with unusual ardor, press my hand;
Contrive just after me to take the Glass,
Nor wou'd you let the least occasion pass,
Which oft I fear'd, I did not mind alone,
And blushing sate for things which you have done;
Then murmur'd to my self, he'll for my sake
Do any thing, I hope 'twas no mistake:
Oft have I read within this pleasing Grove,
Under my Name those Charming words, *I Love*,
I frowning, seem'd not to believe your Flame,
But now, alas, am come to write the same.
  If I were capable to do amiss,
I could not but be sensible of this.
For oh! your Face has such peculiar charms,
That who can hold from flying to your arms?
But what I ner'e can have without offence,
May some blest Maid possess with innocence.
Pleasure may tempt, but vertue more should move,
O Learn of me to want the thing you Love.
What you desire is sought by all mankind:
As you have eyes, so others are not blind.
Like you they see, like you my charms adore,
They wish not less, but you dare venture more:
Oh! had you then upon our Coasts been brought,
My Virgin Love, when thousand Rivals sought,
You had I seen, you should have had my voice;
Nor could my Husband justly blame my Choice.
For both our hopes, alas you come too late!
Another now is Master of my Fate.
More to my wish I cou'd have liv'd with you,
And yet my present lot can undergo.
Cease to solicit a weak Woman's will,
And urge not her you Love, to so much ill.
But let me live contented as I may,

And make not my unspotted fame your prey.
Some Right you claim, since naked to your eyes
Three Goddesses disputed Beauties prize;
One offer'd Valour, t'other Crowns, but she
Obtain'd her Cause, who smiling promis'd me.
But first I am not of belief so light,
To think such Nymphs wou'd shew you such a sight.
Yet granting this, the other part is feign'd:
A Bribe so mean, your sentence had not gain'd.
With partial eyes I shou'd my self regard,
To think that *Venus* made me her reward:
I humbly am content with human praise;
A Goddesse's applause wou'd envy raise:
But be it as you say, for 'tis confest,
The Men who flatter highest, please us best.
That I suspect it, ought not to displease;
For Miracles are not believ'd with ease.
One joy I have, that I had *Venus* voice;
A greater yet, that you confirm'd her Choice;
That proffer'd Laurels, promis'd Sov'raignty,
Juno and *Pallas* you contemn'd for me.
  Am I your Empire then, and your renown?
What heart of Rock but must by this be won?
And yet bear witness, O you Pow'rs above,
How rude I am in all the Arts of Love!
My hand is yet untaught to write to men;
This is th' Essay of my unpractis'd pen:
Happy those Nymphs, whom use has perfect made;
I think all Crime, and tremble at a shade.
Ev'n while I write, my fearful conscious eyes
Look often back, misdoubting a surprize.
For now the Rumour spreads among the Croud,
At Court in whispers, but in Town aloud:
Dissemble you, what er'e you hear 'em say;
To leave off Loving were your better way,
Yet if you will dissemble it, you may.
Love secretly: the absence of my Lord,
More freedom gives, but does not all afford:
Long is his Journey, long will be his stay;
Call'd by affairs of Consequence away.

To go or not when unresolv'd he stood,
I bid him make what swift return he cou'd:
Then Kissing me, he said I recommend
All to thy Care, but most my *Trojan* Friend.
I smil'd at what he innocently said,
And only answer'd, you shall be obey'd.
Propitious winds have born him far from hence,
But let not this secure your confidence.
Absent he is, yet absent he Commands,
You know the Proverb, Princes have long hands.
My Fame 's my burden, for the more I'm prais'd;
A juster ground of jealousie is rais'd.
Were I less fair, I might have been more blest:
Great Beauty through great danger is possest.
To leave me here his venture was not hard,
Because he thought my vertue was my Guard.
He fear'd my Face, but trusted to my Life,
The Beauty doubted, but believ'd the Wife:
You bid me use th' occasion while I can,
Put in our hands by the good easie man.
I wou'd, and yet I doubt, 'twixt Love and fear;
One draws me from you, and one brings me near.
Our flames are mutual: and my Husband 's gone,
The nights are long; I fear to lie alone.
One House contains us, and weak Walls divide;
And you're too pressing to be long denied:
Let me not live, but every thing conspires,
To joyn our Loves, and yet my fear retires.
You Court with words, when you shou'd force employ,
A Rape is requisite to shamefac'd joy.
Indulgent to the wrongs which we receive,
Our Sex can suffer what we dare not give.
  What have I said! for both of us 'twere best,
Our kindling fires, if each of us suppress.
The Faith of Strangers is too prone to change,
And like themselves their wandring Passions range.
Hypsipyle, and the fond *Minoian* Maid,
Were both by trusting of their Ghests betray'd.
How can I doubt that other men deceive,

190 *Hypsipyle 81–93*: *Hipsypile 80*

When you your self did fair *Oenone* leave?
But lest I shou'd upbraid your treachery,
You make a merit of that Crime to me:
Yet grant you were to faithful Love inclin'd,
Your weary *Trojans* wait but for a wind.
Shou'd you prevail while I assign the night,
Your Sails are hoysted, and you take your flight:
Some bawling Mariner our Love destroys,
And breaks asunder our unfinish'd joys.
But I with you may leave the *Spartan* Port,
To view the *Trojan* Wealth, and *Priam*'s Court.
Shown while I see, I shall expose my Fame:
And fill a foreign Country with my shame.
In *Asia* what reception shall I find?
And what dishonour leave in *Greece* behind?
What will your Brothers, *Priam*, *Hecuba*,
And what will all your modest Matrons say?
Ev'n you, when on this action you reflect,
My future Conduct justly may suspect:
And what er'e Stranger Lands upon your Coast,
Conclude me, by your own example, lost.
I from your rage, a Strumpet's Name shall hear,
While you forget, what part in it you bear.
You my Crimes Authour, will my Crime upbraid:
Deep under ground, Oh let me first be laid!
You boast the Pomp and Plenty of your Land,
And promise all shall be at my Command;
Your *Trojan* Wealth, believe me, I despise;
My own poor Native Land has dearer ties.
Shou'd I be injur'd on your *Phrygian* Shore,
What help of Kindred cou'd I there implore?
Medea was by *Jasons* flatt'ry won:
I may like her believe and be undon.
Plain honest hearts, like mine, suspect no cheat;
And Love contributes to its own deceit.
The Ships about whose sides loud Tempests roar,
With gentle Winds were wafted from the Shore.
Your teeming Mother dreamt a flaming Brand
Sprung from her Womb consum'd the *Trojan* Land.
To second this, old Prophecies conspire,

That *Ilium* shall be burnt with *Grecian* fire:
Both give me fear, nor is it much allai'd,
That *Venus* is oblig'd our Loves to aid.
For they who lost their Cause, revenge will take,
And for one Friend two Enemies you make.
Nor can I doubt, but shou'd I follow you,
The Sword wou'd soon our fatal Crime pursue:
A wrong so great my Husband's rage wou'd rouze,
And my Relations wou'd his Cause espouse.
You boast your Strength and Courage, but alas!
Your words receive small credit from your Face.
Let Heroes in the Dusty field delight,
Those Limbs were fashion'd for another fight.
Bid *Hector* sally from the Walls of *Troy*,
A sweeter quarrel shou'd your arms employ.
  Yet fears like these, shou'd not my mind perplex,
Were I as wise as many of my Sex.
But time and you, may bolder thoughts inspire;
And I perhaps may yield to your desire.
You last demand a private Conference,
These are your words, but I can ghess your sense.
Your unripe hopes their harvest must attend:
Be Rul'd by me, and time may be your friend.
This is enough to let you understand,
For now my Pen has tir'd my tender hand:
My Woman Knows the secret of my heart,
And may hereafter better news impart.

DIDO *to* ÆNEAS

The ARGUMENT

Æneas, *the Son of* Venus *and* Anchises, *having at the Destruction of* Troy, *saved his Gods, his Father and Son* Ascanius *from the Fire, put to Sea with twenty Sail of Ships, and having bin long tost with Tempests, was at last cast upon the Shore of* Lybia, *where Queen* Dido, (*flying from the Cruelty of* Pigmalion *her Brother, who had Killed her Husband* Sichæus,) *had lately built* Carthage. *She entertained* Æneas *and his Fleet with great civility, fell passionately in Love with him, and in the end denyed him not the last*

Favours. But Mercury *admonishing* Æneas *to go in search of* Italy, (*a Kingdom promised to him by the Gods,*) *he readily prepared to Obey him.* Dido *soon perceived it, and having in vain try'd all other means to engage him to stay, at last in Despair, writes to him as follows.*

So, on *Mæander*'s banks, when death is nigh,
The mournful *Swan* sings her own Elegie.
Not that I hope, (for oh, that hope were vain!)
By words your lost affection to regain;
But having lost what ere was worth my care,
Why shou'd I fear to loose a dying pray'r?
'Tis then resolv'd poor *Dido* must be left,
Of Life, of Honour, and of Love bereft!
While you, with loosen'd Sails and Vows, prepare
To seek a Land that flies the Searchers care.
Nor can my rising Tow'rs your flight restrain,
Nor my new Empire, offer'd you in vain.
Built Walls you shun, unbuilt you seek; that Land
Is yet to Conquer; but you this Command.
Suppose you Landed where your wish design'd,
Think what Reception Forreiners would find.
What People is so void of common sence,
To Vote Succession from a Native Prince?
Yet there new Scepters and new Loves you seek;
New Vows to plight, and plighted Vows to break.
When will your Tow'rs the height of *Carthage* know?
Or when, your eyes discern such crowds below?
If such a Town and Subjects you cou'd see,
Still wou'd you want a Wife who lov'd like me.
For, oh, I burn, like fires with incense bright;
Not holy Tapers flame with purer light:
Æneas is my thoughts perpetual Theme:
Their daily longing, and their nightly dream.
Yet he ungrateful and obdurate still:
Fool that I am to place my heart so ill!
My self I cannot to my self restore:
Still I complain, and still I love him more.
Have pity, *Cupid*, on my bleeding heart;
And pierce thy Brothers with an equal dart.

4 affection] affections *83–93* 18 Prince? *81–93*: Prince. *80*

I rave: nor canst thou *Venus'* offspring be,
Love's Mother cou'd not bear a Son like Thee.
From harden'd Oak, or from a Rocks cold womb,
At least thou art from some fierce *Tygress* come,
Or, on rough Seas, from their foundation torn,
Got by the winds, and in a Tempest born:
Like that which now thy trembling Sailors fear:
Like that, whose rage should still detain thee here.
  Behold how high the Foamy Billows ride!
The winds and waves are on the juster side.
To Winter weather, and a stormy Sea,
I'll owe what rather I wou'd owe to thee.
Death thou deserv'st from Heav'ns avenging Laws;
But I'm unwilling to become the cause.
To shun my Love, if thou wilt seek thy Fate,
'Tis a dear purchase, and a costly hate.
Stay but a little, till the Tempest cease;
And the loud winds are lull'd into a peace.
May all thy rage, like theirs, unconstant prove!
And so it will, if there be pow'r in Love.
Know'st thou not yet what dangers Ships sustain,
So often wrack'd, how darst thou tempt the Main?
Which, were it smooth; were every wave asleep,
Ten thousand forms of death are in the deep.
In that abyss the Gods their vengeance store,
For broken Vows of those who falsely swore.
There winged storms on Sea-born *Venus* wait,
To vindicate the Justice of her State.
Thus, I to Thee the means of safety show:
And lost my self, would still preserve my Foe.
False as thou art, I not thy death design:
O rather live to be the cause of mine!
Shou'd some avenging storm thy Vessel tear,
(But Heav'n forbid my words shou'd Omen bear,)
Then, in thy face thy perjur'd Vows would fly;
And my wrong'd Ghost be present to thy eye.
With threatning looks, think thou beholdst me stare,
Gasping my mouth, and clotted all my hair.
Then shou'd fork'd Lightning and red Thunder fall,
What coud'st thou say, but I deserv'd 'em all?

Lest this shou'd happen, make not hast away:
To shun the danger will be worth thy stay.
Have pity on thy Son, if not on me:
My death alone is guilt enough for thee.
What has his Youth, what have thy Gods deserv'd,
To sink in Seas, who were from fires preserv'd?
But neither Gods nor Parent didst thou bear,
(Smooth stories all, to please a Womans ear.)
  False was the tale of thy Romantick life;
Nor yet am I thy first deluded wife.
Left to pursuing Foes *Creüsa* stai'd,
By thee, base man, forsaken and betray'd.
This, when thou told'st me, struck my tender heart,
That such requital follow'd such desert.
Nor doubt I but the Gods, for crimes like these,
Sev'n Winters kept thee wandring on the Seas.
Thy starv'd Companions, cast a Shore, I fed,
Thy self admitted to my Crown and Bed.
To harbour Strangers, succour the distrest,
Was kind enough; but oh too kind the rest!
Curst be the Cave which first my ruin brought:
Where, from the storm, we common shelter sought!
A dreadful howling eccho'd round the place,
The Mountain Nymphs, thought I, my Nuptials grace.
I thought so then, but now too late I know
The Furies yell'd my Funerals from below.
O Chastity and violated Fame,
Exact your dues to my dead Husbands name!
By Death redeem my reputation lost;
And to his Arms restore my guilty Ghost.
Close by my Palace, in a Gloomy Grove,
Is rais'd a Chappel to my murder'd Love.
There, wreath'd with boughs and wool his Statue stands,
The pious Monument of Artful hands:
Last night, methought, he call'd me from the dome,
And thrice with hollow voice, cry'd, *Dido*, come.
She comes: thy Wife thy lawful summons hears:
But comes more slowly, clogg'd with conscious fears.
Forgive the wrong I offer'd to thy bed,

75 away:] away. *80–83*: away, *88 93*

Strong were his charms, who my weak faith misled.
His Goddess Mother, and his aged Sire,
Born on his back, did to my Fall conspire.
O such he was, and is, that were he true,
Without a blush I might his Love pursue.
But cruel Stars my birth day did attend:
And as my Fortune open'd, it must end.
My plighted Lord was at the Altar slain,
Whose wealth was made my bloody Brothers gain:
Friendless, and follow'd by the Murd'rers hate,
To forein Countrey's I remov'd my Fate;
And here, a suppliant, from the Natives hands,
I bought the ground on which my City stands,
With all the Coast that stretches to the Sea;
Ev'n to the friendly Port that sheltred Thee:
Then rais'd these Walls, which mount into the Air,
At once my Neighbours wonder, and their fear.
For now they Arm; and round me Leagues are made
My scarce Establisht Empire to invade.
To Man my new built Walls I must prepare,
An helpless Woman and unskill'd in War.
Yet thousand Rivals to my Love pretend;
And for my Person, would my Crown Defend:
Whose jarring Votes in one complaint agree,
That each unjustly is disdain'd for Thee.
To proud *Hyarbas* give me up a prey;
(For that must follow, if thou go'st away.)
Or to my Husbands Murd'rer leave my life;
That to the Husband he may add the Wife.
Go then; since no complaints can move thy mind:
Go perjur'd man, but leave thy Gods behind.
Touch not those Gods by whom thou art forsworn;
Who will in impious hands no more be born.
Thy Sacrilegious worship they disdain,
And rather wou'd the *Grecian* fires sustain.
Perhaps my greatest shame is still to come;
And part of thee lies hid within my womb.
The Babe unborn must perish by thy hate,
And perish guiltless in his Mothers Fate.

126 stands,] stands. *80–93*

Some God, thou say'st, thy Voyage does command:
Wou'd the same God had barr'd thee from my Land.
The same, I doubt not, thy departure Steers,
Who kept thee out at Sea so many years.
Where thy long labours were a price so great,
As thou to purchase *Troy* wouldst not repeat.
But *Tyber* now thou seek'st; to be at best
When there arriv'd, a poor precarious Ghest.
Yet it deludes thy search: perhaps it will
To thy Old Age lie undiscover'd still.
  A ready Crown and Wealth in Dow'r I bring;
And without Conqu'ring here thou art a King.
Here thou to *Carthage* may'st transfer thy *Troy*;
Here young *Ascanius* may his Arms employ:
And, while we live secure in soft repose,
Bring many Laurells home from Conquer'd Foes.
By *Cupids* Arrows, I adjure thee, stay;
By all the Gods, Companions of thy way.
So may thy *Trojans*, who are yet alive
Live still, and with no future Fortune strive:
So may thy Youthful Son old age attain,
And thy dead Fathers Bones in peace remain,
As thou hast pity on unhappy me,
Who knows no Crime but too much Love of thee.
I am not born from fierce *Achilles*' Line:
Nor did my Parents against *Troy* combine.
To be thy Wife, if I unworthy prove,
By some inferiour name admit my Love.
To be secur'd of still possessing thee,
What wou'd I do, and what wou'd I not be!
Our *Lybian* Coasts their certain seasons know,
When free from Tempests Passengers may go.
But now with Northern Blasts the Billows roar,
And drive the floating Sea-weed to the Shore.
Leave to my care the time to Sail away;
When safe, I will not suffer thee to stay.
Thy weary Men wou'd be with ease content;
Their Sails are tatter'd, and their Masts are spent:
If by no merit I thy mind can move,
What thou deny'st my merit, give my Love.

Stay, till I learn my loss to undergo;
And give me time to struggle with my woe.
If not; know this, I will not suffer long;
My life 's too loathsome, and my love too strong.
Death holds my pen, and dictates what I say,
While cross my lap thy *Trojan* Sword I lay.
My tears flow down; the sharp edge cuts their flood,
And drinks my sorrows, that must drink my blood.
How well thy gift does with my Fate agree!
My Funeral pomp is cheaply made by thee.
To no new wounds my bosom I display:
The Sword but enters where Love made the way.
But thou, dear Sister, and yet dearer friend,
Shalt my cold Ashes to their Urn attend.
Sichæus Wife let not the Marble boast,
I lost that Title when my Fame I lost.
This short Inscription only let it bear,
"Unhappy *Dido* lies in quiet here.
"The cause of death, and Sword by which she dy'd,
"*Æneas* gave: the rest her arm supply'd.

PROLOGUE to *CÆSAR BORGIA*

TH' unhappy man, who once has trail'd a Pen,
Lives not to please himself but other men:
Is always drudging, wasts his Life and Blood,
Yet only eats and drinks what you think good:
What praise soe're the Poetry deserve,
Yet every Fool can bid the Poet starve:
That fumbling Lecher to revenge is bent,
Because he thinks himself or Whore is meant:
Name but a Cuckold, all the City swarms,
From *Leaden-hall* to *Ludgate* is in Arms.
Were there no fear of *Antichrist* or *France*,
In the best times poor Poets live by chance.
Either you come not here, or as you grace
Some old acquaintance, drop into the place,
Careless and qualmish with a yawning Face.
You sleep o're Wit, and by my troth you may,
Most of your Talents lye another way.
You love to hear of some prodigious Tale,
The Bell that toll'd alone, or *Irish* Whale.
News is your Food, and you enough provide,
Both for your selves and all the World beside.
One Theatre there is of vast resort,
Which whilome of Requests was call'd the Court.
But now the great *Exchange* of News 'tis hight,
And full of hum and buzz from Noon till Night:
Up Stairs and down you run as for a Race,
And each man wears three Nations in his Face.
So big you look, tho' Claret you retrench,
That arm'd with bottled Ale, you huff the *French*:
But all your Entertainment still is fed
By Villains, in our own dull Island bred:
Would you return to us, we dare engage
To show you better Rogues upon the Stage:
You know no Poison but plain Rats-bane here,
Death 's more refind, and better bred elsewhere.

Prologue. Text from Lee's Cæsar Borgia; Son of Pope Alexander the Sixth: A Tragedy, *1680, collated with the edition of 1696*
33 you *om. 80 (some copies)*

They have a civil way in *Italy*
By smelling a perfume to make you dye,
A Trick would make you lay your Snuff-box by.
Murder's a Trade—so known and practis'd there,
That 'tis Infallible as is the Chair—
But mark their Feasts, you shall behold such Pranks,
The Pope says Grace, but 'tis the Devil gives Thanks.

PROLOGUE to *THE LOYAL GENERAL*

If yet there be a few that take delight
In that which reasonable Men should write;
To them Alone we Dedicate this Night.
The Rest may satisfie their curious Itch
With City Gazets or some Factious Speech,
Or what-ere Libel for the Publick Good,
Stirs up the Shrove-tide Crew to Fire and Blood!
Remove your Benches you apostate Pit,
And take Above, twelve penny-worth of Wit;
Go back to your dear Dancing on the Rope,
Or see what's worse the Devil and the Pope!
The Plays that take on our Corrupted Stage,
Methinks resemble the distracted Age;
Noise, Madness, all unreasonable Things,
That strike at Sense, as Rebels do at Kings!
The stile of Forty One our Poets write,
And you are grown to judge like Forty Eight.
Such Censures our mistaking Audience make,
That 'tis almost grown Scandalous to Take!
They talk of Feavours that infect the Brains,
But Non-sence is the new Disease that reigns.
Weak Stomacks with a long Disease opprest,
Cannot the Cordials of strong Wit digest:
Therfore thin Nourishment of Farce ye choose,
Decoctions of a Barly-water Muse:
A Meal of Tragedy wou'd make ye Sick,
Unless it were a very tender Chick.
Some Scenes in Sippets wou'd be worth our time,
Those wou'd go down; some Love that's poach'd in Rime:

Prologue. Text from Tate's The Loyal General, A Tragedy, *1680*

If these shou'd fail—
We must lie down, and after all our cost,
Keep Holy-day, like Water-men in Frost,
Whil'st you turn Players on the Worlds great Stage,
And Act your selves the Farce of your own Age.

PROLOGUE and SONGS from *THE SPANISH FRYAR*

PROLOGUE

NOW Luck for us, and a kind hearty Pit;
For he who pleases, never failes of Wit:
Honour is yours:
And you, like Kings, at City Treats bestow it;
The Writer kneels, and is bid rise a Poet:
But you are fickle Sovereigns, to our Sorrow,
You dubb to day, and hang a man to morrow;
You cry the same Sense up, and down again,
Just like brass mony once a year in *Spain*:
Take you i'th' mood, what e'er base metal come,
You coin as fast as Groats at *Bromingam*:
Though 'tis no more like Sense in ancient Plays,
Than *Rome*'s Religion like St. *Peter*'s days.
In short, so swift your Judgments turn and wind,
You cast our fleetest Wits a mile behind.
'Twere well your Judgments but in Plays did range,
But ev'n your Follies and Debauches change
With such a Whirl, the Poets of your age
Are tyr'd, and cannot score 'em on the Stage,
Unless each Vice in short-hand they indite,
Ev'n as notcht Prentices whole Sermons write.
The heavy *Hollanders* no Vices know
But what they us'd a hundred years ago,
Like honest Plants, where they were stuck, they grow;

Prologue and Songs. Text from The Spanish Fryar or, The Double Discovery, *1681, collated with the editions of 1686, 1690, 1695*
Prologue. 12–13 *om. 86*

They cheat, but still from cheating Sires they come;
They drink, but they were christ'ned first in Mum.
Their patrimonial Sloth the *Spaniards* keep,
And *Philip* first taught *Philip* how to sleep.
The *French* and we still change, but here 's the Curse,
They change for better, and we change for worse;
They take up our old trade of Conquering,
And we are taking theirs, to dance and sing:
Our Fathers did for change to *France* repair,
And they for change will try our *English* Air.
As Children, when they throw one Toy away,
Strait a more foolish Gugaw comes in play:
So we, grown penitent, on serious thinking,
Leave Whoring, and devoutly fall to Drinking.
Scowring the Watch grows out of fashion wit
Now we set up for Tilting in the Pit,
Where 'tis agreed by Bullies, chicken-hearted,
To fright the Ladies first, and then be parted.
A fair Attempt has twice or thrice been made,
To hire Night-murth'rers, and make Death a Trade.
When Murther 's out, what Vice can we advance?
Unless the new found Pois'ning Trick of *France*:
And when their Art of *Rats-bane* we have got,
By way of thanks, we'll send 'em o'er our *Plot*.

SONGS

I

A Procession of Priests and Choristers in white, with Tapers, follow'd by the Queen and Ladies, goes over the Stage: the Choristers singing.

LOOK down, ye bless'd above, look down,
  Behold our weeping Matron's Tears,
  Behold our tender Virgins Fears,
And with success our Armies crown.

Look down, ye bless'd above, look down:
  Oh! save us, save us, and our State restore;
  For Pitty, Pitty, Pitty, we implore;
For Pitty, Pitty, Pitty, we implore.

II

A SONG

I

FARWELL ungratefull Traytor,
  Farwell my perjur'd Swain,
Let never injur'd Creature
  Believe a Man again.
The Pleasure of Possessing
Surpasses all Expressing,
But 'tis too short a Blessing,
  And Love too long a Pain.

II

'Tis easie to deceive us
  In pity of your Pain,
But when we love you leave us
  To rail at you in vain.
Before we have descry'd it
There is no Bliss beside it,
But she that once has try'd it
  Will never love again.

III

The Passion you pretended
  Was onely to obtain,
But when the Charm is ended
  The Charmer you disdain.
Your Love by ours we measure
Till we have lost our Treasure,
But Dying is a Pleasure,
  When Living is a Pain.

Songs. II. 10 your *86 90 95*: our *81*

EPILOGUE to *TAMERLANE THE GREAT*

LADIES, the Beardless Author of this Day,
Commends to you the Fortune of his Play.
A Woman Wit has often grac'd the Stage,
But he 's the first Boy-Poet of our Age.
Early as is the Year his Fancies blow,
Like young *Narcissus* peeping through the Snow;
Thus *Cowley* Blossom'd soon, yet Flourish'd long,
This is as forward, and may prove as strong.
Youth with the Fair shou'd always Favour find,
Or we are damn'd Dissemblers of our kind.
What 's all this Love they put into our Parts?
'Tis but the pit-a-pat of Two Young Hearts.
Shou'd Hag and Gray-Beard make such tender moan,
Faith you'd e'en trust 'em to themselves alone,
And cry let 's go, here 's nothing to be done.
Since Love's our Business, as 'tis your Delight,
The Young, who best can practise, best can Write.
What though he be not come to his full Pow'r,
He 's mending and improving every hour.
You sly She-Jockies of the Box and Pit,
Are pleas'd to find a hot unbroken Wit,
By management he may in time be made,
But there 's no hopes of an old batter'd Jade;
Faint and unnerv'd he runs into a Sweat,
And always fails you at the Second Heat.

Epilogue. Text from Saunders's Tamerlane the Great. A Tragedy, *1681*

THE EPILOGUE

Spoken to the KING at the opening the PLAY-House at *Oxford* on Saturday last. Being *March* the Nineteenth 1681

As from a darkn'd Roome some Optick glass
Transmits the distant Species as they pass;
The worlds large Landschape is from far descry'd,
And men contracted on the Paper glide;
Thus crowded *Oxford* represents Mankind,
And in these Walls *Great Brittain* seems Confin'd.
Oxford is now the publick *Theater*;
And you both Audience are, and Actors here.
The gazing World on the New Scene attend,
Admire the turns, and wish a prosp'rous end.
This Place the seat of Peace, the quiet Cell
Where Arts remov'd from noisy buisness dwell,
Shou'd calm your Wills, unite the jarring parts,
And with a kind Contagion seize your hearts:
Oh! may its Genius, like soft Musick move,
And tune you all to Concord and to Love.
Our Ark that has in Tempests long been tost,
Cou'd never land on so secure a Coast.
From hence you may look back on Civil Rage,
And view the ruines of the former Age.
Here a New World its glories may unfold,
And here be sav'd the remnants of the Old.
But while your daies on publick thoughts are bent
Past ills to heal, and future to prevent;
Some vacant houres allow to your delight,
Mirth is the pleasing buisness of the Night,
The Kings Prerogative, the Peoples right.
Were all your houres to sullen cares confind,
The Body wou'd be Jaded by the Mind.

The Epilogue. Text from the Oxford version, collated with the London version (*L*). *See Commentary. L is headed* The Epilogue, *with a note in the left margin* Writ by Mr. *Dreyden*, Spoke before His Majesty at *Oxford*, *March* 19. 1680.

17 has in Tempests] hath in Tempest *L*   23 daies on] Day-sun *L*

'Tis Wisdoms part betwixt extreams to Steer:
Be Gods in Senates, but be Mortals here.

The Prologue at OXFORD, 1680

THESPIS, the first Professor of our Art,
At Country Wakes, Sung Ballads from a Cart.
To prove this true, if Latin be no Trespass,
Dicitur & Plaustris, vexisse Poemata Thespis.
But *Escalus*, says *Horace* in some Page,
Was the first Mountebank that trod the Stage:
Yet *Athens* never knew your Learned sport,
Of Tossing Poets in a *Tennis-Court*;
But 'tis the Talent of our *English* Nation,
Still to be Plotting some New Reformation:
And few years hence, if Anarchy goes on,
Jack Presbyter shall here Erect his Throne.
Knock out a Tub with Preaching once a day,
And every Prayer be longer than a Play.
Then all you Heathen Wits shall go to Pot,
For disbelieving of a Popish Plot:
Your Poets shall be us'd like Infidels,
And worst the Author of the *Oxford Bells*:
Nor shou'd we scape the Sentence, to Depart,
Ev'n in our first Original, A Cart.
No Zealous Brother there wou'd want a Stone,
To Maul Us Cardinals, and pelt Pope *Joan*:
Religion, Learning, Wit, wou'd be suppress,
Rags of the Whore, and Trappings of the Beast:
Scot, *Swarez*, *Tom of Aquin*, must go down,
As chief Supporters of the Triple Crown;
And *Aristotle*'s for destruction ripe,
Some say He call'd the Soul an Organ-Pipe,

The Prologue. Text from Miscellany Poems, *1684 and 1692* (*MP*), *collated with Lee's* Sophonisba: or, Hannibal's Overthrow, a Tragedy, *1681, 1685, 1691, 1693 and 1697. See Commentary*

Heading 81–97: Prologue to the University of Oxford 2 from] in *81–97* 6 that] e're *81–97* 11 few] some *81–97* goes] go *81–93* 12 shall] will *81–97* 17–18 *om. 81–97* 19 scape] want *81–97* 21–24 *om. 81–97* 25 *Scot* . . . must] *Occam*, *Dun*, *Scotus* must, though learn'd, *81–97* 27 *Aristotle*'s] *Aristotle*, *81–97*

Which by some little help of Derivation,
Shall then be prov'd a Pipe of Inspiration.
[Your wiser Judgments farther penetrate,
Who late found out one Tare amongst the Wheat.
This is our comfort, none e're cry'd us down,
But who dislik'd both *Bishop* and a *Crown*.]

PROLOGUE and EPILOGUE spoken at *MITHRIDATES*

A PROLOGUE spoken at *MITHRIDATES* King of *PONTUS*, the First Play Acted at the *THEATRE ROYAL* this Year, 1681

AFTER a four Months Fast we hope at length
Your queasie Stomachs have recover'd strength
That You can taste a Play (your old coarse Messe)
As honest and as plain as an Addresse.
And therefore Welcome from your several Parts,
You that have gain'd kind Country Wenches Hearts:
Have watch'd returning Milk-maids in the Dark,
And sinn'd against the Pales of every Park.
Welcom fair Ladies of unblemish'd Faith,
That left Town Bagnio's for the fruitful Bath;
For when the Season 's Hot, and Lover 's there,
The Waters never fail to get an Heir.
Welcom kind Men that did your Wives attend,
And Welcom He that was the Husbands Friend,
Who holding Chat did silently Encroach,
With Treacherous Hand to grabble in the Coach.
Hail you New-Market Brothers of the Switch,
That leap left Strumpets, full of Pox and Itch,
A leap more dangerous than the Devil's Ditch.

30 then be prov'd] thence be call'd *81–97* 31–34 Your . . . *Crown 81–97*: *not in MP*

Prologue and Epilogue. Text from the edition of 1681: see Commentary. L: Luttrell's alterations

Prologue. 6 gain'd] stol'n *L* 12 get] make *L* 18 leap left] use cast *L*

Last Welcom you who never did appear;
Gave out i' th' Country, but lay fluxing here.
Now Crawl abroad with Stick, lean-chapt and thin,
And Fair as Lady that hath new lain in;
This Winter let us reckon you our own,
For all Wise Men will let the State alone:
The Plot 's remov'd, a Witness of Renown
Has lodg'd it safe, at t'other End o'th' Town,
And that it ne're may fail, some pious Whore
Has cast her Mite, and fairly at his Dore
Laid two small squalling Evidences more;
Which well instructed, if we take their words,
In time may grow to hang two Popish Lords;
Heav'n Grant the Babes may Live, for Faith there 's need,
Swearers fall off so fast, if none succeed
The Land 's in danger quite to loose the breed.
Unless you break an Act, which were a Sin,
And for recruit let Irish Cattle in.
Well; after all 'twere better to Compound,
Then let the foolish Frolick still go round,
Both sides have lost and by my Computation
None but *Jack Ketch* has gained in the Nation.

EPILOGUE

POX on this Play-house, 'tis an old tir'd Jade,
'Twill do no longer, we must force a Trade;
What if we all turn Witness of the Plot?
That 's overstockt, there 's nothing to be got.
Shall we take Orders? That will Parts require,
Our Colledges give no Degrees for Hire,
Would *Salamancha* was a little nigher.
Will nothing do? Oh now 'tis found I hope;
Have not you seen the Dancing of the Rope?
When *Andrew*'s Wit was clean run off the Score,
And *Jacob*'s Cap'ring Tricks could do no more,
A Damsel does to the Ladders Top advance
And with two heavy Buckets drags a Dance;

21 th'] the *L* 32 grow] come *L* 41 gained in the] gain'd in all the *L*
Epilogue. 3 Witness of the] witnesses o' th' *L* 6 Our *L*: And *81*

The Yawning Crowd perk't up to see the sight,
And slav'r'd at the Mouth for vast Delight:
Oh Friends there's nothing to Enchant the Mind,
Nothing like that cleft Sex to draw Mankind:
The Foundred Horse that switching will not stir,
Trots to the Mare, afore without a Spur.
Faith I'le go scoure the Scene-room and Engage
Some Toy within to save the falling Stage. *Exit.*

Re-Enters with Mrs. Cox.

Who have we here again, what Nump's i'th' Stocks?
Your most Obedient Slave, sweet Madam *Cox.*
You'd best be Coy, and Blush for a pretence,
For Shame say something in your own Defence.
Mrs. Cox. What shall I say? I have been hence so long
I've e'ne almost forgot my Mother Tongue;
If I can Act I wish I were ten Fathom
Beneath—
M. Goodman. —Oh Lord, Pray, no swearing, Madam;
Mrs. Cox. Why Sir, If I had sworn, to save the Nation
I could find out some Mental Reservation.
Well in plain Termes, Gallants, without a Shamm,
Will you be pleas'd to take me as I am.
Quite out of Countenance, with a down cast look,
Just like a Truant that returnes to Book:
Yet I'me not old, but if I were this place
Ne're wanted Art to peice a ruin'd Face.
When Grey-Beards Govern'd I forsook the Stage,
You know 'tis piteous work to Act with Age;
Though there's no sence amongst these Beardless Boys,
There's what we Women love, that's Mirth and Noise,
These young Beginners may grow up in time,
And the Devil's in't if I'me past my Prime.

14 perk'[t] *L*: pearch't *81* 15 for] with *L* 17 cleft *L*: sweet *81* 21 save] prop *L* 22 Nump's *L*: Nymphs *81* 23 Slave *L*: Servant *81* 30 Why Sir . . . save] If I had sworn, yet sure to serve *L* 40 sence *L*: sex *81*

ABSALOM AND ACHITOPHEL

A POEM

—Si Propiùs stes
Te Capiet Magis—

TO THE READER

'Tis not my intention to make an Apology for my Poem: Some will think it needs no Excuse; and others will receive none. The Design, I am sure, is honest: but he who draws his Pen for one Party, must expect to make Enemies of the other. For, Wit and Fool, are Consequents of Whig and Tory: And every man is a Knave or an Ass to the contrary side. There's a Treasury of Merits in the Phanatick Church, as well as in the Papist; and a Pennyworth to be had of Saintship, Honesty, and Poetry, for the Leud, the Factious, and the Blockheads: But the longest Chapter in Deuteronomy, has not Curses enow for an Anti-Bromingham. My Comfort is, their manifest Prejudice to my Cause, will render their Judgment of less Authority against me. Yet if a Poem have a Genius, it will force its own reception in the World. For there's a sweetness in good Verse, which Tickles even while it Hurts: And, no man can be heartily angry with him, who pleases him against his will. The Commendation of Adversaries, is the greatest Triumph of a Writer; because it never comes unless Extorted. But I can be satisfied on more easy termes: If I happen to please the more Moderate sort, I shall be sure of an honest Party; and, in all probability, of the best Judges; for, the least Concern'd, are commonly the least Corrupt: And, I confess, I have laid in for those, by rebating the Satyre, (where Justice woud allow it) from carrying too sharp an Edge. They, who can Criticize so weakly, as to imagine I have done my Worst, may be Convinc'd, at their own Cost, that I can write Severely, with more ease, than I can Gently. I have but laught at some mens Follies, when I coud have declaim'd against their Vices; and, other mens Vertues I have commended, as freely as I have tax'd their Crimes. And now, if you are a Malitious Reader, I expect you should return upon me, that I affect to be thought more Impartial than I am. But, if men are not to be judg'd by their Professions, God forgive you Common-wealths-men, for professing so plausibly for the Government. You cannot be so Unconscionable, as to charge me for not

Absalom and Achitophel. Text from the first edition, 1681 (A), collated with the subsequent London editions of 1681 (B and C), 1682 (D, E and F), Miscellany Poems *1684 (G) and 1692 (H), and the separate edition of 1692 (I). See Commentary*

To the Reader. 8 *enow*] *enough C–I*

Subscribing of my Name; for that woud reflect too grosly upon your own Party, who never dare, though they have the advantage of a Jury to secure them. If you like not my Poem, the fault may, possibly, be in my Writing: (though 'tis hard for an Authour to judge against himself;) But, more probably, 'tis in your Morals, which cannot bear the truth of it. The Violent, on both sides, will condemn the Character of Absalom, as either too favourably, or too hardly drawn. But, they are not the Violent, whom I desire to please. The fault, on the right hand, is to Extenuate, Palliate and Indulge; and, to confess freely, I have endeavour'd to commit it. Besides the respect which I owe his Birth, I have a greater for his Heroique Vertues; and, David himself, coud not be more tender of the Young-man's Life, than I woud be of his Reputation. But, since the most excellent Natures are always the most easy; and, as being such, are the soonest perverted by ill Counsels, especially when baited with Fame and Glory; 'tis no more a wonder that he withstood not the temptations of Achitophel, than it was for Adam, not to have resisted the two Devils; the Serpent, and the Woman. The conclusion of the Story, I purposely forbore to prosecute; because, I coud not obtain from my self, to shew Absalom Unfortunate. The Frame of it, was cut out, but for a Picture to the Wast; and, if the Draught be so far true, 'tis as much as I design'd.

Were I the Inventour, who am only the Historian, I shoud certainly conclude the Piece, with the Reconcilement of Absalom to David. And, who knows but this may come to pass? Things were not brought to an Extremity where I left the Story: There seems, yet, to be room left for a Composure; hereafter, there may only be for pity. I have not, so much as an uncharitable Wish against Achitophel; but, am content to be Accus'd of a good natur'd Errour; and, to hope with Origen, that the Devil himself may, at last, be sav'd. For which reason, in this Poem, he is neither brought to set his House in order, nor to dispose of his Person afterwards, as he in Wisedom shall think fit. God is infinitely merciful; and his Vicegerent is only not so, because he is not Infinite.

The true end of Satyre, is the amendment of Vices by correction. And he who writes Honestly, is no more an Enemy to the Offendour, than the Physician to the Patient, when he prescribes harsh Remedies to an inveterate Disease: for those, are only in order to prevent the Chyrurgeon's work of an Ense rescindendum, which I wish not to my very Enemies. To conclude all, If the Body Politique have any Analogy to the Natural, in my weak judgment, an Act of Oblivion were as necessary in a Hot, Distemper'd State, as an Opiate woud be in a Raging Fever.

ABSALOM AND ACHITOPHEL

A Poem

IN pious times, e'r Priest-craft did begin,
Before *Polygamy* was made a sin;
When man, on many, multiply'd his kind,
E'r one to one was, cursedly, confind:
When Nature prompted, and no law deny'd
Promiscuous use of Concubine and Bride;
Then, *Israel*'s Monarch, after Heaven's own heart,
His vigorous warmth did, variously, impart
To Wives and Slaves: And, wide as his Command,
Scatter'd his Maker's Image through the Land.
Michal, of Royal blood, the Crown did wear,
A Soyl ungratefull to the Tiller's care:
Not so the rest; for several Mothers bore
To Godlike *David*, several Sons before.
But since like slaves his bed they did ascend,
No True Succession could their seed attend.
Of all this Numerous Progeny was none
So Beautifull, so brave as *Absolon*:
Whether, inspir'd by some diviner Lust,
His Father got him with a greater Gust;
Or that his Conscious destiny made way
By manly beauty to Imperiall sway.
Early in Foreign fields he won Renown,
With Kings and States ally'd to *Israel*'s Crown:
In Peace the thoughts of War he coud remove,
And seem'd as he were only born for love.
What e'r he did was done with so much ease,
In him alone, 'twas Natural to please.
His motions all accompanied with grace;
And *Paradise* was open'd in his face.
With secret Joy, indulgent *David* view'd
His Youthfull Image in his Son renew'd:
To all his wishes Nothing he deny'd,
And made the Charming *Annabel* his Bride.

Absalom and Achitophel. 9 To] Two *C* (*some copies*) 18 Beautifull, *B F–I*: Beautifull *A* 19 by *C–I*: with *A B*

What faults he had (for who from faults is free?)
His Father coud not, or he woud not see.
Some warm excesses, which the Law forbore,
Were constru'd Youth that purg'd by boyling o'r:
And *Amnon*'s Murther, by a specious Name,
Was call'd a Just Revenge for injur'd Fame.
Thus Prais'd, and Lov'd, the Noble Youth remain'd,
While *David*, undisturb'd, in *Sion* raign'd.
But Life can never be sincerely blest:
Heaven punishes the bad, and proves the best.
The *Jews*, a Headstrong, Moody, Murmuring race,
As ever try'd th' extent and stretch of grace;
God's pamper'd people whom, debauch'd with ease,
No King could govern, nor no God could please;
(Gods they had tri'd of every shape and size
That God-smiths could produce, or Priests devise:)
These *Adam*-wits, too fortunately free,
Began to dream they wanted libertie;
And when no rule, no president was found
Of men, by Laws less circumscrib'd and bound,
They led their wild desires to Woods and Caves,
And thought that all but Savages were Slaves.
They who when *Saul* was dead, without a blow,
Made foolish *Ishbosheth* the Crown forgo;
Who banisht *David* did from *Hebron* bring,
And, with a Generall Shout, proclaim'd him King:
Those very *Jewes*, who, at their very best,
Their Humour more than Loyalty exprest,
Now, wondred why, so long, they had obey'd
An Idoll Monarch which their hands had made:
Thought they might ruine him they could create;
Or melt him to that Golden Calf, a State.
But these were randome bolts: No form'd Design,
Nor Interest made the Factious Croud to joyn:
The sober part of *Israel*, free from stain,
Well knew the value of a peacefull raign:
And, looking backward with a wise afright,
Saw Seames of wounds, dishonest to the sight;

50 devise: *C–I*: devise *A B* 58 *Ishbosheth C–I: Isbosheth A B* 64 made: *C–I:* made. *A B*

In contemplation of whose ugly Scars,
They Curst the memory of Civil Wars.
The moderate sort of Men, thus qualifi'd,
Inclin'd the Ballance to the better side:
And *David*'s mildness manag'd it so well,
The Bad found no occasion to Rebell.
But, when to Sin our byast Nature leans,
The carefull Devil is still at hand with means;
And providently Pimps for ill desires:
The Good old Cause reviv'd, a Plot requires.
Plots, true or false, are necessary things,
To raise up Common-wealths, and ruin Kings.
  Th' inhabitants of old *Jerusalem*
Were *Jebusites*: the Town so call'd from them;
And their's the Native right—
But when the chosen people grew more strong,
The rightfull cause at length became the wrong:
And every loss the men of *Jebus* bore,
They still were thought God's enemies the more.
Thus, worn and weaken'd, well or ill content,
Submit they must to *David*'s Government:
Impoverisht, and depriv'd of all Command,
Their Taxes doubled as they lost their Land,
And, what was harder yet to flesh and blood,
Their Gods disgrac'd, and burnt like common wood.
This set the Heathen Priesthood in a flame;
For Priests of all Religions are the same:
Of whatsoe'r descent their Godhead be,
Stock, Stone, or other homely pedigree,
In his defence his Servants are as bold
As if he had been born of beaten gold.
The *Jewish Rabbins* thô their Enemies,
In this conclude them honest men and wise:
For 'twas their duty, all the Learned think,
T'espouse his Cause by whom they eat and drink.
From hence began that Plot, the Nation's Curse,
Bad in it self, but represented worse.
Rais'd in extremes, and in extremes decry'd;
With Oaths affirm'd, with dying Vows deny'd.
Not weigh'd, or winnow'd by the Multitude;

But swallow'd in the Mass, unchew'd and Crude.
Some Truth there was, but dash'd and brew'd with Lyes;
To please the Fools, and puzzle all the Wise.
Succeeding times did equal folly call,
Believing nothing, or believing all.
Th' *Egyptian* Rites the *Jebusites* imbrac'd;
Where Gods were recommended by their Tast.
Such savory Deities must needs be good,
As serv'd at once for Worship and for Food.
By force they could not Introduce these Gods;
For Ten to One, in former days was odds.
So Fraud was us'd, (the Sacrificers trade,)
Fools are more hard to Conquer than Perswade.
Their busie Teachers mingled with the *Jews*;
And rak'd, for Converts, even the Court and Stews:
Which *Hebrew* Priests the more unkindly took,
Because the Fleece accompanies the Flock.
Some thought they God's Anointed meant to Slay
By Guns, invented since full many a day:
Our Authour swears it not; but who can know
How far the Devil and *Jebusites* may go?
This Plot, which fail'd for want of common Sense,
Had yet a deep and dangerous Consequence:
For, as when raging Fevers boyl the Blood,
The standing Lake soon floats into a Flood;
And every hostile Humour, which before
Slept quiet in its Channels, bubbles o'r:
So, several Factions from this first Ferment,
Work up to Foam, and threat the Government.
Some by their Friends, more by themselves thought wise,
Oppos'd the Power, to which they could not rise.
Some had in Courts been Great, and thrown from thence,
Like Feinds, were harden'd in Impenitence.
Some by their Monarch's fatal mercy grown,
From Pardon'd Rebels, Kinsmen to the Throne;
Were rais'd in Power and publick Office high:
Strong Bands, if Bands ungratefull men could tye.

Of these the false *Achitophel* was first:

117 all. *B–I*: all, *A*   121 As *B–I*: And *A*   149 could] cuold *A* (*some copies*)
150 *Editor's paragraph*

A Name to all succeeding Ages Curst.
For close Designs, and crooked Counsels fit;
Sagacious, Bold, and Turbulent of wit:
Restless, unfixt in Principles and Place;
In Power unpleas'd, impatient of Disgrace.
A fiery Soul, which working out its way,
Fretted the Pigmy Body to decay:
And o'r inform'd the Tenement of Clay.
A daring Pilot in extremity;
Pleas'd with the Danger, when the Waves went high
He sought the Storms; but for a Calm unfit,
Would Steer too nigh the Sands, to boast his Wit.
Great Wits are sure to Madness near ally'd;
And thin Partitions do their Bounds divide:
Else, why should he, with Wealth and Honour blest,
Refuse his Age the needful hours of Rest?
Punish a Body which he coud not please;
Bankrupt of Life, yet Prodigal of Ease?
And all to leave, what with his Toyl he won,
To that unfeather'd, two Leg'd thing, a Son:
Got, while his Soul did hudled Notions try;
And born a shapeless Lump, like Anarchy.
In Friendship False, Implacable in Hate:
Resolv'd to Ruine or to Rule the State.
To Compass this the Triple Bond he broke;
The Pillars of the publick Safety shook:
And fitted *Israel* for a Foreign Yoke.
Then, seiz'd with Fear, yet still affecting Fame,
Usurp'd a Patriott's All-attoning Name.
So easie still it proves in Factious Times,
With publick Zeal to cancel private Crimes:
How safe is Treason, and how sacred ill,
Where none can sin against the Peoples Will:
Where Crouds can wink; and no offence be known,
Since in anothers guilt they find their own.
Yet, Fame deserv'd, no Enemy can grudge;
The Statesman we abhor, but praise the Judge.

152 Counsels *C–I*: Counsell *A B* 153 Bold] Kold *A* (*some copies*) 154 Principles *C–I*: Principle *A B* 157 Body] Kody *A* (*some copies*) 179 Usurp'd *C–I*: Assum'd *A B* Patriott's *B–I*: Patron's *A* (*some copies*) 180–91 *added in C, D–I. Text from C. See Commentary*

In *Israels* Courts ne'r sat an *Abbethdin*
With more discerning Eyes, or Hands more clean:
Unbrib'd, unsought, the Wretched to redress;
Swift of Dispatch, and easie of Access.
Oh, had he been content to serve the Crown,
With vertues only proper to the Gown;
Or, had the rankness of the Soyl been freed
From Cockle, that opprest the Noble seed:
David, for him his tunefull Harp had strung,
And Heaven had wanted one Immortal song.
But wilde Ambition loves to slide, not stand;
And Fortunes Ice prefers to Vertues Land:
Achitophel, grown weary to possess
A lawfull Fame, and lazy Happiness;
Disdain'd the Golden fruit to gather free,
And lent the Croud his Arm to shake the Tree.
Now, manifest of Crimes, contriv'd long since,
He stood at bold Defiance with his Prince:
Held up the Buckler of the Peoples Cause,
Against the Crown; and sculk'd behind the Laws.
The wish'd occasion of the Plot he takes,
Some Circumstances finds, but more he makes.
By buzzing Emissaries, fills the ears
Of listning Crowds, with Jealosies and Fears
Of Arbitrary Counsels brought to light,
And proves the King himself a *Jebusite*:
Weak Arguments! which yet he knew full well,
Were strong with People easie to Rebell.
For, govern'd by the *Moon*, the giddy *Jews*
Tread the same track when she the Prime renews:
And once in twenty Years, their Scribes Record,
By natural Instinct they change their Lord.
Achitophel still wants a Chief, and none
Was found so fit as Warlike *Absolon*:
Not, that he wish'd his Greatness to create,
(For Polititians neither love nor hate:)
But, for he knew, his Title not allow'd,
Would keep him still depending on the Crowd:
That Kingly power, thus ebbing out, might be

214 full well *C–I*. fulwell *A B*

Drawn to the dregs of a Democracy.
Him he attempts, with studied Arts to please,
And sheds his Venome, in such words as these.
  Auspicious Prince! at whose Nativity
Some Royal Planet rul'd the Southern sky;
Thy longing Countries Darling and Desire;
Their cloudy Pillar, and their guardian Fire:
Their second *Moses*, whose extended Wand
Divides the Seas, and shews the promis'd Land:
Whose dawning Day, in every distant age,
Has exercis'd the Sacred Prophets rage:
The Peoples Prayer, the glad Deviners Theam,
The Young-mens Vision, and the Old mens Dream!
Thee, *Saviour*, Thee, the Nations Vows confess;
And, never satisfi'd with seeing, bless:
Swift, unbespoken Pomps, thy steps proclaim,
And stammerring Babes are taught to lisp thy Name.
How long wilt thou the general Joy detain;
Starve, and defraud the People of thy Reign?
Content ingloriously to pass thy days
Like one of Vertues Fools that feeds on Praise;
Till thy fresh Glories, which now shine so bright,
Grow Stale and Tarnish with our daily sight.
Believe me, Royal Youth, thy Fruit must be,
Or gather'd Ripe, or rot upon the Tree.
Heav'n, has to all allotted, soon or late,
Some lucky Revolution of their Fate:
Whose Motions, if we watch and guide with Skill,
(For humane Good depends on humane Will,)
Our Fortune rolls, as from a smooth Descent,
And, from the first Impression, takes the Bent:
But, if unseiz'd, she glides away like wind;
And leaves repenting Folly far behind.
Now, now she meets you, with a glorious prize,
And spreads her Locks before her as she flies.
Had thus Old *David*, from whose Loyns you spring,
Not dar'd, when Fortune call'd him, to be King,
At *Gath* an Exile he might still remain,
And heavens Anointing Oyle had been in vain.

235 Divides *C–I*: Shuts up *A B*

Let his successfull Youth your hopes engage,
But shun th' example of Declining Age:
Behold him setting in his Western Skies,
The Shadows lengthning as the Vapours rise.
He is not now, as when on *Jordan*'s Sand
The Joyfull People throng'd to see him Land,
Cov'ring the *Beach*, and blackning all the *Strand*:
But, like the Prince of Angels from his height,
Comes tumbling downward with diminish'd light;
Betray'd by one poor Plot to publick Scorn,
(Our only blessing since his Curst Return:)
Those heaps of People which one Sheaf did bind,
Blown off and scatter'd by a puff of Wind.
What strength can he to your Designs oppose,
Naked of Friends, and round beset with Foes?
If *Pharaoh*'s doubtfull Succour he shoud use,
A Foreign Aid woud more Incense the *Jews*:
Proud *Egypt* woud dissembled Friendship bring;
Foment the War, but not support the King:
Nor woud the Royal Party e'r unite
With *Pharaoh*'s Arms, t'assist the *Jebusite*;
Or if they shoud, their Interest soon woud break,
And with such odious Aid make *David* weak.
All sorts of men by my successfull Arts,
Abhorring Kings, estrange their alter'd Hearts
From *David*'s Rule: And 'tis the general Cry,
Religion, Common-wealth, and Liberty.
If you as Champion of the publique Good,
Add to their Arms a Chief of Royal Blood;
What may not *Israel* hope, and what Applause
Might such a General gain by such a Cause?
Not barren Praise alone, that Gaudy Flower,
Fair only to the sight, but solid Power:
And Nobler is a limited Command,
Giv'n by the Love of all your Native Land,
Than a Successive Title, Long, and Dark,
Drawn from the Mouldy Rolls of *Noah*'s Ark.
  What cannot Praise effect in Mighty Minds,
When Flattery Sooths, and when Ambition Blinds!
Desire of Power, on Earth a Vitious Weed,

Yet, sprung from High, is of Cælestial Seed:
In God 'tis Glory: And when men Aspire,
'Tis but a Spark too much of Heavenly Fire.
Th' Ambitious Youth, too Covetous of Fame,
Too full of Angells Metal in his Frame;
Unwarily was led from Vertues ways;
Made Drunk with Honour, and Debauch'd with Praise.
Half loath, and half consenting to the Ill,
(For Loyal Blood within him strugled still)
He thus reply'd—And what Pretence have I
To take up Arms for Publick Liberty?
My Father Governs with unquestion'd Right;
The Faiths Defender, and Mankinds Delight:
Good, Gracious, Just, observant of the Laws;
And Heav'n by Wonders has Espous'd his Cause.
Whom has he Wrong'd in all his Peaceful Reign?
Who sues for Justice to his Throne in Vain?
What Millions has he Pardon'd of his Foes,
Whom Just Revenge did to his Wrath expose?
Mild, Easy, Humble, Studious of our Good;
Enclin'd to Mercy, and averse from Blood.
If Mildness Ill with Stubborn *Israel* Suite,
His Crime is God's beloved Attribute.
What could he gain, his People to Betray,
Or change his Right, for Arbitrary Sway?
Let Haughty *Pharaoh* Curse with such a Reign,
His Fruitfull *Nile*, and Yoak a Servile Train.
If *David*'s Rule *Jerusalem* Displease,
The *Dog-star* heats their Brains to this Disease.
Why then shoud I, Encouraging the Bad,
Turn Rebell, and run Popularly Mad?
Were he a Tyrant who, by Lawless Might,
Opprest the *Jews*, and Rais'd the *Jebusite*,
Well might I Mourn; but Natures Holy Bands
Woud Curb my Spirits, and Restrain my Hands:
The People might assert their Liberty;
But what was Right in them, were Crime in me.
His Favour leaves me nothing to require;
Prevents my Wishes, and outruns Desire.

314 Loyal] Royal *D–I*

What more can I expect while *David* lives,
All but his Kingly Diadem he gives;
And that: But there he Paus'd; then Sighing, said,
Is Justly Destin'd for a Worthier Head.
For when my Father from his Toyls shall Rest,
And late Augment the Number of the Blest:
His Lawfull Issue shall the Throne ascend,
Or the *Collateral* Line where that shall end.
His Brother, though Opprest with Vulgar Spight,
Yet Dauntless and Secure of Native Right,
Of every Royal Vertue stands possest;
Still Dear to all the Bravest, and the Best.
His Courage Foes, his Friends his Truth Proclaim;
His Loyalty the King, the World his Fame.
His Mercy even th' Offending Crowd will find,
For sure he comes of a Forgiving Kind.
Why shoud I then Repine at Heavens Decree;
Which gives me no Pretence to Royalty?
Yet oh that Fate Propitiously Enclind,
Had rais'd my Birth, or had debas'd my Mind;
To my large Soul, not all her Treasure lent,
And then Betray'd it to a mean Descent.
I find, I find my mounting Spirits Bold,
And *David*'s Part disdains my Mothers Mold.
Why am I Scanted by a Niggard Birth?
My Soul Disclaims the Kindred of her Earth:
And made for Empire, Whispers me within;
Desire of Greatness is a Godlike Sin.
  Him Staggering so when Hells dire Agent found,
While fainting Vertue scarce maintain'd her Ground,
He pours fresh Forces in, and thus Replies:
  Th' Eternal God Supreamly Good and Wise,
Imparts not these Prodigious Gifts in vain;
What Wonders are Reserv'd to bless your Reign?
Against your will your Arguments have shown,
Such Vertue's only given to guide a Throne.
Not that your Father's Mildness I contemn;
But Manly Force becomes the Diadem.
'Tis true, he grants the People all they crave;

369 Birth? *C–I*: Birth, *A B*   381 contemn *C–I*: condemn *A B*

And more perhaps than Subjects ought to have:
For Lavish grants suppose a Monarch tame,
And more his Goodness than his Wit proclaim.
But when shoud People strive their Bonds to break,
If not when Kings are Negligent or Weak?
Let him give on till he can give no more,
The Thrifty Sanhedrin shall keep him poor:
And every Sheckle which he can receive,
Shall cost a Limb of his Prerogative.
To ply him with new Plots, shall be my care,
Or plunge him deep in some Expensive War;
Which when his Treasure can no more Supply,
He must, with the Remains of Kingship, buy.
His faithful Friends, our Jealousies and Fears,
Call *Jebusites*; and *Pharaoh*'s Pentioners:
Whom, when our Fury from his Aid has torn,
He shall be Naked left to publick Scorn.
The next Successor, whom I fear and hate,
My Arts have made Obnoxious to the State;
Turn'd all his Vertues to his Overthrow,
And gain'd our Elders to pronounce a Foe.
His Right, for Sums of necessary Gold,
Shall first be Pawn'd, and afterwards be Sold:
Till time shall Ever-wanting *David* draw,
To pass your doubtfull Title into Law:
If not; the People have a Right Supreme
To make their Kings; for Kings are made for them.
All Empire is no more than Pow'r in Trust,
Which when resum'd, can be no longer Just.
Succession, for the general Good design'd,
In its own wrong a Nation cannot bind:
If altering that, the People can relieve,
Better one Suffer, than a Nation grieve.
The *Jews* well know their power: e'r *Saul* they Chose,
God was their King, and God they durst Depose.
Urge now your Piety, your Filial Name,
A Father's Right, and fear of future Fame;
The publick Good, that Universal Call,
To which even Heav'n Submitted, answers all.

416 Nation *C–I*: Million *A B*

Nor let his Love Enchant your generous Mind;
'Tis Natures trick to Propagate her Kind.
Our fond Begetters, who woud never dye,
Love but themselves in their Posterity.
Or let his Kindness by th' Effects be try'd,
Or let him lay his vain Pretence aside.
God said he lov'd your Father; coud he bring
A better Proof, than to Anoint him King?
It surely shew'd he lov'd the Shepherd well,
Who gave so fair a Flock as *Israel*.
Woud *David* have you thought his Darling Son?
What means he then, to Alienate the Crown?
The name of Godly he may blush to bear:
'Tis after God's own heart to Cheat his Heir.
He to his Brother gives Supreme Command;
To you a Legacy of Barren Land:
Perhaps th' old Harp, on which he thrums his Layes:
Or some dull *Hebrew* Ballad in your Praise.
Then the next Heir, a Prince, Severe and Wise,
Already looks on you with Jealous Eyes;
Sees through the thin Disguises of your Arts,
And markes your Progress in the Peoples Hearts.
Though now his mighty Soul its Grief contains;
He meditates Revenge who least Complains.
And like a Lyon, Slumbring in the way,
Or Sleep-dissembling, while he waits his Prey,
His fearless Foes within his Distance draws;
Constrains his Roaring, and Contracts his Paws;
Till at the last, his time for Fury found,
He shoots with suddain Vengeance from the Ground:
The Prostrate Vulgar, passes o'r, and Spares;
But with a Lordly Rage, his Hunters teares.
Your Case no tame Expedients will afford;
Resolve on Death, or Conquest by the Sword,
Which for no less a Stake than Life, you Draw;
And Self-defence is Natures Eldest Law.
Leave the warm People no Considering time;
For then Rebellion may be thought a Crime.
Prevail your self of what Occasion gives,
But try your Title while your Father lives:

And that your Arms may have a fair Pretence,
Proclaim, you take them in the King's Defence:
Whose Sacred Life each minute woud Expose,
To Plots, from seeming Friends, and secret Foes.
And who can sound the depth of *David*'s Soul?
Perhaps his fear, his kindness may Controul.
He fears his Brother, though he loves his Son,
For plighted Vows too late to be undone.
If so, by Force he wishes to be gain'd,
Like womens Leachery, to seem Constrain'd:
Doubt not, but when he most affects the Frown,
Commit a pleasing Rape upon the Crown.
Secure his Person to secure your Cause;
They who possess the Prince, possess the Laws.
  He said, And this Advice above the rest,
With *Absalom*'s Mild nature suited best;
Unblam'd of Life (Ambition set aside,)
Not stain'd with Cruelty, nor puft with Pride;
How happy had he been, if Destiny
Had higher plac'd his Birth, or not so high!
His Kingly Vertues might have claim'd a Throne,
And blest all other Countries but his own:
But charming Greatness, since so few refuse;
'Tis Juster to Lament him, than Accuse.
Strong were his hopes a Rival to remove,
With blandishments to gain the publick Love;
To Head the Faction while their Zeal was hot,
And Popularly prosecute the Plot.
To farther this, *Achitophel* Unites
The Malecontents of all the *Israelites*;
Whose differing Parties he could wisely Joyn,
For several Ends, to serve the same Design.
The Best, and of the Princes some were such,
Who thought the power of Monarchy too much:
Mistaken Men, and Patriots in their Hearts;
Not Wicked, but Seduc'd by Impious Arts.
By these the Springs of Property were bent,
And wound so high, they Crack'd the Government.
The next for Interest sought t' embroil the State,

482 high! *C–I*: high? *A B*

To sell their Duty at a dearer rate;
And make their *Jewish* Markets of the Throne,
Pretending publick Good, to serve their own.
Others thought Kings an useless heavy Load,
Who Cost too much, and did too little Good.
These were for laying Honest *David* by,
On Principles of pure good Husbandry.
With them Joyn'd all th' Haranguers of the Throng,
That thought to get Preferment by the Tongue.
Who follow next, a double Danger bring,
Not only hating *David*, but the King,
The *Solymæan* Rout; well Verst of old,
In Godly Faction, and in Treason bold;
Cowring and Quaking at a Conqueror's Sword,
But Lofty to a Lawfull Prince Restor'd;
Saw with Disdain an *Ethnick* Plot begun,
And Scorn'd by *Jebusites* to be Out-done.
Hot *Levites* Headed these; who pul'd before
From th' *Ark*, which in the Judges days they bore,
Resum'd their Cant, and with a Zealous Cry,
Pursu'd their old belov'd Theocracy.
Where Sanhedrin and Priest inslav'd the Nation,
And justifi'd their Spoils by Inspiration;
For who so fit for Reign as *Aaron*'s Race,
If once Dominion they could found in Grace?
These led the Pack; tho not of surest scent,
Yet deepest mouth'd against the Government.
A numerous Host of dreaming Saints succeed;
Of the true old Enthusiastick breed:
'Gainst Form and Order they their Power employ;
Nothing to Build and all things to Destroy.
But far more numerous was the herd of such,
Who think too little, and who talk too much.
These, out of meer instinct, they knew not why,
Ador'd their fathers God, and Property:
And, by the same blind benefit of Fate,
The Devil and the *Jebusite* did hate:
Born to be sav'd, even in their own despight;
Because they could not help believing right.

522 Pursu'd] Pursue *B*   530 old *om.* *C* (*some copies*) *D*

Such were the tools; but a whole Hydra more
Remains, of sprouting heads too long, to score.
  Some of their Chiefs were Princes of the Land:
In the first Rank of these did *Zimri* stand:
A man so various, that he seem'd to be
Not one, but all Mankinds Epitome.
Stiff in Opinions, always in the wrong;
Was every thing by starts, and nothing long:
But, in the course of one revolving Moon,
Was Chymist, Fidler, States-Man, and Buffoon:
Then all for Women, Painting, Rhiming, Drinking;
Besides ten thousand freaks that dy'd in thinking.
Blest Madman, who coud every hour employ,
With something New to wish, or to enjoy!
Rayling and praising were his usual Theams;
And both (to shew his Judgment) in Extreams:
So over Violent, or over Civil,
That every man, with him, was God or Devil.
In squandring Wealth was his peculiar Art:
Nothing went unrewarded, but Desert.
Begger'd by Fools, whom still he found too late:
He had his Jest, and they had his Estate.
He laught himself from Court, then sought Relief
By forming Parties, but coud ne're be Chief:
For, spight of him, the weight of Business fell
On *Absalom* and wise *Achitophel*:
Thus, wicked but in will, of means bereft,
He left not Faction, but of that was left.
  Titles and Names 'twere tedious to Reherse
Of Lords, below the Dignity of Verse.
Wits, warriors, Common-wealthsmen, were the best:
Kind Husbands and meer Nobles all the rest.
And, therefore in the name of Dulness, be
The well hung *Balaam* and cold *Caleb* free.
And Canting *Nadab* let Oblivion damn,
Who made new porridge for the Paschal Lamb.
Let Friendships holy band some Names assure:
Some their own Worth, and some let Scorn secure.

543 *Editor's paragraph* 553 Madman] Madam *D* 563 Relief *C–I*: Releif *A B* 571 Wits, Warriors, *C–I*: Wits warriors *A B*

Nor shall the Rascall Rabble here have Place,
Whom Kings no Titles gave, and God no Grace:
Not Bull-fac'd *Jonas*, who could Statutes draw
To mean Rebellion, and make Treason Law.
But he, tho bad, is follow'd by a worse,
The wretch, who Heavens Annointed dar'd to Curse.
Shimei, whose Youth did early Promise bring
Of Zeal to God, and Hatred to his King;
Did wisely from Expensive Sins refrain,
And never broke the Sabbath, but for Gain:
Nor ever was he known an Oath to vent,
Or Curse unless against the Government.
Thus, heaping Wealth, by the most ready way
Among the *Jews*, which was to Cheat and Pray;
The City, to reward his pious Hate
Against his Master, chose him Magistrate:
His Hand a Vare of Justice did uphold;
His Neck was loaded with a Chain of Gold.
During his Office, Treason was no Crime.
The Sons of *Belial* had a glorious Time:
For *Shimei*, though not prodigal of pelf,
Yet lov'd his wicked Neighbour as himself:
When two or three were gather'd to declaim
Against the Monarch of *Jerusalem*,
Shimei was always in the midst of them.
And, if they Curst the King when he was by,
Woud rather Curse, than break good Company.
If any durst his Factious Friends accuse,
He pact a Jury of dissenting *Jews*:
Whose fellow-feeling, in the godly Cause,
Would free the suffring Saint from Humane Laws.
For Laws are only made to Punish those,
Who serve the King, and to protect his Foes.
If any leisure time he had from Power,
(Because 'tis Sin to misimploy an hour;)
His business was, by Writing, to Persuade,
That Kings were Useless, and a Clog to Trade:
And, that his noble Stile he might refine,

581 Bull-fac'd *Jonas* *C–I*: Bull-fac'd-*Jonas* *A B* 585 Youth did early *C–I*: early Youth did *A B* 596 loaded] loaden *D* 610 are] were *F*

No *Rechabite* more shund the fumes of Wine.
Chast were his Cellars, and his Shrieval Board
The Grossness of a City Feast abhor'd:
His Cooks, with long disuse, their Trade forgot;
Cool was his Kitchen, tho his Brains were hot.
Such frugal Vertue Malice may accuse,
But sure 'twas necessary to the *Jews*:
For Towns once burnt, such Magistrates require
As dare not tempt Gods Providence by fire.
With Spiritual food he fed his Servants well,
But free from flesh, that made the *Jews* Rebel:
And *Moses*'s Laws he held in more account,
For forty days of Fasting in the Mount.
  To speak the rest, who better are forgot,
Would tyre a well breath'd Witness of the Plot:
Yet, *Corah*, thou shalt from Oblivion pass;
Erect thy self thou Monumental Brass:
High as the Serpent of thy mettall made,
While Nations stand secure beneath thy shade.
What tho his Birth were base, yet Comets rise
From Earthy Vapours ere they shine in Skies.
Prodigious Actions may as well be done
By Weavers issue, as by Princes Son.
This Arch-Attestor for the Publick Good,
By that one Deed Enobles all his Bloud.
Who ever ask'd the Witnesses high race,
Whose Oath with Martyrdom did *Stephen* grace?
Ours was a *Levite*, and as times went then,
His Tribe were Godalmightys Gentlemen.
Sunk were his Eyes, his Voyce was harsh and loud,
Sure signs he neither Cholerick was, nor Proud:
His long Chin prov'd his Wit; his Saintlike Grace
A Church Vermilion, and a *Moses*'s Face;
His Memory, miraculously great,
Could Plots, exceeding mans belief, repeat;
Which, therefore cannot be accounted Lies,
For humane Wit could never such devise.
Some future Truths are mingled in his Book;
But, where the witness faild, the Prophet Spoke:

630 *Editor's paragraph*

Some things like Visionary flights appear;
The Spirit caught him up, the Lord knows where:
And gave him his *Rabinical* degree
Unknown to Foreign University.
His Judgment yet his Memory did excel;
Which peic'd his wondrous Evidence so well:
And suited to the temper of the times;
Then groaning under *Jebusitick* Crimes.
Let *Israels* foes suspect his heav'nly call,
And rashly judge his Writ Apocryphal;
Our Laws for such affronts have forfeits made:
He takes his life, who takes away his trade.
Were I my self in witness *Corahs* place,
The wretch who did me such a dire disgrace,
Should whet my memory, though once forgot,
To make him an Appendix of my Plot.
His Zeal to heav'n, made him his Prince despise,
And load his person with indignities:
But Zeal peculiar priviledg affords;
Indulging latitude to deeds and words.
And *Corah* might for *Agag*'s murther call,
In terms as course as *Samuel* us'd to *Saul*.
What others in his Evidence did Joyn,
(The best that could be had for love or coyn,)
In *Corah*'s own predicament will fall:
For *witness* is a Common Name to all.
  Surrounded thus with Freinds of every sort,
Deluded *Absalom*, forsakes the Court:
Impatient of high hopes, urg'd with renown,
And Fir'd with near possession of a Crown:
Th' admiring Croud are dazled with surprize,
And on his goodly person feed their eyes:
His joy conceal'd, he sets himself to show;
On each side bowing popularly low:
His looks, his gestures, and his words he frames,
And with familiar ease repeats their Names.
Thus, form'd by Nature, furnish'd out with Arts,
He glides unfelt into their secret hearts:

665 Writ *C–I*: Wit *A B*. *Cf.* The Second Part, *l.* 95 680 fall: *C–I*: fall? *A B*
685 Crown: *C–I*: Crown, *A B* 688 His joy conceal'd *C–I*: Dissembling Joy *A B*

Then with a kind compassionating look,
And sighs, bespeaking pity ere he spoak,
Few words he said; but easy those and fit:
More slow than Hybla drops, and far more sweet.
  I mourn, my Countrymen, your lost Estate;
Tho far unable to prevent your fate:
Behold a Banisht man, for your dear cause
Expos'd a prey to Arbitrary laws!
Yet oh! that I alone cou'd be undone,
Cut off from Empire, and no more a Son!
Now all your Liberties a spoil are made;
Ægypt and *Tyrus* intercept your Trade,
And *Jebusites* your Sacred Rites invade.
My Father, whom with reverence yet I name,
Charm'd into Ease, is careless of his Fame:
And, brib'd with petty summs of Forreign Gold,
Is grown in *Bathsheba*'s Embraces old:
Exalts his Enemies, his Freinds destroys:
And all his pow'r against himself employs.
He gives, and let him give my right away:
But why should he his own, and yours betray?
He only, he can make the Nation bleed,
And he alone from my revenge is freed.
Take then my tears (with that he wip'd his Eyes)
'Tis all the Aid my present power supplies:
No Court Informer can these Arms accuse,
These Arms may Sons against their Fathers use,
And, tis my wish, the next Successors Reign
May make no other *Israelite* complain.
  Youth, Beauty, Graceful Action, seldom fail:
But Common Interest always will prevail:
And pity never Ceases to be shown
To him, who makes the peoples wrongs his own.
The Croud, (that still believe their Kings oppress)
With lifted hands their young *Messiah* bless:
Who now begins his Progress to ordain;
With Chariots, Horsemen, and a numerous train:
From East to West his Glories he displaies:
And, like the Sun, the promis'd land survays.

695 spoak,] spoak: *A–F*: spoke, *G–I*   727 believe *C–I*: believes *A B*

Fame runs before him, as the morning Star;
And shouts of Joy salute him from afar:
Each house receives him as a Guardian God;
And Consecrates the Place of his aboad:
But hospitable treats did most Commend
Wise *Issachar*, his wealthy western friend.
This moving Court, that caught the peoples Eyes,
And seem'd but Pomp, did other ends disguise:
Achitophel had form'd it, with intent
To sound the depths, and fathom where it went,
The Peoples hearts; distinguish Friends from Foes;
And try their strength, before they came to blows:
Yet all was colour'd with a smooth pretence
Of specious love, and duty to their Prince.
Religion, and Redress of Grievances,
Two names, that always cheat and always please,
Are often urg'd; and good King *David*'s life
Indanger'd by a Brother and a Wife.
Thus, in a Pageant Show, a Plot is made;
And Peace it self is War in Masquerade.
Oh foolish *Israel*! never warn'd by ill,
Still the same baite, and circumvented still!
Did ever men forsake their present ease,
In midst of health Imagine a desease;
Take pains Contingent mischiefs to foresee,
Make Heirs for Monarks, and for God decree?
What shall we think! can People give away
Both for themselves and Sons, their Native sway?
Then they are left Defensless, to the Sword
Of each unbounded Arbitrary Lord:
And Laws are vain, by which we Right enjoy,
If Kings unquestiond can those laws destroy.
Yet, if the Crowd be Judge of fit and Just,
And Kings are onely Officers in trust,
Then this resuming Cov'nant was declar'd
When Kings were made, or is for ever bar'd:
If those who gave the Scepter, coud not tye
By their own deed their own Posterity,

739 Eyes, *C–H*: Eyes. *A B I* 742 depths *C–I*: depth *A B* went, *C–I*: went: *A B* 743 hearts; *C–I*: hearts, *A B*

How then coud *Adam* bind his future Race?
How coud his forfeit on mankind take place?
Or how coud heavenly Justice damn us all,
Who nere consented to our Fathers fall?
Then Kings are slaves to those whom they Command,
And Tenants to their Peoples pleasure stand.
Add, that the Pow'r for Property allowd,
Is mischeivously seated in the Crowd:
For who can be secure of private Right,
If Sovereign sway may be dissolv'd by might?
Nor is the Peoples Judgment always true:
The most may err as grosly as the few.
And faultless Kings run down, by Common Cry,
For Vice, Oppression, and for Tyranny.
What Standard is there in a fickle rout,
Which, flowing to the mark, runs faster out?
Nor only Crowds, but Sanhedrins may be
Infected with this publick Lunacy:
And Share the madness of Rebellious times,
To Murther Monarchs for Imagin'd crimes.
If they may Give and Take when e'r they please,
Not Kings alone, (the Godheads Images,)
But Government it self at length must fall
To Natures state; where all have Right to all.
Yet, grant our Lords the People Kings can make,
What Prudent men a setled Throne woud shake?
For whatsoe'r their Sufferings were before,
That Change they Covet makes them suffer more.
All other Errors but disturb a State;
But Innovation is the Blow of Fate.
If ancient Fabricks nod, and threat to fall,
To Patch the Flaws, and Buttress up the Wall,
Thus far 'tis Duty; but here fix the Mark:
For all beyond it is to touch our Ark.
To change Foundations, cast the Frame anew,
Is work for Rebels who base Ends pursue:
At once Divine and Humane Laws controul;
And mend the Parts by ruine of the Whole.
The Tampering World is subject to this Curse,

777 Add, that the Pow'r *C–I*: That Pow'r, which is *A B*

To Physick their Disease into a worse.
  Now what Relief can Righteous *David* bring?
How Fatall 'tis to be too good a King!
Friends he has few, so high the Madness grows,
Who dare be such, must be the Peoples Foes:
Yet some there were, ev'n in the worst of days;
Some let me name, and Naming is to praise.
  In this short File *Barzillai* first appears;
Barzillai crown'd with Honour and with Years:
Long since, the rising Rebells he withstood
In Regions Waste, beyond the *Jordans* Flood:
Unfortunately Brave to buoy the State;
But sinking underneath his Masters Fate:
In Exile with his Godlike Prince he Mourn'd;
For him he Suffer'd, and with him Return'd.
The Court he practis'd, not the Courtier's art:
Large was his Wealth, but larger was his Heart:
Which, well the Noblest Objects knew to choose,
The Fighting Warriour, and Recording Muse.
His Bed coud once a Fruitfull Issue boast:
Now more than half a Father's Name is lost.
His Eldest Hope, with every Grace adorn'd,
By me (so Heav'n will have it) always Mourn'd,
And always honour'd, snatcht in Manhoods prime
By' unequal Fates, and Providences crime:
Yet not before the Goal of Honour won,
All parts fulfill'd of Subject and of Son;
Swift was the Race, but short the Time to run.
Oh Narrow Circle, but of Pow'r Divine,
Scanted in Space, but perfect in thy Line!
By Sea, by Land, thy Matchless Worth was known;
Arms thy Delight, and War was all thy Own:
Thy force, Infus'd, the fainting *Tyrians* prop'd:
And Haughty *Pharaoh* found his Fortune stop'd.
Oh Ancient Honour, Oh Unconquer'd Hand,
Whom Foes unpunish'd never coud withstand!
But *Israel* was unworthy of thy Name:
Short is the date of all Immoderate Fame.
It looks as Heaven our Ruine had design'd,

846 thy Name: *C*: thy Birth; *A B*: his Name: *D–I* 847 Fame *C–I*: Worth *A B*

And durst not trust thy Fortune and thy Mind.
Now, free from Earth, thy disencumbred Soul
Mounts up, and leaves behind the Clouds and Starry Pole:
From thence thy kindred legions mayst thou bring
To aid the guardian Angel of thy King.
Here stop my Muse, here cease thy painfull flight;
No Pinions can pursue Immortal height:
Tell good *Barzillai* thou canst sing no more,
And tell thy Soul she should have fled before;
Or fled she with his life, and left this Verse
To hang on her departed Patron's Herse?
Now take thy steepy flight from heaven, and see
If thou canst find on earth another *He*;
Another He would be too hard to find,
See then whom thou canst see not far behind.
Zadock the Priest, whom, shunning Power and Place,
His lowly mind advanc'd to *David*'s Grace:
With him the *Sagan* of *Jerusalem*,
Of hospitable Soul and noble Stem;
Him of the Western dome, whose weighty sense
Flows in fit words and heavenly eloquence.
The Prophets Sons by such example led,
To Learning and to Loyalty were bred:
For *Colleges* on bounteous Kings depend,
And never Rebell was to Arts a friend.
To these succeed the Pillars of the Laws,
Who best cou'd plead and best can judge a Cause.
Next them a train of Loyal Peers ascend:
Sharp judging *Adriel* the Muses friend,
Himself a Muse—In Sanhedrins debate
True to his Prince; but not a Slave of State.
Whom *David*'s love with Honours did adorn,
That from his disobedient Son were torn.
Jotham of piercing wit and pregnant thought,
Indew'd by nature, and by learning taught
To move Assemblies, who but onely try'd
The worse awhile, then chose the better side;
Nor chose alone, but turn'd the balance too;
So much the weight of one brave man can doe.

861 *He*; *C–I*: *He*, *A B* 882 piercing *C–I*: ready *A B*

Hushai the friend of *David* in distress,
In publick storms of manly stedfastness;
By foreign treaties he inform'd his Youth;
And join'd experience to his native truth.
His frugal care supply'd the wanting Throne,
Frugal for that, but bounteous of his own:
'Tis easy conduct when Exchequers flow,
But hard the task to manage well the low:
For Soveraign power is too deprest or high,
When Kings are forc'd to sell, or Crowds to buy.
Indulge one labour more my weary Muse,
For *Amiel*, who can *Amiel*'s praise refuse?
Of ancient race by birth, but nobler yet
In his own worth, and without Title great:
The Sanhedrin long time as chief he rul'd,
Their Reason guided and their Passion coold;
So dexterous was he in the Crown's defence,
So form'd to speak a Loyal Nation's Sense,
That as their band was *Israel*'s Tribes in small,
So fit was he to represent them all.
Now rasher Charioteers the Seat ascend,
Whose loose Carriers his steady Skill commend:
They like th' unequal Ruler of the Day,
Misguide the Seasons and mistake the Way;
While he withdrawn at their mad Labour smiles,
And safe enjoys the Sabbath of his Toyls.
  These were the chief, a small but faithful Band
Of Worthies, in the Breach who dar'd to stand,
And tempt th' united Fury of the Land.
With grief they view'd such powerful Engines bent,
To batter down the lawful Government.
A numerous Faction with pretended frights,
In Sanhedrins to plume the Regal Rights.
The true Successour from the Court remov'd:
The Plot, by hireling Witnesses improv'd.
These Ills they saw, and as their Duty bound,
They shew'd the King the danger of the Wound:
That no Concessions from the Throne woud please,
But Lenitives fomented the Disease:
That *Absalom*, ambitious of the Crown,

Was made the Lure to draw the People down:
That false *Achitophel*'s pernitious Hate,
Had turn'd the Plot to Ruine Church and State:
The Councill violent, the Rabble worse
That *Shimei* taught *Jerusalem* to Curse.
  With all these loads of Injuries opprest,
And long revolving, in his carefull Breast,
Th' event of things; at last his patience tir'd,
Thus from his Royal Throne by Heav'n inspir'd,
The God-like *David* spoke: with awfull fear
His Train their Maker in their Master hear.
  Thus long have I, by native mercy sway'd,
My wrongs dissembl'd, my revenge delay'd:
So willing to forgive th' Offending Age,
So much the Father did the King asswage.
But now so far my Clemency they slight,
Th' Offenders question my Forgiving Right.
That one was made for many, they contend:
But 'tis to Rule, for that 's a Monarch's End.
They call my tenderness of Blood, my Fear:
Though Manly tempers can the longest bear.
Yet, since they will divert my Native course,
'Tis time to shew I am not Good by Force.
Those heap'd Affronts that haughty Subjects bring,
Are burthens for a Camel, not a King:
Kings are the publick Pillars of the State,
Born to sustain and prop the Nations weight:
If my Young *Samson* will pretend a Call
To shake the Column, let him share the Fall:
But oh that yet he woud repent and live!
How easie 'tis for Parents to forgive!
With how few Tears a Pardon might be won
From Nature, pleading for a Darling Son!
Poor pitied Youth, by my Paternal care,
Rais'd up to all the Height his Frame coud bear:
Had God ordain'd his fate for Empire born,
He woud have given his Soul another turn:
Gull'd with a Patriots name, whose Modern sense
Is one that would by Law supplant his Prince:

939 I,] I *C–I* 957–60 *added in C, D–I* 966 supplant *C–I*: destroy *A B*

The Peoples Brave, the Politicians Tool;
Never was Patriot yet, but was a Fool.
Whence comes it that Religion and the Laws
Should more be *Absalom*'s than *David*'s Cause?
His old Instructor, e're he lost his Place,
Was never thought indu'd with so much Grace.
Good Heav'ns, how Faction can a Patriot Paint!
My Rebel ever proves my Peoples Saint:
Would *They* impose an Heir upon the Throne?
Let Sanhedrins be taught to give their Own.
A King's at least a part of Government,
And mine as requisite as their Consent:
Without my Leave a future King to choose,
Infers a Right the Present to Depose:
True, they Petition me t' approve their Choise,
But *Esau*'s Hands suite ill with *Jacob*'s Voice.
My Pious Subjects for my Safety pray,
Which to Secure they take my Power away.
From Plots and Treasons Heaven preserve my years,
But Save me most from my Petitioners.
Unsatiate as the barren Womb or Grave;
God cannot Grant so much as they can Crave.
What then is left but with a Jealous Eye
To guard the Small remains of Royalty?
The Law shall still direct my peacefull Sway,
And the same Law teach Rebels to Obey:
Votes shall no more Establish'd Pow'r controul,
Such Votes as make a Part exceed the Whole:
No groundless Clamours shall my Friends remove,
Nor Crowds have power to Punish e're they Prove:
For Gods, and Godlike Kings their Care express,
Still to Defend their Servants in distress.
Oh that my Power to Saving were confin'd:
Why am I forc'd, like Heaven, against my mind,
To make Examples of another Kind?
Must I at length the Sword of Justice draw?
Oh curst Effects of necessary Law!
How ill my Fear they by my Mercy scan,
Beware the Fury of a Patient Man.
Law they require, let Law then shew her Face;

They coud not be content to look on Grace,
Her hinder parts, but with a daring Eye
To tempt the terror of her Front, and Dye.
By their own arts 'tis Righteously decreed,
Those dire Artificers of Death shall bleed.
Against themselves their Witnesses will Swear,
Till Viper-like their Mother Plot they tear:
And suck for Nutriment that bloody gore
Which was their Principle of Life before.
Their *Belial* with their *Belzebub* will fight;
Thus on my Foes, my Foes shall do me Right:
Nor doubt th' event: for Factious crowds engage
In their first Onset, all their Brutal Rage;
Then, let 'em take an unresisted Course,
Retire and Traverse, and Delude their Force:
But when they stand all Breathless, urge the fight,
And rise upon 'em with redoubled might:
For Lawfull Pow'r is still Superiour found,
When long driven back, at length it stands the ground.
  He said. Th' Almighty, nodding, gave Consent;
And Peals of Thunder shook the Firmament.
Henceforth a Series of new time began,
The mighty Years in long Procession ran:
Once more the Godlike *David* was Restor'd,
And willing Nations knew their Lawfull Lord.

PROLOGUE and EPILOGUE to *THE UNHAPPY FAVOURITE*

PROLOGUE

Spoken to the King and Queen at their coming to the House, and Written on purpose

WHEN first the Ark was Landed on the Shore,
And Heaven had vow'd to curse the Ground no more,
When Tops of Hills the Longing Patriark saw,
And the new Scene of Earth began to draw;
The Dove was sent to View the Waves Decrease,
And first brought back to Man the Pledge of Peace:
'Tis needless to apply when those appear
Who bring the Olive, and who Plant it here.
We have before our eyes the Royal Dove,
Still Innocence is Harbinger to Love,
The Ark is open'd to dismiss the Train,
And People with a better Race the Plain.
Tell me you Powers, why should vain Man pursue,
With endless Toyl, each object that is new,
And for the seeming substance leave the true—
Why should he quit for hopes his certain good,
And loath the Manna of his dayly food?
Must *England* still the Scene of Changes be,
Tost and Tempestuous like our Ambient Sea?
Must still our Weather and our Wills agree?
Without our Blood our Liberties we have,
Who that is Free would Fight to be a Slave?
Or what can Wars to after Times Assure,
Of which our Present Age is not secure?
All that our Monarch would for us Ordain,
Is but t' Injoy the Blessings of his Reign.
Our Land 's an *Eden*, and the Main 's our Fence,
While we Preserve our State of Innocence;

Prologue and Epilogue. Text from Banks's The Unhappy Favourite: or The Earl of Essex. A Tragedy, *1682, collated with the editions of 1685, 1693, and (Epilogue only)* Miscellany Poems, *1684 and 1692*

That lost, then Beasts their Brutal Force employ,
And first their Lord, and then themselves destroy:
What Civil Broils have cost we know too well,
Oh let it be enough that once we fell,
And every Heart conspire with every Tongue,
Still to have such a King, and this King Long.

EPILOGUE

WE Act by Fits and Starts, like drowning Men,
But just Peep up, and then Dop down again;
Let those who call us Wicked change their Sence,
For never Men liv'd more on Providence,
Not Lott'ry Cavaliers are half so poor,
Nor Broken Cits, nor a Vacation Whore,
Not Courts nor Courtiers living on the Rents,
Of the Three last ungiving Parliaments.
So wretched that if *Pharoah* could Divine,
He might have spar'd his Dream of Seven lean Kine,
And chang'd his Vision for the Muses Nine.
The Comet that they say Portends a Dearth,
Was but a Vapour drawn from Play-house Earth,
Pent there since our last Fire, and *Lilly* sayes,
Fore-shows our change of State and thin Third dayes.
'Tis not our want of Wit that keeps us Poor,
For then the Printers Press would suffer more:
Their Pamphleteers each day their Venom spit,
They thrive by Treason and we starve by Wit.
Confess the truth, which of you has not laid [*To the Upper Gallery.*
Four Farthings out to buy the *Hatfield* Maid?
Or which is duller yet, and more wou'd spight us,
Democritus his Wars with *Heraclitus*?
Such are the Authors who have run us down,
And Exercis'd you Critticks of the Town;

31 know *85 93*: knew *82*
Epilogue. Heading in 84 92: An Epilogue for the Kings House
11 his *84 92*: the *82 85 93* 12 that *84 92*: which *82 85 93* 14 there *84 92*: here *82 85 93* 18 each day their Venom *84 92*: their Venom dayly *82 85 93* 20 Stage direction. *Looking above. 84 92* 22 which *84 92*: what *82 85 93* wou'd *84 92*: to *82*: does *85 93* 24 Such *84 92*: These *82 85 93* who *84 92*: that *82 85 93* 25 Exercis'd *84 92*: Exercise *82 85 93*

Yet these are Pearls to your Lampooning Rhimes,
Y'abuse your selves more dully than the Times;
Scandal, the Glory of the *English* Nation,
Is worn to Rags and Scribled out of Fashion;
Such harmless thrusts, as if like Fencers Wise,
They had agreed their Play before their Prize.
Faith they may hang their Harps upon the Willows,
'Tis just like Children when they Box with Pillows.
Then put an end to Civil Wars for shame,
Let each Knight Errant who has wrong'd a Dame,
Throw down his Pen, and give her as he can,
The satisfaction of a Gentleman.

PROLOGUE and EPILOGUE to *THE LOYAL BROTHER*

A PROLOGUE

Written by Mr. Dryden, *to a New Play, call'd,*
The Loyal Brother, *&c.*

POETS, like Lawfull Monarchs, rul'd the Stage,
Till Criticks, like Damn'd Whiggs, debauch'd our Age.
Mark how they jump: Criticks wou'd regulate
Our Theatres, and Whiggs reform our State:
Both pretend love, and both (Plague rot 'em) hate.
The Critick humbly seems Advice to bring,
The fawning Whigg Petitions to the King:
But ones advice into a Satyr slides;
T'others Petition a Remonstrance hides.
These will no Taxes give, and those no Pence:
Criticks wou'd starve the Poet, Whiggs the Prince.

31 They . . . their . . . their *84 92*: You . . . your . . . the *82 85 93* 32 they . . . their *84 92*: you . . . your *82 85 93* 36 as *84 92*: if *82 85 93*
Prologue and Epilogue. Text from the separate edition of 1682, collated with the first edition of Southerne's The Loyal Brother or The Persian Prince. A Tragedy, *1682. See Commentary*

The Critick all our troops of friends discards;
Just so the Whigg wou'd fain pull down the Guards.
Guards are illegal, that drive foes away,
As watchfull Shepherds, that fright beasts of prey.
Kings, who Disband such needless Aids as these,
Are safe—as long as e're their Subjects please.
And that wou'd be till next Queen *Besses* night:
Which thus, grave penny Chroniclers endite.
Sir *Edmond-berry*, first, in wofull wise,
Leads up the show, and Milks their Maudlin eyes.
There's not a Butcher's Wife but Dribs her part,
And pities the poor Pageant from her heart;
Who, to provoke revenge, rides round the fire,
And, with a civil congee, does retire.
But guiltless blood to ground must never fall:
There's *Antichrist* behind, to pay for all.
The Punk of *Babylon* in Pomp appears,
A lewd Old Gentleman of Seventy years.
Whose Age in vain our Mercy wou'd implore;
For few take pity on an Old-cast Whore.
The Devil, who brought him to the shame, takes part;
Sits cheek by jowl, in black, to cheer his heart:
Like Theef and Parson in a *Tyburn*-Cart.
The word is giv'n; and with a loud Huzzaw
The Miter'd Moppet from his Chair they draw:
On the slain Corps contending Nations fall;
Alas, what's one poor Pope among 'em all!
He burns; now all true hearts your Triumphs ring;
And next (for fashion) cry, *God save the King*.
A needful Cry in midst of such Alarms:
When Forty thousand Men are up in Arms.
But after he's once sav'd, to make amends,
In each succeeding Health they Damn his Friends:
So God begins, but still the Devil ends.
What if some one inspir'd with Zeal, shou'd call,
Come let's go cry, God save him at *White-Hall*?
His best friends wou'd not like this over-care:
Or think him e're the safer for that pray'r.
Five Praying Saints are by an Act allow'd:
But not the whole Church-Militant, in crowd.

Yet, should heav'n all the true Petitions drain
Of *Presbyterians*, who wou'd Kings maintain;
Of Forty thousand, five wou'd scarce remain.

The EPILOGUE *by the same Hand*

Spoken by Mrs. Sarah Cook

A VIRGIN Poet was serv'd up to day;
Who till this hour, ne're cackled for a Play:
He 's neither yet a Whigg nor Tory-Boy;
But, like a Girl, whom several wou'd enjoy,
Begs leave to make the best of his own natural Toy.
Were I to play my callow Author's game,
The King's House wou'd instruct me, by the Name:
There 's Loyalty to one: I wish no more:
A Commonwealth sounds like a Common Whore.
Let Husband or Gallant be what they will,
One part of Woman is true Tory still.
If any Factious spirit shou'd rebell,
Our Sex, with ease, can every rising quell.
Then, as you hope we shou'd your failings hide,
An honest Jury for our play provide:
Whiggs, at their Poets never take offence;
They save dull Culpritts who have Murther'd Sense:
Tho Nonsense is a nauseous heavy Mass,
The Vehicle call'd Faction makes it pass.
Faction in Play 's the Commonwealths man's bribe:
The leaden farthing of the Canting Tribe:
Though void in payment Laws and Statutes make it,
The Neighbourhood, that knows the Man, will take it.
'Tis Faction buys the Votes of half the Pit;
Theirs is the Pention-Parliament of wit.
In City-Clubs their venom let 'em vent;
For there 'tis safe, in its own Element:
Here, where their madness can have no pretence,
Let 'em forget themselves an hour in sense.
In one poor Isle, why shou'd two Factions be?
Small diff'rence in your Vices I can see;
In Drink and Drabs both sides too well agree.

Wou'd there were more Preferments in the Land;
If Places fell, the party cou'd not stand.
Of this damn'd grievance ev'ry Whigg complains;
They grunt like Hogs, till they have got their Grains.
Mean time you see what Trade our Plots advance,
We send each year good Money into *France*:
And they, that know what Merchandise we need,
Send o're true Protestants, to mend our breed.

THE MEDALL

A SATYRE AGAINST SEDITION

Per Graiûm populos, mediæque per Elidis Urbem
Ibat ovans; Divumque sibi poscebat Honores

EPISTLE To the WHIGS

FOR to whom can I dedicate this Poem, with so much justice as to you? 'Tis the representation of your own Heroe: 'tis the Picture drawn at length, which you admire and prize so much in little. None of your Ornaments are wanting; neither the Landscap of the Tower, nor the Rising Sun; nor the Anno Domini of your New Sovereign's Coronation. This must needs be a gratefull undertaking to your whole Party: especially to those who have not been so happy as to purchase the Original. I hear the Graver has made a good Market of it: all his Kings are bought up already; or the value of the remainder so inhanc'd, that many a poor Polander who would be glad to worship the Image, is not able to go to the cost of him: But must be content to see him here. I must confess I am no great Artist; but Sign-post painting will serve the turn to remember a Friend by; especially when better is not to be had. Yet for your comfort the lineaments are true: and though he sate not five times to me, as he did to B. yet I have consulted History; as the Italian Painters doe, when they wou'd draw a Nero or a Caligula; though they have not seen the Man, they can help their Imagination by a Statue of him, and find out the Colouring from Suetonius and Tacitus. Truth is, you might have spar'd one side of your Medall: the Head wou'd be seen to more advantage, if it were plac'd on a Spike of the Tower; a little nearer to the Sun. Which wou'd then break out to better purpose. You tell us in your Preface to the No-protestant Plot, that you shall be forc'd hereafter to leave off your Modesty: I suppose you mean that little which is left you: for it was worn to rags when you put out this Medall. Never was there practis'd such a piece of notorious Impudence in the face of an Establish'd Government. I believe, when he is dead, you will wear him in Thumb-Rings, as the Turks did Scanderbeg; as if there were virtue in his Bones to preserve you against Monarchy. Yet all this while you pretend not onely zeal for the Publick good; but a due veneration for the person of the King. But all men who can see an inch before them, may easily detect those gross fallacies. That it is necessary for men in your circumstances to pretend both, is granted you; for without them there could be no ground to raise a Faction. But I would ask you one civil question, what right has any man

The Medall. Text from the first edition, 1682 (82), collated with the Edinburgh and Dublin editions of 1682, Miscellany Poems, 1684 (84; reprinted 1692), and 'The Third Edition', 1692 (92)

among you, or any Association of men, (to come nearer to you,) who out of Parliament, cannot be consider'd in a publick Capacity, to meet, as you daily doe, in Factious Clubs, to vilify the Government, in your Discourses, and to libel it in all your Writings? who made you Judges in Israel? or how is it consistent with your Zeal of the publick Welfare, to promote Sedition? Does your definition of loyal, which is to serve the King according to the Laws, allow you the licence of traducing the Executive Power, with which you own he is invested? You complain that his Majesty has lost the love and confidence of his People; and by your very urging it, you endeavour what in you lies, to make him lose them. All good Subjects abhor the thought of Arbitrary Power, whether it be in one or many: if you were the Patriots you would seem, you would not at this rate incense the Multitude to assume it; for no sober man can fear it, either from the King's Disposition, or his Practice; or even, where you would odiously lay it, from his Ministers. Give us leave to enjoy the Government and the benefit of Laws under which we were born, and which we desire to transmit to our Posterity. You are not the Trustees of the publick Liberty: and if you have not right to petition in a Crowd, much less have you to intermeddle in the management of Affairs; or to arraign what you do not like: which in effect is every thing that is done by the King and Council. Can you imagine that any reasonable man will believe you respect the person of his Majesty, when 'tis apparent that your Seditious Pamphlets are stuff'd with particular Reflexions on him? If you have the confidence to deny this, 'tis easy to be evinc'd from a thousand Passages, which I onely forbear to quote, because I desire they should die and be forgotten. I have perus'd many of your Papers; and to show you that I have, the third part of your No-protestant Plot is much of it stolen, from your dead Authour's Pamphlet call'd, the Growth of Popery; as manifestly as Milton's defence of the English People, is from Buchanan, de jure regni apud Scotos: or your first Covenant, and new Association, from the holy League of the French Guisards. Any one who reads Davila, may trace your Practices all along. There were the same pretences for Reformation, and Loyalty, the same Aspersions of the King, and the same grounds of a Rebellion. I know not whether you will take the Historian's word, who says it was reported, that Poltrot a Hugonot, murther'd Francis Duke of Guise by the instigations of Theodore Beza: or that it was a Hugonot Minister, otherwise call'd a Presbyterian, (for our Church abhors so devilish a Tenent) who first writ a Treatise of the lawfulness of deposing and murthering Kings, of a different Perswasion in Religion: But I am able to prove from the Doctrine of Calvin, and Principles of Buchanan, that they set the People above the Magistrate; which if I mistake not, is your own Fundamental; and which carries your Loyalty no farther than your likeing. When a Vote of the House of

64 Tenent] Tenet 84 92

Commons goes on your side, you are as ready to observe it, as if it were pass'd into a Law: But when you are pinch'd with any former, and yet unrepealed Act of Parliament, *you declare that in some cases, you will not be oblig'd by it. The Passage is in the same third part of the* No-protestant Plot*; and is too plain to be denied. The late Copy of your intended Association, you neither wholly justify nor condemn; But, as the Papists, when they are unoppos'd, fly out into all the Pageantry's of Worship; but in times of War, when they are hard press'd by Arguments, lie close intrench'd behind the* Council of Trent*: So, now, when your Affairs are in a low condition, you dare not pretend that to be a legal Combination, but whensoever you are afloat, I doubt not but it will be maintain'd and justify'd to purpose. For indeed there is nothing to defend it but the Sword: 'tis the proper time to say any thing, when men have all things in their power.*

In the mean time you wou'd fain be nibbling at a parallel betwixt this Association, and that in the time of Queen Elizabeth. *But there is this small difference betwixt them, that the ends of the one are directly opposite to the other: one with the Queen's approbation, and conjunction, as head of it; the other without either the consent, or knowledge of the King, against whose Authority it is manifestly design'd. Therefore you doe well to have recourse to your last Evasion, that it was contriv'd by your Enemies, and shuffled into the Papers that were seiz'd: which yet you see the Nation is not so easy to believe as your own Jury; But the matter is not difficult, to find twelve men in* New-gate, *who wou'd acquit a Malefactour.*

I have one onely favour to desire of you at parting, that when you think of answering this Poem, *you wou'd employ the same Pens against it, who have combated with so much success against* Absalom and Achitophel*: for then you may assure your selves of a clear Victory, without the least reply. Raile at me abundantly; and, not to break a Custome, doe it without wit: By this method you will gain a considerable point, which is wholly to wave the answer of my Arguments. Never own the botome of your Principles, for fear they shou'd be Treason. Fall severely on the miscarriages of Government; for if scandal be not allow'd, you are no freeborn subjects. If God has not bless'd you with the Talent of Rhiming, make use of my poor Stock and wellcome: let your Verses run upon my feet: and for the utmost refuge of notorious Block-heads, reduc'd to the last extremity of sense, turn my own lines upon me, and in utter despaire of your own Satyre, make me Satyrize my self. Some of you have been driven to this Bay already; But above all the rest commend me to the Non-conformist Parson, who writ the* Whip and Key. *I am afraid it is not read so much as the Piece deserves, because the Bookseller is every week crying help at the end of his* Gazette, *to get it off. You see I am charitable enough to doe him a kindness, that it may be*

84 *of the one*] *of one 84 92*

publish'd as well as printed; and that so much skill in Hebrew Derivations, may not lie for Wast-paper in the Shop. Yet I half suspect he went no farther for his learning, than the Index of Hebrew Names and Etymologies, which is printed at the end of some English *Bibles. If* Achitophel *signify the Brother of a Fool, the Authour of that Poem will pass with his Readers for the next of kin. And perhaps 'tis the Relation that makes the kindness. Whatever the Verses are; buy 'em up I beseech you out of pity; for I hear the Conventicle is shut up, and the Brother of* Achitophel *out of service.*

Now Footmen, you know, have the generosity to make a Purse, for a Member of their Society, who has had his Livery pull'd over his Ears: and even Protestant Socks are bought up among you, out of veneration to the name. A Dissenter in Poetry from Sense and English, will make as good a Protestant Rhymer, as a Dissenter from the Church of England *a Protestant Parson. Besides, if you encourage a young Beginner, who knows but he may elevate his stile a little, above the vulgar Epithets of prophane, and sawcy Jack, and Atheistick Scribler, with which he treats me, when the fit of Enthusiasm is strong upon him: by which well-mannerd and charitable Expressions, I was certain of his Sect, before I knew his name. What wou'd you have more of a man? he has damn'd me in your Cause from* Genesis *to the* Revelations*: And has half the Texts of both the* Testaments *against me, if you will be so civil to your selves as to take him for your Interpreter; and not to take them for* Irish *Witnesses. After all, perhaps you will tell me, that you retain'd him onely for the opening of your Cause, and that your main Lawyer is yet behind. Now if it so happen he meet with no more reply than his Predecessours, you may either conclude, that I trust to the goodness of my Cause, or fear my Adversary, or disdain him, or what you please, for the short on't is, 'tis indifferent to your humble servant, whatever your Party says or thinks of him.*

THE MEDALL

A Satyre Against Sedition

Of all our Antick Sights, and Pageantry
Which *English* Ideots run in crowds to see,
The *Polish Medall* bears the prize alone:
A Monster, more the Favourite of the Town
Than either Fayrs or Theatres have shown.
Never did Art so well with Nature strive;
Nor ever Idol seem'd so much alive:

111 *is*] *are* 84 92

So like the Man; so golden to the sight,
So base within, so counterfeit and light.
One side is fill'd with Title and with Face;
And, lest the King shou'd want a regal Place,
On the reverse, a Tow'r the Town surveys;
O'er which our mounting Sun his beams displays.
The Word, pronounc'd aloud by Shrieval voice,
Lætamur, which, in *Polish*, is *rejoyce.*
The Day, Month, Year, to the great Act are join'd:
And a new Canting Holiday design'd.
Five daies he sate, for every cast and look;
Four more than God to finish *Adam* took.
But who can tell what Essence Angels are,
Or how long Heav'n was making *Lucifer*?
Oh, cou'd the Style that copy'd every grace,
And plough'd such furrows for an Eunuch face,
Cou'd it have form'd his ever-changing Will,
The various Piece had tir'd the Graver's Skill!
A Martial Heroe first, with early care,
Blown, like a Pigmee by the Winds, to war.
A beardless Chief, a Rebel, e'r a Man:
(So young his hatred to his Prince began.)
Next this, (How wildly will Ambition steer!)
A Vermin, wriggling in th' Usurper's Ear.
Bart'ring his venal wit for sums of gold
He cast himself into the Saint-like mould;
Groan'd, sigh'd and pray'd, while Godliness was gain;
The lowdest Bagpipe of the squeaking Train.
But, as 'tis hard to cheat a Juggler's Eyes,
His open lewdness he cou'd ne'er disguise.
There split the Saint: for Hypocritique Zeal
Allows no Sins but those it can conceal.
Whoring to Scandal gives too large a scope:
Saints must not trade; but they may interlope.
Th' ungodly Principle was all the same;
But a gross Cheat betrays his Partner's Game.
Besides, their pace was formal, grave and slack:
His nimble Wit outran the heavy Pack.
Yet still he found his Fortune at a stay;
Whole droves of Blockheads choaking up his way;

They took, but not rewarded, his advice;
Villain and Wit exact a double price.
Pow'r was his aym: but, thrown from that pretence,
The Wretch turn'd loyal in his own defence;
And Malice reconcil'd him to his Prince.
Him, in the anguish of his Soul he serv'd;
Rewarded faster still than he deserv'd.
Behold him now exalted into trust;
His Counsel's oft convenient, seldom just.
Ev'n in the most sincere advice he gave
He had a grudging still to be a Knave.
The Frauds he learnt in his Fanatique years
Made him uneasy in his lawfull gears.
At best as little honest as he cou'd:
And, like white Witches, mischievously good.
To his first byass, longingly he leans;
And *rather* wou'd be great by wicked means.
Thus, fram'd for ill, he loos'd our Triple hold;
(Advice unsafe, precipitous, and bold.)
From hence those tears! that *Ilium* of our woe!
Who helps a pow'rfull Friend, fore-arms a Foe.
What wonder if the Waves prevail so far
When He cut down the Banks that made the bar?
Seas follow but their Nature to invade;
But He by Art our native Strength betray'd.
So *Sampson* to his Foe his force confest;
And, to be shorn, lay slumb'ring on her breast.
But, when this fatal Counsel, found too late,
Expos'd its Authour to the publique hate;
When his just Sovereign, by no impious way,
Cou'd be seduc'd to Arbitrary sway;
Forsaken of that hope, he shifts the sayle;
Drives down the Current with a pop'lar gale;
And shews the Fiend confess'd, without a vaile.
He preaches to the Crowd, that Pow'r is lent,
But not convey'd to Kingly Government;
That Claimes successive bear no binding force;
That Coronation Oaths are things of course;
Maintains the Multitude can never err;
And sets the People in the Papal Chair.

The reason 's obvious; *Int'rest never lyes;*
The most have still their Int'rest in their eyes;
The pow'r is always theirs, and pow'r is ever wise.
Almighty Crowd, thou shorten'st all dispute;
Pow'r is thy Essence; Wit thy Attribute!
Nor Faith nor Reason make thee at a stay,
Thou leapst o'r all eternal truths, in thy *Pindarique* way!
Athens, no doubt, did righteously decide,
When *Phocion* and when *Socrates* were try'd:
As righteously they did those dooms repent;
Still they were wise, what ever way they went.
Crowds err not, though to both extremes they run;
To kill the Father, and recall the Son.
Some think the Fools were most, as times went then;
But now the World 's o'r stock'd with prudent men.
The common Cry is ev'n Religion's Test;
The *Turk*'s is, at *Constantinople*, best;
Idols in *India*, Popery at *Rome*;
And our own Worship onely true at home.
And true, but for the time, 'tis hard to know
How long we please it shall continue so.
This side to day, and that to morrow burns;
So all are God-a'mighties in their turns.
A Tempting Doctrine, plausible and new:
What Fools our Fathers were, if this be true!
Who, to destroy the seeds of Civil War,
Inherent right in Monarchs did declare:
And, that a lawfull Pow'r might never cease,
Secur'd Succession, to secure our Peace.
Thus, Property and Sovereign Sway, at last
In equal Balances were justly cast:
But this new *Jehu* spurs the hot mouth'd horse;
Instructs the Beast to know his native force;
To take the Bit between his teeth and fly
To the next headlong Steep of Anarchy.
Too happy *England*, if our good we knew;
Wou'd we possess the freedom we pursue!
The lavish Government can give no more:
Yet we repine; and plenty makes us poor.
God try'd us once; our Rebel-fathers fought;

He glutted 'em with all the pow'r they sought:
Till, master'd by their own usurping Brave,
The free-born Subject sunk into a Slave.
We loath our Manna, and we long for Quails;
Ah, what is man, when his own wish prevails!
How rash, how swift to plunge himself in ill;
Proud of his Pow'r, and boundless in his Will!
That Kings can doe no wrong we must believe:
None can they doe, and must they all receive?
Help Heaven! or sadly we shall see an hour,
When neither wrong nor right are in their pow'r!
Already they have lost their best defence,
The benefit of Laws, which they dispence.
No justice to their righteous Cause allow'd;
But baffled by an Arbitrary Crowd.
And Medalls grav'd, their Conquest to record,
The Stamp and Coyn of their adopted Lord.
The Man who laugh'd but once, to see an Ass
Mumbling to make the cross-grain'd Thistles pass;
Might laugh again, to see a Jury chaw
The prickles of unpalatable Law.
The Witnesses, that, Leech-like, liv'd on bloud,
Sucking for them were med'cinally good;
But, when they fasten'd on *their* fester'd Sore,
Then, Justice and Religion they forswore;
Their Mayden Oaths debauch'd into a Whore.
Thus Men are rais'd by Factions, and decry'd;
And Rogue and Saint distinguish'd by their Side.
They rack ev'n Scripture to confess their Cause;
And plead a Call to preach, in spight of Laws.
But that 's no news to the poor injur'd Page;
It has been us'd as ill in every Age:
And is constrain'd, with patience, all to take;
For what defence can Greek and Hebrew make?
Happy who can this talking Trumpet seize;
They make it speak whatever Sense they please!
'Twas fram'd, at first, our Oracle t' enquire;
But, since our Sects in prophecy grow higher,
The Text inspires not them; but they the Text inspire.
London, thou great *Emporium* of our Isle,

O, thou too bounteous, thou too fruitfull *Nile*,
How shall I praise or curse to thy desert!
Or separate thy sound, from thy corrupted part!
I call'd thee *Nile*; the parallel will stand:
Thy tydes of Wealth o'rflow the fattend Land;
Yet Monsters from thy large increase we find;
Engender'd on the Slyme thou leav'st behind.
Sedition has not wholly seiz'd on thee;
Thy nobler Parts are from infection free.
Of *Israel*'s Tribes thou hast a numerous band;
But still the *Canaanite* is in the Land.
Thy military Chiefs are brave and true;
Nor are thy disinchanted Burghers few.
The Head is loyal which thy Heart commands;
But what 's a Head with two such gouty Hands?
The wise and wealthy love the surest way;
And are content to thrive and to obey.
But Wisedom is to Sloath too great a Slave;
None are so busy as the Fool and Knave.
Those let me curse; what vengeance will they urge,
Whose Ordures neither Plague nor Fire can purge;
Nor sharp Experience can to duty bring,
Nor angry Heav'n, nor a forgiving King!
In Gospel phrase their Chapmen they betray:
Their Shops are Dens, the Buyer is their Prey.
The Knack of Trades is living on the Spoyl;
They boast, ev'n when each other they beguile.
Customes to steal is such a trivial thing,
That 'tis their Charter, to defraud their King.
All hands unite of every jarring Sect;
They cheat the Country first, and then infect.
They, for God's Cause their Monarchs dare dethrone;
And they'll be sure to make his Cause their own.
Whether the plotting Jesuite lay'd the plan
Of murth'ring Kings, or the *French* Puritan,
Our Sacrilegious Sects their Guides outgo;
And Kings and Kingly Pow'r wou'd murther too.
  What means their Trait'rous Combination less,

174 Engender'd on] *Noyes records a copy of 82 with* Enlivend by   179–80, 181–2 *transposed in Noyes's copy*   182 a] the *Noyes's copy*

Too plain t'evade, too shamefull to confess.
But Treason is not own'd when tis descry'd;
Successfull Crimes alone are justify'd.
The Men, who no Conspiracy wou'd find,
Who doubts, but had it taken, they had join'd.
Joyn'd, in a mutual Cov'nant of defence;
At first without, at last against their Prince.
If Sovereign Right by Sovereign Pow'r they scan,
The same bold Maxime holds in God and Man:
God were not safe, his Thunder cou'd they shun
He shou'd be forc'd to crown another Son.
Thus, when the Heir was from the Vineyard thrown,
The rich Possession was the Murth'rers own.
In vain to Sophistry they have recourse:
By proving theirs no Plot, they prove 'tis worse;
Unmask'd Rebellion, and audacious Force.
Which, though not Actual, yet all Eyes may see
'Tis working, in th' immediate Pow'r to be;
For, from pretended Grievances they rise,
First to dislike, and after to despise.
Then, *Cyclop*-like in humane Flesh to deal;
Chop up a Minister, at every meal:
Perhaps not wholly to melt down the King;
But clip his regal Rights within the Ring.
From thence, t'assume the pow'r of Peace and War;
And ease him by degrees of publique Care.
Yet, to consult his Dignity and Fame,
He shou'd have leave to exercise the Name;
And hold the Cards, while Commons play'd the game.
For what can Pow'r give more than Food and Drink,
To live at ease, and not be bound to think?
These are the cooler methods of their Crime;
But their hot Zealots think 'tis loss of time:
On utmost bounds of Loyalty they stand;
And grinn and whet like a *Croatian* Band;
That waits impatient for the last Command.
Thus Out-laws open Villany maintain:
They steal not, but in Squadrons scoure the Plain:
And, if their Pow'r the Passengers subdue;

237 their] the *84 92* 238 time: *84 92*: time; *82*

The Most have right, the wrong is in the Few.
Such impious Axiomes foolishly they show;
For, in some Soyles Republiques will not grow:
Our Temp'rate Isle will no extremes sustain,
Of pop'lar Sway, or Arbitrary Reign:
But slides between them both into the best;
Secure in freedom, in a Monarch blest.
And though the Clymate, vex't with various Winds,
Works through our yielding Bodies, on our Minds,
The wholsome Tempest purges what it breeds;
To recommend the Calmness that succeeds.
  But thou, the Pander of the Peoples hearts,
(O Crooked Soul, and Serpentine in Arts,)
Whose blandishments a Loyal Land have whor'd,
And broke the Bonds she plighted to her Lord;
What Curses on thy blasted Name will fall!
Which Age to Age their Legacy shall call;
For all must curse the Woes that must descend on all.
Religion thou hast none: thy *Mercury*
Has pass'd through every Sect, or theirs through Thee.
But what thou giv'st, that Venom still remains;
And the pox'd Nation feels Thee in their Brains.
What else inspires the Tongues, and swells the Breasts
Of all thy bellowing Renegado Priests,
That preach up Thee for God; dispence thy Laws;
And with thy Stumm ferment their fainting Cause?
Fresh Fumes of Madness raise; and toile and sweat
To make the formidable Cripple great.
Yet, shou'd thy Crimes succeed, shou'd lawless Pow'r
Compass those Ends thy greedy Hopes devour,
Thy Canting Friends thy Mortal Foes wou'd be;
Thy God and Theirs will never long agree.
For thine, (if thou hast any,) must be one
That lets the World and Humane-kind alone:
A jolly God, that passes hours too well
To promise Heav'n, or threaten us with Hell.
That unconcern'd can at Rebellion sit;
And Wink at Crimes he did himself commit.
A Tyrant theirs; the Heav'n their Priesthood paints
A Conventicle of gloomy sullen Saints;

A Heav'n, like *Bedlam*, slovenly and sad;
Fore-doom'd for Souls, with false Religion, mad.
  Without a Vision Poets can fore-show
What all but Fools, by common Sense may know:
If true Succession from our Isle shou'd fail,
And Crowds profane, with impious Arms prevail,
Not Thou, nor those thy Factious Arts ingage
Shall reap that Harvest of Rebellious Rage,
With which thou flatter'st thy decrepit Age.
The swelling Poyson of the sev'ral Sects,
Which wanting vent, the Nations Health infects
Shall burst its Bag; and fighting out their way
The various Venoms on each other prey.
The *Presbyter*, puft up with spiritual Pride,
Shall on the Necks of the lewd Nobles ride:
His Brethren damn, the Civil Pow'r defy;
And parcel out Republique Prelacy.
But short shall be his Reign: his rigid Yoke
And Tyrant Pow'r will puny Sects provoke;
And Frogs and Toads, and all the Tadpole Train
Will croak to Heav'n for help, from this devouring Crane.
The Cut-throat Sword and clamorous Gown shall jar,
In shareing their ill-gotten Spoiles of War:
Chiefs shall be grudg'd the part which they pretend;
Lords envy Lords, and Friends with every Friend
About their impious Merit shall contend.
The surly Commons shall respect deny;
And justle Peerage out with Property.
Their Gen'ral either shall his Trust betray,
And force the Crowd to Arbitrary sway;
Or they suspecting his ambitious Aym,
In hate of Kings shall cast anew the Frame;
And thrust out *Collatine* that bore their Name.
  Thus inborn Broyles the Factions wou'd ingage;
Or Wars of Exil'd Heirs, or Foreign Rage,
Till halting Vengeance overtook our Age:
And our wild Labours, wearied into Rest,
Reclin'd us on a rightfull Monarch's Breast.
        —*Pudet hæc opprobria, vobis*
Et dici potuisse, & non potuisse refelli.

323–4 *Added in 82, second issue*

PROLOGUE To His *ROYAL HIGHNESS* Upon His first appearance at the *DUKE'S THEATRE* since his Return from *SCOTLAND*

Spoken by Mr. Smith

IN those cold Regions which no Summers chear,
When brooding darkness covers half the year,
To hollow Caves the shivering Natives go;
Bears range abroad, and hunt in tracks of Snow:
But when the tedious Twilight wears away,
And Stars grow paler at th' approach of Day,
The longing Crowds to frozen Mountains run,
Happy who first can see the glimmering Sun!
The surly Salvage Off-spring disappear;
And curse the bright Successour of the Year.
Yet, though rough Bears in Covert seek defence,
White Foxes stay, with seeming Innocence:
That crafty kind with day-light can dispense.
Still we are throng'd so full with *Reynard*'s race,
That Loyal Subjects scarce can find a place:
Thus modest Truth is cast behind the Crowd:
Truth speaks too Low; Hypocrisie too Loud.
Let 'em be first, to flatter in success;
Duty can stay; but Guilt has need to press.
Once, when true Zeal the Sons of God did call,
To make their solemn show at Heaven's *White-hall*,
The fawning Devil appear'd among the rest,
And made as good a Courtier as the best.
The Friends of *Job*, who rail'd at him before,
Came Cap in hand when he had three times more.
Yet, late Repentance may, perhaps, be true;
Kings can forgive if Rebels can but sue:
A Tyrant's Pow'r in rigour is exprest:
The Father yearns in the true Prince's Breast.
We grant an O'regrown Whig no grace can mend;
But most are Babes, that know not they offend.

Prologue To His Royal Highness. Text from the first edition, 1682
30 O'regrown] Ore'grown *82*

The Crowd, to restless motion still enclin'd,
Are Clouds, that rack according to the Wind.
Driv'n by their Chiefs they storms of Hail-stones pour:
Then mourn, and soften to a silent showre.
O welcome to this much offending Land
The Prince that brings forgiveness in his hand!
Thus Angels on glad Messages appear:
Their first Salute commands us not to fear:
Thus Heav'n, that cou'd constrain us to obey,
(With rev'rence if we might presume to say,)
Seems to relax the rights of Sov'reign sway:
Permits to Man the choice of Good and Ill;
And makes us Happy by our own Free-will.

PROLOGUE To The Dutchess On Her Return from SCOTLAND

WHEN Factious Rage to cruel Exile, drove
The Queen of Beauty, and the Court of Love;
The Muses Droop'd, with their forsaken Arts,
And the sad *Cupids* broke their useless Darts.
Our fruitfull Plains to Wilds and Desarts turn'd,
Like *Edens* Face when banish'd Man it mourn'd:
Love was no more when Loyalty was gone,
The great Supporter of his Awfull Throne.
Love cou'd no longer after Beauty stay,
But wander'd Northward to the verge of day,
As if the Sun and He had lost their way.
But now th' Illustrious Nymph return'd again,
Brings every Grace triumphant in her Train:
The wondring *Nereids*, though they rais'd no storm,
Foreslow'd her passage to behold her form:
Some cry'd a *Venus*, some a *Thetis* past:
But this was not so fair, nor that so chast.
Far from her sight flew Faction, Strife and Pride:
And Envy did but look on her, and dy'd.

Prologue To The Dutchess. Text from the first edition, 1682

What e'er we suffer'd from our sullen Fate,
Her sight is purchas'd at an easy rate:
Three gloomy Years against this day were set:
But this one mighty Sum has clear'd the Debt.
Like *Joseph*'s Dream, but with a better doom;
The Famine past, the Plenty still to come.
For Her the weeping Heav'ns become serene,
For Her the Ground is clad in cheerfull green:
For Her the Nightingales are taught to sing,
And Nature has for her delay'd the Spring.
The Muse resumes her long-forgotten Lays,
And Love, restor'd, his Ancient Realm surveys;
Recalls our Beauties, and revives our Plays.
His Wast Dominions peoples once again,
And from Her presence dates his Second Reign.
But awfull Charms on her fair Forehead sit,
Dispensing what she never will admit.
Pleasing, yet cold, like *Cynthia*'s silver Beam,
The Peoples Wonder, and the Poets Theam.
Distemper'd Zeal, Sedition, canker'd Hate,
No more shall vex the Church, and tear the State;
No more shall Faction civil Discords move,
Or onely discords of too tender love:
Discord like that of Musicks various parts,
Discord that makes the harmony of Hearts,
Discord that onely this dispute shall bring,
Who best shall love the Duke, and serve the King.

MAC FLECKNOE

ALL humane things are subject to decay,
And, when Fate summons, Monarchs must obey:
This *Fleckno* found, who, like *Augustus*, young
Was call'd to Empire, and had govern'd long:
In Prose and Verse, was own'd, without dispute
Through all the Realms of *Non-sense*, absolute.
This aged Prince now flourishing in Peace,
And blest with issue of a large increase,
Worn out with business, did at length debate
To settle the succession of the State:
And pond'ring which of all his Sons was fit
To Reign, and wage immortal War with Wit;
Cry'd, 'tis resolv'd; for Nature pleads that He
Should onely rule, who most resembles me:
Sh—— alone my perfect image bears,
Mature in dullness from his tender years.
Sh—— alone, of all my Sons, is he
Who stands confirm'd in full stupidity.
The rest to some faint meaning make pretence,
But *Sh*—— never deviates into sense.
Some Beams of Wit on other souls may fall,
Strike through and make a lucid intervall;
But *Sh*——'s genuine night admits no ray,
His rising Fogs prevail upon the Day:
Besides his goodly Fabrick fills the eye,
And seems design'd for thoughtless Majesty:
Thoughtless as Monarch Oakes, that shade the plain,
And, spread in solemn state, supinely reign.
Heywood and *Shirley* were but Types of thee,
Thou last great Prophet of Tautology:
Even I, a dunce of more renown than they,
Was sent before but to prepare thy way;
And coursly clad in *Norwich* Drugget came

Mac Flecknoe. Text from Miscellany Poems, *1684 (reprinted 1692), collated with the first edition, 1682. See Commentary*

The title in 82 runs: Mac Flecknoe, or A Satyr upon the *True-Blew-Protestant* Poet, T. S. By the Author of *Absalom & Achitophel*

11 was] were *82*   12 War] Wars *82*   15 et passim *Sh*——] *Shad*—— *82*

33 And coursly clad in *Norwich* Drugget] I coursly Cloath'd in Drugget Russet, *82*

To teach the Nations in thy greater name.
My warbling Lute, the Lute I whilom strung
When to King *John* of *Portugal* I sung,
Was but the prelude to that glorious day,
When thou on silver *Thames* did'st cut thy way,
With well tim'd Oars before the Royal Barge,
Swell'd with the Pride of thy Celestial charge;
And big with Hymn, Commander of an Host,
The like was ne'er in *Epsom* Blankets tost.
Methinks I see the new *Arion* Sail,
The Lute still trembling underneath thy nail.
At thy well sharpned thumb from Shore to Shore
The Treble squeaks for fear, the Bases roar:
Echoes from *Pissing-Ally*, *Sh*—— call,
And *Sh*—— they resound from *A*—— *Hall*.
About thy boat the little Fishes throng,
As at the Morning Toast, that Floats along.
Sometimes as Prince of thy Harmonious band
Thou weild'st thy Papers in thy threshing hand.
St. *Andre*'s feet ne'er kept more equal time,
Not ev'n the feet of thy own *Psyche*'s rhime:
Though they in number as in sense excell;
So just, so like tautology they fell,
That, pale with envy, *Singleton* forswore
The Lute and Sword which he in Triumph bore,
And vow'd he ne'er would act *Villerius* more.
Here stopt the good old *Syre*; and wept for joy
In silent raptures of the hopefull boy.
All arguments, but most his Plays, perswade,
That for anointed dullness he was made.
  Close to the Walls which fair *Augusta* bind,
(The fair *Augusta* much to fears inclin'd)
An ancient fabrick, rais'd t'inform the sight,
There stood of yore, and *Barbican* it hight:
A watch Tower once; but now, so Fate ordains,
Of all the Pile an empty name remains.

37 the] a *82* 41 Commander] Commanders *82* 44 trembling] Trembles *82* 47 Echoes] Eccho *82* 48 *A*—— *Hall*] *Aston-Hall 82* 50 As . . . along] And gently waft the over all along *82* 52 Papers] Paper *82* 53 *Andre*'s] *Andrew's 82* 58 bore] wore *82* 64 to] by *82* 69 Of . . . name] An Empty name of all the Pile *82*

From its old Ruins Brothel-houses rise,
Scenes of lewd loves, and of polluted joys.
Where their vast Courts the Mother-Strumpets keep,
And, undisturb'd by Watch, in silence sleep.
Near these a Nursery erects its head,
Where Queens are form'd, and future Hero's bred;
Where unfledg'd Actors learn to laugh and cry,
Where infant Punks their tender Voices try,
And little *Maximins* the Gods defy.
Great *Fletcher* never treads in Buskins here,
Nor greater *Johnson* dares in Socks appear.
But gentle *Simkin* just reception finds
Amidst this Monument of vanisht minds:
Pure Clinches, the suburbian Muse affords;
And *Panton* waging harmless War with words.
Here *Fleckno*, as a place to Fame well known,
Ambitiously design'd his *Sh*——'s Throne.
For ancient *Decker* prophesi'd long since,
That in this Pile should Reign a mighty Prince,
Born for a scourge of Wit, and flayle of Sense:
To whom true dulness should some *Psyches* owe,
But Worlds of *Misers* from his pen should flow;
Humorists and *Hypocrites* it should produce,
Whole *Raymond* families, and Tribes of *Bruce*.
Now Empress *Fame* had publisht the Renown
Of *Sh*——'s Coronation through the Town.
Rows'd by report of Fame, the Nations meet,
From near *Bun-Hill*, and distant *Watling-street*.
No *Persian* Carpets spread th' Imperial way,
But scatter'd Limbs of mangled Poets lay:
From dusty shops neglected Authors come,
Martyrs of Pies, and Reliques of the Bum.
Much *Heywood*, *Shirly*, *Ogleby* there lay,
But loads of *Sh*—— almost choakt the way.
Bilk't *Stationers* for Yeomen stood prepar'd,
And *H*—— was Captain of the Guard.
The hoary Prince in Majesty appear'd,

71 loves] Love *82*   82 this Monument] these Monuments *82*   vanisht] Varnisht *82* (*some copies*)   88 Pile] Isle *82*   92 *Hypocrites*] *Editor's italics*   it] his Pen *82*   94 Renown *82*: renown, *84 92*   96 Fame] Pomp *82*   97 and] to *82*   98 Carpets] Carpet *82*   105 *H*——] *Herringman 82*

High on a Throne of his own Labours rear'd.
At his right hand our young *Ascanius* sate
Rome's other hope, and pillar of the State.
His Brows thick fogs, instead of glories, grace,
And lambent dullness plaid arround his face.
As *Hannibal* did to the Altars come,
Sworn by his *Syre* a mortal Foe to *Rome*;
So *Sh*—— swore, nor should his Vow bee vain,
That he till Death true dullness would maintain;
And in his father's Right, and Realms defence,
Ne'er to have peace with Wit, nor truce with Sense.
The King himself the sacred Unction made,
As King by Office, and as Priest by Trade:
In his sinister hand, instead of Ball,
He plac'd a mighty Mug of potent Ale;
Love's Kingdom to his right he did convey,
At once his Sceptre and his rule of Sway;
Whose righteous Lore the Prince had practis'd young,
And from whose Loyns recorded *Psyche* sprung.
His Temples last with Poppies were o'erspread,
That nodding seem'd to consecrate his head:
Just at that point of time, if Fame not lye,
On his left hand twelve reverend *Owls* did fly.
So *Romulus*, 'tis sung, by *Tyber*'s *Brook*,
Presage of Sway from twice six Vultures took.
Th' admiring throng loud acclamations make,
And Omens of his future Empire take.
The *Syre* then shook the honours of his head,
And from his brows damps of oblivion shed
Full on the filial dullness: long he stood,
Repelling from his Breast the raging God;
At length burst out in this prophetick mood:
  Heavens bless my Son, from *Ireland* let him reign
To farr *Barbadoes* on the Western main;
Of his Dominion may no end be known,

107 Throne] State *82* 108 sate *82 92*: sat *84* 110 glories, grace] Glories-Grace *82* 111 arround] about *82* 114 swore] Sworn *82* 115 till] to *82* 117 Ne'er . . . Sense] Wou'd bid defiance unto Wit and Sense *82* 121 He] Was *82* 122 *Love's Kingdom*] *Editor's italics* 124 Lore] Love *82* 126 Poppies] Poppey *82* 132 admiring] advancing *82* 133 his] the *82* 134 of] on *82* 135–6 shed . . . dullness:] Shed: . . . Dulness *82* 136 on] of *82* 139 Heavens] Heaven *82* 140 farr] fair *82*

And greater than his Father's be his Throne.
Beyond loves Kingdom let him stretch his Pen;
He paus'd, and all the people cry'd *Amen.*
Then thus, continu'd he, my Son advance
Still in new Impudence, new Ignorance.
Success let others teach, learn thou from me
Pangs without birth, and fruitless Industry.
Let *Virtuoso's* in five years be Writ;
Yet not one thought accuse thy toyl of wit.
Let gentle *George* in triumph tread the Stage,
Make *Dorimant* betray, and *Loveit* rage;
Let *Cully*, *Cockwood*, *Fopling*, charm the Pit,
And in their folly shew the Writers wit.
Yet still thy fools shall stand in thy defence,
And justifie their Author's want of sense.
Let 'em be all by thy own model made
Of dullness, and desire no foreign aid:
That they to future ages may be known,
Not Copies drawn, but Issue of thy own.
Nay let thy men of wit too be the same,
All full of thee, and differing but in name;
But let no alien *S—dl—y* interpose
To lard with wit thy hungry *Epsom* prose.
And when false flowers of *Rhetorick* thou would'st cull,
Trust Nature, do not labour to be dull;
But write thy best, and top; and in each line,
Sir *Formal*'s oratory will be thine.
Sir *Formal*, though unsought, attends thy quill,
And does thy *Northern Dedications* fill.
Nor let false friends seduce thy mind to fame,
By arrogating *Johnson*'s Hostile name.
Let Father *Fleckno* fire thy mind with praise,
And Uncle *Ogleby* thy envy raise.
Thou art my blood, where *Johnson* has no part;
What share have we in Nature or in Art?
Where did his wit on learning fix a brand,

143 Kingdom] Kingdoms *82* let him] may he *82* 148 and] a *82* 150 toyl] Soul *82* 151 in] with *82* 153 *Cully*,] Cully *82* 157 by] of *82* 159 future] after *82* 160 Issue] Issues *82* thy] thine *82* 162 full of] like to *82* 163 *S—dl—y*] *Sydney 82* 167 best, and top] best on th' top *82* 168 will] Wit *82* 170 does] doth *82* 175 has] hath *82* 177 on] or *82*

And rail at Arts he did not understand?
Where made he love in Prince *Nicander*'s vein,
Or swept the dust in *Psyche*'s humble strain?
Where sold he Bargains, Whip-stitch, kiss my Arse,
Promis'd a Play and dwindled to a Farce?
When did his Muse from *Fletcher* scenes purloin,
As thou whole *Eth'ridg* dost transfuse to thine?
But so transfus'd as Oyl on Waters flow,
His always floats above, thine sinks below.
This is thy Province, this thy wondrous way,
New Humours to invent for each new Play:
This is that boasted Byas of thy mind,
By which one way, to dullness, 'tis inclin'd.
Which makes thy writings lean on one side still,
And in all changes that way bends thy will.
Nor let thy mountain belly make pretence
Of likeness; thine 's a tympany of sense.
A Tun of Man in thy Large bulk is writ,
But sure thou'rt but a Kilderkin of wit.
Like mine thy gentle numbers feebly creep,
Thy Tragick Muse gives smiles, thy Comick sleep.
With whate'er gall thou sett'st thy self to write,
Thy inoffensive Satyrs never bite.
In thy fellonious heart, though Venom lies,
It does but touch thy *Irish* pen, and dyes.
Thy Genius calls thee not to purchase fame
In keen Iambicks, but mild Anagram:
Leave writing Plays, and chuse for thy command
Some peacefull Province in Acrostick Land.
There thou maist wings display and Altars raise,
And torture one poor word Ten thousand ways.
Or if thou would'st thy diff'rent talents suit,
Set thy own Songs, and sing them to thy lute.
He said, but his last words were scarcely heard,
For *Bruce* and *Longvil* had a *Trap* prepar'd,
And down they sent the yet declaiming Bard.

178 And] Or *82*   181 my] *mine 82*   183 When] Where *82*   *Fletcher*] *Fletchers 82*   185 Oyl] Oyls *82*   Waters] Water *82*   187 Province] Promise *82*   189 thy] the *82*   191 lean] lame *82*   192 changes] Charges *82*   196 thou'rt but] thou art *82*   199 sett'st] sets *82*   202 does] doth *82*   204 mild] wild *82*   209 talents] Talent *82*   210 own] one *82*   213 declaiming] declining *82*

Sinking he left his Drugget robe behind,
Born upwards by a subterranean wind.
The Mantle fell to the young Prophet's part,
With double portion of his Father's Art.

214 his] the *82* robe] Robes *82* 217 double] doubled *82*

THE SECOND PART OF
ABSALOM AND ACHITOPHEL
A POEM

—Si Quis tamen Hæc quoque, Si Quis
Captus Amore Leget—

SINCE Men like Beasts, each others Prey were made,
Since Trade began, and Priesthood grew a Trade,
Since Realms were form'd, none sure so curst as those
That madly their own Happiness oppose;
There Heaven it self, and Godlike Kings, in vain
Showr down the *Manna* of a gentle Reign;
While pamper'd Crowds to mad Sedition run,
And Monarchs by Indulgence are undone.
Thus *David*'s Clemency was fatal grown,
While wealthy Faction aw'd the wanting Throne.
For now their Sov'reigns Orders to contemn
Was held the Charter of *Jerusalem*,
His Rights t' invade, his Tributes to refuse,
A Privilege peculiar to the *Jews*;
As if from Heav'nly Call this Licence fell,
And *Jacob*'s Seed were chosen to rebell!
Achitophel with triumph sees his Crimes
Thus suited to the madness of the Times;
And *Absalom*, to make his hopes succeed,
Of Flattering Charms no longer stands in need;
While fond of Change, though ne'er so dearly bought,
Our Tribes out-strip the Youth's Ambitious Thought;
His swiftest Hopes with swifter Homage meet,
And crowd their servile Necks beneath his Feet.
Thus to his aid while pressing Tides repair,
He mounts and spreads his Streamers in the Air.
The Charms of Empire might his Youth mis-lead,
But what can our besotted *Israel* plead?
Sway'd by a Monarch whose serene Command,

The Second Part, &c. Text from the first edition, 1682 (A), collated with the second edition, 1682 (B)

9 Clemency was *B*: Goodness was e'en *A* 20 Flattering *B*: Flatterie's *A*

Seems half the Blessing of our promis'd Land,
Whose onely Grievance is excess of Ease,
Freedome our Pain, and Plenty our Disease!
Yet, as all Folly wou'd lay claim to Sense,
And Wickedness ne'er wanted a Pretence,
With Arguments they'd make their Treason good,
And righteous *David*'s self with Slanders load:
That Arts of foreign Sway he did affect,
And guilty *Jebusites* from Law protect,
Whose very Chiefs, convict, were never freed,
Nay, we have seen their Sacrificers bleed!
Accusers Infamy is urg'd in vain,
While in the bounds of Sense they did contain,
But soon they launcht into th' unfathom'd Tide,
And in the Depths they knew disdain'd to Ride,
For probable Discoveries to dispence,
Was thought below a pention'd Evidence;
Mere Truth was dull, nor suited with the port
Of pamper'd *Corah*, when advanc't to Court.
No less than Wonders now they will impose,
And Projects void of Grace or Sense disclose.
Such was the Charge on pious *Michal* brought,
Michal that ne'er was cruel e'en in thought,
The best of Queens, and most obedient Wife,
Impeach'd of curst Designs on *David*'s Life!
His Life, the Theam of her eternal Pray'r,
'Tis scarce so much his Guardian Angels Care.
Not Summer Morns such Mildness can disclose,
The *Hermon* Lilly, nor the *Sharon* Rose.
Neglecting each vain Pomp of Majesty,
Transported *Michal* feeds her thoughts on high.
She lives with Angels, and as Angels do,
Quits Heav'n sometimes to bless the World below.
Where cherisht by her Bounties plenteous Spring,
Reviving Widows smile, and Orphans sing.
Oh! when rebellious *Israel*'s Crimes at height,
Are threatned with her Lord's approaching Fate,
The Piety of *Michal* then remain
In Heav'ns Remembrance, and prolong his Reign.

33 as *B*: since *A*　　44 Ride, *A* (*some copies*) *B*: Ride. *A* (*some copies*)

Less Desolation did the Pest persue,
That from *Dan*'s limits to *Beersheba* slew,
Less fatal the repeated Wars of *Tyre*,
And less *Jerusalem*'s avenging Fire.
With gentler terrour these our State o'erran,
Than since our Evidencing Days began!
On every Cheek a pale Confusion sat,
Continu'd Fear beyond the worst of Fate!
Trust was no more, Art, Science useless made,
All occupations lost but *Corah*'s Trade.
Mean while a Guard on modest *Corah* wait,
If not for safety, needfull yet for State.
Well might he deem each Peer and Prince his Slave:
And Lord it o'er the Tribes which he could save:
E'en Vice in him was Vertue—what sad Fate
But for his Honesty had seiz'd our State?
And with what Tyranny had we been curst,
Had *Corah* never prov'd a Villain first?
T' have told his knowledge of th' Intrigue in gross
Had been alas to our Deponent's loss:
The travell'd Levite had th' Experience got,
To husband well, and make the best of's Plot;
And therefore like an Evidence of skill,
With wise Reserves secur'd his Pension still;
Nor quite of future Pow'r himself bereft,
But Limbo's large for unbelievers left.
And now his Writ such Reverence had got,
'Twas worse than Plotting to suspect his Plot.
Some were so well convinc't, they made no doubt,
Themselves to help the founder'd Swearers out.
Some had their Sense impos'd on by their Fear,
But more for Int'rest sake believe and swear:
E'en to that height with some the Frenzy grew,
They rag'd to find their danger not prove true.
Yet, than all these a viler Crew remain,
Who with *Achitophel* the Cry maintain;
Not urg'd by Fear, nor through misguided Sense,
(Blind Zeal, and starving Need had some pretence)
But for the *Good Old Cause* that did excite

80 safety, *B*: safety *A* 95 And *B*: For *A*

Th' Original Rebells Wiles, Revenge and Spight.
These raise the Plot to have the Scandal thrown
Upon the bright Successor of the Crown,
Whose Vertue with such wrongs they had persu'd,
As seem'd all hope of pardon to exclude.
Thus, while on private Ends their Zeal is built
The cheated Crowd applaud and share their Guilt.
  Such Practices as These, too gross to lye
Long unobserv'd by each discerning Eye,
The more judicious *Israelites* Unspell'd,
Though still the Charm the giddy Rabble held.
Ev'n *Absalom* amidst the dazling Beams
Of Empire, and Ambitions flattering Dreams,
Perceives the Plot (too foul to be excus'd)
To aid Designs, no less pernicious, us'd.
And (Filial Sense yet striving in his Breast)
Thus to *Achitophel* his Doubts exprest.
  Why are my Thoughts upon a Crown employ'd,
Which once obtain'd, can be but half Enjoy'd?
Not so when Virtue did my Arms require,
And to my Father's Wars I flew Intire.
My Regal Pow'r how will my Foes resent,
When I my Self have scarce my own Consent?
Give me a Son's unblemisht Truth again,
Or quench the Sparks of Duty that remain.
How slight to force a Throne that Legions guard
The Task to me; to prove Unjust, how hard!
And if th' imagin'd Guilt thus wound my Thought,
What will it when the tragick Scene is wrought?
Dire War must first be conjur'd from below,
The Realm we'd Rule we first must Overthrow.
And when the Civil Furies are on wing
That blind and undistinguisht Slaughters fling,
Who knows what impious chance may reach the King?
Oh! rather let me Perish in the Strife,
Than have my Crown the Price of *David*'s Life!
Or if the Tempest of the War he stand,
In Peace, some vile officious Villain's hand
His Soul's anointed Temple may invade,

118 held.] held, *A B*   134 Unjust, *B*: Unjust *A*   142 Oh! *B*: Or *A*

Or, prest by clamorous Crowds, my Self be made
His Murtherer; rebellious Crowds, whose Guilt
Shall dread his vengeance till his Bloud be spilt.
Which if my filial Tenderness oppose,
Since to the Empire by their Arms I rose,
Those very Arms on Me shall be employ'd,
A new Usurper Crown'd, and I Destroy'd:
The same Pretence of Publick Good will hold,
And new *Achitophels* be found, as bold
To urge the needfull Change, perhaps the Old.
 He said. The Statesman with a Smile replies,
(A smile that did his rising Spleen disguise.)
My thoughts presum'd our labours at an End,
And are we still with Conscience to contend?
Whose Want in Kings, as needfull is allow'd,
As 'tis for them to find it in the Crowd.
Far in the doubtfull Passage you are gone,
And onely can be Safe by pressing on.
The Crowns true Heir, a Prince severe, and wise,
Has view'd your Motions long with Jealous Eyes;
Your Persons Charms, your more prevailing Arts,
And mark't your Progress in the Peoples Hearts:
Whose Patience is th' effect of stinted Pow'r,
But treasures Vengeance for the fatal hour,
And if remote the Perill He can bring,
Your Present Danger 's greater from the King.
Let not a Parent's name deceive your Sense,
Nor trust the Father in a Jealous Prince!
Your trivial Faults if he could so resent,
To doom you little less than Banishment,
What rage must your Presumption Since inspire?
Against his Orders your Return from *Tyre*?
Nor onely so, but with a Pomp more high,
And open Court of Popularity,
The Factious Tribes—And this Reproof from Thee?
(The Prince replies) O Statesman's winding Skill,
They first Condemn that first Advis'd the Ill!
Illustrious Youth (returned *Achitophel*)
Misconstrue not the Words that mean you well.

166 Eyes;] Eyes: *A B*   168 Hearts:] Hearts, *A B*   170 hour, *B*: hour. *A*

The Course you steer I worthy Blame conclude,
But 'tis because you leave it Unpersu'd.
A Monarch's Crown with Fate surrounded lyes,
Who reach, lay hold on Death that miss the Prize.
Did you for this expose your self to Show,
And to the Crowd bow popluarly low?
For this your Glorious Progress next ordain,
With Chariots, Horsemen, and a numerous Train,
With Fame before you like the Morning Starr,
And Shouts of Joy saluting from afarr?
Oh from the Heights you've reach't but take a View,
Scarce leading *Lucifer* cou'd Fall like You!
And must I here my Ship-wrackt Arts bemoan?
Have I for this so oft made *Israel* groan!
Your single Interest with the Nation weigh'd,
And turn'd the Scale where your Desires were laid?
Ev'n when at Helm a Course so dang'rous mov'd
To Land your Hopes, as my Removal prov'd.
  I not dispute (the Royal Youth replyes)
The known Perfection of your Policies,
Nor in *Achitophel* yet grudge, or blame,
The Priviledge that Statesmen ever claim;
Who private Interest never yet persu'd,
But still pretended 'twas for Others good:
What Polititian yet e'er scap't his Fate,
Who saving his own Neck not sav'd the State?
From hence on ev'ry hum'rous Wind that veer'd,
With shifted Sayls a sev'ral Course you Steer'd.
What Form of Sway did *David* e'er persue
That seem'd like Absolute but sprung from You?
Who at your instance quasht each penal Law,
That kept dissenting factious *Jews* in awe;
And who suspends fixt Laws, may abrogate,
That done, form New, and so enslave the State.
Ev'n Property, whose Champion now you stand,
And seem for this the Idol of the Land,
Did ne'er sustain such Violence before,
As when your Counsel shut the Royal Store;
Advice, that Ruine to whole Tribes procur'd,

193 Train,] Train. *A B*   195 afarr?] afarr. *A B*

But secret kept till your own Banks secur'd.
Recount with this the tripple Cov'nant broke,
And *Israel* fitted for a Foreign Yoke;
Nor here your Counsels fatal Progress staid,
But sent our levied Pow'rs to *Pharaoh*'s Aid.
Hence *Tyre* and *Israel*, low in Ruins laid,
And *Egypt* once their Scorn, their common Terrour made.
Ev'n yet of such a Season we can dream,
When Royal Rights you made your darling Theam.
For Pow'r unlimited could Reasons draw,
And place Prerogative above the Law;
Which on your fall from Office grew Unjust,
The Laws made King, the King a Slave in Trust:
Whom with State-craft (to Int'rest onely True)
You now Accuse of ills contriv'd by You.
  To this Hell's Agent—Royal Youth fix here,
Let Int'rest be the Star by which I Steer.
Hence to repose your Trust in Me was wise,
Whose Int'rest most in your Advancement lies.
A Tye so firm as always will avail
When Friendship, Nature and Religion fail;
On ours the Safety of the Crowd depends,
Secure the Crowd and we obtain our Ends,
Whom I will cause so far our Guilt to share
Till they are made our Champions by their Fear.
What Opposition can your Rival bring,
While Sanhedrims are Jealous of the King?
His Strength as yet in *David*'s Friendship lies,
And what can *David*'s Self without Supplies?
Who with Exclusive Bills must now Dispence,
Debarr the Heir, or Starve in his Defence.
Conditions which our Elders ne'er will quit,
And *David*'s Justice never can admit.
Or forc't by Wants his Brother to betray,
To your Ambition next he clears the Way;
For if Succession once to Nought they bring,
Their next Advance removes the present King:
Persisting else his Senates to dissolve,
In equal Hazzard shall his Reign involve.

227 Yoke; *B*: Yoke, *A*

Our Tribes, whom *Pharaoh*'s Pow'r so much Alarms,
Shall rise without their Prince t' oppose his Arms;
Nor boots it on what Cause at first they Joyn,
Their Troops once up, are Tools for our Design.
At least such subtle Covenants shall be made,
Till Peace it self is War in Masquerade.
Associations of Mysterious Sense,
Against, but seeming for the King's Defence:
Ev'n on their Courts of Justice Fetters draw,
And from our Agents Muzzle up their Law.
By which, a Conquest if we fail to make,
'Tis a drawn Game at worst, and we secure our Stake.
He said, and for the dire Success depends
On various Sects, by common Guilt made Friends:
Whose Heads, though ne'er so diff'ring in their Creed,
I' th' point of Treason yet were well Agreed.
'Mongst these, Extorting *Ishban* first appears,
Persu'd b' a meager Troop of Bankrupt Heirs.
Blest times, when *Ishban*, He whose Occupation
So long has been to Cheat, Reformes the Nation!
Ishban of Conscience suited to his Trade,
As good a Saint as Usurer e'er made.
Yet *Mammon* has not so engrost him quite,
But *Belial* lays as large a Claim of Spight;
Who, for those Pardons from his Prince he draws,
Returns Reproaches, and cries up the Cause.
That Year in which the City he did sway,
He left Rebellion in a hopefull way.
Yet his Ambition once was found so bold,
To offer Talents of Extorted Gold;
Cou'd *David*'s Wants have So been brib'd to shame
And scandalize our Peerage with his Name;
For which, his dear Sedition he'd forswear,
And e'en turn Loyal to be made a Peer.
Next him, let Railing *Rabsheka* have place,
So full of Zeal He has no need of Grace;
A Saint that can both Flesh and Spirit use,
Alike haunt Conventicles and the Stews:
Of whom the Question difficult appears,

277 Friends:] Friends. *A B*

If most i' th' Preachers or the Bawds Arrears.
What Caution cou'd appear too much in Him
That keeps the Treasure of *Jerusalem*!
Let *David*'s Brother but approach the Town,
Double our Guards, (He cries) *We are undone.*
Protesting that He dares not Sleep in's Bed
Lest he shou'd rise next Morn without his Head.
  Next these, a Troop of buisy Spirits press,
Of little Fortunes, and of Conscience Less;
With them the Tribe, whose Luxury had drain'd
Their Banks, in former Sequestrations gain'd:
Who Rich and Great by past Rebellions grew,
And long to fish the troubled Streams anew.
Some future Hopes, some present Payment draws,
To Sell their Conscience and espouse the Cause,
Such Stipends those vile Hirelings best befit,
Priests without Grace, and Poets without Wit.
Shall that false *Hebronite* escape our Curse,
Judas that keeps the Rebells Pension-Purse;
Judas that pays the Treason-writers Fee,
Judas that well deserves his Namesake's Tree;
Who at *Jerusalem*'s own Gates Erects
His College for a Nursery of Sects.
Young Prophets with an early Care secures,
And with the Dung of his own Arts manures.
What have the Men of *Hebron* here to doe?
What part in *Israel*'s promis'd Land have you?
Here *Phaleg* the Lay *Hebronite* is come,
'Cause like the rest he could not live at Home;
Who from his own Possessions cou'd not drain
An *Omer* even of *Hebronitish* Grain,
Here Struts it like a Patriot, and talks high
Of Injur'd Subjects, alter'd Property:
An Emblem of that buzzing Insect Just,
That mounts the Wheell, and thinks she raises Dust.
Can dry Bones Live? or *Skeletons* produce
The Vital Warmth of Cuckoldizing Juice?
Slim *Phaleg* cou'd, and at the Table fed,
Return'd the gratefull product to the Bed.

315 Streams *B*: Waves *A*

A Waiting-man to Trav'ling Nobles chose,
He, his own Laws, wou'd Sawcily impose;
Till Bastinado'd back again he went,
To Learn those Manners he to Teach was sent.
Chastiz'd, he ought to have retreated Home,
But He reads Politicks to *Absalom.*
For never *Hebronite* though Kickt and Scorn'd,
To his own Country willingly return'd.
— But leaving famish'd *Phaleg* to be fed,
And to talk Treason for his daily Bread,
Let *Hebron*, nay let Hell produce a Man
So made for Mischief as *Ben-Jochanan.*
A *Jew* of Humble Parentage was He,
By Trade a Levite though of low Degree:
His Pride no higher than the Desk aspir'd,
But for the Drudgery of Priests was hir'd
To Reade and Pray in Linen Ephod brave,
And pick up single Sheckles from the Grave.
Married at last, and finding Charge come faster,
He cou'd not live by God, but chang'd his Master:
Inspir'd by Want, was made a Factious Tool,
They Got a Villain, and we lost a Fool.
Still Violent, whatever Cause he took,
But most against the Party he forsook,
For Renegadoes, who ne'er turn by halves,
Are bound in Conscience to be double Knaves.
So this Prose-Prophet took most monstrous Pains,
To let his Masters see he earn'd his Gains.
But as the Dev'l ows all his Imps a Shame,
He chose th' *Apostate* for his proper Theme;
With little Pains he made the Picture true,
And from Reflexion took the Rogue he drew.
A wondrous Work to prove the *Jewish* Nation,
In every Age a Murmuring Generation;
To trace 'em from their Infancy of Sinning,
And shew 'em Factious from their First Beginning.
To prove they cou'd Rebell, and Rail, and Mock,
Much to the Credit of the Chosen Flock;
A strong Authority which must Convince,
That Saints own no Allegiance to their Prince.

As 'tis a Leading-Card to make a Whore,
To prove her Mother had turn'd up before.
But, tell me, did the Drunken Patriarch Bless
The Son that shew'd his Father's Nakedness?
Such Thanks the present Church thy Pen will give,
Which proves Rebellion was so Primitive.
Must Ancient Failings be Examples made?
Then Murtherers from *Cain* may learn their Trade.
As thou the Heathen and the Saint hast drawn,
Methinks th' Apostate was the better man:
And thy hot *Father* (waving my respect)
Not of a mother Church, but of a Sect.
And Such he needs must be of thy Inditing,
This Comes of drinking Asses milk and writing.
If *Balack* should be cal'd to leave his place
(As profit is the loudest call of Grace,)
His Temple dispossess'd of one, wou'd be
Replenish'd with seven Devils more by thee.
Levi, thou art a load, I'll lay thee down,
And shew Rebellion bare, without a Gown;
Poor Slaves in metre, dull and adle-pated,
Who Rhime below ev'n *David*'s Psalms translated.
Some in my Speedy pace I must outrun,
As lame *Mephibosheth* the Wisard's Son:
To make quick way I'll Leap o'er heavy blocks,
Shun rotten *Uzza* as I wou'd the Pox;
And hasten *Og* and *Doeg* to rehearse,
Two Fools that Crutch their Feeble sense on Verse;
Who by my Muse, to all succeeding times,
Shall live in spight of their own Dogrell Rhimes.
Doeg, though without knowing how or why,
Made still a blund'ring kind of Melody;
Spurd boldly on, and Dash'd through Thick and Thin,
Through Sense and Non-sense, never out nor in;
Free from all meaning, whether good or bad,
And in one word, Heroically mad:
He was too warm on Picking-work to dwell,
But Faggotted his Notions as they fell,
And if they Rhim'd and Rattl'd all was well.

384 Patriarch *B*: Patriot *A* 388 made?] made, *A B* 389 Trade.] Trade? *A B*

Spightfull he is not, though he wrote a Satyr,
For still there goes some *thinking* to ill-Nature:
He needs no more than Birds and Beasts to think,
All his occasions are to eat and drink.
If he call Rogue and Rascal from a Garrat,
He means you no more Mischief than a Parat:
The words for Friend and Foe alike were made,
To Fetter 'em in Verse is all his Trade.
For Almonds he'll cry Whore to his own Mother:
And call Young *Absalom* King *David*'s Brother.
Let him be Gallows-Free by my consent,
And nothing suffer since he nothing meant;
Hanging Supposes humane Soul and reason,
This Animal's below committing Treason:
Shall he be hang'd who never cou'd Rebell?
That 's a preferment for *Achitophel.*
The Woman that Committed Buggary,
Was rightly Sentenc'd by the Law to die;
But 'twas hard Fate that to the Gallows led,
The Dog that never heard the Statute read.
Railing in other Men may be a crime,
But ought to pass for mere instinct in him;
Instinct he follows and no farther knows,
For to write Verse with him is to *Transprose.*
'Twere pity treason at his Door to lay,
Who makes Heaven's gate a Lock to its own Key:
Let him rayl on, let his invective muse
Have four and Twenty letters to abuse,
Which if he Jumbles to one line of Sense,
Indict him of a Capital Offence.
In Fire-works give him leave to vent his spight,
Those are the onely Serpents he can write;
The height of his Ambition is we know
But to be Master of a Puppet-show:
On that one Stage his works may yet appear,
And a months Harvest keeps him all the Year.
Now stop your noses Readers, all and some,
For here's a tun of Midnight-work to come,
Og from a Treason Tavern rowling home.

454 Puppet-show:] Puppet-show, *A B*

Round as a Globe, and Liquor'd ev'ry chink,
Goodly and Great he Sayls behind his Link;
With all this Bulk there 's nothing lost in *Og*
For ev'ry inch that is not Fool is Rogue:
A Monstrous mass of foul corrupted matter,
As all the Devils had spew'd to make the batter.
When wine has given him courage to Blaspheme,
He Curses God, but God before Curst him;
And if man cou'd have reason none has more,
That made his Paunch so rich and him so poor.
With wealth he was not trusted, for Heav'n knew
What 'twas of Old to pamper up a *Jew*;
To what wou'd he on Quail and Pheasant swell,
That ev'n on Tripe and Carrion cou'd rebell?
But though Heav'n made him poor, (with rev'rence speaking,)
He never was a Poet of God's making;
The Midwife laid her hand on his Thick Skull,
With this Prophetick blessing—*Be thou Dull;*
Drink, Swear and Roar, forbear no lew'd delight
Fit for thy Bulk, doe any thing but write:
Thou art of lasting Make like thoughtless men,
A strong Nativity—but for the Pen;
Eat Opium, mingle Arsenick in thy Drink,
Still thou mayst live avoiding Pen and Ink.
I see, I see 'tis Counsell given in vain,
For Treason botcht in Rhime will be thy bane;
Rhime is the Rock on which thou art to wreck,
'Tis fatal to thy Fame and to thy Neck:
Why shoud thy Metre good King *David* blast?
A Psalm of his will Surely be thy last.
Dar'st thou presume in verse to meet thy foes,
Thou whom the Penny Pamphlet foil'd in prose?
Doeg, whom God for Mankinds mirth has made,
O'er-tops thy tallent in thy very Trade;
Doeg to thee, thy paintings are so Course,
A Poet is, though he 's the Poets Horse.
A Double Noose thou on thy Neck dost pull,
For Writing Treason, and for Writing dull;
To die for Faction is a Common evil,

But to be hang'd for Non-sense is the Devil:
Had'st thou the Glories of thy King exprest,
Thy praises had been Satyr at the best;
But thou in Clumsy verse, unlickt, unpointed,
Hast Shamefully defi'd the Lord's Anointed:
I will not rake the Dunghill of thy Crimes,
For who wou'd reade thy Life that reads thy rhimes?
But of King *David*'s Foes be this the Doom,
May all be like the Young-man *Absalom*;
And for my Foes may this their Blessing be,
To talk like *Doeg*, and to Write like Thee.
  Achitophel each Rank, Degree and Age,
For various Ends neglects not to Engage;
The Wise and Rich for Purse and Counsell brought,
The Fools and Beggars for their Number sought:
Who yet not onely on the Town depends,
For Ev'n in Court the Faction had its Friends;
These thought the Places they possest too small,
And in their Hearts wisht Court and King to fall:
Whose Names the Muse disdaining holds i' th' Dark,
Thrust in the Villain Herd without a Mark;
With Parasites and Libell-spawning Imps,
Intriguing Fopps, dull Jesters and worse Pimps.
Disdain the Rascal Rabble to persue,
Their Sett Caballs are yet a viler Crew;
See where involv'd in Common Smoak they sit;
Some for our Mirth, some for our Satyr fit:
These Gloomy, Thoughtfull and on Mischief bent,
While those for mere good Fellowship frequent
Th' Appointed Clubb, can let Sedition pass,
Sense, Non-sence, anything t' employ the Glass;
And who believe in their dull honest Hearts,
The Rest talk Treason but to shew their Parts;
Who n'er had Wit or Will for Mischief yet,
But pleas'd to be reputed of a Set.
  But in the Sacred Annals of our Plot,
Industrious *AROD* never be forgot:
The Labours of this Midnight-Magistrate,
May Vie with *Corah*'s to preserve the State;

528 Clubb,] Clubb *A B*

In search of Arms, He fail'd not to lay hold
On War's most powerfull dang'rous Weapon, *GOLD.*
And last, to take from *Jebusites*, all Odds,
Their Altars pillag'd, stole their very Gods;
Oft wou'd He Cry, when Treasure He surpriz'd,
'Tis Baalish *Gold in* David's *Coyn Disguiz'd.*
Which to his House with *richer Relicts* came,
While Lumber Idols onely fed the Flame:
For our wise Rabble ne'er took pains t' enquire,
What 'twas he burnt, so 't made a rousing Fire.
With which our Elder was enricht no more
Than False *Gehazi* with the *Syrian*'s Store;
So Poor, that when our Choosing-Tribes were met,
Ev'n for his Stinking Votes He ran in Debt;
For Meat the Wicked, and as Authours think,
The Saints He Chous'd for His Electing Drink;
Thus, ev'ry Shift and subtle Method past,
And All to be no *Zaken* at the Last.
  Now, rais'd on *Tyre*'s sad Ruines, *Pharaoh*'s Pride
Soar'd high, his Legions threatning far and wide;
As when a battring Storm ingendred high,
By Winds upheld, hangs hov'ring in the Skye,
Is gaz'd upon by ev'ry trembling Swain,
This for his Vineyard fears, and that his Grain:
For blooming Plants, and Flow'rs new Opening, These
For Lambs ean'd lately, and far-lab'ring Bees;
To Guard his Stock each to the Gods does call,
Uncertain where the Fire-charg'd Clouds will Fall:
Ev'n so the doubtfull Nations watch his Arms,
With Terrour each expecting his Alarms.
Where *Judah*, where was now, thy Lyons Roar?
Thou onely cou'dst the Captive Lands restore;
But Thou, with inbred Broils, and Faction prest,
From *Egypt* needst a Guardian with the Rest.
Thy Prince from Sanhedrims no Trust allow'd,
Too much the Representers of the Crow'd,
Who for their own Defence give no Supply,
But what the Crowns Prerogatives must buy:
As if their Monarch's Rights to violate,
More needfull were than to preserve the State!

From present Dangers they divert their Care,
And all their Fears are of the Royal Heir;
Whom now the reigning Malice of his Foes
Unjudg'd wou'd Sentence, and e'er Crown'd, Depose.
Religion the Pretence, but their Decree
To barr his Reign, whate'er his Faith shall be!
By Sanhedrims, and clam'rous Crowds, thus prest
What passions rent the Righteous *David*'s Breast?
Who knows not how t' oppose, or to comply,
Unjust to Grant, and dangerous to Deny!
How near in this dark Juncture *Israel*'s Fate,
Whose Peace one sole Expedient cou'd create,
Which yet th' extremest Virtue did require,
Ev'n of that Prince whose Downfall they conspire!
His Absence *David* does with Tears advise,
T' appease their Rage, Undaunted He Complies;
Thus he who prodigal of Bloud, and Ease,
A Royal Life expos'd to Winds and Seas,
At once contending with the Waves and Fire,
And heading Danger in the Wars of *Tyre*,
Inglorious now forsakes his Native Sand,
And like an Exile quits the promis'd Land!
Our Monarch scarce from pressing Tears refrains,
And painfully his Royal State maintains,
Who now embracing on th' extremest Shore
Almost Revokes what he Injoyn'd before:
Concludes at last more Trust to be allow'd,
To Storms and Seas, than to the raging Crow'd!
Forbear, rash Muse, the parting Scene to draw,
With Silence charm'd as deep as theirs that saw!
Not onely our attending Nobles weep,
But hardy Saylers swell with Tears the Deep!
The Tyde restrain'd her Course, and more amaz'd,
The Twyn-Stars on the Royal Brothers gaz'd:
While this sole Fear—
Does Trouble to our suff'ring Heroe bring
Lest next the Popular Rage oppress the King!
Thus parting, each for th' others Danger griev'd,
The Shore the King, and Seas the Prince receiv'd.
Go injur'd Heroe while propitious Gales,

Soft as thy Consorts breath, inspire thy Sails;
Well may She trust her Beauties on a Flood,
Where thy Triumphant Fleets so oft have rode!
Safe on thy Breast reclin'd her Rest be deep,
Rockt like a *Nereid* by the Waves asleep;
While happiest Dreams her Fancy entertain,
And to *Elysian Fields* convert the Main!
Go injur'd Heroe while the Shores of *Tyre*,
At thy Approach so Silent shall admire,
Who on thy Thunder still their Thoughts imploy,
And greet thy Landing with a trembling Joy.
  On Heroes thus the Prophet's Fate is thrown,
Admir'd by ev'ry Nation but their Own;
Yet while our factious *Jews* his Worth deny,
Their Aking Conscience gives their Tongue the Lye.
Ev'n in the worst of Men the noblest Parts
Confess him, and he Triumphs in their Hearts,
Whom to his King the best Respects commend
Of Subject, Souldier, Kinsman, Prince and Friend;
All Sacred Names of most divine Esteem,
And to Perfection all sustain'd by Him,
Wise, Just and Constant, Courtly without Art,
Swift to discern and to reward Desert;
No Hour of His in fruitless Ease destroy'd,
But on the noblest Subjects still employ'd:
Whose steddy Soul ne'er learnt to Separate
Between his Monarch's Int'rest and the State,
But heaps those Blessings on the Royal Head,
Which He well knows must be on Subjects shed.
  On what Pretence cou'd then the Vulgar Rage
Against his Worth, and native Rights engage?
Religious Fears their Argument are made,
Religious Fears his Sacred Rights invade!
Of future Superstition They complain,
And *Jebusitick* Worship in His Reign;
With such Alarms his Foes the Crowd deceive,
With Dangers fright, which not Themselves believe.
  Since nothing can our Sacred Rites remove,
Whate'er the Faith of the Successour prove:

618 breath,] breath *A B*

Our *Jews* their Ark shall undisturb'd retain,
At least while their Religion is their Gain,
Who know by old Experience *Baal*'s Commands
Not onely claim'd their Conscience, but their Lands;
They grutch God's Tythes, how therefore shall they yield
An Idol full possession of the Field?
Grant such a Prince enthron'd, we must confess
The People's Suff'rings than that Monarch's less,
Who must to hard Conditions still be bound,
And for his Quiet with the Crowd compound;
Or shou'd his thoughts to Tyranny incline,
Where are the means to compass the design?
Our Crowns Revenues are too short a Store,
And Jealous Sanedrims wou'd give no more!
As vain our Fears of *Egypt*'s potent Aid,
Not so has *Pharaoh* learnt Ambition's Trade,
Nor ever with such Measures can comply,
As Shock the common Rules of Policy;
None dread like Him the Growth of *Israel*'s King,
And He alone sufficient Aids can bring;
Who knows that Prince to *Egypt* can give Law,
That on our Stubborn Tribes his Yoak cou'd draw,
At such profound Expence He has not stood,
Nor dy'd for this his Hands so deep in Blood;
Wou'd nere through Wrong and Right his Progress take,
Grudge his own Rest, and keep the World awake,
To fix a Lawless Prince on *Judah*'s Throne,
First to Invade our Rights, and then his Own;
His dear-gaind Conquests cheaply to despoil,
And Reap the Harvest of his Crimes and Toil.
We grant his Wealth Vast as our Ocean's Sand,
And Curse its Fatal Influence on our Land,
Which our Brib'd *Jews* so num'rously pertake,
That even an Host his Pensioners wou'd make;
From these Deceivers our Divisions spring,
Our Weakness, and the Growth of *Egypt*'s King;
These with pretended Friendship to the State,
Our Crowd's Suspition of their Prince Create,
Both pleas'd and frighten'd with the specious Cry,
To Guard their Sacred Rights and Property;

To Ruin, thus, the Chosen Flock are Sold,
While Wolves are tane for Guardians of the Fold;
Seduc'd by these, we groundlesly complain,
And loath the Manna of a gentle Reign:
Thus our Fore-fathers crooked Paths are trod,
We trust our Prince, no more then They their God.
But all in vain our Reasoning Prophets Preach,
To those whom sad Experience ne're cou'd Teach,
Who can commence new Broils in Bleeding Scars,
And fresh Remembrance of Intestine Wars;
When the same Houshold Mortal Foes did yeild,
And Brothers stain'd with Brothers Blood the Feild;
When Sons Curst Steel the Fathers Gore did Stain,
And Mothers Mourn'd for Sons by Fathers Slain!
When thick, as *Egypt*'s Locusts on the Sand,
Our Tribes lay Slaughter'd through the promis'd Land,
Whose few Survivers with worse Fate remain,
To drag the Bondage of a Tyrants Reign:
Which Scene of Woes, unknowing We renew,
And madly, ev'n those ills we Fear, persue;
While *Pharaoh* laughs at our Domestick Broils,
And safely crowds his Tents with Nations Spoils.
Yet our fierce Sanedrim in restless Rage,
Against our absent Heroe still engage,
And chiefly urge, (such did their frenzy prove),
The only Suit their Prince forbids to move,
Which till obtain'd, they cease Affairs of State,
And real Dangers wave, for groundless Hate.
Long *David*'s patience waits Relief to bring,
With all th' Indulgence of a lawful King,
Expecting till the troubled Waves wou'd cease,
But found the raging Billows still increase.
The Crowd, whose Insolence Forbearance swells,
While he forgives too far, almost Rebels.
At last his deep Resentments silence broke,
Th' Imperial Pallace shook, while thus he spoke,
  Then Justice wake, and Rigour take her time,
For Lo! Our Mercy is become our Crime.
While haulting Punishment her stroke delays,
Our Sov'reign Right, Heav'ns Sacred Trust, decays;

For whose support ev'n Subjects Interest calls,
Wo! to that Kingdom where the Monarch Falls.
That Prince who yields the least of Regal Sway,
So far his Peoples Freedom does Betray.
Right lives by Law, and Law subsists by Pow'r,
Disarm the Shepherd, Wolves the Flock devour.
Hard Lot of Empire o're a stubborn Race,
Which Heav'n it Self in vain has try'd with Grace!
When will our Reasons long-charm'd Eyes unclose,
And *Israel* judge between her Friends and Foes?
When shall we see expir'd Deceivers Sway,
And credit what our God and Monarchs say?
Dissembled Patriots brib'd with *Egypts* Gold,
Ev'n Sanedrims in blind Obedience hold;
Those Patriots Falshood in their Actions see,
And judge by the pernicious Fruit the Tree;
If ought for which so loudly they declaim
Religion, Laws, and Freedom were their Aim;
Our Senates in due Methods they had led,
T' avoid those Mischeifs which they seem'd to dread;
But first e're yet they propt the sinking State,
T' impeach and charge, as urg'd by private Hate;
Proves that they ne're beleiv'd the Fears they prest,
But Barb'rously destroy'd the Nations Rest!
O! Whither will ungovern'd Senates drive,
And to what Bounds licentious Votes arrive?
When their Injustice We are prest to share,
The Monarch urg'd t' exclude the lawful Heir;
Are Princes thus distinguish'd from the Crowd,
And this the Priviledge of Royal Blood?
But grant we shou'd Confirm the Wrongs they press,
His Sufferings yet were, than the Peoples, less;
Condem'd for Life the Murdring Sword to weild,
And on their Heirs entail a Bloody Feild:
Thus madly their own Freedom they betray,
And for th' Oppression which they fear, make way;
Succession fixt by Heav'n the Kingdoms Bar,
Which once dissolv'd, admits the Flood of War;
Wast, Rapine, Spoil, without th' Assault begin,
And our mad Tribes Supplant the Fence within.

Since then their Good they will not understand,
'Tis time to take the Monarchs Pow'r in hand;
Authority, and Force to joyn with Skill,
And save the Lunaticks against their Will.
The same rough Means that swage the Crowd, appease
Our Senates raging with the Crowds Disease.
Henceforth unbiass'd Measures let 'em draw
From no false Gloss, but Genuine Text of Law;
Nor urge those Crimes upon Religions score
Themselves so much, in *Jebusites* abhor.
Whom Laws convict (and only they) shall Bleed,
Nor Pharisees by Pharisees be Freed.
Impartial Justice from our Throne shall Shou'r,
All shall have Right, and We our Sov'reign Pow'r.
  He said, th' Attendants heard with awful Joy,
And glad Presages their fixt Thoughts employ;
From *Hebron* now the suffering Heir Return'd,
A Realm that long with Civil Discor'd Mourn'd;
Till his Approach, like some Arriving God,
Compos'd, and heal'd the place of his Aboad;
The Deluge checkt that to *Judea* spread,
And stopt Sedition at the Fountain's Head.
Thus in forgiving *David*'s Paths he drives,
And chas'd from *Israel*, *Israels* Peace contrives.
The Feild confest his Pow'r in Arms before,
And Seas proclaim'd his Tryumphs to the Shore;
As nobly has his Sway in *Hebron* shown,
How fit t' Inherit Godlike *Davids* Throne.
Through *Sion's*-Streets his glad Arrivals spread,
And Conscious Faction shrinks her snaky head;
His Train their Sufferings think o'repaid, to see
The Crowds Applause with Vertue once agree.
Success charms All, but Zeal for Worth distrest
A Virtue proper to the Brave and Best;
'Mongst whom was *Jothran*, *Jothran* always bent
To serve the Crown and Loyal by Descent.
Whose Constancy so Firm, and Conduct Just,
Deserv'd at once Two Royal Masters Trust;
Who *Tyre*'s proud Arms had Manfully withstood

804 Throne.] Throne? *A B*

On Seas, and gather'd Lawrels from the Flood;
Of Learning yet no Portion was deny'd,
Friend to the Muses, and the Muses Pride.
Nor can *Benaiah*'s Worth forgotten lie,
Of steddy Soul when Publick Storms were high;
Whose Conduct, while the *Moor* fierce Onsets made,
Secur'd at once our Honour and our Trade.
Such were the Chiefs, who most his Suff'rings mourn'd,
And view'd with silent Joy the Prince return'd;
While those that sought his Absence to Betray,
Press first their Nauseous False Respects to pay;
Him still th' officious Hypocrites Molest,
And with malicious Duty break his Rest.
  While real Transports thus his Friends Employ,
And Foes are Loud in their dissembled Joy,
His Tryumphs so resounded far and near,
Mist not his Young Ambitious Rival's Ear;
And as when joyful Hunters clam'rous Train,
Some Slumbring Lion Wakes in *Moab*'s Plain,
Who oft had forc'd the bold Assailants Yeild,
And scatter'd his Persuers through the Feild,
Disdaining, furls his Main, and tears the Ground,
His Eyes enflaming all the Desart Round,
With Roar of Seas directs his Chasers Way,
Provokes from far, and dares them to the Fray:
Such Rage storm'd now in *Absalom*'s fierce Breast,
Such Indignation his fir'd Eyes Confest;
Where now was the Instructer of his Pride?
Slept the Old Pilot in so rough a Tide?
Whose Wiles had from the happy Shore betray'd,
And thus on Shelves the cred'lous Youth convey'd.
In deep revolving Thoughts He weighs his State,
Secure of Craft, nor doubts to baffle Fate,
At least, if his storm'd Bark must go adrift,
To baulk his Charge, and for himself to shift,
In which his dextrous Wit had oft been shown,
And in the wreck of Kingdoms sav'd his own;
But now with more then Common Danger prest,

816 Flood;] Flood *A B* 829 *Editor's paragraph* 840 Fray:] Fray; *A B*
846 convey'd.] convey'd; *A B*

Of various Resolutions stands possest,
Perceives the Crowds unstable Zeal decay,
Least their Recanting Chief the Cause betray,
Who on a Father's Grace his Hopes may ground,
And for his Pardon with their Heads compound.
Him therefore, e're his Fortune slip her Time,
The Statesman Plots t' engage in some bold Crime
Past Pardon, whether to Attempt his Bed,
Or Threat with open Arms the Royal Head,
Or other daring Method, and Unjust,
That may confirm him in the Peoples Trust.
But failing thus t' ensnare him, nor secure
How long his foil'd Ambition may endure,
Plots next to lay him by, as past his Date,
And try some new Pretenders luckier Fate;
Whose Hopes with equal Toil he wou'd persue,
Nor cares what Claimer's Crownd, except the True.
Wake *Absalom*, approaching Ruin shun,
And see, O see, for whom thou art Undone!
How are thy Honours and thy Fame betray'd,
The Property of desp'rate Villains made?
Lost Pow'r and Conscious Fears their Crimes Create,
And Guilt in them was little less than Fate;
But why shou'dst Thou, from ev'ry Grievance free,
Forsake thy Vineyards for their Stormy Sea?
For Thee did *Canaan*'s Milk and Honey flow,
Love drest thy Bow'rs, and Lawrels sought thy Brow,
Preferment, Wealth and Pow'r thy Vassals were,
And of a Monarch all things but the Care.
Oh shou'd our Crimes, again, that Curse draw down,
And Rebel-Arms once more attempt the Crown,
Sure Ruin waits unhappy *Absalon*,
Alike by Conquest or Defeat undone;
Who cou'd relentless see such Youth and Charms,
Expire with wretched Fate in Impious Armes?
A Prince so form'd with Earth's, and Heav'ns Applause,
To Tryumph ore Crown'd Heads in *David*'s Cause:
Or grant him Victor, still his Hopes must fail,
Who, Conquering, wou'd not for himself prevail;

864 confirm *B*: secure *A*

The Faction whom He trusts for future Sway,
Him and the Publique wou'd alike Betray;
Amongst themselves divide the Captive State,
And found their *Hydra*-Empire in his Fate!
Thus having beat the Clouds with painful Flight,
The pitty'd Youth, with Scepters in his Sight,
(So have their Cruel Politicks Decreed,)
Must by that Crew that made him Guilty, Bleed!
For cou'd their Pride brook any Prince's Sway,
Whom but mild *David* wou'd they choose t' Obey?
Who once at such a gentle Reign Repine,
The Fall of Monarchy it self Design;
From Hate to That their Reformations spring,
And *David* not their Grievance, but the King.
Seiz'd now with pannick Fear the Faction lies,
Least this clear Truth strike *Absaloms* charm'd Eyes,
Least He percieve, from long Enchantment free,
What all, beside the flatter'd Youth, must see.
But whate're doubts his troubled Bosome swell,
Fair Carriage still became *Achitophel.*
Who now an envious Festival enstalls,
And to survey their Strength the Faction calls,
Which Fraud, Religious Worship too must Guild;
But oh how weakly does Sedition Build!
For Lo! the Royal Mandate Issues forth,
Dashing at once their Treason, Zeal, and Mirth!
So have I seen disastrous Chance Invade,
Where careful Emmits had their Forrage laid,
Whether fierce *Vulcan*'s Rage, the Furzy Plain
Had seiz'd, Engendred by some careless Swain;
Or swelling *Neptune* lawless Inroads made,
And to their Cell of Store his Flood convey'd;
The Common-Wealth broke up distracted go,
And in wild Hast their loaded Mates o'rethrow:
Ev'n so our scatter'd Guests confus'dly meet,
With Boil'd, Bak'd, Roast, all Justling in the Street;
Dejected all, and rufully dismai'd,
For *Sheckle* without Treat, or Treason paid.
   Seditions dark Eclipse now fainter shows,

898 Sight,] Sight; *A B*   916 Build!] Build? *A B*

More bright each Hour the Royal Plannet grows,
Of Force the Clouds of Envy to disperse,
In kind Conjunction of Assisting Stars.
Here lab'ring Muse those Glorious Chiefs relate,
That turn'd the doubtful Scale of *David*'s Fate;
The rest of that Illustrious Band rehearse,
Immortalliz'd in Lawrell'd *Asaph*'s Verse:
Hard task! yet will I not thy Flight recall,
View Heav'n and then enjoy thy glorious Fall.
First Write *Bezaliel*, whose Illustrious Name
Forestals our Praise, and gives his Poet Fame.
The *Kenites* Rocky Province his Command,
A barren Limb of Fertile *Canaans* Land;
Which for its gen'rous Natives yet cou'd be
Held Worthy such a President as He!
Bezaliel with each Grace, and Virtue Fraught,
Serene his Looks, Serene his Life and Thought,
On whom so largly Nature heapt her Store,
There scarce remain'd for Arts to give him more!
To Aid the Crown and State his greatest Zeal,
His Second Care that Service to Conceal;
Of Dues Observant, Firm in ev'ry Trust,
And to the Needy always more than Just.
Who Truth from specious falshood can divide,
Has all the Gown-mens Skill without their Pride;
Thus crown'd with worth from heights of honor won,
Sees all his Glories copyed in his Son,
Whose forward Fame should every Muse engage:
Whose Youth boasts skill denyed to others Age.
Men, Manners, Language, Books of noblest kind
Already are the Conquest of his Mind.
Whose Loyalty before its Date was prime;
Nor waited the dull course of rowling Time:
The Monster *Faction* early he dismaid,
And *David*'s Cause long since confest his Aid.
Brave *Abdael* o're the Prophets School was plac'd;
Abdael with all his Fathers Virtue grac'd;
A Heroe, who, while Stars look'd wondring down,

958 copyed] coppied *A* (*some copies*) 960 denyed] denied *A* (*some copies*)
963 its] it's *A* (*some copies*) 967 Prophets] Prophet's *A B*

Without one *Hebrew*'s Bloud restor'd the Crown.
That Praise was His; what therefore did remain
For following Chiefs, but boldly to maintain
That Crown restor'd; and in this Rank of Fame,
Brave *Abdael* with the First a place must claim.
Proceed illustrious, happy Chief, proceed,
Foreseize the Garlands for thy Brow decreed,
While th' inspir'd Tribe attend with noblest strein
To Register the Glories thou shalt gain:
For sure, the Dew shall *Gilboah*'s Hills forsake,
And *Jordan* mix his Streams with *Sodom*'s Lake;
Or Seas retir'd their secret Stores disclose,
And to the Sun their scaly Brood expose,
Or swell'd above the Clifts, their Billows raise,
Before the Muses leave their Patron's Praise.
  Eliab our next Labour does invite,
And hard the Task to doe *Eliab* right:
Long with the royal Wanderer he rov'd,
And firm in all the Turns of Fortune prov'd!
Such ancient Service and Desert so large,
Well claim'd the Royal Houshold for his Charge.
His Age with only one mild Heiress blest,
In all the Bloom of smiling Nature drest,
And blest again to see his Flow'r ally'd
To *David*'s Stock, and made young *Othniel*'s Bride!
The bright Restorer of his Father's Youth,
Devoted to a Son's and Subject's Truth:
Resolv'd to bear that prize of Duty home,
So bravely sought (while sought) by *Absalom*.
Ah Prince! th' illustrious Planet of thy Birth,
And thy more powerful Virtue guard thy worth;
That no *Achitophel* thy Ruine boast;
Israel too much in one such Wreck has lost.
  Ev'n Envy must consent to *Helon*'s Worth,
Whose Soul (though *Egypt* glories in his Birth)
Cou'd for our Captive-Ark its Zeal retain,
And *Pharaoh*'s Altars in their Pomp disdain:

975 happy] happy, *A* (*some copies*) *B*   985 does] do's *A* (*some copies*)   986 doe] do *A* (*some copies*)   988 Fortune] Fortunes *A B*   994 *Othniel*'s] *Othriel*'s *A B*   1004 though] tho' *A* (*some copies*)   1006 *Pharaoh*'s] *Pharoab*'s *A* (*some copies*)

To slight his Gods was small; with nobler pride,
He all th' Allurements of his Court defi'd.
Whom Profit nor Example cou'd betray,
But *Israel*'s Friend and true to *David*'s Sway.
What acts of favour in his Province fall;
On Merit he confers, and Freely all.
Our List of Nobles next let *Amri* grace,
Whose Merits claim'd the *Abethdins* high place;
Who, with a Loyalty that did excell,
Brought all th' endowments of *Achitophel*.
Sincere was *Amri*, and not only knew,
But *Israel*'s Sanctions into practice drew;
Our Laws, that did a boundless Ocean seem,
Were coasted all, and fathom'd all by Him.
No *Rabbin* speaks like him their mystick Sense,
So just, and with such Charms of Eloquence:
To whom the double Blessing does belong,
With *Moses* Inspiration, *Aaron*'s Tongue.
Than *Sheva*, none more loyal Zeal have shown,
Wakefull, as *Judah*'s Lion for the Crown,
Who for that Cause still combats in his Age,
For which his Youth with danger did engage.
In vain our factious Priests the Cant revive,
In vain seditious Scribes with Libels strive
T' enflame the Crow'd, while He with watchfull Eye
Observes, and shoots their Treasons as They fly.
Their weekly Frauds his keen Replies detect,
He undeceives more fast than they infect.
So *Moses* when the Pest on *Legions* prey'd,
Advanc'd his Signal and the Plague was stay'd.
Once more, my fainting Muse, thy Pinnions try,
And Strengths exhausted store let *Love* supply.
What Tribute, *Asaph*, shall we render Thee?
We'll crown thee with a Wreath from thy own Tree!
Thy Lawrell Grove no Envye's flash can blast.
The Song of *Asaph* shall for ever last!

1015 excell] excel *A* (*some copies*) 1024 *Moses*] *Mose*'s *A*: *Moses*'s *B* 1026 Wakefull] Wakeful *A* (*some copies*) Crown, *B*: Crown. *A* 1031 Crow'd] Crowd *A* (*some copies*) watchfull] watchful *A* (*some copies*) 1037 more,] more *A* (*some copies*) Muse,] Muse *A* (*some copies*) 1039 Tribute, *Asaph*,] Tribute *Asaph A* (*some copies*) 1041 blast.] blast; *B*

With wonder late Posterity shall dwell
On *Absalom*, and false *Achitophel*:
Thy streins shall be our slumbring Prophets dream,
And when our *Sion* Virgins sing, their Theam.
Our *Jubilees* shall with thy Verse be grac't,
The Song of *Asaph* shall for ever last!
How fierce his Satyr loos'd, restrain'd how tame,
How tender of th' offending *Young man*'s Fame!
How well his worth, and brave Adventures still'd,
Just to his Vertues, to his Errour mild.
No Page of thine that fears the strictest view,
But teems with just Reproof, or Praise, as due;
Not *Eden* cou'd a fairer Prospect yield,
All *Paradise* without one barren Field:
Whose Wit the Censure of his Foes has past,
The Song of *Asaph* shall for ever last!
What Praise for such rich Strains shall we allow?
What just Rewards the gratefull Crown bestow?
While Bees in Flow'rs rejoyce, and Flow'rs in Dew,
While Stars and Fountains to their Course are true;
While *Judah*'s Throne, and *Sion*'s Rock stand fast,
The Song of *Asaph* and the Fame shall last.
  Still *Hebrons* honour'd happy Soil Retains
Our Royal Heroes beauteous dear remains;
Who now sails off with Winds nor Wishes slack,
To bring his Suff'rings bright Companion back:
But e're such Transport can our sense employ
A bitter grief must poyson half our Joy;
Nor can our Coasts restor'd those Blessings see
Without a Bribe to envious Destiny!
Curs'd *Sodom*'s Doom for ever fix the Tyde
Where by inglorious Chance the Valiant dy'd.
Give not insulting *Askalon* to know,
Nor let *Gath*'s Daughters triumph in our Woe!
No Sailer with the News swell *Egypt*'s Pride,
By what inglorious Fate our Valiant dy'd!
Weep *Arnon*! *Jordan* weep thy Fountains dry

1045 streins] strains *A* (*some copies*) 1046 sing, *B*: sing *A* 1049 restrain'd how tame,] restrain'd, how tame *A* (*some copies*) *B* 1052 Errour] Error *A* (*some copies*) 1060 gratefull] grateful *A* (*some copies*) 1068 back:] back, *A B*

While *Sion*'s Rock dissolves for a Supply!
Calm were the Elements, Night's silence deep,
The Waves scarce murm'ring, and the Winds asleep;
Yet Fate for Ruine takes so still an hour,
And treacherous Sands the Princely Barque devour;
Then Death unworthy seiz'd a gen'rous Race,
To Virtues scandal, and the Stars disgrace!
Oh! had th' Indulgent Pow'rs vouchsaf't to yield,
Instead of faithless Shelves, a listed Field;
A listed Field of Heav'ns and *David*'s Foes,
Fierce as the Troops that did his Youth oppose,
Each Life had on his slaughter'd heap retir'd,
Not Tamely, and Unconqu'ring thus expir'd:
But Destiny is now their only Foe,
And dying, ev'n o're that they tryumph too;
With loud last Breaths their Master's 'Scape applaud,
Of whom kind Force cou'd scarce the Fates defraud;
Who for such Followers lost, O matchless Mind!
At his own Safety now almost repin'd!
Say Royal Sir, by all your Fame in Arms,
Your Praise in Peace, and by *Urania*'s Charms;
If all your Suff'rings past so nearly prest,
Or pierct with half so painful Grief your Breast?
  Thus some Diviner Muse her *Heroe* forms,
Not sooth'd with soft Delights, but tost in storms.
Not stretcht on Roses in the Myrtle Grove,
Nor Crowns his Days with Mirth, his Nights with Love,
But far remov'd in Thundring Camps is found,
His Slumbers short, his Bed the herbless Ground:
In Tasks of Danger always seen the First,
Feeds from the Hedg, and slakes with Ice his Thirst.
Long must his Patience strive with Fortunes Rage
And long, opposing Gods themselves engage,
Must see his Country Flame, his Friends destroy'd,
Before the promis'd Empire be enjoy'd,
Such Toil of Fate must build a Man of Fame,
And such, to *Israel*'s Crown, the God-like *David* came.

1094 o're] o'er *A* (*some copies*) tryumph] triumph *A* (*some copies*) 1095 'Scape] Scape *A* (*some copies*) 1103 *new paragraph in B* 1106 Love, *B*: Love *A*

What suddain Beams dispel the Clouds so fast,
Whose drenching Rains laid all our Vineyards waste?
The Spring so far behind her Course delay'd,
On th' Instant is in all her Bloom array'd,
The Winds breath low, the Element serene;
Yet mark what Motion in the Waves is seen!
Thronging and busie as *Hyblæan* Swarms,
Or stragled Souldiers Summon'd to their Arms.
See where the Princely Barque in loosest Pride,
With all her Guardian Fleet, Adorns the Tide!
High on her Deck the Royal Lovers stand,
Our Crimes to Pardon e're they toucht our Land.
Welcome to *Israel* and to *David*'s Breast!
Here all your Toils, here all your Suff'rings Rest.
This year did *Ziloah* Rule *Jerusalem*,
And boldly all Sedition's Syrges stem,
How e're incumbred with a viler Pair
Than *Ziph* or *Shimei* to assist the Chair;
Yet *Ziloah*'s loyal Labours so prevail'd
That Faction at the next Election fail'd,
When ev'n the common Cry did Justice Sound,
And Merrit by the Multitude was Crown'd:
With *David* then was *Israel*'s peace restor'd,
Crowds Mournd their Errour and Obey'd their Lord.

1117 fast,] fast! *A B*

RELIGIO LAICI

or A Laymans Faith

A POEM

Ornari res ipsa negat; contenta doceri

THE PREFACE

A POEM with so bold a Title, and a Name prefix'd, from which the handling of so serious a Subject wou'd not be expected, may reasonably oblige the Author, to say somewhat in defence both of himself, and of his undertaking. In the first place, if it be objected to me that being a *Layman*, I ought not to have concern'd my self with Speculations, which belong to the Profession of *Divinity*; I cou'd Answer, that perhaps, Laymen, with equal advantages of Parts and Knowledge, are not the most incompetent Judges of Sacred things; But in the due sense of my own weakness and want of Learning, I plead not this: I pretend not to make my self a Judge of Faith, in others, but onely to make a Confession of my own; I lay no unhallow'd hand upon the Ark; but wait on it, with the Reverence that becomes me at a distance: In the next place I will ingenuously confess, that the helps I have us'd in this small Treatise, were many of them taken from the Works of our own Reverend Divines of the Church of *England*; so that the Weapons with which I Combat Irreligion, are already Consecrated; though I suppose they may be taken down as lawfully as the Sword of *Goliah* was by *David*, when they are to be employed for the common Cause, against the Enemies of Piety. I intend not by this to intitle them to any of my errours; which, yet, I hope are only those of Charity to Mankind; and such as my *own* Charity has caus'd me to commit, that of *others* may more easily excuse. Being naturally inclin'd to Scepticism in Philosophy, I have no reason to impose my Opinions, in a Subject which is above it: But whatever they are, I submit them with all reverence to my Mother Church, accounting them no further mine, than as they are Authoriz'd, or at least, uncondemn'd by her. And, indeed, to secure my self on this side, I have us'd the necessary Pre-

Religio Laici. Text from the first edition, 1682 (82a), collated with the second edition, 1682 (82b), and the third, 1683

The Preface. 13 ingenuously] ingeniously *82b*

caution, of showing this Paper before it was Publish'd to a judicious and learned Friend, a Man indefatigably zealous in the service of the Church and State: and whose Writings, have highly deserv'd of both. He was pleas'd to approve the body of the Discourse, and I hope he is more my Friend, than to do it out of Complaisance: 'Tis true he had too good a tast to like it all; and amongst some other faults recommended to my second view, what I have written, perhaps too boldly on St. *Athanasius*: which he advised me wholy to omit. I am sensible enough that I had done more *prudently* to have follow'd his opinion: But then I could not have satisfied my self, that I had done honestly not to have written what was my own. It has always been my *thought*, that Heathens, who never did, nor without Miracle cou'd hear of the name of Christ were yet in a possibility of Salvation. Neither will it enter easily into my belief, that before the coming of our Saviour, the whole World, excepting only the Jewish Nation, shou'd lye under the inevitable necessity of everlasting Punishment, for want of that Revelation, which was confin'd to so small a spot of ground as that of *Palæstine*. Among the Sons of *Noah* we read of one onely who was accurs'd; and if a blessing in the ripeness of time was reserv'd for *Japhet*, (of whose Progeny we are,) it seems unaccountable to me, why so many Generations of the same Offspring, as preceeded our Saviour in the Flesh, shou'd be all involv'd in one common condemnation, and yet that their Posterity shou'd be Intitled to the hopes of Salvation: As if a Bill of Exclusion had passed only on the Fathers, which debar'd not the Sons from their Succession. Or that so many Ages had been *deliver'd over* to Hell, and so many *reserv'd* for Heaven, and that the Devil had the first choice, and God the next. Truly I am apt to think, that the revealed Religion which was taught by *Noah* to all his Sons, might continue for some Ages in the whole Posterity. That afterwards it was included wholly in the Family of *Sem* is manifest: but when the Progenies of *Cham* and *Japhet* swarm'd into Colonies, and those Colonies were subdivided into many others; in process of time their Descendants lost by little and little the Primitive and Purer Rites of Divine Worship, retaining onely the notion of one Deity; to which succeeding Generations added others: (for Men took their Degrees in those Ages from Conquerours to Gods.) Revelation being thus Eclipsed to almost all Mankind, the light of Nature as the next in Dignity was substituted; and that is it which St. *Paul* concludes to be the Rule of the Heathens; and by which they are hereafter to be judg'd. If my supposition be true, then the consequence which I have assum'd in my Poem may be also true; namely, that Deism, or the

Principles of Natural Worship, are onely the faint remnants or dying flames of reveal'd Religion in the Posterity of *Noah*: And that our Modern Philosophers, nay and some of our Philosophising Divines have too much exalted the faculties of our Souls, when they have maintain'd that by their force, mankind has been able to find out that there is one Supream Agent or Intellectual Being which we call God: that Praise and Prayer are his due Worship; and the rest of those deducements, which I am confident are the remote effects of Revelation, and unatainable by our Discourse, I mean as simply considerd, and without the benefit of Divine Illumination. So that we have not lifted up our selves to God, by the weak Pinions of our Reason, but he has been pleasd to descend to us: and what *Socrates* said of him, what *Plato* writ, and the rest of the Heathen Philosophers of several Nations, is all no more than the Twilight of Revelation, after the Sun of it was set in the Race of *Noah*. That there is some thing above us, some Principle of *motion*, our Reason can apprehend, though it cannot discover what it is, by its own Vertue. And indeed 'tis very improbable, that we, who by the strength of our faculties cannot enter into the knowledg of any *Beeing*, not so much as of our *own*, should be able to find out by them, that Supream Nature, which we cannot otherwise define, than by saying it is Infinite; as if Infinite were definable, or Infinity a Subject for our narrow understanding. They who wou'd prove Religion by Reason, do but weaken the cause which they endeavour to support: 'tis to take away the Pillars from our Faith, and to prop it onely with a twig: 'tis to design a Tower like that of *Babel*, which if it were possible (as it is not) to reach Heaven, would come to nothing by the confusion of the Workmen. For every man is Building a several way; impotently conceipted of his own Model, and his own Materials: Reason is always striving, and always at a loss, and of necessity it must so come to pass, while 'tis exercis'd about that which is not its proper object. Let us be content at last, to know God, by his own Methods; at least so much of him, as he is pleas'd to reveal to us, in the sacred Scriptures; to apprehend them to be the word of God, is all our Reason has to do; for all beyond it is the work of Faith, which is the Seal of Heaven impress'd upon our humane understanding.

And now for what concerns the Holy Bishop *Athanasius*, the Preface of whose Creed seems inconsistent with my opinion; which is, That Heathens may possibly be sav'd; in the first place I desire it may be consider'd that it is the Preface onely, not the Creed it self, which, (till

97 its proper] its own proper *82b*

I am better inform'd) is of too hard a digestion for my Charity. 'Tis not that I am ignorant how many several Texts of Scripture seemingly support that Cause; but neither am I ignorant how all those Texts may receive a kinder, and more mollified Interpretation. Every man who is read in Church History, knows *that* Belief was drawn up after a long contestation with *Arrius*, concerning the Divinity of our Blessed Saviour, and his being one Substance with the Father; and that thus compild, it was sent abroad among the Christian Churches, as a kind of Test, which whosoever took, was look'd on as an Orthodox Believer. 'Tis manifest from hence, that the Heathen part of the Empire was not concerned in it: for its business was not to distinguish betwixt Pagans and Christians, but betwixt Heriticks and true Believers. This, well consider'd, takes off the heavy weight of Censure, which I wou'd willingly avoid from so venerable a Man; for if this Proportion, *whosoever will be sav'd*, be restrained onely, to those to whom it was intended, and for whom it was compos'd, I mean the Christians; then the Anathema, reaches not the Heathens, who had never heard of Christ, and were nothing interessed in that dispute. After all, I am far from blaming even that Prefatory addition to the Creed, and as far from cavilling at the continuation of it in the Liturgy of the Church; where on the days appointed, 'tis publickly read: For I suppose there is the same reason for it now, in opposition to the Socinians, as there was then against the Arrians; the one being a Heresy, which seems to have been refin'd out of the other; and with how much more plausibility of Reason it combats our Religion, with so much more caution to be avoided: and therefore the prudence of our Church is to be commended which has interpos'd her Authority for the recommendation of this Creed. Yet to such as are grounded in the true belief, those explanatory Creeds, the *Nicene* and this of *Athanasius* might perhaps be spar'd: for what is supernatural, will always be a mystery in spight of Exposition: and for my own part the plain Apostles Creed, is most sutable to my weak understanding; as the simplest diet is the most easy of Digestion.

I have dwelt longer on this Subject than I intended; and longer than, perhaps, I ought; for having laid down, as my Foundation, that the Scripture is a Rule; that in all things needfull to Salvation, it is clear, sufficient, and ordain'd by God Almighty for that purpose, I have left my self no right to interpret obscure places, such as concern the possibility of eternal happiness to Heathens: because whatsoever is obscure is concluded not necessary to be known.

But, by asserting the Scripture to be the Canon of our Faith, I have unavoidably created to my self two sorts of Enemies: The Papists indeed, more directly, because they have kept the Scripture from us, what they cou'd; and have reserv'd to themselves a right of Interpreting what they have deliver'd under the pretence of Infalibility: and the Fanaticks more collaterally, because they have assum'd what amounts to an Infalibility, in the private Spirit: and have detorted those Texts of Scripture, which are not necessary to Salvation, to the damnable uses of Sedition, disturbance and destruction of the Civil Government. To begin with the Papists, and to speak freely, I think them the less dangerous (at least in appearance) to our present State; for not onely the Penal Laws are in Force against them, and their number is contemptible; but also their Peerage and Commons are excluded from Parliaments, and consequently those Laws in no probability of being Repeal'd. A General and Uninterrupted Plot of their Clergy, ever since the Reformation, I suppose all Protestants believe. For 'tis not reasonable to think but that so many of their Orders, as were outed from their fat possessions, wou'd endeavour a reentrance against those whom they account Hereticks. As for the late design, Mr. *Colemans* Letters, for ought I know are the best Evidence; and what they discover, without wyre-drawing their Sence, or malicious Glosses, all Men of reason conclude credible. If there be any thing more than this requir'd of me, I must believe it as well as I am able, in spight of the Witnesses, and out of a decent conformity to the Votes of Parliament: For I suppose the Fanaticks will not allow the private Spirit in this Case: Here the Infallibility is at least in one part of the Government; and our understandings as well as our wills are represented. But to return to the Roman Catholicks, how can we be secure from the practice of Jesuited Papists in that Religion? For not two or three of that Order, as some of them would impose upon us, but almost the whole Body of them are of opinion, that their Infallible Master has a right over Kings, not onely in Spirituals but Temporals. Not to name *Mariana*, *Bellarmine*, *Emanuel Sa*, *Molina*, *Santarel*, *Simancha*, and at the least twenty others of Foreign Countries; we can produce of our own Nation, *Campian*, and *Doleman* or *Parsons*, besides many are nam'd whom I have not read, who all of them attest this Doctrine, that the Pope can Depose and give away the Right of any Sovereign Prince, *si vel paulum deflexerit*, if he shall never so little Warpe: but if he once comes to be Excommunicated, then the Bond of obedience is taken off from Subjects; and they may and ought to drive him like another *Nebuchadnezzar*, *ex hominum Christianorum Dominatu*, from exercising Dominion over Christians: and to this they are bound by virtue of Divine Precept, and by all the tyes of Conscience under no less Penalty than Damnation. If they answer me (as a Learned Priest has lately Written,) that this Doctrine of the Jesuits is not *de fide*, and that consequently they are not oblig'd by it, they must pardon me, if I think they have said nothing to the purpose; for 'tis a Maxim in their Church, where Points of Faith are not decided, and that Doctors are of contrary opinions, they may follow which part they please; but more safely the most receiv'd and most Authoriz'd. And their Champion *Bellarmine* has told the World, in his Apology, that the King of *England* is a Vassal to the Pope, *ratione directi Dominii*, and that he holds in Villanage of his Roman Landlord. Which is no new claim put in for *England*. Our Chronicles are his Authentique Witnesses, that, King *John* was depos'd by the same Plea, and *Philip Augustus* admitted Tenant. And which makes the more for *Bellarmine*, the French King was again ejected when our King submitted to the Church, and the Crown receiv'd under the sordid Condition of a Vassalage.

'Tis not sufficient for the more moderate and well-meaning Papists, (of which I doubt not there are many) to produce the Evidences of their Loyalty to the late King, and to declare their Innocency in this Plot; I will grant their behaviour in the first, to have been as Loyal and as brave as they desire; and will be willing to hold them excus'd as to the second, (I mean when it comes to my turn, and after my betters; for 'tis a madness to be sober alone, while the Nation continues Drunk:) but that saying of their Father *Cres:* is still running in my head, that they may be dispens'd with in their Obedience to an Heretick Prince, while the necessity of the times shall oblige them to it: (for that (as another of them tells us,) is onely the effect of Christian Prudence) but when once they shall get power to shake him off, an Heretick is no lawful King, and consequently to rise against him is no Rebellion. I should be glad therefore, that they wou'd follow the advice which was charitably given them by a Reverend Prelate of our Church; namely, that they would joyn in a publick Act of disowning and detesting those Jesuitick Principles; and subscribe to all Doctrines which deny the Popes Authority of Deposing Kings, and releasing Subjects from their Oath of Allegiance: to which I shou'd think they might easily be induc'd, if it be true that this present Pope has condemn'd the Doctrine of King-killing (a Thesis of the Jesuites) amongst others *ex Cathedra* (as they call it) or in open consistory.

Leaving them, therefore, in so fair a way (if they please themselves) of satisfying all reasonable Men, of their sincerity and good meaning to the Government, I shall make bold to consider that other extream of our Religion, I mean the Fanaticks, or Schismaticks, of the English Church. Since the Bible has been Translated into our Tongue, they have us'd it so, as if their business was not to be sav'd but to be damnd by its Contents. If we consider onely them, better had it been for the English Nation, that it had still remain'd in the original Greek and Hebrew, or at least in the honest Latine of St. *Jerome*, than that several Texts in it, should have been prevaricated to the destruction of that Government, which put it into so ungrateful hands.

How many Heresies the first Translation of *Tyndal* produced in few years, let my Lord *Herbert*'s History of *Henry* the Eighth inform you; Insomuch that for the gross errours in it, and the great mischiefs it occasion'd, a Sentence pass'd on the first Edition of the Bible, too shamefull almost to be repeated. After the short Reign of *Edward* the Sixth (who had continued to carry on the Reformation, on other principles than it was begun) every one knows that not onely the chief promoters of that work, but many others, whose Consciences wou'd not dispence with Popery, were forc'd, for fear of persecution, to change Climates: from whence returning at the beginning of Queen *Elizabeth*'s Reign, many of them who had been in *France*, and at *Geneva*, brought back the rigid opinions and imperious discipline of *Calvin*, to graffe upon our Reformation. Which, though they cunningly conceal'd at first, (as well knowing how nauseously that Drug wou'd go down in a lawfull Monarchy, which was prescrib'd for a rebellious Common-wealth) yet they always kept it in reserve; and were never wanting to themselves either in Court or Parliament, when either they had any prospect of a numerous Party of Fanatique Members in the one, or the encouragement of any Favourite in the other, whose Covetousness was gaping at the Patrimony of the Church. They who will consult the Works of our venerable *Hooker*, or the account of his Life, or more particularly the Letter written to him on this Subject, by *George Cranmer*, may see by what gradations they proceeded; from the dislike of Cap and Surplice, the very next step was Admonitions to the Parliament against the whole Government Ecclesiastical: then came out Volumes in English and Latin in defence of their Tenets: and immediately, practices were set on foot to erect their Discipline without Authority. Those not succeeding, Satyre and Rayling was the next: And *Martin Mar-Prelate* (the *Marvel* of those times) was the first Presbyterian Scribler, who sanctify'd Libels and Scurrility to the use of the Good Old Cause. Which was done

231 had it] it had *82b*

(says my Authour) upon this account; that (their serious Treatises having been fully answered and refuted) they might compass by rayling what they had lost by reasoning; and when their Cause was sunk in Court and Parliament, they might at least hedge in a stake amongst the Rabble: for to their ignorance all things are Wit which are abusive; but if Church and State were made the Theme, then the Doctoral Degree of Wit was to be taken at *Billingsgate*: even the most Saintlike of the Party, though they durst not excuse this contempt and villifying of the Government, yet were pleas'd, and grin'd at it with a pious smile; and call'd it a judgment of God against the Hierarchy. Thus Sectaries, we may see, were born with teeth, foul-mouth'd and scurrilous from their Infancy: and if Spiritual Pride, Venome, Violence, Contempt of Superiours and Slander had been the marks of Orthodox Belief; the Presbytery and the rest of our Schismaticks, which are their Spawn, were always the most visible Church in the Christian World.

'Tis true, the Government was too strong at that time for a Rebellion; but to shew what proficiency they had made in *Calvin*'s School, even *Then* their mouths water'd at it: for two of their gifted Brotherhood (*Hacket* and *Coppinger*) as the Story tells us, got up into a Pease-Cart, and harangued the People, to dispose them to an insurrection, and to establish their Discipline by force: so that however it comes about, that now they celebrate Queen *Elizabeth*'s Birth-night, as that of their Saint and Patroness; yet then they were for doing the work of the Lord by Arms against her; and in all probability, they wanted but a Fanatique Lord Mayor and two Sheriffs of their Party to have compass'd it.

Our venerable *Hooker*, after many Admonitions which he had given them, toward the end of his Preface, breaks out into this Prophetick speech. "*There is in every one of these Considerations most just cause to fear,* "*lest our hastiness to embrace a thing of so perilous Consequence* (meaning the "Presbyterian Discipline) *should cause Postery to feel those Evils, which as yet* "*are more easy for us to prevent, than they would be for them to remedy.*

How fatally this *Cassandra* has foretold we know too well by sad experience: the Seeds were sown in the time of Queen *Elizabeth*, the bloudy Harvest ripened in the Reign of King *Charles* the Martyr: and because all the Sheaves could not be carried off without shedding some of the loose Grains, another Crop is too like to follow; nay I fear 'tis unavoidable if the Conventiclers be permitted still to scatter.

283 *Then 82a (second issue) 82b 83*: then *82a (first issue)* 295–6 (meaning . . . Discipline)] *italics in 82a (first issue)*

A man may be suffer'd to quote an Adversary to our Religion, when he speaks Truth: and 'tis the observation of *Meimbourg* in his History of Calvinism, that where-ever that Discipline was planted and embrac'd, Rebellion, Civil War and Misery attended it. And how indeed should it happen otherwise? Reformation of Church and State has always been the ground of our Divisions in *England.* While we were Papists, our Holy Father rid us, by pretending authority out of the Scriptures to depose Princes, when we shook off his Authority, the Sectaries furnish'd themselves with the same Weapons, and out of the same Magazine, the Bible. So that the Scriptures, which are in themselves the greatest security of Governours, as commanding express obedience to them, are now turn'd to their destruction; and never since the Reformation has there wanted a Text of their interpreting to authorize a Rebel. And 'tis to be noted by the way, that the Doctrines of King-killing and Deposing, which have been taken up onely by the worst Party of the Papists, the most frontless Flatterers of the Pope's Authority, have been espous'd, defended and are still maintain'd by the whole Body of Nonconformists and Republicans. 'Tis but dubbing themselves the People of God, which 'tis the interest of their Preachers to tell them they are, and their own interest to believe; and after that, they cannot dip into the Bible, but one Text or another will turn up for their purpose: If they are under Persecution (as they call it,) then that is a mark of their Election; if they flourish, then God works Miracles for their Deliverance, and the Saints are to possess the Earth.

They may think themselves to be too roughly handled in this Paper; but I who know best how far I could have gone on this Subject, must be bold to tell them they are spar'd: though at the same time I am not ignorant that they interpret the mildness of a Writer to them, as they do the mercy of the Government; in the one they think it Fear, and conclude it Weakness in the other. The best way for them to confute me, is, as I before advis'd the Papists, to disclaim their Principles, and renounce their Practices. We shall all be glad to think them true Englishmen when they obey the King, and true Protestants when they conform to the Church Discipline.

It remains that I acquaint the Reader, that the Verses were written for an ingenious young Gentleman my Friend; upon his Translation of *The Critical History of the Old Testament*, compos'd by the learned Father

311–12 *after* Princes, *82a* (*first issue only*) *has* (a Doctrine which, though some Papists may reject, no Pope has hitherto deny'd, nor ever will,)   340 compos'd *82a* (*second issue*) *82b*: written *82a* (*first issue*) *83*

Simon: The Verses therefore are address'd to the Translatour of that Work, and the style of them is, what it ought to be, Epistolary.

If any one be so lamentable a Critique as to require the Smoothness, the Numbers and the Turn of Heroick Poetry in this Poem; I must tell him, that if he has not read *Horace*, I have studied him, and hope the style of his Epistles is not ill imitated here. The Expressions of a Poem, design'd purely for Instruction, ought to be Plain and Natural, and yet Majestick: for here the Poet is presum'd to be a kind of Law-giver, and those three qualities which I have nam'd are proper to the Legislative style. The Florid, Elevated and Figurative way is for the Passions; for Love and Hatred, Fear and Anger, are begotten in the Soul by shewing their Objects out of their true proportion; either greater than the Life, or less; but Instruction is to be given by shewing them what they naturally are. A Man is to be cheated into Passion, but to be reason'd into Truth.

RELIGIO LAICI

DIM, as the borrow'd beams of Moon and Stars
To *lonely*, *weary*, *wandring* Travellers,
Is *Reason* to the *Soul*: And as on high,
Those rowling Fires *discover* but the Sky
Not light us *here*; So *Reason*'s glimmering Ray
Was lent, not to *assure* our *doubtfull* way,
But *guide* us upward to a *better Day*.
And as those nightly Tapers disappear
When Day's bright Lord ascends our Hemisphere;
So pale grows *Reason* at *Religions* sight;
So *dyes*, and so *dissolves* in *Supernatural Light*.
Some few, whose Lamp shone brighter, have been led
From Cause to Cause, to *Natures* secret head;
And found that *one first principle* must be:
But *what*, or *who*, that *UNIVERSAL HE*;
Whether some *Soul* incompassing this Ball
Unmade, *unmov'd*; yet *making*, *moving All*;
Or various *Atoms* interfering Dance
Leapt into *Form*, (the Noble work of *Chance*;)

Religio Laici. 18 *Atoms*] *Atom's*, *82a 82b 83*

Or this great *All* was from *Eternity*;
Not ev'n the *Stagirite* himself could see;
And *Epicurus Guess'd* as well as He:
As *blindly grop'd* they for a *future State*;
As *rashly Judg'd* of *Providence* and *Fate*:

Opinions of the several Sects of Philosophers concerning the Summum Bonum.

But least of all could their Endeavours find
What most concern'd the good of Humane kind:
For *Happiness* was never to be found;
But vanish'd from 'em, like Enchanted ground.
One thought *Content* the Good to be enjoy'd:
This, every little *Accident* destroy'd:
The *wiser Madmen* did for *Vertue* toyl:
A Thorny, or at best a barren Soil:
In *Pleasure* some their glutton Souls would steep;
But found their Line too short, the Well too deep;
And leaky Vessels which no *Bliss* cou'd keep.
Thus, *anxious Thoughts* in *endless Circles* roul,
Without a *Centre* where to fix the *Soul*:
In this wilde Maze their vain Endeavours end.
How can the *less* the *Greater* comprehend?
Or *finite Reason* reach *Infinity*?
For what cou'd *Fathom GOD* were *more* than *He*.

Systeme of Deisme.

The *Deist* thinks he stands on firmer ground;
Cries ἕυρεκα: the mighty Secret's found:
God is that *Spring* of *Good*; *Supreme*, and *Best*;
We, made to *serve*, and in that Service *blest*;
If so, some *Rules* of Worship must be given,
Distributed alike to all by Heaven:
Else *God* were *partial*, and to *some* deny'd
The Means his Justice shou'd for *all* provide.
This *general Worship* is to *PRAISE*, and *PRAY*:
One part to *borrow* Blessings, one to *pay*:
And when frail Nature slides into *Offence*,
The *Sacrifice* for *Crimes* is *Penitence*.
Yet, since th' Effects of Providence, we find
Are variously dispens'd to Humane kind;
That *Vice Triumphs*, and *Vertue suffers* here,
(A Brand that Sovereign Justice cannot bear;)
Our Reason prompts us to a *future* State:
The *last Appeal* from *Fortune*, and from *Fate*:

Where God's all-righteous ways will be declar'd;
The *Bad* meet *Punishment*, the *Good*, *Reward*.
Thus Man by his own strength to Heaven wou'd soar: *Of Reveal'd Religion.*
And wou'd not be Oblig'd to God for more.
Vain, wretched Creature, how art thou misled
To think thy Wit these God-like Notions bred!
These Truths are not the product of thy Mind,
But dropt from Heaven, and of a Nobler kind.
Reveal'd Religion first inform'd thy Sight,
And *Reason* saw not, till *Faith* sprung the Light.
Hence all thy *Natural Worship* takes the *Source*:
'Tis *Revelation* what thou thinkst *Discourse.*
Else, how com'st *Thou* to see these truths so clear,
Which so obscure to *Heathens* did appear?
Not *Plato* these, nor *Aristotle* found:
Nor He whose Wisedom *Oracles* renown'd. *Socrates.*
Hast thou a Wit so deep, or so sublime,
Or canst thou lower dive, or higher climb?
Canst *Thou*, by *Reason*, more of *God-head* know
Than *Plutarch*, *Seneca*, or *Cicero*?
Those Gyant Wits, in happyer Ages born,
(When *Arms*, and *Arts* did *Greece* and *Rome* adorn)
Knew no such *Systeme*: no such Piles cou'd raise
Of *Natural Worship*, built on *Pray'r* and *Praise*,
To One sole GOD.
Nor did Remorse, to Expiate Sin, prescribe:
But slew their fellow Creatures for a Bribe:
The guiltless *Victim* groan'd for their Offence;
And *Cruelty*, and *Blood* was *Penitence.*
If *Sheep* and *Oxen* cou'd Attone for Men
Ah! at how cheap a rate the *Rich* might Sin!
And great Oppressours might Heavens Wrath beguile
By offering his own Creatures for a Spoil!
Dar'st thou, poor Worm, offend *Infinity*?
And must the Terms of Peace be given by *Thee*?
Then *Thou* art *Justice* in the *last Appeal*;
Thy easie God instructs Thee to *rebell*:
And, like a King remote, and weak, must take
What Satisfaction *Thou* art pleas'd to make.
But if there be a *Pow'r* too *Just*, and *strong*

To wink at *Crimes*, and bear unpunish'd *Wrong*;
Look humbly upward, see his Will disclose:
The *Forfeit* first, and then the *Fine* impose:
A *Mulct thy* Poverty cou'd never pay
Had not *Eternal Wisedom* found the way:
And with Cœlestial Wealth supply'd thy Store:
His Justice makes the *Fine*, *his Mercy* quits the *Score*.
See God descending in thy Humane Frame;
Th' *offended*, suff'ring in th' *Offenders* Name:
All thy Misdeeds to him imputed see,
And all his Righteousness devolv'd on thee.
  For granting we have Sin'd, and that th' offence
Of *Man*, is made against *Omnipotence*,
Some Price, that bears *proportion*, must be paid;
And *Infinite* with *Infinite* be weigh'd.
See then the *Deist lost: Remorse* for *Vice*,
Not paid, or *paid*, *inadequate* in price:
What farther means can *Reason* now direct,
Or what Relief from *humane Wit* expect?
That shews us *sick*; and sadly are we sure
Still to be *Sick*, till *Heav'n* reveal the *Cure*:
If then *Heaven*'s *Will* must needs be understood,
(Which must, if we want *Cure*, and *Heaven*, be *Good*)
Let all Records of *Will reveal'd* be shown;
With *Scripture*, all in equal ballance thrown,
And *our one Sacred Book* will be *That one*.
  Proof needs not here, for whether we compare
That Impious, Idle, Superstitious Ware
Of *Rites*, *Lustrations*, *Offerings*, (which before,
In various Ages, various Countries bore)
With *Christian Faith* and *Vertues*, we shall find
None answ'ring the great ends of humane kind
But *This one Rule of Life: That* shews us best
How *God* may be *appeas'd*, and *Mortals blest*.
Whether from length of *Time* its worth we draw,
The *World* is scarce more *Ancient* than the *Law*:
Heav'ns early Care prescrib'd for every Age;
First, in the *Soul*, and after, in the *Page*.
Or, whether more abstractedly we look,
Or on the *Writers*, or the *written Book*,

Whence, but from *Heav'n*, cou'd men unskill'd in Arts,
In several Ages born, in several parts,
Weave such *agreeing Truths*? or *how*, or *why*
Shou'd *all* conspire to cheat us with a *Lye*?
Unask'd their *Pains*, *ungratefull* their *Advice*,
Starving their *Gain*, and *Martyrdom* their *Price*.
If on the Book it self we cast our view,
Concurrent Heathens prove the Story *True*:
The *Doctrine*, *Miracles*; which must convince,
For *Heav'n* in *Them* appeals to *humane Sense*:
And though they *prove* not, they *Confirm* the Cause,
When what is *Taught* agrees with *Natures Laws*.
Then for the *Style*; *Majestick* and *Divine*,
It speaks no less than God in every Line:
Commanding words; whose *Force* is still the same
As the first *Fiat* that produc'd our Frame.
All Faiths *beside*, or did by *Arms* ascend;
Or *Sense* indulg'd has made *Mankind* their *Friend*:
This *onely* Doctrine does our *Lusts* oppose:
Unfed by Natures Soil, in which it grows;
Cross to our *Interests*, curbing Sense, and Sin;
Oppress'd without, and undermin'd within,
It thrives through pain; its own Tormentours tires;
And with a stubborn patience still aspires.
To what can *Reason* such Effects assign
Transcending *Nature*, but to *Laws Divine*?
Which in that Sacred Volume are contain'd;
Sufficient, clear, and for that use ordain'd.

Objection of the Deist.

But stay: the *Deist* here will urge anew,
No *Supernatural Worship* can be *True*:
Because a *general Law* is that alone
Which must to *all*, and every *where* be known:
A Style so large as not *this* Book can claim
Nor ought that bears *reveal'd* Religions *Name*.
'Tis said the sound of a *Messiah*'s *Birth*
Is gone through all the habitable Earth:
But still that Text must be confin'd alone
To what was *Then* inhabited, and known:
And what Provision cou'd from *thence* accrue
To *Indian* Souls, and Worlds discover'd *New*?

In other parts it helps, that Ages past,
The Scriptures there were *known*, and were *imbrac'd*,
Till Sin spread once again the Shades of Night:
What 's that to these who never *saw* the Light?

The Objection answer'd.

Of all Objections this indeed is chief
To startle Reason, stagger frail Belief:
We grant, 'tis true, that Heav'n from humane Sense
Has hid the secret paths of *Providence*:
But *boundless Wisedom, boundless Mercy*, may
Find ev'n for those *be-wildred* Souls, a *way*:
If from his *Nature Foes* may Pity claim,
Much more may *Strangers* who ne'er heard his *Name.*
And though *no Name* be for *Salvation* known,
But that of his *Eternal Sons* alone;
Who knows how far transcending Goodness can
Extend the *Merits* of *that Son* to *Man*?
Who knows what *Reasons* may his *Mercy* lead;
Or *Ignorance invincible* may plead?
Not onely *Charity* bids hope the *best*,
But *more* the great Apostle has exprest:
That, if the Gentiles, (whom no Law inspir'd,)
By Nature did what was by *Law requir'd;*
They, who the written Rule had never known,
Were to themselves both Rule and Law alone:
To Natures plain indictment they shall plead;
And, by their Conscience, be condemn'd or freed.
Most righteous Doom! because a *Rule reveal'd*
Is *none* to *Those*, from whom it was *conceal'd*.
Then those who follow'd *Reasons* Dictates right;
Liv'd up, and lifted high their *Natural Light*;
With *Socrates* may see their Maker's Face,
While Thousand *Rubrick-Martyrs* want a place.
Nor does it baulk my *Charity*, to find
Th' *Egyptian* Bishop of another mind:
For, though his *Creed Eternal Truth* contains,
'Tis hard for *Man* to doom to *endless pains*
All who believ'd not all, his Zeal requir'd;
Unless he first cou'd prove he was inspir'd.
Then let us either think he meant to say
This Faith, where *publish'd*, was the onely way;

Or else conclude that, *Arius* to confute,
The good old Man, too eager in dispute,
Flew high; and as his *Christian* Fury rose
Damn'd all for *Hereticks* who durst *oppose*.

Digression to the Translatour of Father Simon's *Critical History of the Old Testament.*

Thus far my Charity this path has try'd;
(A much unskilfull, but well meaning guide:)
Yet what they are, ev'n these crude thoughts were bred
By reading that, which better thou hast read,
Thy Matchless Author's work: which thou, my Friend,
By well translating better dost commend:
Those youthfull hours which, of thy Equals most
In *Toys* have *squander'd*, or in *Vice* have *lost*,
Those hours hast thou to Nobler use employ'd;
And the severe Delights of Truth enjoy'd.
Witness this weighty Book, in which appears
The crabbed Toil of many thoughtfull years,
Spent by thy Authour, in the Sifting Care
Of *Rabbins* old Sophisticated Ware
From Gold Divine; which he who well can sort
May afterwards make *Algebra* a Sport.
A Treasure, which if *Country-Curates* buy,
They *Junius*, and *Tremellius* may defy:
Save pains in various readings, and Translations;
And without *Hebrew* make most learn'd quotations.
A Work so full with various Learning fraught,
So nicely pondred, yet so strongly wrought,
As Natures height and Arts last hand requir'd:
As much as Man cou'd compass, uninspir'd.
Where we may see what *Errours* have been made
Both in the *Copiers* and *Translaters Trade*:
How *Jewish*, *Popish*, Interests have prevail'd,
And where *Infallibility* has *fail'd*.

For some, who have his secret meaning ghes'd,
Have found our Authour not too *much* a *Priest*:
For *Fashion-sake* he seems to have recourse
To *Pope*, and *Councils*, and *Traditions* force:
But he that *old* Traditions cou'd subdue,
Cou'd not but find the weakness of the *New*:
If *Scripture*, though deriv'd from *heav'nly birth*,

224 has] hath *83*

Has been but carelesly preserv'd on *Earth*;
If *God*'s *own People*, who of *God* before
Knew what we know, and had been promis'd more,
In fuller Terms, of Heaven's assisting Care,
And who did neither *Time*, nor *Study* spare
To keep this Book *untainted*, *unperplext*;
Let in gross *Errours* to corrupt the *Text*:
Omitted *paragraphs*, embroyl'd the *Sense*;
With vain *Traditions* stopt the gaping Fence,
Which every common hand pull'd up with ease:
What Safety from such *brushwood-helps* as these?
If *written words* from time are not secur'd,
How can we think have *oral Sounds* endur'd?
Which *thus* transmitted, if *one* Mouth has fail'd,
Immortal Lyes on *Ages* are intail'd:
And that some such have been, is prov'd too plain;
If we consider *Interest*, *Church*, and *Gain*.

Of the Infallibility of Tradition, in General.

Oh but says one, *Tradition* set aside,
Where can we hope for an *unerring Guid*?
For since th' *original* Scripture has been lost,
All Copies *disagreeing*, *maim'd* the *most*,
Or *Christian Faith* can have no *certain* ground,
Or *Truth* in *Church Tradition* must be found.

Such an *Omniscient* Church we wish indeed;
'Twere worth *Both Testaments*, and cast in the *Creed*:
But if *this Mother* be a *Guid* so sure,
As can all *doubts resolve*, all *truth secure*,
Then her *Infallibility*, as well
Where Copies are *corrupt*, or *lame*, can tell;
Restore *lost Canon* with as little pains,
As *truly explicate* what still *remains*:
Which yet no *Council* dare *pretend* to doe;
Unless like *Esdras*, they cou'd *write* it new:
Strange Confidence, still to *interpret* true,
Yet not be sure that all they have explain'd,
Is in the blest *Original* contain'd.
More Safe, and much more modest 'tis, to say
God wou'd not leave Mankind without a way:
And that the *Scriptures*, though not *every where*
Free from Corruption, or intire, or clear,

Are uncorrupt, sufficient, clear, intire,
In *all* things which our needfull *Faith* require.
If *others* in the *same Glass better* see
'Tis for *Themselves* they look, but not for *me*:
For *MY* Salvation must its Doom receive
Not from what *OTHERS*, but what *I* believe.

Objection in behalf of Tradition; urg'd by Father Simon.

Must *all Tradition* then be set aside?
This to affirm were Ignorance, or Pride.
Are there not many points, some needfull sure
To saving Faith, that Scripture leaves obscure?
Which every Sect will wrest a several way
(For what *one* Sect Interprets, *all* Sects *may*:)
We hold, and say we prove from Scripture plain,
That *Christ* is *GOD*; the bold *Socinian*
From the *same* Scripture urges he's but *MAN*.
Now what Appeal can end th' important Suit;
Both parts *talk* loudly, but the *Rule* is *mute*?
Shall I speak plain, and in a Nation free
Assume an honest *Layman's Liberty*?
I think (according to my little Skill,
To my own Mother-Church submitting still:)
That many have been sav'd, and many may,
Who never heard this Question brought in play.
Th' *unletter'd* Christian, who believes in *gross*,
Plods on to *Heaven*; and ne'er is at a loss:
For the *Streight-gate* wou'd be made *streighter* yet,
Were *none* admitted there but men of *Wit*.
The few, by Nature form'd, with Learning fraught,
Born to instruct, as others to be taught,
Must Study well the Sacred Page; and see
Which Doctrine, this, or that, does best agree
With the whole Tenour of the Work Divine:
And plainlyest points to Heaven's reveal'd Design:
Which Exposition flows from *genuine Sense*;
And which is *forc'd* by *Wit* and *Eloquence*.
Not that Traditions parts are useless here:
When general, old, disinteress'd and clear:
That Ancient Fathers thus expound the Page,
Gives *Truth* the reverend Majesty of *Age*:
Confirms its force, by biding every *Test*;

For best *Authority*'s next *Rules* are *best*.
And still the nearer to the Spring we go
More limpid, more unsoyl'd the Waters flow.
Thus, *first Traditions* were a proof alone;
Cou'd we be *certain* such they *were*, so *known*:
But since some Flaws in long descent may be,
They make not *Truth* but *Probability*.
Even *Arius* and *Pelagius* durst provoke
To what the *Centuries preceding* spoke.
Such difference is there in an oft-told Tale:
But Truth by its own Sinews will prevail.
Tradition written therefore more commends
Authority, than what from *Voice* descends:
And this, as perfect as its kind can be,
Rouls down to us the Sacred History:
Which, from the *Universal Church receiv'd*,
Is *try'd*, and *after*, for its *self* believ'd.

The Second Objection.

The partial *Papists* wou'd infer from hence
Their Church, in last resort, shou'd Judge the *Sense*.

Answer to the Objection.

But first they wou'd assume, with wondrous Art,
Themselves to be the *whole*, who are but *part*
Of that vast Frame, the Church; yet grant they were
The handers down, can they from thence infer
A right t' interpret? or wou'd they alone
Who brought the Present, claim it for their own?
The *Book*'s a *Common Largess* to *Mankind*;
Not more for *them*, than *every* Man design'd:
The *welcome News* is in the *Letter* found;
The *Carrier*'s not Commission'd to *expound*.
It *speaks* it *Self*, and what it does contain,
In all things *needfull* to be *known*, is *plain*.
In times o'ergrown with Rust and Ignorance,
A gainfull Trade their Clergy did advance:
When want of Learning kept the *Laymen* low,
And none but *Priests* were *Authoriz'd* to *know*:
When what small Knowledge was, in them did dwell;
And he a *God* who cou'd but *Reade* or *Spell*;
Then *Mother Church* did mightily prevail:
She parcel'd out the Bible by *retail*:

368 it *Self*] its *Self* 83

But still *expounded* what She *sold* or *gave*;
To keep it in *her Power* to *Damn* and *Save*:
Scripture was *scarce*, and as the Market went,
Poor *Laymen* took *Salvation* on *Content*;
As needy men take Money, good or bad:
God's Word they had not, but the *Priests* they had.
Yet, whate'er *false Conveyances* they made,
The *Lawyer* still was *certain* to be paid.
In those dark times they learn'd their knack so well,
That by long use they grew *Infallible*:
At last, a knowing Age began t' enquire
If *they* the *Book*, or *That* did *them* inspire:
And, making narrower search they found, thô late,
That what they thought the *Priest*'s, was *Their* Estate:
Taught by the *Will produc'd*, (the written Word)
How long they had been *cheated* on *Record*.
Then, every man who saw the Title fair,
Claim'd a Child's part, and put in for a Share:
Consulted Soberly his private good;
And sav'd himself as cheap as e'er he cou'd.
'Tis true, my Friend, (and far be Flattery hence)
This good had full as bad a Consequence:
The Book thus put in every vulgar hand,
Which each presum'd he best cou'd understand,
The *Common Rule* was made the *common Prey*;
And at the mercy of the *Rabble* lay.
The tender Page with horney Fists was gaul'd;
And he was gifted most that loudest baul'd:
The *Spirit* gave the *Doctoral Degree*:
And every member of a *Company*
Was of *his Trade*, and of the *Bible free*.
Plain *Truths* enough for needfull *use* they found;
But men wou'd still be itching to *expound*:
Each was ambitious of th' obscurest place,
No measure ta'n from *Knowledge*, all from *GRACE*.
Study and *Pains* were now no more their Care;
Texts were explain'd by *Fasting*, and by *Prayer*:
This was the Fruit the *private Spirit* brought;
Occasion'd by *great Zeal*, and *little Thought*.
While Crouds unlearn'd, with rude Devotion warm,

About the Sacred Viands buz and swarm,
The *Fly-blown Text* creates a *crawling Brood*;
And turns to *Maggots* what was meant for *Food.*
A Thousand daily Sects rise up, and dye;
A Thousand more the perish'd Race supply.
So all we make of Heavens discover'd Will
Is, not to have it, or to use it ill.
The Danger's much the same; on several Shelves
If *others* wreck *us*, or *we* wreck our *selves.*
  What then remains, but, waving each Extreme,
The Tides of Ignorance, and Pride to stem?
Neither so rich a Treasure to forgo;
Nor proudly seek beyond our pow'r to know:
Faith is not built on disquisitions vain;
The things we *must* believe, are *few*, and *plain*:
But since men *will* believe more than they *need*;
And every man will make *himself* a Creed:
In doubtfull questions 'tis the safest way
To learn what unsuspected Ancients say:
For 'tis not likely *we* shou'd higher Soar
In search of Heav'n, than *all the Church before*:
Nor can we be deceiv'd, unless we see
The *Scripture*, and the *Fathers disagree.*
If after all, they stand suspected still,
(For no man's Faith depends upon his Will;)
'Tis some Relief, that points not clearly known,
Without much hazard may be let alone:
And, after hearing what our Church can say,
If still our Reason runs another way,
That private Reason 'tis more Just to curb,
Than by Disputes the publick Peace disturb.
For points obscure are of small use to learn:
But *Common quiet* is *Mankind's concern.*
  Thus have I made my own Opinions clear:
Yet neither Praise expect, nor Censure fear:
And this unpolish'd, rugged Verse, I chose;
As fittest for Discourse, and nearest Prose:
For, while from *Sacred Truth* I do not swerve,
Tom Sternhold's, or *Tom Shadwell*'s *Rhimes* will serve.

456 *Shadwell's*] *Sha—ll's 82a (second issue) 82b 83*

PROLOGUE and EPILOGUE To the King and Queen

PROLOGUE TO THE King and Queen, AT THE OPENING OF Their THEATRE

Spoken by Mr. *Batterton*

SINCE Faction ebbs, and Rogues grow out of Fashion,
Their penny-Scribes take care t' inform the Nation,
How well men thrive in this or that Plantation.

How *Pensilvania*'s Air agrees with Quakers,
And *Carolina*'s with Associators:
Both e'en too good for Madmen and for Traitors.

Truth is, our Land with Saints is so run o'er,
And every Age produces such a store,
That now there's need of two *New-Englands* more.

What's this, you'll say, to Us and our Vocation?
Onely thus much, that we have left our Station,
And made this Theatre our new Plantation.

The Factious Natives never cou'd agree;
But aiming, as they call'd it, to be Free,
Those Play-house Whiggs set up for Property.

Some say they no Obedience paid of late;
But wou'd new Fears and Jealousies create;
Till topsy-turvy they had turn'd the State.

Plain Sense, without the Talent of Foretelling,
Might guess 'twou'd end in down-right knocks and quelling:
For seldome comes there better of Rebelling.

When Men will, needlesly, their Freedom barter
For Lawless Pow'r, sometimes they catch a Tartar:
(There's a damn'd word that rhimes to this call'd Charter.)

But, since the Victory with Us remains,
You shall be call'd to Twelve in all our Gains:
(If you'll not think us sawcy for our pains.)

Prologue and Epilogue. Text from the first edition, 1683

Old Men shall have good old Plays to delight 'em:
And you, fair Ladys and Gallants that slight 'em,
We'll treat with good new Plays; if our new Wits can
  write 'em.

We'll take no blundring Verse, no fustian Tumour,
No dribling Love, from this or that Presumer:
No dull fat Fool shamm'd on the Stage for humour.

For, faith, some of 'em such vile stuff have made,
As none but Fools or Fairies ever Play'd;
But 'twas, as Shopmen say, to force a Trade.

We've giv'n you Tragedies, all Sense defying:
And singing men, in wofull Metre dying;
This 'tis when heavy Lubbers will be flying.

All these disasters we well hope to weather;
We bring you none of our old Lumber hether:
Whigg Poets and Whigg Sheriffs may hang together.

EPILOGUE

Spoken by Mr. *Smith*

NEW Ministers, when first they get in place
Must have a care to Please; and that's our Case:
Some Laws for publick Welfare we design,
If You, the Power supreme, will please to joyn:
There are a sort of Pratlers in the Pit,
Who either have, or who pretend to Wit:
These noisie Sirs so loud their Parts rehearse,
That oft the Play is silenc'd by the Farce:
Let such be dumb, this Penalty to shun,
Each to be thought my Lady's Eldest Son.
But stay: methinks some Vizard Masque I see,
Cast out her Lure from the mid Gallery:
About her all the flutt'ring Sparks are rang'd;
The Noise continues though the Scene is chang'd:
Now growling, sputtring, wauling, such a clutter,
'Tis just like Puss defendant in a Gutter:
Fine Love no doubt, but e'er two days are o'er ye,
The Surgeon will be told a wofull story.

Let Vizard Masque her naked Face expose,
On pein of being thought to want a Nose:
Then for your Lacqueys, and your Train beside,
(By what e'er Name or Title dignify'd)
They roar so loud, you'd think behind the Stairs
Tom Dove, and all the Brotherhood of Bears:
They're grown a Nuisance, beyond all Disasters,
We've none so great but their unpaying Masters.
We beg you, Sirs, to beg your Men, that they
Wou'd please to give you leave to hear the Play.
Next, in the Play-house spare your pretious Lives;
Think, like good Christians, on your Bearns and Wives:
Think on your Souls; but by your lugging forth,
It seems you know how little they are Worth:
If none of these will move the Warlike Mind,
Think on the helpless Whore you leave behind!
We beg you last, our Scene-room to forbear,
And leave our Goods and Chattels to our Care:
Alas, our Women are but washy Toys,
And wholly taken up in Stage employs:
Poor willing Tits they are: but yet I doubt
This double Duty soon will wear 'em out.
Then you are watcht besides, with jealous care;
What if my Lady's Page shoud find you there?
My Lady knows t'a tittle what there's in ye;
No passing your guilt Shilling for a Guiney.
Thus, Gentlemen, we have summ'd up in short,
Our Grievances, from Country, Town and Court:
Which humbly we submit to your good pleasure;
But first vote Money, then Redress at leasure.

PROLOGUE, EPILOGUES and SONG from *THE DUKE OF GUISE*

PROLOGUE TO THE Duke of GUISE

Spoken by Mr. *Smith*

OUR Play's a Parallel: The Holy League
Begot our Cov'nant: Guisards got the Whigg:
Whate'er our hot-brain'd Sheriffs did advance,
Was, like our Fashions, first produc'd in *France*:
And, when worn out, well scourg'd, and banish'd there,
Sent over, like their godly Beggars here.
Cou'd the same Trick, twice play'd, our Nation gull?
It looks as if the Devil were grown dull;
Or serv'd us up, in scorn, his broken Meat,
And thought we were not worth a better Cheat.
The fulsome Cov'nant, one wou'd think in reason,
Had giv'n us all our Bellys-full of Treason:
And yet, the Name but chang'd, our nasty Nation
Chaws its own Excrement, th' Association.
'Tis true we have not learn'd their pois'ning way,
For that 's a mode but newly come in play;
Besides, your Drug's uncertain to prevail;
But your true Protestant can never fail,
With that compendious Instrument, a Flail.
Go on; and bite, ev'n though the Hook lies bare;
Twice in one Age expell the lawfull Heir:
Once more decide Religion by the Sword;
And purchase for us a new Tyrant Lord.
Pray for your King; but yet your Purses spare;
Make him not two-Pence richer by your Prayer.
To show you love him much, chastise him more;
And make him very Great, and very Poor.
Push him to Wars, but still no Pence advance;

Prologue and Epilogues. Text from the separate edition, 1683, collated with editions of the play 1683, 1687, and 1699. See Commentary
25 your] his *99*

Let him lose *England* to recover *France.*
Cry Freedom up with Popular noisy Votes:
And get enough to cut each others Throats.
Lop all the Rights that fence your Monarch's Throne;
For fear of too much Pow'r, pray leave him none.
A noise was made of Arbitrary Sway;
But in Revenge, you Whiggs, have found a way,
An Arbitrary Duty now to pay.
Let his own Servants turn, to save their stake;
Glean from his plenty, and his wants forsake.
But let some *Judas* near his Person stay,
To swallow the last Sop, and then betray.
Make *London* independant of the Crown:
A Realm apart; the Kingdom of the Town.
Let *Ignoramus* Juries find no Traitors:
And *Ignoramus* Poets scribble Satyres.
And, that your meaning none may fail to scan,
Doe, what in Coffee-houses you began;
Pull down the Master, and Set up the Man.

EPILOGUE

Spoken by Mrs. *Cooke*

MUCH Time and Trouble this poor Play has cost;
And, faith, I doubted once the Cause was lost.
Yet no one Man was meant; nor Great nor Small;
Our Poets, like frank Gamesters, threw at all.
They took no single Aim:—
But, like bold Boys, true to their Prince and hearty,
Huzza'd, and fir'd Broad-sides at the whole Party.
Duells are Crimes; but when the Cause is right,
In Battel, every Man is bound to fight.
For what shou'd hinder Me to sell my Skin
Dear as I cou'd, if once my hand were in?
Se defendendo never was a Sin.
'Tis a fine World, my Masters, right or wrong,
The Whiggs must talk, and Tories hold their tongue.
They must doe all they can—
But We, forsooth, must bear a Christian mind;

And fight, like Boys, with one Hand ty'd behind;
Nay, and when one Boy's down, 'twere wondrous wise,
To cry, Box fair, and give him time to rise.
When Fortune favours, none but Fools will dally:
Wou'd any of you Sparks, if *Nan* or *Mally*
Tipt you th' inviting Wink, stand shall I, shall I?
A *Trimmer* cry'd, (that heard me tell this Story)
Fie, Mistress *Cooke*! faith you're too rank a Tory!
Wish not Whiggs hang'd, but pity their hard Cases;
You Women love to see Men make wry Faces.
Pray, Sir, said I, don't think me such a *Jew*;
I say no more, but give the Dev'l his due.
Lenitives, says he, suit best with our Condition.
Jack Ketch, says I, 's an excellent Physician.
I love no Bloud—. Nor I, Sir, as I breath;
But hanging is a fine dry kind of Death.
We *Trimmers* are for holding all things even:
Yes—just like him that hung 'twixt Hell and Heaven.
Have we not had Mens Lives enow already?
Yes sure:—but you're for holding all things steddy:
Now since the Weight hangs all on one side, Brother,
You *Trimmers* shou'd, to poize it, hang on t'other.
Damn'd Neuters, in their middle way of steering,
Are neither Fish, nor Flesh, nor good Red-Herring:
Not Whiggs, nor Tories they; nor this, nor that;
Not Birds, nor Beasts; but just a kind of Bat:
A Twilight Animal; true to neither Cause,
With Tory Wings, but Whiggish Teeth and Claws.

ANOTHER EPILOGUE

Intended to have been Spoken to the PLAY, before it was forbidden, last Summer

TWO Houses joyn'd, two Poets to a Play?
You noisy Whiggs will sure be pleas'd to day;
It looks so like two Shrieves the City way.

Epilogue. 23 this] the *87* 27 such] so much *99*

But since our Discords and Divisions cease,
You, Bilbo Gallants, learn to keep the Peace:
Make here no Tilts: let our Poor Stage alone;
Or if a decent Murther must be done,
Pray take a Civil turn to *Marybone.*
If not, I swear we'll pull up all our Benches;
Not for your sakes, but for our Orange-Wenches:
For you thrust wide sometimes; and many a Spark,
That misses one, can hit the other Mark.
This makes our Boxes full; for Men of Sense
Pay their four Shillings in their own defence:
That safe behind the Ladies they may stay;
Peep o'er the Fan, and Judg the bloudy Fray.
But other Foes give Beauty worse alarms;
The *Posse Poetarum*'s up in Arms:
No Womans Fame their Libells has escap'd;
Their Ink runs Venome, and their Pens are Clap'd.
When Sighs and Pray'rs their Ladies cannot move,
They Rail, write Treason, and turn Whiggs to love.
Nay, and I fear they worse Designs advance,
There's a damn'd Love-trick new brought o'er from *France,*
We charm in vain, and dress, and keep a Pother,
While those false Rogues are Ogling one another.
All Sins besides, admit some expiation;
But this against our Sex is plain Damnation.
They joyn for Libells too, these Women-haters;
And as they club for Love, they club for Satyrs:
The best on't is they hurt not: for they wear
Stings in their Tayls; their onely Venom's there.
'Tis true, some Shot at first the Ladies hit,
Which able Markesmen made and Men of Wit:
But now the Fools give fire, whose Bounce is louder;
And yet, like mere Train-bands, they shoot but Powder.
Libells, like Plots, sweep all in their first Fury;
Then dwindle like an *Ignoramus* Jury:
Thus Age begins with Towzing and with Tumbling;
But Grunts, and Groans, and ends at last in Fumbling.

A SONG in the Fifth ACT of the DUKE of GUISE

Shepherdess. TELL me *Thirsis*, tell your Anguish,
why you Sigh, and why you Languish;
when the Nymph whom you Adore,
grants the Blessing of Possessing,
what can Love and I do more?
what can Love, what can Love and I do more?

Shepherd. Think it's Love beyond all measure,
makes me faint away with Pleasure;
strength of Cordial may destroy,
and the Blessing of Possessing
kills me with excess of Joy.

Shepherdess. *Thirsis*, how can I believe you?
but confess, and I'le forgive you;
Men are false, and so are you;
never Nature fram'd a Creature
to enjoy, and yet be true;
never Nature fram'd a Creature
to enjoy, and yet be true;
to enjoy, and yet be true,
Soft. and yet be true.

Shepherd. Mine's a Flame beyond expiring,
still possessing, still desiring,
fit for Love's Imperial Crown;
ever shining, and refining,
still the more 'tis melted down.

Chorus together. Mine's a Flame beyond expiring,
still possessing, still desiring,
fit for Love's Imperial Crown;
ever shining, and refining,
still the more 'tis melted down.

A Song. Text from The Duke of Guise. A Tragedy, *1683, collated with the editions of 1687 and 1699*
6, 17–20 *om. 87 99*   20 *Soft.*] *Direction in the music*   26–30 *om. 87 99*

[*An Epigram of* Agathias]

C*HERONEAN PLUTARCH*, to thy deathless praise,
Does Martial *Rome* this grateful Statue raise:
Because both *Greece* and she thy fame have shar'd;
(Their Heroes written, and their Lives compar'd:)
But thou thy self cou'dst never write thy own;
Their Lives have Parallels but thine has none.

An Epigram. Text from Plutarchs Lives. Translated From the Greek by Several Hands *... 1683.*

THE ART OF POETRY

Written in *French* by The *SIEUR de Boileau*, Made *English*

CANTO I

RASH Author, 'tis a vain presumptuous Crime
To undertake the Sacred Art of Rhyme;
If at thy Birth the Stars that rul'd thy Sence
Shone not with a Poetic Influence:
In thy strait Genius thou wilt still be bound,
Find *Phœbus* deaf, and *Pegasus* unsound.
You then, that burn with the desire to try
The dangerous Course of charming Poetry;
Forbear in fruitless Verse to lose your time,
Or take for Genius the desire of Rhyme:
Fear the allurements of a specious Bait,
And well consider your own Force and Weight.
Nature abounds in Wits of every kind,
And for each Author can a Talent find:
One may in Verse describe an Amorous Flame,
Another sharpen a short Epigram:
Waller a Hero's mighty Acts extol;
Spencer Sing *Rosalind* in Pastoral:
But Authors that themselves too much esteem,
Lose their own Genius, and mistake their Theme;
Thus in times past **Dubartas* vainly Writ,
Allaying Sacred Truth with trifling Wit,
Impertinently, and without delight,
Describ'd the *Israelites* Triumphant Flight,
And following *Moses* o're the Sandy Plain,
Perish'd with *Pharaoh* in th' *Arabian* Main.
What-e're you write of Pleasant or Sublime,
Always let sence accompany your Rhyme:

* Dubartas *Translated by* Sylvester.

The Art of Poetry. Text from the first edition, 1683. See Commentary
27 of *83* (*errata*): or *83* (*text*)

Falsely they seem each other to oppose;
Rhyme must be made with Reason's Laws to close:
And when to conquer her you bend your force,
The Mind will Triumph in the Noble Course;
To Reason's yoke she quickly will incline,
Which, far from hurting, renders her Divine:
But, if neglected, will as easily stray,
And master Reason, which she should obey.
Love Reason then: and let what e're you Write
Borrow from her its Beauty, Force, and Light.
Most Writers, mounted on a resty Muse,
Extravagant, and Senceless Objects chuse;
They Think they erre, if in their Verse they fall
On any thought that's Plain, or Natural:
Fly this excess; and let *Italians* be
Vain Authors of false glitt'ring Poetry.
All ought to aim at Sence; but most in vain
Strive the hard Pass, and slipp'ry Path to gain:
You drown, if to the right or left you stray;
Reason to go has often but one way.
Sometimes an Author, fond of his own Thought,
Pursues his Object till it's over-wrought:
If he describes a House, he shews the Face,
And after walks you round from place to place;
Here is a *Vista*, there the Doors unfold,
Balcone's here are Ballustred with Gold;
Then counts the Rounds and Ovals in the Halls,
** The Festoons, Freezes, and the Astragals:*
Tir'd with his tedious Pomp, away I run,
And skip o're twenty Pages to be gon.
Of such Descriptions the vain Folly see,
And shun their barren Superfluity.
All that is needless carefully avoid,
The Mind once satisfi'd, is quickly cloy'd:
He cannot Write, who knows not to give o're;
To mend one Fault, he makes a hundred more:
A Verse was weak, you turn it much too strong,
And grow Obscure, for fear you should be Long.
Some are not Gaudy, but are Flat and Dry;

* *Verse of* Scudery.

Not to be low, another soars too high.
Would you of every one deserve the Praise?
In Writing, vary your Discourse, and Phrase;
A frozen Stile, that neither Ebs or Flows,
Instead of pleasing, makes us gape and doze.
Those tedious Authors are esteem'd by none
Who tire us, Humming the same heavy Tone.
Happy, who in his Verse can gently steer,
From Grave, to Light; from Pleasant, to Severe:
His Works will be admir'd where-ever found,
And oft with Buyers will be compass'd round.
In all you Write, be neither Low nor Vile:
The meanest Theme may have a proper Stile.
  The dull Burlesque appear'd with impudence,
And pleas'd by Novelty, in Spite of Sence.
All, except trivial points, grew out of date;
Parnassus spoke the Cant of *Belinsgate*:
Boundless and Mad, disorder'd Rhyme was seen:
Disguis'd *Apollo* chang'd to *Harlequin*.
This Plague, which first in Country Towns began,
Cities and Kingdoms quickly over-ran;
The dullest Scriblers some Admirers found,
And the **Mock-Tempest* was a while renown'd:
But this low stuff the Town at last despis'd,
And scorn'd the Folly that they once had pris'd;
Distinguish'd Dull, from Natural and Plain,
And left the Villages to *Fleckno*'s Reign.
Let not so mean a Stile your Muse debase;
But learn from †*Butler* the Buffooning grace:
And let Burlesque in Ballads be employ'd;
Yet noisy Bumbast carefully avoid,
Nor think to raise (tho' on *Pharsalia*'s Plain)
‡*Millions of mourning Mountains of the Slain:*
§Nor, with *Dubartas*, bridle up the Floods,
And Periwig with Wool the bald-pate Woods.
Chuse a just Stile; be Grave without constraint,
Great without Pride, and Lovely without Paint:

* *The* Mock-Tempest, *a Play, written by Mr.* Duffet.
† *Hudebrass.* ‡ Verse of *Brebeuf.* § Verse of *Dubartas.*

102 Woods.] Woods, *83*

Write what your Reader may be pleas'd to hear;
And, for the Measure, have a careful Ear.
On easie Numbers fix your happy choice;
Of jarring Sounds avoid the odious noise:
The fullest Verse and the most labor'd Sence,
Displease us, if the Ear once take offence.
  Our ancient Verse, (as homely as the Times,)
Was rude, unmeasur'd, only Tagg'd with Rhimes:
Number and Cadence, that have Since been Shown,
To those unpolish'd Writers were unknown.
**Fairfax* was He, who, in that Darker Age,
By his just Rules restrain'd Poetic Rage;
Spencer did next in Pastorals excel,
And taught the Noble Art of Writing well:
To stricter Rules the Stanza did restrain,
And found for Poetry a richer Veine.
Then *D'Avenant* came; who, with a new found Art,
Chang'd all, spoil'd all, and had his way apart:
His haughty Muse all others did despise,
And thought in Triumph to bear off the Prize,
Till the Sharp-sighted Critics of the Times
In their Mock-*Gondibert* expos'd his Rhimes;
The Lawrels he pretended did refuse,
And dash'd the hopes of his aspiring Muse.
This head-strong Writer, falling from on high,
Made following Authors take less Liberty.
Waller came last, but was the first whose Art
Just Weight and Measure did to Verse impart;
That of a well-plac'd Word could teach the force,
And shew'd for Poetry a nobler Course:
His happy Genius did our Tongue Refine,
And easie Words with pleasing Numbers joyn:
His Verses to good method did apply,
And chang'd harsh Discord to Soft Harmony.
All own'd his Laws; which, long approv'd and try'd,
To present Authors now may be a *Guide*.

* *Fairfax* in his Translation of *Godfrey of Bullen*.

---

111 *Editor's paragraph*

Tread boldly in his Steps, secure from Fear,
And be, like him, in your Expressions clear.
If in your Verse you drag, and Sence delay,
My Patience tires, my Fancy goes astray,
And from your vain Discourse I turn my mind,
Nor search an Author troublesom to find.
There is a kind of Writer pleas'd with Sound,
Whose Fustian head with clouds is compass'd round,
No Reason can disperse 'em with its Light:
Learn then to Think, e're you pretend to Write.
As your Idea 's clear, or else obscure,
Th' Expression follows perfect, or impure:
What we conceive, with ease we can express;
Words to the Notions flow with readiness.
  Observe the Language well in all you Write,
And swerve not from it in your loftiest flight.
The smoothest Verse, and the exactest Sence
Displease us, if ill *English* give offence:
A barb'rous Phrase no Reader can approve;
Nor Bombast, Noise, or Affectation Love.
In short, without pure Language, what you Write,
Can never yield us Profit, or Delight.
Take time for thinking; never work in hast;
And value not your self for writing fast.
A rapid Poem, with such fury writ,
Shews want of Judgment, not abounding Wit.
More pleas'd we are to see a River lead
His gentle Streams along a flow'ry Mead,
Than from high Banks to hear loud Torrents roar,
With foamy Waters on a Muddy Shore.
Gently make haste, of Labour not afraid;
A hundred times consider what you've said:
Polish, repolish, every Colour lay,
And sometimes add; but oft'ner take away.
Tis not enough, when swarming Faults are writ,
That here and there are scattered Sparks of Wit;
Each Object must be fix'd in the due place,
And diff'ring parts have Corresponding Grace:
Till, by a curious Art dispos'd, we find

150 Write.] Write, *83*

One perfect whole, of all the pieces join'd.
Keep to your Subject close, in all you say;
Nor for a sounding Sentence ever stray.
  The publick Censure for your Writings fear,
And to your self be Critic most severe.
Fantastic Wits their darling Follies love;
But find You faithful Friends that will reprove,
That on your Works may look with careful Eyes,
And of your Faults be zealous Enemies:
Lay by an Author's Pride and Vanity,
And from a Friend a Flatterer descry,
Who seems to like, but means not what he says:
Embrace true Counsel, but suspect false Praise.
A Sycophant will every thing admire;
Each Verse, each Sentence sets his Soul on Fire:
All is Divine! there's not a Word amiss!
He shakes with Joy, and weeps with Tenderness;
He over-pow'rs you with his mighty Praise.
Truth never moves in those impetuous ways:
A Faithful Friend is careful of your Fame,
And freely will your heedless Errors blame;
He cannot pardon a neglected Line,
But Verse to Rule and Order will confine.
Reprove of words the too affected sound;
Here the Sence flags and your expression's round,
Your Fancy tires and your Discourse grows vain,
Your Terms improper, make them just and plain.
Thus 'tis a faithful Friend will freedom use;
But Authors, partial to their Darling Muse,
Think to protect it they have just pretence,
And at your Friendly Counsel take offence.
Said you of this, that the Expression's flat?
Your Servant, Sir; you must excuse me that,
He answers you. This word has here no grace,
Pray leave it out: That, Sir, 's the proper'st place.
This Turn I like not: 'Tis approv'd by all.
Thus, resolute not from a fault to fall,
If there's a Syllable of which you doubt,
'Tis a sure Reason not to blot it out.

183 *Editor's paragraph*   206 improper,] improper *83*   216 fall,] fall. *83*

Yet still he says you may his Faults confute,
And over him your pow'r is absolute:
But of his feign'd Humility take heed;
'Tis a Bait lay'd, to make you hear him read:
And when he leaves you, happy in his Muse,
Restless he runs some other to abuse,
And often finds; for in our scribling times
No Fool can want a Sot to praise his Rhymes:
The flattest work has ever, in the Court,
Met with some Zealous *Ass* for its support:
And in all times a forward, Scribling Fop
Has found some greater Fool to cry him up.

CANTO II

Pastoral

As a fair Nymph, when Rising from her bed,
With sparkling Diamonds dresses not her head;
But, without Gold, or Pearl, or costly Scents,
Gathers from neighb'ring Fields her Ornaments:
Such, lovely in its dress, but plain withal,
Ought to appear a Perfect *Pastoral*:
Its humble method nothing has of fierce,
But hates the ratling of a lofty Verse:
There, Native beauty pleases, and excites,
And never with harsh Sounds the Ear affrights.
But in this stile a Poet often spent,
In rage throws by his *Rural Instrument,
And vainly, when disorder'd thoughts abound,
Amid'st the Eclogue makes the Trumpet Sound:
Pan flyes, Alarm'd, into the neighb'ring Woods,
And frighted Nymphs dive down into the Floods.
Oppos'd to this another, low in stile,
Makes Shepherds speak a Language base and vile:
His Writings, flat and heavy, without Sound,
Kissing the Earth, and creeping on the ground;
You'd swear that *Randal*, in his Rustick Strains,

* *Flute* Pipe.

Again was quav'ring to the Country Swains,
And changing, without care of Sound or Dress,
Strephon and *Phyllis*, into *Tom* and *Bess*.
'Twixt these extreams 'tis hard to keep the right;
For Guides take *Virgil*, and read *Theocrite*:
Be their just Writings, by the Gods inspir'd,
Your constant Pattern, practis'd and admir'd.
By them alone you'l easily comprehend
How Poets, without shame, may condescend
To sing of Gardens, Fields, of Flow'rs, and Fruit,
To stir up Shepherds, and to tune the Flute,
Of Love's rewards to tell the happy hour,
Daphne a Tree, *Narcissus* made a Flower,
And by what means the Eclogue yet has pow'r
*To make the Woods worthy a Conqueror:
This of their Writings is the grace and flight;
Their risings lofty, yet not out of Sight.

Elegy

The *Elegy*, that loves a mournful stile,
With unbound hair weeps at a Funeral Pile,
It paints the Lovers Torments, and Delights,
A Mistress Flatters, Threatens, and Invites:
But well these Raptures if you'l make us see,
You must know Love, as well as Poetry.
I hate those Lukewarm Authors, whose forc'd Fire
In a cold stile describe a hot Desire,
That sigh by Rule, and raging in cold blood
Their sluggish Muse whip to an Amorous mood:
Their feign'd Transports appear but flat and vain;
They always sigh, and always hug their Chain,
Adore their Prison, and their Suff'rings bless,
Make Sence and Reason quarrel as they please.
'Twas not of old in this affected Tone
That Smooth *Tibullus* made his Amorous moan;
Nor *Ovid*, when, Instructed from above,
By Nature's Rules he taught the Art of Love.
The Heart in *Elegies* forms the Discourse.

* *Virg*. Eclog. 4.

Ode

The *Ode* is bolder, and has greater force.
Mounting to Heav'n in her Ambitious flight,
Amongst the Gods and Heroes takes delight;
Of *Pisa*'s Wrestlers tells the Sin'ewy force,
And sings the dusty Conqueror's glorious Course:
To *Simois* streams does fierce *Achilles* bring,
And makes the *Ganges* bow to *Britan*'s King.
Sometimes she flies, like an Industrious Bee,
And robs the Flow'rs by Nature's Chymistry,
Describes the Shepherds Dances, Feasts, and Bliss,
And boasts from *Phyllis* to surprise a Kiss,
When gently she resists with feign'd remorse,
That what she grants may seem to be by force:
Her generous stile at random oft will part,
And by a brave disorder shows her Art.
Unlike those fearful Poets, whose cold Rhyme
In all their Raptures keep exactest time,
That sing th' Illustrious Hero's mighty praise
(Lean Writers!) by the terms of Weeks and Dayes;
And dare not from least Circumstances part,
But take all Towns by strictest Rules of Art:
Apollo drives those Fops from his abode;
And some have said, that once the humorous God
Resolving all such Scriblers to confound
For the short *Sonnet* order'd this strict bound:
Set Rules for the just Measure, and the Time,
The easie running, and alternate Rhyme;
But, above all, those Licences deny'd
Which in these Writings the lame Sence Supply'd;
Forbad an useless Line should find a place,
Or a repeated Word appear with grace.
A faultless *Sonnet*, finish'd thus, would be
Worth tedious Volumes of loose Poetry.
A hundred Scribling Authors, without ground
Believe they have this only Phœnix found:
When yet th' exactest scarce have two or three
Among whole Tomes, from Faults and Censure free.
The rest, but little read, regarded less,

Are shovel'd to the Pastry from the Press.
Closing the Sence within the measur'd time,
'Tis hard to fit the Reason to the Rhyme.

Epigram

The *Epigram*, with little art compos'd,
Is one good sentence in a Distich clos'd.
These points, that by *Italians* first were priz'd,
Our ancient Authors knew not, or despis'd:
The Vulgar, dazled with their glaring Light,
To their false pleasures quickly they invite;
But publick Favor so increas'd their pride,
They overwhelm'd *Parnassus* with their Tide.
The *Madrigal* at first was overcome,
And the proud *Sonnet* fell by the same Doom;
With these grave *Tragedy* adorn'd her flights,
And mournful *Elegy* her Funeral Rites:
A Hero never fail'd 'em on the Stage,
Without his Point a Lover durst not rage;
The Amorous Shepherds took more care to prove
True to their Point, than Faithful to their Love.
Each word, like *Janus*, had a double face:
And Prose, as well as Verse allow'd it place:
The Lawyer with Conceits adorn'd his Speech,
The Parson without Quibling could not Preach.
At last affronted Reason look'd about,
And from all serious matters shut 'em out:
Declar'd that none should use 'em without Shame,
Except a scattering in the *Epigram*;
Provided that, by Art, and in due time
They turn'd upon the Thought, and not the Rhime.
Thus in all parts disorders did abate:
Yet Quiblers in the Court had leave to prate:
Insipid Jesters, and unpleasant Fools,
A Corporation of dull Punning Drolls.
'Tis not, but that sometimes a dextrous Muse
May with advantage a turn'd Sence abuse,
And, on a word, may trifle with address;
But above all avoid the fond excess,

342 his] this *83* 344 their *83* (*text*): his *83* (*errata*) 348 Preach.] Preach, *83*

And think not, when your Verse and Sence are lame,
With a dull Point to Tag your *Epigram.*
  Each Poem his Perfection has apart;
The *Brittish Round* in plainness shows his Art;
The *Ballad*, tho the pride of Ancient time,
Has often nothing but his humorous Rhyme;
The **Madrigal* may softer Passions move,
And breath the tender Ecstasies of Love:
Desire to show it self, and not to wrong
Arm'd Virtue first with *Satyr* in its Tongue.

Satyr

  Lucilius was the man who bravely bold,
To *Roman* Vices did this Mirror hold,
Protected humble Goodness from reproach,
Show'd Worth on foot and Rascals in the Coach:
Horace his pleasing Wit to this did add,
And none uncensur'd could be Fool, or mad;
Unhappy was that Wretch, whose name might be
Squar'd to the Rules of their Sharp Poetry.
Persius, obscure, but full of Sence and Wit,
Affected brevity in all he writ!
And *Juvenal*, Learn'd as those times could be,
Too far did stretch his sharp Hyperbole;
Tho horrid Truths thro all his labors shine,
In what he writes there's something of Divine:
Whether he blames the *Caprean* Debauch,
Or of *Sejanus* Fall tells the approach,
Or that he makes the trembling Senate come
To the stern Tyrant, to receive their Doom;
Or *Roman* Vice in coursest Habits shews,
And paints an Empress reeking from the Stews:
In all he Writes appears a noble Fire;
To follow such a Master then desire.
Chaucer alone fix'd on this solid Base;
In his old Stile, conserves a modern grace:
Too happy, if the freedom of his Rhymes
Offended not the method of our Times.
The *Latin* Writers, Decency neglect;

* *An old way of Writing, which began and ended with the same Measure.*

But modern Readers challenge our respect,
And at immodest Writings take offence,
If clean Expression cover not the Sence.
I love sharp Satyr, from obsceneness free;
Not Impudence, that Preaches Modesty:
Our *English*, who in Malice never fail,
Hence, in Lampoons and Libels, learnt to Rail;
Pleasant Detraction, that by Singing goes
From mouth to mouth, and as it marches grows!
Our freedom in our Poetry we see,
That Child of Joy, begot by Liberty.
But, vain Blasphemer, tremble, when you chuse
God for the Subject of your Impious Muse:
At last, those Jeasts which Libertines invent
Bring the lewd Author to just punishment.
Ev'n in a Song there must be Art, and Sence;
Yet sometimes we have seen, that Wine, or Chance
Have warm'd cold Brains, and given dull Writers Mettle,
And furnish'd out a Scene for Mr. *S*——:
But for one lucky Hit, that made thee please,
Let not thy Folly grow to a Disease,
Nor think thy self a Wit: for in our Age
If a warm Fancy does some Fop ingage;
He neither eats nor sleeps, 'till he has Writ,
But plagues the World with his Adulterate Wit.
Nay, 'tis a wonder, if, in his dire rage,
He Prints not his dull Follies for the Stage;
And, in the Front of all his Senceless Plays,
Makes **David Logan* Crown his head with Bayes.

CANTO III

Tragedy

THERE'S not a Monster bred beneath the Sky
But, well dispos'd by Art, may please the Eye:
A curious Workman, by his Skill Divine,
From an ill Object makes a good Design.

* *D. Logan* a Graver.

414 punishment.] punishment, *83* 421 Wit:] Wit; *83*

Thus, to Delight us, *Tragedy*, in Tears
For **Oedipus*, provokes our Hopes, and Fears:
For Parricide *Orestes* asks relief;
And, to encrease our pleasure, causes grief.
You then, that in this noble Art would rise,
Come; and in lofty Verse dispute the Prize.
Would you upon the Stage acquire renown,
And for your Judges summon all the Town?
Would you your Works for ever should remain,
And, after Ages past, be sought again?
In all you Write, observe with Care and Art
To move the Passions, and incline the Heart.
If, in a labour'd Act, the pleasing Rage
Cannot our Hopes and Fears by turns ingage,
Nor in our mind a feeling Pity raise;
In vain with Learned Scenes you fill your Plays:
Your cold Discourse can never move the mind
Of a stern Critic, nat'urally unkind;
Who, justly tir'd with your Pedantic flight,
Or falls asleep, or censures all you Write.
The Secret is, Attention first to gain;
To move our minds, and then to entertain:
That, from the very op'ning of the Scenes,
The first may show us what the Author means.
I'm tir'd to see an Actor on the Stage
That knows not whether he's to Laugh, or Rage;
Who, an Intrigue unravelling in vain,
Instead of pleasing, keeps my mind in pain:
I'de rather much the nauseous Dunce should say
Downright, my name is *Hector* in the Play;
Than with a Mass of Miracles, ill joyn'd,
Confound my Ears, and not instruct my Mind.
The Subject's never soon enough exprest;
Your place of Action must be fix'd, and rest.
A *Spanish* Poet may, with good event,
In one day's space whole Ages represent;
There oft the Hero of a wandring Stage
Begins a Child, and ends the Play of Age:

* Writ by Mr. *Dryden*.

433 us,] as *83* (*text*): us *83* (*errata*)

But we, that are by Reason's Rules confin'd,
Will, that with Art the Poem be design'd,
That unity of Action, Time, and Place
Keep the Stage full, and all our Labors grace.
Write not what cannot be with ease conceiv'd;
Some Truths may be too strong to be believ'd.
A foolish Wonder cannot entertain:
My mind's not mov'd, if your Discourse be vain.
You may relate, what would offend the Eye:
Seeing, indeed, would better satisfy;
But there are objects, that a curious Art
Hides from the Eyes, yet offers to the Heart.
The mind is most agreably surpris'd,
When a well-woven Subject, long disguis'd,
You on a sudden artfully unfold,
And give the whole another face, and mould.

*At first the *Tragedy* was void of Art;
A Song; where each man Danc'd, and Sung his Part,
And of God *Bacchus* roaring out the praise
Sought a good Vintage for their Jolly dayes:
Then Wine, and Joy, were seen in each man's Eyes,
And a fat Goat was the best Singer's prize.
Thespis was first, who, all besmear'd with Lee,
Began this pleasure for Posterity:
And, with his Carted Actors, and a Song,
Amus'd the People as he pass'd along.
Next *Æschylus* the diff'rent Persons plac'd,
And with a better Masque his Players grac'd:
Upon a Theater his Verse express'd,
And show'd his Hero with a Buskin dress'd.
Then *Sophocles*, the Genius of his Age,
Increas'd the Pomp, and Beauty of the Stage,
Ingag'd the Chorus Song in every part,
And polish'd rugged Verse by Rules of Art:
He, in the *Greek*, did those perfections gain
Which the weak *Latin* never could attain.
Our pious Fathers, in their Priest-rid Age,
As Impious, and Prophane, abhorr'd the Stage:

* *The beginning and progress of* Tragedies.

---

487 *Editor's paragraph*

A Troop of silly Pilgrims, as 'tis said,
Foolishly zealous, scandalously Play'd
(Instead of Heroes, and of Love's complaints)
The Angels, God, the Virgin, and the Saints.
At last, right Reason did his Laws reveal,
And show'd the Folly of their ill-plac'd Zeal,
Silenc'd those Nonconformists of the Age,
And rais'd the lawful Heroes of the Stage:
Only th' *Athenian* Masque was lay'd aside,
And Chorus by the Musick was supply'd.
Ingenious Love, inventive in new Arts,
Mingled in Playes, and quickly touch'd our Hearts:
This Passion never could resistance find,
But knows the shortest passage to the mind.
  Paint then, I'm pleas'd my Hero be in Love;
But let him not like a tame Shepherd move:
Let not *Achilles* be like *Thyrsis* seen,
Or for a *Cyrus* show an **Artamen*;
That, strugling oft, his Passions we may find,
The Frailty, not the Virtue of his mind.
Of Romance Heroes shun the low Design;
Yet to great Hearts some Human frailties joyn:
Achilles must with *Homer*'s heat ingage;
For an affront I'm pleas'd to see him rage.
Those little Failings in your Hero's heart
Show that of Man and Nature he has part:
To leave known Rules you cannot be allow'd;
Make *Agamemnon* covetous, and proud,
Æneas in Religious Rites austere,
Keep to each man his proper Character.
Of Countryes and of Times the humors know;
From diff'rent Climates, diff'ring Customs grow:
And strive to shun their fault, who vainly dress
An Antique Hero like some modern Ass;
Who make old *Romans* like our *English* move,
Show *Cato* Sparkish, or make *Brutus* Love.

* Artamen, *the name of* Cyrus *in* Scuderies *Romance.*

---

523 *Editor's paragraph*

In a Romance those errors are excus'd:
There 'tis enough that, Reading, we're amus'd:
Rules too severe would then be useless found;
But the strict Scene must have a juster bound:
Exact Decorum we must always find.
If then you form some Hero in your mind,
Be sure your Image with it self agree;
For what he first appears, he still must be.
Affected Wits will nat'urally incline
To paint their Figures by their own design:
Your Bully Poets, Bully Heroes write:
Chapman, in *Bussy D'Ambois* took delight,
And thought perfection was to Huff, and Fight.
Wise Nature by variety does please;
Cloath diff'ring Passions in a diff'ring Dress:
Bold Anger, in rough haughty words appears;
Sorrow is humble, and dissolves in Tears.
Make not your **Hecuba* with fury rage,
And show a Ranting grief upon the Stage;
Or tell in vain how the rough *Tanais* bore
His seven-fold Waters to the *Euxine* Shore:
These swoln expressions, this affected noise
Shows like some Pedant, that declaims to Boys.
In sorrow, you must softer methods keep;
And, to excite our tears, your self must weep:
Those noisie words with which ill Plays abound,
Come not from hearts that are in sadness drown'd.
The Theatre for a young Poet's Rhymes
Is a bold venture in our knowing times:
An Author cannot eas'ly purchase Fame;
Critics are always apt to hiss, and blame:
You may be Judg'd by every Ass in Town,
The Priviledge is bought for half a Crown.
To please, you must a hundred Changes try;
Sometimes be humble, then must soar on high:
In noble thoughts must every where abound,
Be easy, pleasant, solid, and profound:
To these you must surprising Touches joyn,
And show us a new wonder in each Line;

* *Seneca Trag.*

That all in a just method well design'd,
May leave a strong Impression in the mind.
These are the Arts that *Tragedy* maintain:

The Epic

But the *Heroic* claims a Loftier Strain.
In the Narration of some great Design,
Invention, Art, and Fable all must joyn:
Here Fiction must employ its utmost grace;
All must assume a Body, Mind, and Face:
Each Virtue a Divinity is seen;
Prudence is *Pallas*, Beauty *Paphos* Queen.
'Tis not a Cloud from whence swift Lightnings fly;
But *Jupiter*, that thunders from the Sky:
Nor a rough Storm, that gives the Sailor pain;
But angry *Neptune*, plowing up the Main:
Echo's no more an empty Airy Sound;
But a fair Nymph that weeps, her Lover drown'd.
Thus in the endless Treasure of his mind,
The Poet does a thousand Figures find,
Around the work his Ornaments he pours,
And strows with lavish hand his op'ning Flow'rs.
'Tis not a wonder if a Tempest bore
The *Trojan* Fleet against the *Libyan* Shore;
From faithless Fortune this is no surprise,
For every day 'tis common to our eyes;
But angry *Juno*, that she might destroy,
And overwhelm the rest of ruin'd *Troy*:
That *Æolus* with the fierce Goddess joyn'd,
Op'ned the hollow Prisons of the Wind;
Till angry *Neptune*, looking o're the Main,
Rebukes the Tempest, calms the Waves again,
Their Vessels from the dang'rous quick-sands steers;
These are the Springs that move our hopes and fears.
Without these Ornaments before our Eyes,
Th' unsinew'd Poem languishes, and dyes:
Your Poet in his art will always fail,
And tell you but a dull insipid Tale.

585 mind.] mind, *83*

In vain have our mistaken Authors try'd
These ancient Ornaments to lay aside,
Thinking our God, and Prophets that he sent,
Might Act like those the Poets did invent,
To fright poor Readers in each Line with Hell,
And talk of *Satan*, *Ashtaroth*, and *Bel*;
The Mysteries which Christians must believe,
Disdain such shifting Pageants to receive:
The Gospel offers nothing to our thoughts
But penitence, or punishment for faults;
And mingling falshoods with those Mysteries,
Would make our Sacred Truths appear like Lyes.
Besides, what pleasure can it be to hear
The howlings of repining *Lucifer*,
Whose rage at your imagin'd Hero flyes,
And oft with God himself disputes the prize?
Tasso, you'l say, has done it with applause;
It is not here I mean to Judge his Cause:
Yet, tho our Age has so extoll'd his name,
His Works had never gain'd immortal Fame,
If holy *Godfrey* in his Ecstasies
Had only Conquer'd *Satan* on his knees;
If *Tancred*, and *Armida*'s pleasing form,
Did not his melancholy Theme adorn.
'Tis not, that Christian Poems ought to be
Fill'd with the Fictions of Idolatry;
But in a common Subject to reject
The Gods, and Heathen Ornaments neglect;
To banish Tritons who the Seas invade,
To take *Pan*'s Whistle, or the Fates degrade,
To hinder *Charon* in his leaky Boat
To pass the Shepherd with the Man of Note,
Is with vain Scruples to disturb your mind,
And search Perfection you can never find:
As well they may forbid us to present
Prudence or Justice for an Ornament,
To paint old *Janus* with his front of Brass,
And take from Time his Scythe, his Wings and Glass,
And every where, as't were Idolatry,

632 hear] hear, *83*

Banish Descriptions from our Poetry.
Leave 'em their pious Follys to pursue;
But let our Reason such vain fears subdue:
And let us not, amongst our Vanities,
Of the true God create a God of Lyes.
In Fable we a thousand pleasures see,
And the smooth names seem made for Poetry;
As *Hector*, *Alexander*, *Helen*, *Phillis*,
Ulysses, *Agamemnon*, and *Achilles*:
In such a Crowd, the Poet were to blame
To chuse King *Chilp'eric* for his Hero's name.
Sometimes, the name being well or ill apply'd,
Will the whole Fortune of your Work decide.
  Would you your Reader never should be tir'd?
Chuse some great Hero, fit to be admir'd,
In Courage signal, and in Virtue bright,
Let ev'n his very failings give delight;
Let his great Actions our attention bind,
Like *Cæsar*, or like *Scipio*, frame his mind,
And not like *Oedipus* his perjur'd Race;
A common Conqueror is a Theme too base.
Chuse not your Tale of Accidents too full;
Too much variety may make it dull:
Achilles rage alone, when wrought with skill,
Abundantly does a whole *Iliad* fill.
Be your Narrations lively, short, and smart;
In your Descriptions show your noblest Art:
There 'tis your Poetry may be employ'd;
Yet you must trivial Accidents avoid.
Nor imitate that *Fool, who, to describe
The wondrous Marches of the Chosen Tribe,
Plac'd on the sides, to see their Armyes pass,
The Fishes staring through the liquid Glass;
Describ'd a Child, who with his little hand,
Pick'd up the shining Pebbles from the sand.
Such objects are too mean to stay our sight;
Allow your Work a just and nobler flight.
Be your beginning plain; and take good heed

* St. *Amant.*

672 *Editor's paragraph*

Too soon you mount not on the Airy Steed:
Nor tell your Reader, in a Thund'ring Verse,
**I sing the Conqueror of the Universe.*
What can an Author after this produce?
The lab'ring Mountain must bring forth a Mouse.
Much better are we pleas'd with his †Address
Who, without making such vast promises,
Sayes, in an easier Stile and plainer Sence,
"I sing the Combats of that pious Prince
"Who from the *Phrygian* Coast his Armies bore,
"And landed first on the *Lavinian* shore.
His op'ning Muse sets not the World on fire,
And yet performs more than we can require:
Quickly you'l hear him celebrate the fame,
And future glory of the *Roman* Name;
Of *Styx* and *Acheron* describe the Floods,
And *Cæsars* wandring in th' *Elysian* Woods:
With Figures numberless his Story grace,
And every thing in beauteous Colours trace.
At once you may be pleasing, and sublime;
I hate a heavy melancholy Rhyme:
I'de rather read *Orlando*'s Comic Tale,
Than a dull Author always stiff and stale,
Who thinks himself dishonour'd in his stile,
If on his Works the Graces do but smile.
'Tis said, that *Homer*, Matchless in his Art,
Stole *Venus* Girdle, to ingage the Heart:
His Works indeed vast Treasures do unfold,
And whatsoe're he touches, turns to Gold:
All in his hands new beauty does acquire;
He always pleases, and can never tire.
A happy Warmth he every where may boast;
Nor is he in too long Digressions lost:
His Verses without Rule a method find,
And of themselves appear in order joyn'd:
All without trouble answers his intent;
Each Syllable is tending to th' Event.
Let his example your indeavours raise:
To love his Writings, is a kind of praise.

* *The first line of* Scuderies Alaric. † Virgils *Eneids*.

A Poem, where we all perfections find,
Is not the work of a Fantastick mind:
There must be Care, and Time, and Skill, and Pains;
Not the first heat of unexperienc'd Brains.
Yet sometimes Artless Poets, when the rage
Of a warm Fancy does their minds engage,
Puff'd with vain pride, presume they understand,
And boldly take the Trumpet in their hand;
Their Fustian Muse each Accident confounds;
Nor can she fly, but rise by leaps and bounds,
Till their small stock of Learning quickly spent,
Their Poem dyes for want of nourishment:
In vain Mankind the hot-brain'd fools decryes,
No branding Censures can unveil their eyes;
With Impudence the Laurel they invade,
Resolv'd to like the Monsters they have made.
Virgil, compar'd to them, is flat and dry;
And *Homer* understood not Poetry:
Against their merit if this Age Rebel,
To future times for Justice they appeal.
But waiting till Mankind shall do 'em right,
And bring their Works Triumphantly to Light;
Neglected heaps we in by-corners lay,
Where they become to Worms and Moths a prey;
Forgot, in Dust and Cobwebs let 'em rest,
Whilst we return from whence we first digrest.
The great Success which Tragic Writers found,
In *Athens* first the *Comedy* renown'd,
Th' abusive *Grecian* there, by pleasing wayes,
Dispers'd his nat'ural malice in his Playes:
Wisdom, and Virtue, Honor, Wit, and Sence,
Were Subject to Buffooning insolence:
Poets were publickly approv'd, and sought,
That Vice extol'd, and Virtue set at naught;
A *Socrates* himself, in that loose Age,
Was made the Pastime of a Scoffing Stage.
At last the Public took in hand the Cause,
And cur'd this Madness by the pow'r of Laws;
Forbad at any time, or any place,

749 their] his *83*

To name the Person, or describe the Face.
The Stage its ancient Fury thus let fall,
And Comedy diverted without Gall:
By mild reproofs, recover'd minds diseas'd,
And, sparing Persons, innocently pleas'd.
Each one was nicely shown in this new Glass,
And smil'd to think He was not meant the Ass:
A Miser oft would laugh the first, to find
A faithful Draught of his own sordid mind;
And Fops were with such care and cunning writ,
They lik'd the Piece for which themselves did sit.
  You then, that would the Comic Lawrels wear,
To study Nature be your only Care:
Who e're knows man, and by a curious art
Discerns the hidden secrets of the heart;
He who observes, and naturally can Paint
The Jealous Fool, the fawning Sycophant,
A Sober Wit, an enterprising Ass,
A humorous *Otter*, or a *Hudibras*;
May safely in these noble Lists ingage,
And make 'em Act and Speak upon the Stage:
Strive to be natural in all you Write,
And paint with Colours that may please the Sight.
Nature in various Figures does abound;
And in each mind are diff'rent Humors found:
A glance, a touch, discovers to the wise;
But every man has not discerning eyes.
All-changing Time does also change the mind;
And diff'rent Ages, diff'rent pleasures find:
Youth, hot and furious, cannot brook delay,
By flattering Vice is eas'ly led away;
Vain in discourse, inconstant in desire,
In Censure, rash; in pleasures, all on fire.
The Manly age does steadier thoughts enjoy;
Pow'r, and Ambition do his Soul employ:
Against the turns of Fate he sets his mind;
And by the past the future hopes to find.
Decrepit Age, still adding to his Stores,
For others heaps the Treasure he adores.

786 *Editor's paragraph*

In all his actions keeps a frozen pace;
Past Times extols, the present to debase:
Incapable of pleasures Youth abuse,
In others blames, what age does him refuse.
Your Actors must by Reason be control'd;
Let young men speak like young, old men like old:
Observe the Town, and study well the Court;
For thither various Characters resort:
Thus 'twas great *Johnson* purchas'd his renown,
And in his Art had born away the Crown;
If less desirous of the Peoples praise,
He had not with low Farce debas'd his Playes;
Mixing dull Buffoonry with Wit refin'd,
And *Harlequin* with noble *Terence* joyn'd.
When in the *Fox* I see the Tortois hist,
I lose the Author of the *Alchymist*.
The Comic Wit, born with a smiling Air,
Must Tragic grief, and pompous Verse forbear;
Yet may he not, as on a Market-place,
With Baudy jests amuse the Populace:
With well-bred Conversation you must please,
And your Intrigue unravel'd be with ease:
Your Action still should Reason's Rules obey,
Nor in an empty Scene may lose its way.
Your humble Stile must sometimes gently rise;
And your Discourse Sententious be, and Wise:
The Passions must to Nature be confin'd,
And Scenes to Scenes with Artful weaving joyn'd:
Your Wit must not unseasonably play;
But follow Bus'ness, never lead the way.
Observe how *Terence* does this error shun;
A careful Father chides his Am'orous Son:
Then see that Son, whom no advice can move,
Forget those Orders, and pursue his Love:
'Tis not a well-drawn Picture we discover;
'Tis a true Son, a Father, and a Lover.
I like an Author that Reforms the Age,
And keeps the right Decorum of the Stage;
That alwayes pleases by just Reason's Rule:

830 *Editor's paragraph* 850 Age,] Age; *83* 851 Stage;] Stage, *83*

But for a tedious Droll, a Quibling Fool,
Who with low nauseous Baudry fills his Plays;
Let him begon and on two Tressels raise
Some *Smithfield* Stage, where he may act his Pranks,
And make *Jack Puddings* speak to Mountebanks.

CANTO IV

IN *Florence* dwelt a Doctor of Renown,
The Scourge of God, and Terror of the Town,
Who all the Cant of Physick had by heart,
And never Murder'd but by rules of Art.
The Public mischief was his Private gain;
Children their slaughter'd Parents sought in vain:
A Brother here his poyson'd Brother wept;
Some bloodless dy'd, and some by *Opium* slept.
Colds, at his presence, would to Frenzies turn;
And Agues, like Malignant Fevers, burn.
Hated, at last, his Practice gives him o'er:
One Friend, unkill'd by Drugs, of all his Store,
In his new Country-house affords him place,
'Twas a rich Abbot, and a Building Ass:
Here first the Doctor's Talent came in play,
He seems Inspir'd, and talks like * *Wren* or *May*:
Of this new Portico condemns the Face,
And turns the Entrance to a better place;
Designs the Stair-case at the other end.
His Friend approves, does for his Mason send,
He comes; the Doctor's Arguments prevail.
In short, to finish this our hum'rous Tale,
He *Galen*'s dang'erous Science does reject,
And from ill Doctor turn good Architect.
  In this Example we may have our part:
Rather be Mason, ('tis an useful Art!)
Than a dull Poet; for that Trade accurst,
Admits no mean betwixt the Best and Worst.
In other Sciences, without disgrace
A Candidate may fill a second place;

* *The Kings* Archetects.

But Poetry no Medium can admit,
No Reader suffers an indiff'rent Wit:
The ruin'd Stationers against him baul,
And *Herringman* degrades him from his Stall.
Burlesque, at least our Laughter may excite:
But a cold Writer never can delight.
The *Counter-Scuffle* has more Wit and Art,
Than the stiff Formal Stile of *Gondibert.*
Be not affected with that empty praise
Which your vain Flatterers will sometimes raise,
And when you read, with Ecstasie will say,
The finish'd Piece! The admirable Play!
Which, when expos'd to Censure and to Light,
Cannot indure a Critic's piercing sight.
A hundred Authors Fates have been foretold,
And *Sh* —— *ll*'s Works are Printed, but not Sold.
Hear all the World; consider every Thought;
A Fool by chance may stumble on a Fault:
Yet, when *Apollo* does your Muse inspire,
Be not impatient to expose your Fire;
Nor imitate the *Settles* of our Times,
Those Tuneful Readers of their own dull Rhymes,
Who seize on all th' Acquaintance they can meet,
And stop the Passengers that walk the Street;
There is no Sanctuary you can chuse
For a Defence from their pursuing Muse.
I've said before, Be patient when they blame;
To alter for the better is no shame.
Yet yield not to a Fool's Impertinence:
Sometimes conceited Sceptics void of Sence,
By their false taste condemn some finish'd part,
And blame the noblest flights of Wit and Art.
In vain their fond Opinions you deride,
With their lov'd Follies they are satisfy'd;
And their weak Judgment, void of Sence and Light,
Thinks nothing can escape their feeble sight:
Their dang'rous Counsels do not cure, but wound;
To shun the Storm, they run your Verse aground,
And thinking to escape a Rock, are drown'd.

903 *Sh* —— *ll*'s] *Sh* ——*le*'s *83*

Chuse a sure Judge to Censure what you Write,
Whose Reason leads, and Knowledge gives you light,
Whose steady hand will prove your Faithful Guide,
And touch the darling follies you would hide:
He, in your doubts, will carefully advise,
And clear the Mist before your feeble eyes.
'Tis he will tell you, to what noble height
A generous Muse may sometimes take her flight;
When, too much fetter'd with the Rules of Art,
May from her stricter Bounds and Limits part:
But such a perfect Judge is hard to see,
And every Rhymer knows not Poetry;
Nay some there are, for Writing Verse extol'd,
Who know not *Lucan*'s Dross from *Virgil*'s Gold.
Would you in this great Art acquire Renown?
Authors, observe the Rules I here lay down.
In prudent Lessons every where abound;
With pleasant, joyn the useful and the sound:
A Sober Reader, a vain Tale will slight;
He seeks as well Instruction, as Delight.
Let all your Thoughts to Virtue be confin'd,
Still off'ring nobler Figures to our Mind:
I like not those loose Writers, who employ
Their guilty Muse, good Manners to destroy;
Who with false Colours still deceive our Eyes,
And show us Vice dress'd in a fair Disguise.
Yet do I not their sullen Muse approve
Who from all modest Writings banish Love;
That strip the Play-house of its chief Intrigue,
And make a Murderer of *Roderigue*:
*The lightest Love, if decently exprest,
Will raise no Vitious motions in our brest.
Dido in vain may weep, and ask relief;
I blame her Folly, whil'st I share her Grief.
A Virtuous Author, in his Charming Art,
To please the Sense needs not corrupt the Heart:
His Heat will never cause a guilty Fire:
To follow Virtue then be your desire.
In vain your Art and Vigor are exprest;

* The *Cid*. Translated into *English*.

Th' obscene expression shows th' Infected breast.
But above all, base Jealousies avoid,
In which detracting Poets are employ'd:
A noble Wit dares lib'rally commend;
And scorns to grudge at his deserving Friend.
Base Rivals, who true Wit and Merit hate,
Caballing still against it with the Great,
Maliciously aspire to gain Renown
By standing up, and pulling others down.
Never debase your self by Treacherous ways,
Nor by such abject methods seek for praise:
Let not your only bus'ness be to Write;
Be Virtuous, Just, and in your Friends delight.
'Tis not enough your Poems be admir'd;
But strive your Conversation be desir'd:
Write for immortal Fame; nor ever chuse
Gold for the object of a gen'erous Muse.
I know a noble Wit may, without Crime,
Receive a lawful Tribute for his time:
Yet I abhor those Writers, who despise
Their Honour; and alone their Profit prize;
Who their *Apollo* basely will degrade,
And of a noble Science, make a Trade.
Before kind Reason did her Light display,
And Government taught Mortals to obey,
Men, like wild Beasts, did Nature's Laws pursue,
They fed on Herbs, and drink from Rivers drew;
Their Brutal force, on Lust and Rapine bent
Committed Murders without Punishment:
Reason at last, by her all-conquering Arts,
Reduc'd these Savages, and Tun'd their hearts;
Mankind from Bogs, and Woods, and Caverns calls,
And Towns and Cities fortifies with Walls:
Thus fear of Justice made proud Rapine cease,
And shelter'd Innocence by Laws and Peace.
  These Benefits from Poets we receiv'd,
From whence are rais'd those Fictions since believ'd,
That *Orpheus*, by his soft Harmonious strains,
Tam'd the fierce Tigers of the *Thracian* Plains;
Amphion's Notes, by their melodious pow'rs,

Drew Rocks and Woods, and rais'd the *Theban* Tow'rs:
These Miracles from numbers did arise,
Since which, in Verse Heav'n taught his Mysteries,
And by a Priest, possess'd with rage Divine,
Apollo spoke from his Prophetick Shrine.
Soon after *Homer* the old Heroes prais'd,
And noble minds by great Examples rais'd;
Then *Hesiod* did his *Græcian* Swains incline
To Till the Fields, and Prune the bounteous Vine.
Thus useful Rules were by the Poets aid,
In easy numbers, to rude men convey'd,
And pleasingly their Precepts did impart;
First Charm'd the Ear, and then ingag'd the Heart:
The Muses thus their Reputation rais'd,
And with just Gratitude in *Greece* were prais'd.

With pleasure Mortals did their Wonders see,
And Sacrific'd to their Divinity:
But Want, at last base Flatt'ry entertain'd,
And old *Parnassus* with this Vice was stain'd:
Desire of gain dazling the Poets Eyes,
Their Works were fill'd with fulsome flatteries.
Thus needy Wits a vile revenue made,
And Verse became a mercenary Trade.
Debase not with so mean a Vice thy Art:
If Gold must be the Idol of thy heart,
Fly, fly th' unfruitful *Heliconian* strand,
Those streams are not inrich'd with Golden Sand:
Great Wits, as well as Warriors, only gain
Laurels and Honors for their Toyl and Pain:
But, what? an Author cannot live on Fame,
Or pay a Reck'ning with a lofty Name:
A Poet to whom Fortune is unkind,
Who when he goes to bed has hardly din'd;
Takes little pleasure in *Parnassus* Dreams,
Or relishes the *Heliconian* streams.
Horace had Ease and Plenty when he writ,
And free from cares for money or for meat,
Did not expect his dinner from his wit.
'Tis true; but Verse is cherish'd by the Great,

1021 *Editor's paragraph*

And now none famish who deserve to eat:
What can we fear, when Virtue, Arts, and Sence,
Receive the Stars propitious Influence;
When a sharp-sighted Prince, by early Grants
Rewards your Merits, and prevents your Wants?
Sing then his Glory, celebrate his Fame;
Your noblest Theme is his immortal Name.
  Let mighty *Spencer* raise his reverend head,
Cowley and *Denham* start up from the dead;
Waller his age renew, and Off'rings bring,
Our Monarch's praise let bright-ey'd Virgins sing;
Let *Dryden* with new Rules our Stage refine,
And his great Models form by this Design:
But where's a Second *Virgil*, to Rehearse
Our Hero's Glories in his Epic Verse?
What *Orpheus* sing his Triumphs o'er the Main,
And make the Hills and Forests move again;
Shew his bold Fleet on the *Batavian* shore,
And *Holland* trembling as his Canons roar;
Paint *Europe*'s Balance in his steady hand,
Whilst the two Worlds in expectation stand
Of Peace or War, that wait on his Command?
But, as I speak, new Glories strike my Eyes,
Glories, which Heav'n it Self does give, and prize,
Blessings of Peace; that with their milder Rayes
Adorn his Reign, and bring *Saturnian* Dayes:
Now let Rebellion, Discord, Vice, and Rage,
That have in Patriots Forms debauch'd our Age,
Vanish, with all the Ministers of Hell;
His Rayes their poys'nous Vapours shall dispel:
'Tis He alone our safety did create,
His own firm Soul secur'd the Nation's Fate,
Oppos'd to all the *boutfeaus* of the State.
Authors, for Him your great indeavours raise;
The loftiest Numbers will but reach his praise.
For me, whose Verse in Satyr has been bred,
And never durst Heroic Measures tread;
Yet you shall see me, in that famous Field
With Eyes and Voice, my best assistance yield;

1052 *Editor's paragraph*

Offer you Lessons, that my Infant Muse
Learnt, when she *Horace* for her Guide did chuse:
Second your Zeal with Wishes, Heart and Eyes,
And afar off hold up the glorious Prize.
But pardon too, if, Zealous for the Right,
A strict observer of each Noble flight,
From the fine Gold I separate th' Allay,
And show how hasty Writers sometimes stray:
Apter to blame, than knowing how to mend;
A sharp, but yet a necessary Friend.

THE EPILOGUE TO *CONSTANTINE* the *GREAT*

OUR Hero's happy in the Plays Conclusion,
The holy Rogue at last has met Confusion:
Tho' *Arius* all along appear'd a Saint,
The last Act shew'd him a true Protestant.
Eusebius, (for you know I read Greek Authors,)
Reports, that after all these Plots and Slaughters,
The Court of *Constantine* was full of Glory,
And every *Trimmer* turn'd Addressing *Tory*;
They follow'd him in Heards as they were mad:
When *Clause* was King, then all the World was glad.
Whigs kept the Places they possest before,
And most were in a Way of getting more;
Which was as much as saying, Gentlemen,
Here's Power and Money to be Rogues again.
Indeed there were a sort of peaking Tools,
Some call them Modest, but I call 'em Fools,
Men much more Loyal, tho' not half so loud;
But these poor Devils were cast behind the Croud.
For bold Knaves thrive without one grain of Sence,
But good men starve for want of Impudence.
Besides all these, there were a sort of Wights,
(I think my Author calls them *Teckelites*;)
Such hearty Rogues, against the King and Laws,
They favour'd even a Foreign Rebel's Cause.
When their own damn'd Design was quash'd and aw'd,
At least they gave it their good Word abroad.
As many a Man, who, for a quiet Life,
Breeds out his Bastard, not to nose his Wife;
Thus o're their Darling Plot, these *Trimmers* cry;
And tho' they cannot keep it in their Eye,
They bind it Prentice to Count *Teckely*.

The Epilogue. Text from A True Coppy of the Epilogue to Constantine the Great. That which was first Published being false printed and surreptitious, *1684*, *collated with* The Prologue and Epilogue, To the Last New Play; Constantine the Great, *1683* (*83*), *and the first edition of the play*, *1684* (*84*). *See Commentary* 10 *Clause*] *CAUSE 83* 13 as much as saying, *84*: much as saying, *True Coppy*: as much as to say — *83* 26 least] last *83* 28 Breeds] Sends *83* 29 Plot, these] *Treason 83* 30 cannot keep it in their Eye] dare not Her, it wants Supply *83*

They believe not the last Plot; may I be curst,
If I believe they e're believ'd the first;
No wonder their own Plot, no Plot they think;
The Man that makes it, never smells the Stink.
And, now it comes into my Head, I'le tell
Why these damn'd *Trimmers* lov'd the *Turks* so well.
The Original *Trimmer*, tho' a Friend to no man,
Yet in his heart ador'd a pretty Woman:
He knew that *Mahomet* laid up for ever,
Kind black-eyed Rogues, for every true Believer:
And, which was more than mortal Man e're tasted,
One Pleasure that for threescore Twelve-months lasted:
To turn for this, may surely be forgiven:
Who'd not be circumcis'd for such a Heav'n!

32 Plot;] Plot, *True Coppy 83* 37 these] those *83* lov'd the *Turks*] love the *TURK 83* 45 Heav'n!] HEAVEN? *83*

POEMS FROM *MISCELLANY POEMS* By the most Eminent Hands

(*1684*)

SEVERAL OF OVID'S ELEGIES, BOOK II

ELEGY the NINETEENTH

If for thy self thou wilt not watch thy Whore,
Watch her for me that I may love her more;
What comes with ease we nauseously receive,
Who but a Sot wou'd scorn to love with leave?
With hopes and fears my Flames are blown up higher,
Make me despair, and then I can desire.
Give me a Jilt to tease my Jealous mind,
Deceits are Vertues in the Female kind.
Corinna my Fantastick humour knew,
Play'd trick for trick, and kept her self still new:
She, that next night I might the sharper come,
Fell out with me, and sent me fasting home;
Or some pretence to lye alone wou'd take,
When e'er she pleas'd her head and teeth wou'd ake:
Till having won me to the highest strain,
She took occasion to be sweet again.
With what a Gust, ye Gods, we then imbrac'd!
How every kiss was dearer than the last!
  Thou whom I now adore be edify'd,
Take care that I may often be deny'd.
Forget the promis'd hour, or feign some fright,
Make me lye rough on Bulks each other Night.
These are the Arts that best secure thy reign,
And this the Food that must my Fires maintain.
Gross easie Love does like gross diet, pall,
In squeasie Stomachs Honey turns to Gall.

Poems. Text from the first edition, 1684, collated with the second edition, 1692

Had *Danae* not been kept in brazen Tow'rs,
Jove had not thought her worth his Golden Show'rs.
When *Juno* to a Cow turn'd *Io*'s Shape,
The Watchman helpt her to a second Leap.
Let him who loves an easie Whetstone Whore,
Pluck leaves from Trees, and drink the Common Shore.
The Jilting Harlot strikes the surest blow,
A truth which I by sad Experience know.
The kind poor constant Creature we despise,
Man but pursues the Quarry while it flies.
  But thou dull Husband of a Wife too fair,
Stand on thy Guard, and watch the pretious Ware;
If creaking Doors, or barking Dogs thou hear,
Or Windows scratcht, suspect a Rival there;
An Orange-wench wou'd tempt thy Wife abroad,
Kick her, for she's a Letter-bearing Bawd:
In short be Jealous as the Devil in Hell;
And set my Wit on work to cheat thee well.
The sneaking City Cuckold is my Foe,
I scorn to strike, but when he Wards the blow.
Look to thy hits, and leave off thy Conniving,
I'll be no Drudge to any Wittall living;
I have been patient and forborn thee long,
In hope thou wou'dst not pocket up thy wrong:
If no Affront can rouse thee, understand
I'll take no more Indulgence at thy hand.
What, ne'er to be forbid thy House and Wife!
Damn him who loves to lead so dull a life.
Now I can neither sigh, nor whine, nor pray,
All those occasions thou hast ta'ne away.
Why art thou so incorrigibly Civil?
Doe somewhat I may wish thee at the Devil.
For shame be no Accomplice in my Treason,
A Pimping Husband is too much in reason.
  Once more wear horns before I quite forsake her,
In hopes whereof I rest thy Cuckold-maker.

AMARYLLIS
Or the Third *Idyllium* of *THEOCRITUS* Paraphras'd

To *Amaryllis* Love compells my way,
My browzing *Goats* upon the Mountains stray:
O *Tityrus*, tend them well, and see them fed
In Pastures fresh, and to their watring led;
And 'ware the Ridgling with his butting head.
Ah beauteous Nymph, can you forget your Love,
The conscious *Grottos*, and the shady Grove;
Where stretch'd at ease your tender Limbs were laid,
Your nameless Beauties nakedly display'd?
Then I was call'd your darling, your desire,
With Kisses such as set my Soul on Fire:
But you are chang'd; yet I am still the same,
My heart maintains for both a double Flame.
Griev'd, but unmov'd, and patient of your scorn,
So faithfull I, and you so much forsworn!
I dye, and Death will finish all my pain,
Yet e'er I dye, behold me once again:
Am I so much deform'd, so chang'd of late?
What partial Judges are our Love and hate!
Ten Wildings have I gather'd for my Dear,
How ruddy like your Lips their streaks appear!
Far off you view'd them with a longing Eye
Upon the topmost branch (the Tree was high;)
Yet nimbly up, from bough to bough I swerv'd;
And for to Morrow have Ten more reserv'd.
Look on me Kindly and some pity shew,
Or give me leave at least to look on you.
Some God transform me by his Heavenly pow'r
Ev'n to a *Bee* to buzz within your Bow'r,
The winding Ivy-chaplet to invade,
And folded Fern that your fair Forehead shade.
Now to my cost the force of Love I find;
The heavy hand he bears on humane kind!

Amaryllis 12 chang'd;] chang'd, *84 92* 28 transform] transforms *92*

The Milk of *Tygers* was his Infant food,
Taught from his tender years the tast of bloud;
His Brother whelps and he ran wild about the wood.
Ah Nymph, train'd up in his Tyrannick Court,
To make the suff'rings of your Slaves your sport!
Unheeded Ruine! treacherous delight!
O polish'd hardness soften'd to the sight!
Whose radiant Eyes your Ebon Brows adorn,
Like Midnight those, and these like break of Morn!
Smile once again, revive me with your Charms;
And let me dye contented in your Armes.
I would not ask to live another Day,
Might I but sweetly Kiss my Soul away!
Ah, why am I from empty Joys debar'd,
For Kisses are but empty, when Compar'd!
I rave, and in my raging fit shall tear
The Garland which I wove for you to wear,
Of Parsley with a wreath of Ivy bound;
And border'd with a Rosie edging round.
What pangs I feel, unpity'd, and unheard!
Since I must dye, why is my Fate defer'd!
I strip my Body of my Shepherds Frock,
Behold that dreadfull downfall of a Rock,
Where yon old *Fisher* views the Waves from high!
'Tis that Convenient leap I mean to try.
You would be pleas'd to see me plunge to shoar,
But better pleas'd, if I should rise no more.
I might have read my Fortune long agoe,
When, seeking my success in Love to know,
I try'd th' infallible Prophetique way,
A Poppy leaf upon my palm to lay;
I struck, and yet no lucky crack did follow,
Yet I struck hard, and yet the leaf lay hollow.
And which was worse, If any worse cou'd prove,
The withring leaf foreshew'd your withring Love.
Yet farther (Ah, how far a Lover dares!)
My last recourse I had to Seive and Sheeres;
And told the Witch *Agreo* my desease,
(*Agreo* that in Harvest us'd to lease;

52 round.] round *84 92*

But Harvest done, to Chare-work did aspire;
Meat, drink, and Two-pence was her daily hire:)
To work she went, her Charms she mutter'd o'er,
And yet the resty Seive wagg'd ne'er the more;
I wept for Woe, the testy Beldame swore.
And foaming with her God, foretold my Fate;
That I was doom'd to Love, and you to Hate.
A milk-white Goat for you I did provide;
Two milk-white Kids run frisking by her side,
For which the Nut-brown Lass, *Erithacis*,
Full often offer'd many a savoury Kiss;
Hers they shall be, since you refuse the price,
What Madman would o'erstand his Market twice?
My right Eye itches, some good-luck is near,
Perhaps my *Amaryllis* may appear,
I'll set up such a Note as she shall hear.
What Nymph but my melodious Voice would move?
She must be Flint, if she refuse my Love.
Hippomenes, who ran with Noble strife
To win his Lady, or to loose his Life,
(What shift some men will make to get a Wife?)
Threw down a Golden Apple in her way,
For all her haste she could not chuse but stay:
Renown said run, the glitt'ring Bribe cry'd hold,
The Man might have been hang'd but for his Gold.
Yet some suppose 'twas Love (some few indeed,)
That stopt the fatal fury of her Speed:
She saw, she sigh'd; her nimble Feet refuse
Their wonted Speed, and she took pains to loose.
A Prophet some, and some a Poet cry,
(No matter which, so neither of them lye,)
From steepy *Othrys* top, to *Pylus* drove
His herd; and for his pains enjoy'd his Love:
If such another Wager shou'd be laid,
I'll find the Man, if you can find the Maid.
Why name I Men, when Love extended finds
His pow'r on high, and in Celestial Minds?
Venus the Shepherd's homely habit took,
And manag'd something else besides the Crook.

101 wonted] wanted *92* 103 lye,] lye. *84 92*

Nay, when *Adonis* dy'd, was heard to roar,
And never from her heart forgave the Boar.
How blest is fair *Endymion* with his Moon,
Who sleeps on *Latmos* top from Night to Noon!
What *Jason* from *Medea*'s Love possest,
You shall not hear, but know 'tis like the rest.
My aking Head can scarce support the pain;
This cursed Love will surely turn my Brain:
Feel how it shoots, and yet you take no Pity,
Nay then 'tis time to end my dolefull Ditty.
A clammy Sweat does o'er my Temples creep;
My heavy Eyes are urg'd with Iron sleep:
I lay me down to gasp my latest Breath,
The Wolves will get a Breakfast by my Death;
Yet scarce enough their hunger to supply,
For Love has made me Carrion e'er I dye.

PROLOGUE, To the University of *Oxon.*

Spoken by Mr. Hart, *at the Acting of the* Silent Woman

WHAT *Greece*, when Learning flourish'd, onely Knew,
(*Athenian* Judges,) you this day Renew.
Here too are Annual Rites to *Pallas* done,
And here Poetique prizes lost or won.
Methinks I see you, Crown'd with Olives sit,
And strike a sacred Horrour from the Pit.
A Day of Doom is this of your Decree,
Where even the Best are but by Mercy free:
A Day which none but *Johnson* durst have wish'd to see.
Here they who long have known the usefull Stage,
Come to be taught themselves to teach the Age.
As your Commissioners our Poets goe,
To Cultivate the Virtue which you sow:
In your *Lycæum*, first themselves refind,
And Delegated thence to Humane kind.
But as Embassadours, when long from home,
For new Instructions to their Princes come;

Prologue. There is a version of Prologue and Epilogue in Bodl. MS. Rawl. Poet. 19, ff. 149, 152. MS. heading 'Prologue'
7 is this of] it is at *MS* 8 Where] When *MS* 13 the] that *MS*

So Poets who your Precepts have forgot,
Return, and beg they may be better taught:
Follies and Faults elsewhere by them are shown,
But by your Manners they Correct their Own.
Th' illiterate Writer, Emperique like, applies
To minds diseas'd, unsafe, chance Remedies:
The Learn'd in Schools, where Knowledge first began,
Studies with Care th' Anatomy of Man;
Sees Vertue, Vice, and Passions in their Cause,
And Fame from Science, not from Fortune draws.
So Poetry, which is in *Oxford* made
An Art, in *London* onely is a Trade.
There Haughty Dunces whose unlearned Pen
Could ne'er Spell Grammar, would be reading Men.
Such build their Poems the *Lucretian* way,
So many Huddled Atoms make a Play,
And if they hit in Order by some Chance,
They call that Nature, which is Ignorance.
To such a Fame let mere Town-Wits aspire,
And their Gay Nonsense their own Citts admire.
Our Poet, could he find Forgiveness here
Would wish it rather than a *Plaudit* there.
He owns no Crown from those *Prætorian* bands,
But knows *that* Right is in this Senates hands.
Not Impudent enough to hope your Praise,
Low at the Muses feet, his Wreath he lays,
And where he took it up Resigns his Bays.
Kings make their Poets whom themselves think fit,
But 'tis your Suffrage makes Authentique Wit.

EPILOGUE, *Spoken by the same*

NO poor *Dutch* Peasant, wing'd with all his Fear,
Flies with more haste, when the *French* arms draw near,
Than We with our Poetique train come down
For refuge hither, from th' infected Town;

20 and Faults] *om. MS* 24 where] whence *MS* 28 Poetry] Poesy *MS* 34 And] which *MS* 39 wish it rather] rather wish it *MS* 41 this] the *92* 46 *MS adds* Mr Driden's Prologue for ye Players at Oxford.

Epilogue 2 haste] speed *MS* draw] are *MS*

Heaven for our Sins this Summer has thought fit
To visit us with all the Plagues of Wit.
 A *French* Troop first swept all things in its way,
But those Hot *Monsieurs* were too quick to stay;
Yet, to our Cost in that short time, we find
They left their Itch of Novelty behind.
 Th' *Italian* Merry-Andrews took their place,
And quite Debauch'd the Stage with lewd Grimace;
Instead of Wit, and Humours, your Delight
Was there to see two Hobby-horses Fight,
Stout *Scaramoucha* with Rush Lance rode in,
And ran a Tilt at Centaure *Arlequin*.
For Love you heard how amorous Asses bray'd,
And Cats in Gutters gave their Serenade.
Nature was out of Countenance, and each Day
Some new born Monster shewn you for a Play.
 But when all fail'd, to strike the Stage quite Dumb,
Those wicked Engines call'd Machines are come.
Thunder and Lightning now for Wit are Play'd,
And shortly Scenes in *Lapland* will be Lay'd:
Art Magique is for Poetry profest,
And Cats and Dogs, and each obscener Beast
To which *Ægyptian* Dotards once did Bow,
Upon our *English* stage are worship'd now.
Witchcraft reigns there, and raises to Renown
Macbeth, the *Simon Magus* of the Town.
Fletcher's despis'd, your *Johnson* out of Fashion,
And Wit the onely Drug in all the Nation.
In this low Ebb our Wares to you are shown,
By you those Staple Authours worth is known,
For Wit's a Manufacture of your Own.
When you, who onely can, their Scenes have prais'd,
We'll boldly back, and say their Price is rais'd.

9 Cost] costs *MS* 13 Humours] humour *MS* 15 *Scaramoucha*] Staramouch *MS* 21 But when all] When all this *MS* 30 the *Simon*] and *Simon* *92* 31 *Johnson*] Johnsons *MS* 32 Wit] Wit's *MS* 34 By] To *MS*

PROLOGUE, *to the University of* Oxford, 1674

Spoken by Mr. Hart

POETS, your Subjects, have their Parts assign'd
T' unbend, and to divert their Sovereign's mind;
When tyr'd with following Nature, you think fit
To seek repose in the cool shades of Wit,
And from the sweet Retreat, with Joy survey
What rests, and what is conquer'd, of the way.
Here free your selves, from Envie, Care and Strife,
You view the various turns of humane Life:
Safe in our Scene, through dangerous Courts you go,
And Undebauch'd, the Vice of Cities know.
Your Theories are here to Practice brought,
As in Mechanick operations wrought;
And Man the Little world before you set,
As once the Sphere of Chrystal, shew'd the Great:
Blest sure are you above all Mortal kind,
If to your Fortunes you can Suit your Mind.
Content to see, and shun, those Ills we show,
And Crimes, on Theatres alone, to know:
With joy we bring what our dead Authours writ,
And beg from you the value of their Wit.
That *Shakespear*'s, *Fletcher*'s, and great *Johnson*'s claim
May be Renew'd from those, who gave them fame.
None of our living Poets dare appear,
For Muses so severe are worshipt here;
That conscious of their Faults they shun the Eye,
And as Prophane, from Sacred places fly,
Rather than see th' offended God, and dye.
We bring no Imperfections, but our own,
Such Faults as made, are by the Makers shown.
And you have been so kind, that we may boast,
The greatest Judges still can Pardon most.
Poets must stoop, when they would please our Pit,
Debas'd even to the Level of their Wit.
Disdaining that, which yet they know, will Take,
Hating themselves, what their Applause must make:

Prologue. 15 kind, *92*: kind: *84*

But when to Praise from you they would Aspire
Though they like Eagles Mount, your *Jove* is Higher.
So far your Knowledge, all their Pow'r transcends,
As what *should* be, beyond what *Is*, extends.

EPILOGUE To *OXFORD*

Spoken by *Mrs. Marshal*

OFT has our Poet wisht, this happy Seat
Might prove his fading Muses last retreat:
I wonder'd at his wish, but now I find
He sought for quiet, and content of mind;
Which noisfull Towns, and Courts can never know,
And onely in the shades like Laurels grow.
Youth, e'er it sees the World, here studies rest,
And Age returning thence concludes it best.
What wonder if we court that happiness
Yearly to share, which hourly you possess,
Teaching ev'n you, (while the vext World we show,)
Your Peace to value more, and better know?
'Tis all we can return for favours past,
Whose holy Memory shall ever last,
For Patronage from him whose care presides
O'er every noble Art, and every Science guides:
Bathurst, a name the learn'd with reverence know,
And scarcely more to his own *Virgil* owe.
Whose Age enjoys but what his Youth deserv'd,
To rule those Muses whom before he serv'd.
His Learning, and untainted Manners too
We find (*Athenians*) are deriv'd to you;
Such Ancient hospitality there rests
In yours, as dwelt in the first *Grecian* Breasts,
Whose kindness was Religion to their Guests.
Such Modesty did to our sex appear,
As had there been no Laws we need not fear,
Since each of you was our Protector here.

Epilogue. Two versions are printed in 84. Text from 84a, which 92 follows. Epilogue . . . *Marshal 84b*: Epilogue, *Spoken by Mrs.* Boutell *84a*: Epilogue *spoken at* Oxford *by Mrs.* Marshall *92*

4 sought for] here sought *84b* 14 last,] last. *84b* 20 serv'd. *84b*: serv'd, *84a*: serv'd: *92* 25 Whose] Where *84b*

Converse so chast, and so strict Vertue shown,
As might *Apollo* with the Muses own.
Till our return we must despair to find
Judges so just, so knowing, and so kind.

Prologue *to the University of* Oxford

DISCORD, and Plots which have undone our Age
With the same ruine, have o'erwhelm'd the Stage.
Our House has suffer'd in the common Woe,
We have been troubled with *Scotch* Rebels too;
Our Brethren, are from *Thames* to *Tweed* departed,
And of our Sisters, all the kinder hearted,
To *Edenborough* gone, or Coacht, or Carted.
With bonny Blewcap there they act all night
For *Scotch* half Crown, in *English* Three-pence hight.
One Nymph, to whom fat *Sir John Falstaff*'s lean,
There with her single Person fills the Scene.
Another, with long use, and Age decay'd,
Div'd here old Woman, and rose there a Maid.
Our Trusty Door-keepers of former time,
There strutt and swagger in Heroique rhime:
Tack but a Copper-lace to Drugget sute,
And there's a Heroe made without dispute.
And that which was a Capons tayl before,
Becomes a plume for *Indian* Emperour.
But all his Subjects, to express the care
Of Imitation, go, like *Indians*, bare;
Lac'd Linen there wou'd be a dangerous thing,
It might perhaps a new Rebellion bring,
The *Scot* who wore it, wou'd be chosen King.
But why shou'd I these Renegades describe,
When you your selves have seen a lewder Tribe.
Teg has been here, and to this learned Pit,
With *Irish* action slander'd *English* Wit.
You have beheld such barb'rous *Mac's* appear,
As merited a second Massacre.
Such as like *Cain* were branded with disgrace,
And had their Country stampt upon their Face.

Prologue. 32 Face.] Face: *84 92*

When Stroulers durst presume to pick your purse,
We humbly thought our broken Troop not worse,
How ill soe'er our action may deserve,
Oxford's a place, where Wit can never sterve.

PROLOGUE TO THE University of *OXFORD*

THO' Actors cannot much of Learning boast,
Of all who want it, we admire it most.
We love the Praises of a Learned Pit,
As we remotely are ally'd to Wit.
We speak our Poets Wit, and Trade in Ore,
Like those who touch upon the Golden Shore:
Betwixt our Judges can distinction make,
Discern how much, and why, our Poems take.
Mark if the Fools, or Men of Sence, rejoyce,
Whether th' Applause be only Sound or Voice.
When our Fop Gallants, or our City Folly
Clap over-loud, it makes us melancholy:
We doubt that Scene which does their wonder raise,
And, for their ignorance contemn their Praise.
Judge then, if We who Act, and They who Write,
Shou'd not be proud of giving You delight.
London likes grossly, but this nicer Pit
Examines, Fathoms all the depths of Wit:
The ready Finger lays on every Blot,
Knows what shou'd justly please, and what shou'd not.
Nature her self lies open to your view,
You judge by Her what draught of Her is true,
Where out lines false, and Colours seem too faint,
Where Bunglers dawb, and where True Poets Paint.
But by the Sacred Genius of this Place,
By every Muse, by each Domestick Grace,

Prologue. There is a version in Bodl. MS. Eng. Poet. e. 4, f. 178, headed A Prologue to the University of Oxford, at the Act 1676; by his Majesties Servants
2 we] they *MS* 10 Whether th' Applause] Whether applause *MS* 13 that] the *MS* does] doth *MS* 14 contemn] condemn *MS* 15 and] or *MS* 23 too] to *MS* 25 But] Now *MS* 26 by each] and each *MS*

Be kind to Wit, which but endeavours well,
And, where you judge, presumes not to excel.
Our Poets hither for Adoption come,
As Nations su'd to be made Free of *Rome.*
Not in the suffragating Tribes to stand,
But in your utmost, last, Provincial Band.
If His Ambition may those Hopes pursue,
Who with Religion loves Your Arts and You,
Oxford to Him a dearer Name shall be,
Than His own Mother University.
Thebes did His Green, unknowing Youth ingage,
He chuses *Athens* in His Riper Age.

Prologue to ARVIRAGUS REVIV'D

Spoken by Mr. *Hart*

WITH sickly Actors and an old House too,
We're match'd with Glorious Theatres and New,
And with our Alehouse Scenes, and Cloaths bare worn,
Can neither raise Old Plays, nor New adorn.
If all these ills could not undo us quite,
A Brisk *French* Troop is grown your dear delight.
Who with broad bloody Bills call you each day,
To laugh, and break your Buttons at their Play.
Or see some serious Piece, which we presume
Is fal'n from some incomparable Plume;
And therefore, *Messieurs*, if you'l do us grace,
Send Lacquies early to preserve your Place.
We dare not on your Priviledge intrench,
Or ask you why you like 'em? They are *French.*
Therefore some go with Courtesie exceeding,
Neither to Hear nor See, but show their Breeding.
Each Lady striving to out-laugh the rest,
To make it seem they understood the Jest:
Their Countrymen come in, and nothing pay,
To teach Us *English* where to Clap the Play:

27 Wit, which] him, who *MS* 29 Adoption] Adoptions *MS* 32 your] the *MS* 33 those] his *MS*

Civil *Igad*: Our Hospitable Land,
Bears all the charge for them to understand:
Mean time we Languish, and neglected lye,
Like Wives, while You keep better Company;
And wish for our own sakes, without a Satyr,
You'd less good Breeding, or had more good Nature.

Prologue for the Women, when they Acted at the Old THEATRE in LINCOLNS-INN-FIELDS

WERE none of you Gallants e're driven so hard,
As when the poor kind Soul was under guard
And could not do't at home, in some by-street,
To take a Lodging, and in private meet?
Such is our Case, We can't appoint our House,
The Lovers old and wonted Rendezvouz.
But hither to this trusty Nook remove,
The worse the Lodging is, the more the Love.
For much good Pastime, many a dear sweet hug
Is stoln in Garrets on the humble Rugg.
Here's good Accommodation in the Pit,
The Grave demurely in the midst may Sit.
And so the hot *Burgundian* on the Side,
Ply Vizard Masque, and o're the Benches stride:
Here are convenient upper Boxes too,
For those that make the most triumphant show,
All that keep Coaches must not Sit below.
There Gallants, You betwixt the Acts retire,
And at dull Plays have something to admire:
We who look up, can Your Addresses mark;
And see the Creatures Coupled in the Ark:
So we expect the *Lovers*, *Braves*, and *Wits*;
The Gaudy House with Scenes, will serve for *Citts*.

Prologue. 1 WERE] WHere *84 92* 6 wonted] wanted *84 92* 22 *Wits*;] *Wits*, *84 92*

A Prologue spoken at the Opening of the NEW HOUSE, *Mar.* 26. 1674

A PLAIN Built House after so long a stay,
Will send you half unsatisfy'd away;
When, fal'n from your expected Pomp, you find
A bare convenience only is design'd.
You who each day can Theatres behold,
Like *Nero*'s Palace, shining all with Gold,
Our mean ungilded Stage will scorn, we fear,
And for the homely Room, disdain the Chear.
Yet now cheap Druggets to a Mode are grown,
And a plain Sute (since we can make but one)
Is better than to be by tarnisht gawdry known.
They who are by Your Favours wealthy made,
With mighty Sums may carry on the Trade:
We, broken Banquers, half destroy'd by Fire,
With our small Stock to humble Roofs retire;
Pity our Loss, while you their Pomp admire.
For Fame and Honour we no longer strive,
We yield in both, and only beg to Live.
Unable to support their vast Expence,
Who Build, and Treat with such Magnificence;
That like th' Ambitious Monarchs of the Age,
They give the Law to our Provincial Stage:
Great Neighbours enviously promote Excess,
While they impose their Splendor on the less.
But only Fools, and they of vast Estate,
Th' extremity of Modes will imitate,
The dangling Knee-fringe, and the Bib-Cravat.
Yet if some Pride with want may be allow'd,
We in our plainness may be justly proud:
Our Royal Master will'd it should be so,
What e're He's pleas'd to own, can need no show:
That Sacred Name gives Ornament and Grace,
And, like his stamp, makes basest Mettals pass.
'Twere Folly now a stately Pile to raise,
To build a Play-House while You throw down Plays.

A Prologue. 15 retire;] retire, *84 92*

Whilst Scenes, Machines, and empty *Opera's* reign,
And for the Pencil You the Pen disdain.
While Troops of famisht *Frenchmen* hither drive,
And laugh at those upon whose Alms they live:
Old *English* Authors vanish, and give place
To these new Conqu'rors of the *Norman* Race;
More tamely, than your Fathers You submit,
You'r now grown Vassals to 'em in your wit:
Mark, when they Play, how our fine Fops advance
The mighty Merits of these Men of *France*,
Keep Time, cry *Ben*, and humour the Cadence:
Well, please your selves, but sure 'tis understood,
That *French* Machines have ne'r done *England* good:
I wou'd not prophesie our Houses Fate:
But while vain Shows and Scenes you over-rate,
'Tis to be fear'd—
That as a Fire the former House o'rethrew,
Machines and Tempests will destroy the new.

Epilogue by the same Author

THOUGH what our Prologue said was sadly true,
Yet, Gentlemen, our homely House is new,
A Charm that seldom fails with, wicked, You.
A Country Lip may have the Velvet touch,
Tho' She's no Lady, you may think her such,
A strong imagination may do much.
But you, loud Sirs, who thro' your Curls look big,
Criticks in Plume and white vallancy Wig,
Who lolling on our foremost Benches sit,
And still charge first, (the true forlorn of Wit)
Whose favours, like the Sun, warm where you roul,
Yet you like him, have neither heat nor Soul;
So may your Hats your Foretops never press,
Untouch'd your Ribbonds, sacred be your dress;
So may you slowly to Old Age advance,
And have th' excuse of Youth for Ignorance.

47 Well, *92*: Well *84*
Epilogue. 7 thro'] tho' *84 92* 14 Ribbonds] Ribbons *92*

So may Fop corner full of noise remain,
And drive far off the dull attentive train;
So may your Midnight Scowrings happy prove,
And Morning Batt'ries force your way to Love;
So may not *France* your Warlike Hands recall,
But leave you by each others Swords to fall:
As you come here to ruffle Vizard Punk,
When sober, rail and roar when you are drunk.
But to the Wits we can some merit plead,
And urge what by themselves has oft been said:
Our House relieves the Ladies from the frights
Of ill pav'd Streets, and long dark Winter Nights;
The *Flanders* Horses from a cold bleak Road,
Where Bears in Furs dare scarcely look abroad:
The Audience from worn Plays and Fustian Stuff
Of Rhyme, more nauseous than three Boys in Buff.
Though in their House the Poets Heads appear,
We hope we may presume their Wits are here.
The best which they reserv'd they now will Play,
For, like kind Cuckolds, tho' w' have not the way
To please, we'l find you Abler Men who may.
If they shou'd fail, for last recruits we breed
A Troop of frisking Monsieurs to succeed:
(You know the *French* sure cards at time of need.)

Prologue to the Princess of CLEVES

LADIES! (I hope there's none behind to hear,)
I long to whisper something in your Ear:
A Secret, which does much my Mind perplex,
There's Treason in the Play against our Sex.
A Man that's false to Love, that Vows and cheats,
And kisses every living thing he meets!
A Rogue in Mode, I dare not speak too broad,
One that does something to the very Bawd.
Out on him, Traytor, for a filthy Beast,
Nay, and he's like the pack of all the rest;

30 abroad:] abroad. *84 92*

None of 'em stick at mark: They all deceive,
Some *Jew* has chang'd the Text, I half believe,
Their *Adam* cozen'd our poor Grandame *Eve*.
To hide their faults they rap out Oaths and tear:
Now tho' we Lye, w're too well bred to Swear.
So we compound for half the Sin we owe,
But men are dipt for Soul and Body too.
And when found out excuse themselves, Pox cant 'em,
With Latin stuff, *perjuria ridet Amantum*.
I'm not Book Learn'd, to know that word in vogue,
But I suspect 'tis Latin for a Rogue.
I'me sure I never heard that Schritch owl hollow'd
In my poor ears, but Separation follow'd.
How can such perjur'd Villains e're be Saved,
Achitophel's not half so false to *David*.
With Vows and soft expressions to allure,
They stand like Foremen of a Shop, demure,
No sooner out of sight, but they are gadding,
And for the next new Face Ride out a padding.
Yet, by their favour when they have bin Kissing,
We can perceive the ready Mony missing:
Well! we may rail, but 'tis as good e'en wink,
Something we find, and something they will sink.
But since they'r at Renouncing, 'tis our parts,
To trump their Diamonds, as they trump our Hearts.

Epilogue to the Princess of *Cleves*

A QUALM of Conscience brings me back agen
To make amends to you bespatter'd Men!
We Women Love like Cats, that hide their Joys,
By growling, squaling, and a hideous noise.
I rail'd at wild young Sparks, but without lying,
Never was Man worse thought on for high-flying;
The prodigal of Love gives each her part,
And squandring shows, at least, a noble Heart.
I've heard of Men, who in some lew'd Lampoon,
Have hir'd a Friend, to make their valour known.

Prologue. 13 Their] There *92*   35 as] & *92*

That Accusation straight, this question brings,
What is the Man that does such naughty things?
The Spaniel Lover, like a sneaking Fop,
Lyes at our Feet. He's scarce worth taking up;
'Tis true, such Hero's in a Play go far,
But Chamber practice, is not like the Bar.
When Men such vile, such faint Petitions make,
We fear to give, because they fear to take;
Since Modesty's the Vertue of our kind,
Pray let it be to our own Sex confin'd.
When Men usurp it from the Female Nation,
'Tis but a work of Supererrogation.—
We show'd a Princess in the Play, 'tis true,
Who gave her *Cæsar* more than all his due.
Told her own Faults, but I shou'd much abhor,
To choose a Husband for my Confessor.
You see what Fate follow'd the Saint-like Fool,
For telling Tales from out the Nuptial School.
  Our Play a merry Comedy had prov'd,
  Had she Confess't as much to him she lov'd.
  True *Presbyterian*-Wives, the *means* wou'd try,
  But damn'd Confessing is flat Popery.

The Tears of AMYNTA, for the Death of DAMON

SONG

On a bank, beside a Willow,
Heav'n her Cov'ring, Earth her Pillow,
Sad *Amynta* sigh'd alone:
From the chearless Dawn of Morning
Till the Dew's of Night returning
Singing thus she made her mone:
        Hope is banish'd
        Joys are vanish'd;
Damon, my belov'd is gone!

Epilogue. 23 Play, 'tis] Play. 'Tis *84 92*   24 his] is *92*

2

Time, I dare thee to discover
Such a Youth, and such a Lover,
Oh so true, so kind was he!
Damon was the Pride of Nature,
Charming in his every Feature,
Damon liv'd alone for me:
Melting Kisses
Murmuring Blisses,
Who so liv'd and lov'd as we!

3

Never shall we curse the Morning,
Never bless the Night returning,
Sweet Embraces to restore:
Never shall we both ly dying
Nature failing, Love supplying
All the Joyes he drain'd before:
Death, come end me
To befriend me;
Love and *Damon* are no more.

EPILOGUE intended to have been spoken by the Lady Henr. Mar. Wentworth *when* Calisto *was acted at Court*

As *Jupiter* I made my Court in vain,
I'le now assume my native shape again.
I'm weary to be so unkindly us'd,
And would not be a God to be refus'd.
State grows uneasie when it hinders love,
A glorious burden, which the Wise remove.
Now as a Nymph I need not sue nor try
The force of any lightning but the eye.
Beauty and youth more then a God Command;
No *Jove* could e're the force of these withstand.
Tis here that Sovereign Pow'r admits dispute,
Beauty sometimes is justly absolute.

Our sullen *Catoes*, whatsoe're they say,
Even while they frown and dictate Laws, obey.
You, mighty Sir, our Bonds more easie make
And gracefully what all must suffer take.
Above those forms the Grave affect to wear;
For 'tis not to be wise to be severe.
True wisdom may some gallantry admit,
And soften business with the charms of wit.
These peaceful Triumphs with your cares you bought,
And from the midst of fighting Nations brought.
You only hear it thunder from afar,
And sit in peace the Arbiter of War.
Peace, the loath'd Manna, which hot brains despise,
You knew its worth, and made it early prize:
And in its happy leisure sit and see
The promises of more felicity:
Two glorious Nymphs of your one Godlike line,
Whose Morning Rays like Noontide strike and shine;
Whom you to suppliant Monarchs shall dispose,
To bind your Friends and to disarm your Foes.

Epilogue. 28 felicity:] felicity. *84 92* 30 shine;] shine. *84 92*

PROLOGUE To a NEW PLAY, Call'd, The Disappointment: or, The Mother in Fashion.

Spoken by Mr. BETTERTON

HOW comes it, Gentlemen, that now aday's
When all of you so shrewdly judge of Plays,
Our Poets tax you still with want of Sence?
All Prologues treat you at your own Expence.
Sharp Citizens a wiser way can go;
They make you Fools, but never call you so.
They, in good Manners, seldom make a Slip,
But, Treat a Common Whore with Ladyship:
But here each sawcy Wit at Random writes,
And uses Ladies as he uses Knights.
Our Author, Young, and Grateful in his Nature,
Vow's, that from him no Nymph deserves a Satyr.
Nor will he ever Draw—I mean his Rhime,
Against the sweet Partaker of his Crime.
Nor is he yet so bold an Undertaker
To call MEN Fools, 'tis Railing at their MAKER.
Besides, he fears to split upon that Shelf;
He's young enough to be a FOPP himself.
And, if his Praise can bring you all A-bed,
He swears such hopeful Youth no Nation ever bred.
Your Nurses, we presume, in such a Case,
Your Father chose, because he lik'd the Face;
And, often, they supply'd your Mothers place.
The Dry Nurse was your Mothers ancient Maid,
Who knew some former Slip she ne're betray'd.
Betwixt 'em both, for Milk and Sugar Candy,
Your sucking Bottles were well stor'd with Brandy.
Your Father to initiate your Discourse
Meant to have taught you first to Swear and Curse;
But was prevented by each careful Nurse.
For, leaving Dad and Mam, as Names too common,
They taught you certain parts of Man and Woman.

Prologue To a New Play, &c. Text from the separate edition, 1684 (A), collated with Southerne's The Disappointment or The Mother in Fashion, *1684 (B)*
10 uses *B*: use's *A*

I pass your Schools, for there when first you came,
You wou'd be sure to learn the Latin name.
In Colledges you scorn'd their Art of thinking,
But learn'd all Moods and Figures of good Drinking:
Thence, come to Town you practise Play, to know
The Vertues of the High Dice, and the Low.
Each thinks himself a SHARPER most profound:
He cheats by Pence; is cheated by the Pound:
With these Perfections, and what else he Gleans,
The SPARK sets up for Love behind our Scenes;
Hot in pursuit of Princesses and Queens.
There, if they know their Man, with cunning Carriage,
Twenty to one but it concludes in Marriage.
He hires some Homely Room, Love's Fruits to gather,
And, Garret-high, Rebels against his Father.
But he once dead—
Brings her in Triumph, with her Portion down,
A Twillet, Dressing-Box, and Half a Crown.
Some Marry first, and then they fall to Scowring,
Which is, Refining Marriage into Whoring.
Our Women batten well on their good Nature,
All they can rap and rend for the dear Creature.
But while abroad so liberal the DOLT is,
Poor SPOUSE at Home as Ragged as a Colt is.
Last, some there are, who take their first Degrees
Of Lewdness, in our Middle Galleries:
The Doughty BULLIES enter Bloody Drunk,
Invade and grubble one another's PUNK:
They Caterwaul, and make a dismal Rout,
Call SONS of WHORES, and strike, but ne're lugg-out:
Thus while for *Paultry Punk* they roar and stickle,
They make it *Bawdier* than a CONVENTICLE.

60 grubble] grabble *B*

To the Earl of *Roscomon*, on his Excellent *Essay* on *Translated Verse*

WHETHER the fruitful *Nile*, or *Tyrian* Shore,
The seeds of Arts and Infant Science bore,
'Tis sure the noble Plant, translated first,
Advanc'd its head in *Grecian* Gardens nurst.
The *Grecians* added Verse, their tuneful Tongue
Made Nature first, and Nature's God their song.
Nor stopt Translation here: For conquering *Rome*
With *Grecian* Spoils brought *Grecian* Numbers home;
Enrich'd by those *Athenian* Muses more,
Than all the vanquish'd World cou'd yield before.
'Till barb'rous Nations, and more barb'rous Times
Debas'd the majesty of Verse to Rhymes;
Those rude at first: a kind of hobbling Prose:
That limp'd along, and tinckl'd in the close:
But *Italy*, reviving from the trance,
Of *Vandal*, *Goth*, and *Monkish* ignorance,
With pauses, cadence, and well vowell'd Words,
And all the Graces a good Ear affords,
Made Rhyme an Art: and *Dante*'s polish'd page
Restor'd a silver, not a golden Age:
Then *Petrarch* follow'd, and in him we see,
What Rhyme improv'd in all its height can be;
At best a pleasing Sound, and fair barbarity:
The *French* pursu'd their steps; and *Brittain*, last
In Manly sweetness all the rest surpass'd.
The Wit of *Greece*, the Gravity of *Rome*
Appear exalted in the *Brittish* Loome;
The Muses Empire is restor'd agen,
In *Charles* his Reign, and by *Roscomon*'s Pen.
Yet modestly he does his Work survey,
And calls a finish'd Poem an *ESSAY*;
For all the needful Rules are scatter'd here;
Truth smoothly told, and pleasantly severe;
(So well is Art disguis'd, for Nature to appeare.)

To the Earl of Roscomon. Text from An Essay on Translated Verse, *1684, collated with the edition of 1685*

Nor need those Rules, to give Translation light;
His own example is a flame so bright;
That he, who but arrives to copy well,
Unguided will advance; unknowing will excel.
Scarce his own *Horace* cou'd such Rules ordain;
Or his own *Virgil* sing a nobler strain.
How much in him may rising *Ireland* boast,
How much in gaining him has *Britain* lost!
Their Island in revenge has ours reclaim'd,
The more instructed we, the more we still are sham'd.
'Tis well for us his generous bloud did flow
Deriv'd from *British* Channels long ago;
That here his conquering Ancestors were nurst;
And *Ireland* but translated *England* first:
By this Reprisal we regain our right;
Else must the two contending Nations fight,
A nobler quarrel for his Native earth,
Than what divided *Greece* for *Homer*'s birth.
To what perfection will our Tongue arrive,
How will Invention and Translation thrive
When Authors nobly born will bear their part
And not disdain th' inglorious praise of Art!
Great Generals thus descending from command,
With their own toil provoke the Souldiers hand.
How will sweet *Ovid*'s Ghost be pleas'd to hear
His Fame augmented by an *English* Peer, *The Earl of* Mulgrave.
How he embellishes His *Helen*'s loves,
Out does his softness, and his sense improves?
When these translate, and teach Translators too,
Nor Firstling Kid, nor any vulgar vow
Shou'd at *Apollo*'s grateful Altar stand;
Roscomon writes, to that auspicious hand,
Muse feed the Bull that spurns the yellow sand.
Roscomon, whom both Court and Camps commend,
True to his Prince, and faithful to his friend;
Roscomon first in Fields of Honour known,
First in the peaceful Triumphs of the Gown;
He both *Minerva's* justly makes his own.

47 were *85*: was *84*. *See Commentary* 60 *English 85*: *Brittish 84* 72 He] Who *85*

Now let the few belov'd by *Jove*, and they,
Whom infus'd *Titan* form'd of better Clay,
On equal terms with ancient Wit ingage,
Nor mighty *Homer* fear, nor sacred *Virgil*'s page:
Our *English* Palace opens wide in state;
And without stooping they may pass the Gate.

To the MEMORY of Mr. *OLDHAM*

FAREWEL, too little and too lately known,
Whom I began to think and call my own;
For sure our Souls were near ally'd; and thine
Cast in the same Poetick mould with mine.
One common Note on either Lyre did strike,
And Knaves and Fools we both abhorr'd alike:
To the same Goal did both our Studies drive,
The last set out the soonest did arrive.
Thus *Nisus* fell upon the slippery place,
While his young Friend perform'd and won the Race.
O early ripe! to thy abundant store
What could advancing Age have added more?
It might (what Nature never gives the young)
Have taught the numbers of thy native Tongue.
But Satyr needs not those, and Wit will shine
Through the harsh cadence of a rugged line.
A noble Error, and but seldom made,
When Poets are by too much force betray'd.
Thy generous fruits, though gather'd ere their prime
Still shew'd a quickness; and maturing time
But mellows what we write to the dull sweets of Rime.
Once more, hail and farewel; farewel thou young,
But ah too short, *Marcellus* of our Tongue;
Thy Brows with Ivy, and with Laurels bound;
But Fate and gloomy Night encompass thee around.

To the Memory of Mr. Oldham. Text from Remains of Mr. John Oldham in Verse and Prose, *1684, collated with the editions of 1686, 1687, 1693, 1694, 1697*

POEMS FROM SYLVÆ

or, the *Second Part* of *POETICAL MISCELLANIES* (*1685*)

PREFACE

For this last half Year I have been troubled with the disease (as I may call it) of Translation; the cold Prose fits of it, (which are always the most tedious with me) were spent in the History of the League; the hot, (which succeeded them) in this Volume of Verse Miscellanies. The truth is, I fancied to my self a kind of ease in the change of the Paroxism; never suspecting but that the humour wou'd have wasted it self in two or three Pastorals of Theocritus, *and as many Odes of* Horace. *But finding, or at least thinking I found, something that was more pleasing in them, than my ordinary productions, I encourag'd my self to renew my old acquaintance with* Lucretius *and* Virgil*; and immediately fix'd upon some parts of them which had most affected me in the reading. These were my natural Impulses for the undertaking: But there was an accidental motive, which was full as forcible, and God forgive him who was the occasion of it. It was my Lord* Roscomon's Essay *on translated Verse, which made me uneasie till I try'd whether or no I was capable of following his Rules, and of reducing the speculation into practice. For many a fair Precept in Poetry, is like a seeming Demonstration in the Mathematicks; very specious in the Diagram, but failing in the Mechanick Operation. I think I have generally observ'd his instructions; I am sure my reason is sufficiently convinc'd both of their truth and usefulness; which, in other words, is to confess no less a vanity than to pretend that I have at least in some places made Examples to his Rules. Yet withall, I must acknowledge, that I have many times exceeded my Commission; for I have both added and omitted, and even sometimes very boldly made such expositions of my Authors, as no* Dutch *Commentator will forgive me. Perhaps, in such particular passages, I have thought that I discover'd some beauty yet undiscover'd by those Pedants, which none but a Poet cou'd have found. Where I have taken away some of their Expressions, and cut them shorter, it may possibly be on this consideration, that what was beautiful in the* Greek *or* Latin, *wou'd not appear so shining in the* English*: And where I have enlarg'd them, I desire the false Criticks wou'd not*

Poems. Text from the first edition, 1685, collated with the second edition, 1692
Preface. 13 *which 85 (errata): whose 85 (text)*

always think that those thoughts are wholly mine, but that either they are secretly in the Poet, or may be fairly deduc'd from him: or at least, if both those considerations should fail, that my own is of a piece with his, and that if he were living, and an Englishman, *they are such, as he wou'd probably have written.*

For, after all, a Translator is to make his Author appear as charming as possibly he can, provided he maintains his Character, and makes him not unlike himself. Translation is a kind of Drawing after the Life; where every one will acknowledge there is a double sort of likeness, a good one and a bad. 'Tis one thing to draw the Out-lines true, the Features like, the Proportions exact, the Colouring it self perhaps tolerable, and another thing to make all these graceful, by the posture, the shadowings, and chiefly by the Spirit which animates the whole. I cannot without some indignation, look on an ill Copy of an excellent Original: Much less can I behold with patience Virgil, Homer, *and some others, whose beauties I have been endeavouring all my Life to imitate, so abus'd, as I may say to their Faces by a botching Interpreter. What* English *Readers unacquainted with* Greek *or* Latin *will believe me or any other Man, when we commend those Authors, and confess we derive all that is pardonable in us from their Fountains, if they take those to be the same Poets, whom our* Ogleby's *have Translated? But I dare assure them, that a good Poet is no more like himself, in a dull Translation, than his Carcass would be to his living Body. There are many who understand* Greek *and* Latin, *and yet are ignorant of their Mother Tongue. The proprieties and delicacies of the* English *are known to few; 'tis impossible even for a good Wit, to understand and practice them without the help of a liberal Education, long Reading, and digesting of those few good Authors we have amongst us, the knowledge of Men and Manners, the freedom of habitudes and conversation with the best company of both Sexes; and in short, without wearing off the rust which he contracted, while he was laying in a stock of Learning. Thus difficult it is to understand the purity of* English, *and critically to discern not only good Writers from bad, and a proper stile from a corrupt, but also to distinguish that which is pure in a good Author, from that which is vicious and corrupt in him. And for want of all these requisites, or the greatest part of them, most of our ingenious young Men, take up some cry'd up* English *Poet for their Model, adore him, and imitate him as they think, without knowing wherein he is defective, where he is Boyish and trifling, wherein either his thoughts are improper to his Subject, or his Expressions unworthy of his Thoughts, or the turn of both is unharmonious. Thus it appears necessary that a Man shou'd be a nice Critick in his Mother Tongue, before he attempts to Translate a foreign Language. Neither is it sufficient that he be able to Judge of Words and Stile; but he must be a Master of them too: He must perfectly understand his Authors Tongue, and absolutely command his*

33 *charming as* 92: *charming at* 85

own: So that to be a thorow Translatour, he must be a thorow Poet. Neither is it enough to give his Authors sence, in good English, in Poetical expressions, and in Musical numbers: For, though all these are exceeding difficult to perform, there yet remains an harder task; and 'tis a secret of which few Translatours have sufficiently thought. I have already hinted a word or two concerning it; that is, the maintaining the Character of an Author, which distinguishes him from all others, and makes him appear that individual Poet whom you wou'd interpret. For example, not only the thoughts, but the Style and Versification of Virgil and Ovid, are very different: Yet I see, even in our best Poets, who have Translated some parts of them, that they have confounded their several Talents; and by endeavouring only at the sweetness and harmony of Numbers, have made them both so much alike, that if I did not know the Originals, I shou'd never be able to Judge by the Copies, which was Virgil, and which was Ovid. It was objected against a late noble Painter, that he drew many graceful Pictures, but few of them were like. And this happen'd to him, because he always studied himself more than those who sate to him. In such Translatours I can easily distinguish the hand which perform'd the Work, but I cannot distinguish their Poet from another. Suppose two Authors are equally sweet, yet there is a great distinction to be made in sweetness, as in that of Sugar, and that of Honey. I can make the difference more plain, by giving you, (if it be worth knowing) my own method of proceeding, in my Translations out of four several Poets in this Volume; Virgil, Theocritus, Lucretius and Horace. In each of these, before I undertook them, I consider'd, the Genius and distinguishing Character of my Author. I look'd on Virgil, as a succinct and grave Majestick Writer; one who weigh'd not only every thought, but every Word and Syllable. Who was still aiming to crowd his sence into as narrow a compass as possibly he cou'd; for which reason he is so very Figurative, that he requires, (I may almost say) a Grammar apart to construe him. His Verse is every where sounding the very thing in your Ears, whose sence it bears: Yet the Numbers are perpetually varied, to increase the delight of the Reader; so that the same sounds are never repeated twice together. On the contrary, Ovid and Claudian, though they Write in Styles differing from each other, yet have each of them but one sort of Musick in their Verses. All the versification, and little variety of Claudian, is included within the compass of four or five Lines, and then he begins again in the same tenour; perpetually closing his sence at the end of a Verse, and that Verse commonly which they call golden, or two Substantives and two Adjectives with a Verb betwixt them to keep the peace. Ovid with all his sweetness, has as little variety of Numbers and sound as he: He is always as it were upon the Hand-gallop, and his Verse runs upon Carpet ground. He avoids like the other all Synalœpha's, or cutting off one Vowel when it comes before

76 are] art 85 92

another, in the following word: So that minding only smoothness, he wants both Variety and Majesty. But to return to Virgil, though he is smooth where smoothness is requir'd, yet he is so far from affecting it, that he seems rather to disdain it. Frequently makes use of Synalœpha's, and concludes his sence in the middle of his Verse. He is every where above conceipts of Epigrammatick Wit, and gross Hyperboles: He maintains Majesty in the midst of plainess; he shines, but glares not; and is stately without ambition, which is the vice of Lucan. I drew my definition of Poetical Wit from my particular consideration of him: For propriety of thoughts and words are only to be found in him; and where they are proper, they will be delightful. Pleasure follows of necessity, as the effect does the cause; and therefore is not to be put into the definition. This exact propriety of Virgil, I particularly regarded, as a great part of his Character; but must confess to my shame, that I have not been able to Translate any part of him so well, as to make him appear wholly like himself. For where the Original is close, no Version can reach it in the same compass. Hannibal Caro's in the Italian, is the nearest, the most Poetical, and the most Sonorous of any Translation of the Æneids; yet, though he takes the advantage of blank Verse, he commonly allows two Lines for one of Virgil, and does not always hit his sence. Tasso tells us in his Letters, that Sperone Speroni, a great Italian Wit, who was his Contemporary, observ'd of Virgil and Tully; that the Latin Oratour, endeavour'd to imitate the Copiousness of Homer the Greek Poet; and that the Latine Poet, made it his business to reach the conciseness of Demosthenes the Greek Oratour. Virgil therefore being so very sparing of his words, and leaving so much to be imagin'd by the Reader, can never be translated as he ought, in any modern Tongue: To make him Copious is to alter his Character; and to Translate him Line for Line is impossible; because the Latin is naturally a more succinct Language, than either the Italian, Spanish, French, or even than the English, (which by reason of its Monosyllables is far the most compendious of them) Virgil is much the closest of any Roman Poet, and the Latin Hexameter, has more Feet than the English Heroick.

Besides all this, an Author has the choice of his own thoughts and words, which a Translatour has not; he is confin'd by the sence of the Inventor to those expressions, which are the nearest to it: So that Virgil studying brevity, and having the command of his own Language, cou'd bring those words into a narrow compass, which a Translatour cannot render without Circumlocutions. In short they who have call'd him the torture of Grammarians, might also have call'd him the plague of Translatours; for he seems to have studied not to be Translated. I own that endeavouring to turn his Nisus and Euryalus as close as I was able; I have perform'd that Episode too literally; that giving more scope to Mezentius and Lausus, that Version which has more of the Majesty of Virgil, has less of his *conciseness; and all that I can promise for my self, is only that I have done both, better than* Ogleby, *and perhaps as well as* Caro. *So, that methinks I come like a Malefactor, to make a Speech upon the Gallows, and to warn all other Poets, by my sad example, from the Sacrilege of Translating* Virgil. *Yet, by considering him so carefully as I did before my attempt, I have made some faint resemblance of him; and had I taken more time, might possibly have succeeded better; but never so well, as to have satisfied my self.*

He who excells all other Poets in his own Language, were it possible to do him right, must appear above them in our Tongue, which, as my Lord Roscomon *justly observes, approaches nearest to the* Roman *in its Majesty: Nearest indeed, but with a vast interval betwixt them. There is an inimitable grace in* Virgils *words, and in them principally consists that beauty, which gives so unexpressible a pleasure to him who best understands their force; this Diction of his, I must once again say, is never to be Copied, and since it cannot, he will appear but lame in the best Translation. The turns of his Verse, his breakings, his propriety, his numbers, and his gravity, I have as far imitated, as the poverty of our Language, and the hastiness of my performance wou'd allow. I may seem sometimes to have varied from his sence; but I think the greatest variations may be fairly deduc'd from him; and where I leave his Commentators, it may be I understand him better: At least I Writ without consulting them in many places. But two particular Lines in* Mezentius *and* Lausus, *I cannot so easily excuse; they are indeed remotely ally'd to* Virgils *sence; but they are too like the trifling tenderness of* Ovid; *and were Printed before I had consider'd them enough to alter them: The first of them I have forgotten, and cannot easily retrieve, because the Copy is at the Press: The second is this;*

—When *Lausus* dy'd, I was already slain.

This appears pretty enough at first sight, but I am convinc'd for many reasons, that the expression is too bold, that Virgil *wou'd not have said it, though* Ovid *wou'd. The Reader may pardon it, if he please, for the freeness of the confession; and instead of that, and the former, admit these two Lines which are more according to the Author,*

Nor ask I Life, nor fought with that design;
As I had us'd my Fortune, use thou thine.

Having with much ado got clear of Virgil, *I have in the next place to consider the genius of* Lucretius, *whom I have Translated more happily in those parts of him which I undertook. If he was not of the best age of* Roman *Poetry, he was at least of that which preceded it; and he himself refin'd it to that degree of perfection, both in the Language and the thoughts, that he left an easie task to*

156 *observes,*] *observes* 85 92

Virgil; *who as he succeeded him in time, so he Copy'd his excellencies: for the method of the* Georgicks *is plainly deriv'd from him.* Lucretius *had chosen a Subject naturally crabbed; he therefore adorn'd it with Poetical descriptions, and Precepts of Morality, in the beginning and ending of his Books. Which you see* Virgil *has imitated with great success, in those four Books, which in my Opinion are more perfect in their kind, than even his Divine* Æneids. *The turn of his Verse he has likewise follow'd, in those places which* Lucretius *has most labour'd, and some of his very Lines he has transplanted into his own Works, without much variation. If I am not mistaken, the distinguishing Character of* Lucretius, *(I mean of his Soul and Genius) is a certain kind of noble pride, and positive assertion of his Opinions. He is every where confident of his own reason, and assuming an absolute command not only over his vulgar Reader, but even his Patron* Memmius. *For he is always bidding him attend, as if he had the Rod over him; and using a Magisterial authority, while he instructs him. From his time to ours, I know none so like him, as our Poet and Philosopher of* Malmsbury. *This is that perpetual Dictatorship, which is exercis'd by* Lucretius; *who though often in the wrong, yet seems to deal* bonâ fide *with his Reader, and tells him nothing but what he thinks; in which plain sincerity, I believe he differs from our* Hobbs, *who cou'd not but be convinc'd, or at least doubt of some eternal Truths which he has oppos'd. But for* Lucretius, *he seems to disdain all manner of Replies, and is so confident of his cause, that he is before hand with his Antagonists; Urging for them, whatever he imagin'd they cou'd say, and leaving them as he supposes, without an objection for the future. All this too, with so much scorn and indignation, as if he were assur'd of the Triumph, before he enter'd into the Lists. From this sublime and daring Genius of his, it must of necessity come to pass, that his thoughts must be Masculine, full of Argumentation, and that sufficiently warm. From the same fiery temper proceeds the loftiness of his Expressions, and the perpetual torrent of his Verse, where the barrenness of his Subject does not too much constrain the quickness of his Fancy. For there is no doubt to be made, but that he cou'd have been every where as Poetical, as he is in his Descriptions, and in the Moral part of his Philosophy, if he had not aim'd more to instruct in his Systeme of Nature, than to delight. But he was bent upon making* Memmius *a Materialist, and teaching him to defie an invisible power: In short, he was so much an Atheist, that he forgot sometimes to be a Poet. These are the considerations which I had of that Author, before I attempted to translate some parts of him. And accordingly I lay'd by my natural Diffidence and Scepticism for a while, to take up that Dogmatical way of his, which as I said, is so much his Character, as to make him that individual Poet. As for his Opinions concerning the mortality of the Soul, they are so absurd, that I cannot if I wou'd believe them.*

193 Lucretius,] Lucretius; *85 92*

I think a future state demonstrable even by natural Arguments; at least to take away rewards and punishments, is only a pleasing prospect to a Man, who resolves before hand not to live morally. But on the other side, the thought of being nothing after death is a burden unsupportable to a vertuous Man, even though a Heathen. We naturally aim at happiness, and cannot bear to have it confin'd to the shortness of our present Being, especially when we consider that vertue is generally unhappy in this World, and vice fortunate. So that 'tis hope of Futurity alone, that makes this Life tolerable, in expectation of a better. Who wou'd not commit all the excesses to which he is prompted by his natural inclinations, if he may do them with security while he is alive, and be uncapable of punishment after he is dead! If he be cunning and secret enough to avoid the Laws, there is no band of morality to restrain him: For Fame and Reputation are weak ties; many men have not the least sence of them: Powerful men are only aw'd by them, as they conduce to their interest, and that not always when a passion is predominant; and no Man will be contain'd within the bounds of duty, when he may safely transgress them. These are my thoughts abstractedly, and without entring into the Notions of our Christian Faith, which is the proper business of Divines.

But there are other Arguments in this Poem (which I have turn'd into English,) *not belonging to the Mortality of the Soul, which are strong enough to a reasonable Man, to make him less in love with Life, and consequently in less apprehensions of Death. Such as are the natural Satiety, proceeding from a perpetual enjoyment of the same things; the inconveniencies of old age, which make him uncapable of corporeal pleasures; the decay of understanding and memory, which render him contemptible and useless to others; these and many other reasons so pathetically urg'd, so beautifully express'd, so adorn'd with examples, and so admirably rais'd by the* Prosopopeia *of Nature, who is brought in speaking to her Children, with so much authority and vigour, deserve the pains I have taken with them, which I hope have not been unsuccessful, or unworthy of my Author. At least I must take the liberty to own, that I was pleas'd with my own endeavours, which but rarely happens to me, and that I am not dissatisfied upon the review, of any thing I have done in this Author.*

'Tis true, there is something, and that of some moment, to be objected against my Englishing *the Nature of Love, from the Fourth Book of* Lucretius*: And I can less easily answer why I Translated it, than why I thus Translated it. The Objection arises from the Obscenity of the Subject; which is aggravated by the too lively, and alluring delicacy of the Verses. In the first place, without the least Formality of an excuse, I own it pleas'd me: and let my Enemies make the worst they can of this Confession; I am not yet so secure from that passion, but that I want my Authors Antidotes against it. He has given the truest and most Philosophical account both of the Disease and Remedy, which I ever found in any*

Author: For which reasons I Translated him. But it will be ask'd why I turn'd him into this luscious English, (*for I will not give it a worse word:*) *instead of an answer, I wou'd ask again of my Supercilious Adversaries, whether I am not bound when I Translate an Author, to do him all the right I can, and to Translate him to the best advantage? If to mince his meaning, which I am satisfi'd was honest and instructive, I had either omitted some part of what he said, or taken from the strength of his expression, I certainly had wrong'd him; and that freeness of thought and words, being thus cashier'd, in my hands, he had no longer been* Lucretius. *If nothing of this kind be to be read, Physicians must not study Nature, Anatomies must not be seen, and somewhat I cou'd say of particular passages in Books, which to avoid prophaness I do not name: But the intention qualifies the act; and both mine and my Authors were to instruct as well as please. Tis most certain that barefac'd Bawdery is the poorest pretence to wit imaginable: If I shou'd say otherwise, I shou'd have two great authorities against me: The one is the Essay on Poetry, which I publickly valued before I knew the Author of it, and with the commendation of which, my Lord* Roscomon *so happily begins his Essay on Translated Verse: The other is no less than our admir'd* Cowley; *who says the same thing in other words: For in his Ode concerning Wit, he writes thus of it;*

Much less can that have any place
At which a Virgin hides her Face:
Such dross the fire must purge away; 'tis just
The Author blush, there where the Reader must.

Here indeed Mr. Cowley *goes farther than the Essay; for he asserts plainly that obscenity has no place in Wit; the other only says, 'tis a poor pretence to it, or an ill sort of Wit, which has nothing more to support it than bare-fac'd Ribaldry; which is both unmannerly in it self, and fulsome to the Reader. But neither of these will reach my case: For in the first place, I am only the Translatour, not the Inventor; so that the heaviest part of the censure falls upon* Lucretius, *before it reaches me: in the next place, neither he nor I have us'd the grossest words; but the cleanliest Metaphors we cou'd find, to palliate the broadness of the meaning; and to conclude, have carried the Poetical part no farther, than the Philosophical exacted.*

There is one mistake of mine which I will not lay to the Printers charge, who has enough to answer for in false pointings: 'tis in the word Viper: *I wou'd have the Verse run thus,*

The Scorpion, Love, must on the wound be bruis'd.

There are a sort of blundering half-witted people, who make a great deal of noise

297 *Editor's paragraph*

about a Verbal slip; though Horace *wou'd instruct them better in true Criticism:* Non ego paucis, offendar maculis quas aut incuria fudit, aut humana parùm cavit natura. *True judgment in Poetry, like that in Painting, takes a view of the whole together, whether it be good or not; and where the beauties are more than the Faults, concludes for the Poet against the little Judge; 'tis a sign that malice is hard driven, when 'tis forc'd to lay hold on a Word or Syllable; to arraign a Man is one thing, and to cavil at him is another. In the midst of an ill natur'd Generation of Scriblers, there is always Justice enough left in Mankind, to protect good Writers: And they too are oblig'd, both by humanity and interest, to espouse each others cause, against false Criticks, who are the common Enemies. This last consideration puts me in mind of what I owe to the Ingenious and Learned Translatour of* Lucretius*; I have not here design'd to rob him of any part of that commendation, which he has so justly acquir'd by the whole Author, whose Fragments only fall to my Portion. What I have now perform'd, is no more than I intended above twenty years ago: The ways of our Translation are very different; he follows him more closely than I have done; which became an Interpreter of the whole Poem. I take more liberty, because it best suited with my design, which was to make him as pleasing as I could. He had been too voluminous had he us'd my method in so long a work, and I had certainly taken his, had I made it my business to Translate the whole. The preference then is justly his; and I joyn with Mr.* Evelyn *in the confession of it, with this additional advantage to him; that his Reputation is already establish'd in this Poet, mine is to make its Fortune in the World. If I have been any where obscure, in following our common Author, or if* Lucretius *himself is to be condemned, I refer my self to his excellent Annotations, which I have often read, and always with some new pleasure.*

My Preface begins already to swell upon me, and looks as if I were afraid of my Reader, by so tedious a bespeaking of him; and yet I have Horace *and* Theocritus *upon my hands; but the* Greek *Gentleman shall quickly be dispatch'd, because I have more business with the* Roman.

That which distinguishes Theocritus *from all other Poets, both* Greek *and* Latin, *and which raises him even above* Virgil *in his Eclogues, is the inimitable tenderness of his passions; and the natural expression of them in words so becoming of a Pastoral. A simplicity shines through all he writes: he shows his Art and Learning by disguising both. His Shepherds never rise above their Country Education in their complaints of Love: There is the same difference betwixt him and* Virgil, *as there is betwixt* Tasso's Aminta, *and the* Pastor Fido *of* Guarini. Virgils *Shepherds are too well read in the Philosophy of* Epicurus *and of* Plato*; and* Guarini's *seem to have been bred in Courts. But* Theocritus *and* Tasso, *have taken theirs from Cottages and Plains. It was said of* Tasso, *in* *relation to his similitudes,* Mai esce del Bosco: *That he never departed from the Woods, that is, all his comparisons were taken from the Country: The same may be said, of our* Theocritus*; he is softer than* Ovid, *he touches the passions more delicately; and performs all this out of his own* Fond, *without diving into the Arts and Sciences for a supply. Even his Dorick Dialect has an incomparable sweetness in its Clownishness, like a fair Shepherdess in her Country Russet, talking in a* Yorkshire *Tone. This was impossible for* Virgil *to imitate; because the severity of the* Roman *Language denied him that advantage.* Spencer *has endeavour'd it in his Shepherds Calendar; but neither will it succeed in* English, *for which reason I forbore to attempt it. For* Theocritus *writ to* Sicilians, *who spoke that Dialect; and I direct this part of my Translations to our Ladies, who neither understand, nor will take pleasure in such homely expressions. I proceed to* Horace.

Take him in parts, and he is chiefly to be consider'd in his three different Talents, as he was a Critick, a Satyrist, and a Writer of Odes. His Morals are uniform, and run through all of them; For let his Dutch *Commentatours say what they will, his Philosophy was Epicurean; and he made use of Gods and providence, only to serve a turn in Poetry. But since neither his Criticisms (which are the most instructive of any that are written in this Art) nor his Satyrs (which are incomparably beyond* Juvenals, *if to laugh and rally, is to be preferr'd to railing and declaiming,) are any part of my present undertaking, I confine my self wholly to his Odes: These are also of several sorts; some of them are Panegyrical, others Moral, the rest Jovial, or (if I may so call them)* Bacchanalian. *As difficult as he makes it, and as indeed it is, to imitate* Pindar, *yet in his most elevated flights, and in the sudden changes of his Subject with almost imperceptible connexions, that* Theban *Poet is his Master. But* Horace *is of the more bounded Fancy, and confines himself strictly to one sort of Verse, or Stanza in every Ode. That which will distinguish his Style from all other Poets, is the Elegance of his Words, and the numerousness of his Verse; there is nothing so delicately turn'd in all the* Roman *Language. There appears in every part of his Diction, or, (to speak* English) *in all his Expressions, a kind of noble and bold Purity. His Words are chosen with as much exactness as* Virgils*; but there seems to be a greater Spirit in them. There is a secret Happiness attends his Choice, which in* Petronius *is call'd* Curiosa Felicitas, *and which I suppose he had from the* Feliciter audere *of* Horace *himself. But the most distinguishing part of all his Character, seems to me, to be his Briskness, his Jollity, and his good Humour: And those I have chiefly endeavour'd to Coppy; his other Excellencies, I confess are above my Imitation. One Ode, which infinitely pleas'd me in the reading, I have attempted to translate in Pindarique Verse: 'tis that which is inscribed to the present Earl*

362 *any 85 (errata): no 85 (text) 92*

of Rochester, *to whom I have particular Obligations, which this small Testimony of my Gratitude can never pay. 'Tis his Darling in the* Latine, *and I have taken some pains to make it my Master-Piece in* English*: For which reason, I took this kind of Verse, which allows more Latitude than any other. Every one knows it was introduc'd into our Language, in this Age, by the happy Genius of Mr.* Cowley. *The seeming easiness of it, has made it spread; but it has not been considered enough, to be so well cultivated. It languishes in almost every hand but his, and some very few, whom (to keep the rest in countenance) I do not name. He, indeed, has brought it as near Perfection as was possible in so short a time. But if I may be allowed to speak my Mind modestly, and without Injury to his sacred Ashes, somewhat of the Purity of* English, *somewhat of more equal of Thoughts, somewhat of sweetness in the Numbers, in one Word, somewhat of a finer turn and more Lyrical Verse is yet wanting. As for the Soul of it, which consists in the Warmth and Vigor of Fancy, the masterly Figures, and the copiousness of Imagination, he has excelled all others in this kind. Yet, if the kind it self be capable of more Perfection, though rather in the Ornamental parts of it, than the Essential, what Rules of Morality or respect have I broken, in naming the defects, that they may hereafter be amended? Imitation is a nice point, and there are few Poets who deserve to be models in all they write.* Miltons *Paradice Lost is admirable; but am I therefore bound to maintain, that there are no flats amongst his Elevations, when 'tis evident he creeps along sometimes, for above an Hundred lines together? cannot I admire the height of his Invention, and the strength of his expression, without defending his antiquated words, and the perpetual harshness of their sound? 'Tis as much commendation as a Man can bear, to own him excellent; all beyond it is Idolatry. Since* Pindar *was the Prince of* Lyrick *Poets; let me have leave to say, that in imitating him, our numbers shou'd for the most part be Lyrical: For variety, or rather where the Majesty of the thought requires it, they may be stretch'd to the* English *Heroick of five Feet, and to the* French *Alexandrine of Six. But the ear must preside, and direct the Judgment to the choice of numbers: Without the nicety of this, the Harmony of Pindarick Verse can never be compleat; the cadency of one line must be a rule to that of the next; and the sound of the former must slide gently into that which follows; without leaping from one extream into another. It must be done like the shadowings of a Picture, which fall by degrees into a darker colour. I shall be glad if I have so explain'd my self as to be understood, but if I have not,* quod nequeo dicere & sentio tantùm, *must be my excuse. There remains much more to be said on this subject; but to avoid envy, I will be silent. What I have said is the general Opinion of the best Judges, and in a manner has been forc'd from me, by*

388 *whom* (*to*] (*whom to* 84 92   391 *Thoughts* 92: *Thought* 85   394 *Fancy* 92: *Thought* 85

seeing a noble sort of Poetry so happily restor'd by one Man, and so grosly copied, by almost all the rest: A musical eare, and a great genius, if another Mr. Cowley *cou'd arise, in another age may bring it to perfection. In the mean time,*

> —Fungar vice cotis acutum
> Reddere quæ ferrum valet, expers ipsa secandi.

I hope it will not be expected from me, that I shou'd say any thing of my fellow undertakers in this Miscellany. Some of them are too nearly related to me, to be commended without suspicion of partiality: Others I am sure need it not; and the rest I have not perus'd. To conclude, I am sensible that I have written this too hastily and too loosly; I fear I have been tedious, and which is worse, it comes out from the first draught, and uncorrected. This I grant is no excuse; for it may be reasonably urg'd, why did he not write with more leisure, or, if he had it not (which was certainly my case) why did he attempt to write on so nice a subject? The objection is unanswerable, but in part of recompence, let me assure the Reader, that in hasty productions, he is sure to meet with an Authors present sence, which cooler thoughts wou'd possibly have disguisd. There is undoubtedly more of spirit, though not of judgment in these uncorrect Essays, and consequently though my hazard be the greater, yet the Readers pleasure is not the less.

John Dryden.

LUCRETIUS

The beginning of the First Book

DELIGHT of Humane kind, and Gods above;
Parent of *Rome*; Propitious Queen of Love;
Whose vital pow'r, Air, Earth, and Sea supplies;
And breeds what e'r is born beneath the rowling Skies:
For every kind, by thy prolifique might,
Springs, and beholds the Regions of the light:
Thee, Goddess thee, the clouds and tempests fear,
And at thy pleasing presence disappear:
For thee the Land in fragrant Flow'rs is drest,
For thee the Ocean smiles, and smooths her wavy breast;
And Heav'n it self with more serene, and purer light is blest.
For when the rising Spring adorns the Mead,
And a new Scene of Nature stands display'd,
When teeming Budds, and chearful greens appear,
And Western gales unlock the lazy year,
The joyous Birds thy welcome first express,

Whose native Songs thy genial fire confess:
Then salvage Beasts bound o're their slighted food,
Strook with thy darts, and tempt the raging floud:
All Nature is thy Gift; Earth, Air, and Sea:
Of all that breaths, the various progeny,
Stung with delight, is goaded on by thee.
O're barren Mountains, o're the flow'ry Plain,
The leavy Forest, and the liquid Main
Extends thy uncontroul'd and boundless reign.
Through all the living Regions dost thou move,
And scatter'st, where thou goest, the kindly seeds of Love:
Since then the race of every living thing,
Obeys thy pow'r; since nothing new can spring
Without thy warmth, without thy influence bear,
Or beautiful, or lovesome can appear,
Be thou my ayd: My tuneful Song inspire,
And kindle with thy own productive fire;
While all thy Province Nature, I survey,
And sing to *Memmius* an immortal lay
Of Heav'n, and Earth, and every where thy wond'rous pow'r display.
To *Memmius*, under thy sweet influence born,
Whom thou with all thy gifts and graces dost adorn.
The rather, then assist my Muse and me,
Infusing Verses worthy him and thee.
Mean time on Land and Sea let barb'rous discord cease,
And lull the listning world in universal peace.
To thee, Mankind their soft repose must owe,
For thou alone that blessing canst bestow;
Because the brutal business of the War
Is manag'd by thy dreadful Servant's care:
Who oft retires from fighting fields, to prove
The pleasing pains of thy eternal Love:
And panting on thy breast, supinely lies,
While with thy heavenly form he feeds his famish'd eyes:
Sucks in with open lips, thy balmy breath,
By turns restor'd to life, and plung'd in pleasing death.
There while thy curling limbs about him move,
Involv'd and fetter'd in the links of Love,
When wishing all, he nothing can deny,
Thy Charms in that auspicious moment try;

With winning eloquence our peace implore,
And quiet to the weary World restore.

LUCRETIUS

The beginning of the Second Book

Suave Mari magno, &c.

'TIS pleasant, safely to behold from shore
The rowling Ship; and hear the Tempest roar:
Not that anothers pain is our delight;
But pains unfelt produce the pleasing sight.
'Tis pleasant also to behold from far
The moving Legions mingled in the War:
But much more sweet thy lab'ring steps to guide,
To Vertues heights, with wisdom well supply'd,
And all the *Magazins* of Learning fortifi'd:
From thence to look below on humane kind,
Bewilder'd in the Maze of Life, and blind:
To see vain fools ambitiously contend
For Wit and Pow'r; their lost endeavours bend
T' outshine each other, waste their time and health,
In search of honour, and pursuit of wealth.
O wretched man! in what a mist of Life,
Inclos'd with dangers and with noisie strife,
He spends his little Span: And overfeeds
His cramm'd desires, with more than nature needs:
For Nature wisely stints our appetite,
And craves no more than undisturb'd delight;
Which minds unmix'd with cares, and fears, obtain;
A Soul serene, a body void of pain.
So little this corporeal frame requires;
So bounded are our natural desires,
That wanting all, and setting pain aside,
With bare privation, sence is satisfi'd.
If Golden Sconces hang not on the Walls,
To light the costly Suppers and the Balls;
If the proud Palace shines not with the state
Of burnish'd Bowls, and of reflected Plate,

If well tun'd Harps, nor the more pleasing sound
Of Voices, from the vaulted roofs rebound,
Yet on the grass beneath a poplar shade
By the cool stream, our careless limbs are lay'd,
With cheaper pleasures innocently blest,
When the warm Spring with gawdy flow'rs is drest.
Nor will the rageing Feavours fire abate,
With Golden Canopies and Beds of State:
But the poor Patient will as soon be sound,
On the hard mattress, or the Mother ground.
Then since our Bodies are not eas'd the more
By Birth, or Pow'r, or Fortunes wealthy store,
Tis plain, these useless toyes of every kind
As little can relieve the lab'ring mind:
Unless we cou'd suppose the dreadful sight
Of marshall'd Legions moving to the fight
Cou'd with their sound, and terrible array
Expel our fears, and drive the thoughts of death away.
But since the supposition vain appears,
Since clinging cares, and trains of inbred fears,
Are not with sounds to be affrighted thence,
But in the midst of Pomp pursue the Prince,
Not aw'd by arms, but in the presence bold,
Without respect to Purple, or to Gold;
Why shou'd not we these pageantries despise;
Whose worth but in our want of reason lies?
For life is all in wandring errours led;
And just as Children are surpriz'd with dread,
And tremble in the dark, so riper years
Ev'n in broad day light are possest with fears:
And shake at shadows fanciful and vain,
As those which in the breasts of Children reign.
These bugbears of the mind, this inward Hell,
No rayes of outward sunshine can dispel;
But nature and right reason, must display
Their beames abroad, and bring the darksome soul to day.

49 away.] away; *85 92*

TRANSLATION OF THE Latter Part of the Third Book of LUCRETIUS

Against the Fear of Death

WHAT has this Bugbear death to frighten Man,
If Souls can die, as well as Bodies can?
For, as before our Birth we felt no pain
When Punique arms infested Land and Mayn,
When Heav'n and Earth were in confusion hurl'd
For the debated Empire of the World,
Which aw'd with dreadful expectation lay,
Sure to be Slaves, uncertain who shou'd sway:
So, when our mortal frame shall be disjoyn'd,
The lifeless Lump, uncoupled from the mind,
From sense of grief and pain we shall be free;
We shall not feel, because we shall not *Be*.
Though Earth in Seas, and Seas in Heav'n were lost,
We shou'd not move, we only shou'd be tost.
Nay, ev'n suppose when we have suffer'd Fate,
The Soul cou'd feel in her divided state,
What's that to us, for we are only we
While Souls and bodies in one frame agree?
Nay, tho' our Atoms shou'd revolve by chance,
And matter leape into the former dance;
Tho' time our Life and motion cou'd restore,
And make our Bodies what they were before,
What gain to us wou'd all this bustle bring,
The new made man wou'd be another thing;
When once an interrupting pause is made,
That individual Being is decay'd.
We, who are dead and gone, shall bear no part
In all the pleasures, nor shall feel the smart,
Which to that other Mortal shall accrew,
Whom of our Matter Time shall mould anew.

Translation. Editor's paragraphs

For backward if you look, on that long space
Of Ages past, and view the changing face
Of Matter, tost and variously combin'd
In sundry shapes, 'tis easie for the mind
From thence t' infer, that Seeds of things have been
In the same order as they now are seen:
Which yet our dark remembrance cannot trace,
Because a pause of Life, a gaping space
Has come betwixt, where memory lies dead,
And all the wandring motions from the sence are fled.
For who so e're shall in misfortunes live
Must *Be*, when those misfortunes shall arrive;
And since the Man who *Is* not, feels not woe,
(For death exempts him, and wards off the blow,
Which we, the living, only feel and bear)
What is there left for us in death to fear?
When once that pause of life has come between,
'Tis just the same as we had never been.
  And therefore if a Man bemoan his lot,
That after death his mouldring limbs shall rot,
Or flames, or jaws of Beasts devour his Mass,
Know he's an unsincere, unthinking Ass.
A secret Sting remains within his mind,
The fool is to his own cast offals kind;
He boasts no sense can after death remain,
Yet makes himself a part of life again:
As if some other He could feel the pain.
If, while he live, this thought molest his head,
What Wolf or Vulture shall devour me dead,
He wasts his days in idle grief, nor can
Distinguish 'twixt the Body and the Man:
But thinks himself can still himself survive;
And what when dead he feels not, feels alive.
Then he repines that he was born to die,
Nor knows in death there is no other He,
No living He remains his grief to vent,
And o're his senseless Carcass to lament.
If after death 'tis painful to be torn
By Birds and Beasts, then why not so to burn,

43 woe,] woe. *85 92*   69 Beasts, *92*: Beasts *85*

Or drench'd in floods of honey to be soak'd,
Imbalm'd to be at once preserv'd and choak'd;
Or on an ayery Mountains top to lie
Expos'd to cold and Heav'ns inclemency,
Or crowded in a Tomb to be opprest
With Monumental Marble on thy breast?
But to be snatch'd from all thy houshold joys,
From thy Chast Wife, and thy dear prattling boys,
Whose little arms about thy Legs are cast
And climbing for a Kiss prevent their Mothers hast,
Inspiring secret pleasure thro' thy Breast,
All these shall be no more: thy Friends opprest,
Thy Care and Courage now no more shall free:
Ah Wretch, thou cry'st, ah! miserable me,
One woful day sweeps children, friends, and wife,
And all the brittle blessings of my life!
Add one thing more, and all thou say'st is true;
Thy want and wish of them is vanish'd too,
Which well consider'd were a quick relief,
To all thy vain imaginary grief.
For thou shalt sleep and never wake again,
And quitting life, shall quit thy living pain.
But we thy friends shall all those sorrows find,
Which in forgetful death thou leav'st behind,
No time shall dry our tears, nor drive thee from our mind.
The worst that can befall thee, measur'd right,
Is a sound slumber, and a long good night.
Yet thus the fools, that would be thought the Wits,
Disturb their mirth with melancholy fits,
When healths go round, and kindly brimmers flow,
Till the fresh Garlands on their foreheads glow,
They whine, and cry, let us make haste to live,
Short are the joys that humane Life can give.
Eternal Preachers, that corrupt the draught,
And pall the God that never thinks, with thought;
Ideots with all that thought, to whom the worst
Of death, is want of drink, and endless thirst,
Or any fond desire as vain as these.
For ev'n in sleep, the body wrapt in ease,

76 joys, *92*: joys *85*

Supinely lies, as in the peaceful grave,
And wanting nothing, nothing can it crave.
Were that sound sleep eternal it were death,
Yet the first Atoms then, the seeds of breath
Are moving near to sense, we do but shake
And rouze that sense, and straight we are awake.
Then death to us, and deaths anxiety
Is less than nothing, if a less cou'd be.
For then our Atoms, which in order lay,
Are scatter'd from their heap, and puff'd away,
And never can return into their place,
When once the pause of Life has left an empty space.
 And last, suppose Great Natures Voice shou'd call
To thee, or me, or any of us all,
What dost thou mean, ungrateful wretch, thou vain,
Thou mortal thing, thus idly to complain,
And sigh and sob, that thou shalt be no more?
For if thy life were pleasant heretofore,
If all the bounteous blessings I cou'd give
Thou hast enjoy'd, if thou hast known to live,
And pleasure not leak'd thro' thee like a Seive,
Why dost thou not give thanks as at a plenteous feast
Cram'd to the throat with life, and rise and take thy rest?
But if my blessings thou hast thrown away,
If indigested joys pass'd thro' and wou'd not stay,
Why dost thou wish for more to squander still?
If Life be grown a load, a real ill,
And I wou'd all thy cares and labours end,
Lay down thy burden fool, and know thy friend.
To please thee I have empti'd all my store,
I can invent, and can supply no more;
But run the round again, the round I ran before.
Suppose thou art not broken yet with years,
Yet still the self same Scene of things appears,
And wou'd be ever, coud'st thou ever live;
For life is still but Life, there's nothing new to give.
What can we plead against so just a Bill?
We stand convicted, and our cause goes ill.
But if a wretch, a man opprest by fate,
Shou'd beg of Nature to prolong his date,

She speaks aloud to him with more disdain,
Be still thou Martyr fool, thou covetous of pain.
But if an old decrepit Sot lament;
What thou (She cryes) who hast outliv'd content!
Dost thou complain, who hast enjoy'd my store?
But this is still th' effect of wishing more!
Unsatisfy'd with all that Nature brings;
Loathing the present, liking absent things;
From hence it comes thy vain desires at strife
Within themselves, have tantaliz'd thy Life,
And ghastly death appear'd before thy sight
E're thou hadst gorg'd thy Soul, and sences with delight.
Now leave those joys unsuiting to thy age,
To a fresh Comer, and resign the Stage.
  Is Nature to be blam'd if thus she chide?
No sure; for 'tis her business to provide,
Against this ever changing Frames decay,
New things to come, and old to pass away.
One Being worn, another Being makes;
Chang'd but not lost; for Nature gives and takes:
New Matter must be found for things to come,
And these must waste like those, and follow Natures doom.
All things, like thee, have time to rise and rot;
And from each others ruin are begot;
For life is not confin'd to him or thee;
'Tis giv'n to all for use; to none for Property.
Consider former Ages past and gone,
Whose Circles ended long e're thine begun,
Then tell me Fool, what part in them thou hast?
Thus may'st thou judge the future by the past.
What horrour seest thou in that quiet state,
What Bugbear dreams to fright thee after Fate?
No Ghost, no Gobblins, that still passage keep,
But all is there serene, in that eternal sleep.
For all the dismal Tales that Poets tell,
Are verify'd on Earth, and not in Hell.
No *Tantalus* looks up with fearful eye,
Or dreads th' impending Rock to crush him from on high:
But fear of Chance on earth disturbs our easie hours:
Or vain imagin'd wrath, of vain imagin'd Pow'rs.

No *Tityus* torn by Vultures lies in Hell;
Nor cou'd the Lobes of his rank liver swell
To that prodigious Mass for their eternal meal.
Not tho' his monstrous bulk had cover'd o're
Nine spreading Acres, or nine thousand more;
Not tho' the Globe of earth had been the Gyants floor.
Nor in eternal torments cou'd he lie;
Nor cou'd his Corps sufficient food supply.
But he's the *Tityus*, who by Love opprest,
Or Tyrant Passion preying on his breast,
And ever anxious thoughts, is robb'd of rest.
The *Sisiphus* is he, whom noise and strife
Seduce from all the soft retreats of life,
To vex the Government, disturb the Laws;
Drunk with the Fumes of popular applause,
He courts the giddy Crowd to make him great,
And sweats and toils in vain, to mount the sovereign Seat.
For still to aim at pow'r, and still to fail,
Ever to strive and never to prevail,
What is it, but in reasons true account
To heave the Stone against the rising Mount;
Which urg'd, and labour'd, and forc'd up with pain,
Recoils and rowls impetuous down, and smoaks along the plain.
Then still to treat thy ever craving mind
With ev'ry blessing, and of ev'ry kind,
Yet never fill thy rav'ning appetite;
Though years and seasons vary thy delight,
Yet nothing to be seen of all the store,
But still the Wolf within thee barks for more;
This is the Fables moral, which they tell
Of fifty foolish Virgins damn'd in Hell
To leaky Vessels, which the Liquor spill;
To Vessels of their Sex, which none cou'd ever fill.
As for the Dog, the Furies, and their Snakes,
The gloomy Caverns, and the burning Lakes,
And all the vain infernal trumpery,
They neither are, nor were, nor e're can be.
But here on Earth the guilty have in view
The mighty pains to mighty mischiefs due:

199 thoughts,] thoughts *85 92* 202 Laws;] Laws, *85 92* 214 appetite;] appetite, *85 92*

Racks, Prisons, Poisons, the *Tarpeian* Rock,
Stripes, Hangmen, Pitch, and suffocating Smoak,
And last, and most, if these were cast behind,
Th' avenging horrour of a Conscious mind,
Whose deadly fear anticipates the blow,
And sees no end of Punishment and woe:
But looks for more, at the last gasp of breath:
This makes an Hell on Earth, and Life a death.
  Mean time, when thoughts of death disturb thy head;
Consider, *Ancus* great and good is dead;
Ancus thy better far, was born to die,
And thou, dost thou bewail mortality?
So many Monarchs with their mighty State,
Who rul'd the World, were overrul'd by fate.
That haughty King, who Lorded o're the Main,
And whose stupendous Bridge did the wild Waves restrain,
(In vain they foam'd, in vain they threatned wreck,
While his proud Legions march'd upon their back:)
Him death, a greater Monarch, overcame;
Nor spared his guards the more, for their immortal name.
The *Roman* chief, the *Carthaginian* dread,
Scipio the Thunder Bolt of War is dead,
And like a common Slave, by fate in triumph led.
The Founders of invented Arts are lost;
And Wits who made Eternity their boast;
Where now is *Homer* who possest the Throne?
Th' immortal Work remains, the mortal Author's gone.
Democritus perceiving age invade,
His Body weakn'd, and his mind decay'd,
Obey'd the summons with a chearful face;
Made hast to welcom death, and met him half the race.
That stroke, ev'n *Epicurus* cou'd not bar,
Though he in Wit surpass'd Mankind, as far
As does the midday Sun, the midnight Star.
And thou, dost thou disdain to yield thy breath,
Whose very life is little more than death?
More than one half by Lazy sleep possest;
And when awake, thy Soul but nods at best,
Day-Dreams and sickly thoughts revolving in thy breast.
Eternal troubles haunt thy anxious mind,

Whose cause and cure thou never hop'st to find;
But still uncertain, with thy self at strife,
Thou wander'st in the *Labyrinth* of Life.
O, if the foolish race of man, who find
A weight of cares still pressing on their mind,
Cou'd find as well the cause of this unrest,
And all this burden lodg'd within the breast,
Sure they wou'd change their course; nor live as now,
Uncertain what to wish or what to vow.
Uneasie both in Countrey and in Town,
They search a place to lay their burden down.
One restless in his Palace, walks abroad,
And vainly thinks to leave behind the load.
But straight returns; for he's as restless there;
And finds there's no relief in open Air.
Another to his *Villa* wou'd retire,
And spurs as hard as if it were on fire;
No sooner enter'd at his Country door,
But he begins to stretch, and yawn, and snore;
Or seeks the City which he left before.
Thus every man o're works his weary will,
To shun himself, and to shake off his ill;
The shaking Fit returns and hangs upon him still.
No prospect of repose, nor hope of ease;
The Wretch is ignorant of his disease;
Which known wou'd all his fruitless trouble spare;
For he wou'd know the World not worth his care:
Then wou'd he search more deeply for the cause;
And study Nature well, and Natures Laws:
For in this moment lies not the debate;
But on our future, fix'd, Eternal State;
That never changing state which all must keep
Whom Death has doom'd to everlasting sleep.
Why are we then so fond of mortal Life,
Beset with dangers and maintain'd with strife.
A Life which all our care can never save;
One fate attends us; and one common Grave.
Besides we tread but a perpetual round,
We ne're strike out; but beat the former ground,
And the same Maukish joyes in the same track are found.

For still we think an absent blessing best;
Which cloys, and is no blessing when possest;
A new arising wish expells it from the Breast.
The Feav'rish thirst of Life increases still;
We call for more and more and never have our fill:
Yet know not what to morrow we shall try,
What dregs of life in the last draught may lie.
Nor, by the longest life we can attain,
One moment from the length of death we gain;
For all behind belongs to his Eternal reign.
When once the Fates have cut the mortal Thred,
The Man as much to all intents is dead,
Who dyes to day, and will as long be so,
As he who dy'd a thousand years ago.

LUCRETIUS

The Fourth Book

Concerning the Nature of Love;

Beginning at this Line,
Sic igitur, Veneris qui telis accipit ictum, &c.

THUS therefore, he who feels the Fiery dart
Of strong desire transfix his amorous heart,
Whether some beauteous Boys alluring face,
Or Lovelyer Maid with unresisted Grace,
From her each part the winged arrow sends,
From whence he first was struck, he thither tends;
Restless he roams, impatient to be freed,
And eager to inject the sprightly seed.
For fierce desire does all his mind employ,
And ardent Love assures approaching joy.
Such is the nature of that pleasing smart,
Whose burning drops distil upon the heart,
The Feaver of the Soul shot from the fair,
And the cold Ague of succeeding care.

315 attain,] attain; *85 92* *Lucretius The Fourth Book. Editor's paragraphs*

If absent, her Idea still appears;
And her sweet name is chiming in your ears:
But strive those pleasing fantomes to remove,
And shun th' Aerial images of Love;
That feed the flame: When one molests thy mind
Discharge thy loyns on all the leaky kind;
For that's a wiser way than to restrain
Within thy swelling nerves, that hoard of pain.
For every hour some deadlier symptom shows,
And by delay the gath'ring venom grows,
When kindly applications are not us'd;
The Scorpion, Love, must on the wound be bruis'd:
On that one object 'tis not safe to stay,
But force the tide of thought some other way:
The squander'd Spirits prodigally throw,
And in the common Glebe of Nature sow.
Nor wants he all the bliss, that Lovers feign,
Who takes the pleasure, and avoids the pain;
For purer joys in purer health abound,
And less affect the sickly than the sound.
  When Love its utmost vigour does imploy,
Ev'n then, 'tis but a restless wandring joy:
Nor knows the Lover, in that wild excess,
With hands or eyes, what first he wou'd possess:
But strains at all; and fast'ning where he strains,
Too closely presses with his frantique pains:
With biteing kisses hurts the twining fair,
Which shews his joyes imperfect, unsincere:
For stung with inward rage, he flings around,
And strives t' avenge the smart on that which gave the wound.
But love those eager bitings does restrain,
And mingling pleasure mollifies the pain.
For ardent hope still flatters anxious grief,
And sends him to his Foe to seek relief:
Which yet the nature of the thing denies;
For Love, and Love alone of all our joyes
By full possession does but fan the fire,
The more we still enjoy, the more we still desire.

26 The Scorpion, Love, *Dryden's correction, see* Preface, *lines 297–300*: The Viper Love *85 92*

Nature for meat, and drink provides a space;
And when receiv'd they fill their certain place;
Hence thirst and hunger may be satisfi'd,
But this repletion is to Love deny'd:
Form, feature, colour, whatsoe're delight
Provokes the Lovers endless appetite,
These fill no space, nor can we thence remove
With lips, or hands, or all our instruments of love:
In our deluded grasp we nothing find,
But thin aerial shapes, that fleet before the mind.
As he who in a dream with drought is curst,
And finds no real drink to quench his thirst,
Runs to imagin'd Lakes his heat to steep,
And vainly swills and labours in his sleep;
So Love with fantomes cheats our longing eyes,
Which hourly seeing never satisfies;
Our hands pull nothing from the parts they strain,
But wander o're the lovely limbs in vain:
Nor when the Youthful pair more clossely joyn,
When hands in hands they lock, and thighs in thighs they twine;
Just in the raging foam of full desire,
When both press on, both murmur, both expire,
They gripe, they squeeze, their humid tongues they dart,
As each wou'd force their way to t'others heart:
In vain; they only cruze about the coast,
For bodies cannot pierce, nor be in bodies lost:
As sure they strive to be, when both engage,
In that tumultuous momentary rage,
So 'tangled in the Nets of Love they lie,
Till Man dissolves in that excess of joy.
Then, when the gather'd bag has burst its way,
And ebbing tydes the slacken'd nerves betray,
A pause ensues; and Nature nods a while,
Till with recruited rage new Spirits boil;
And then the same vain violence returns,
With flames renew'd th' erected furnace burns.
Agen they in each other wou'd be lost,
But still by adamantine bars are crost;
All wayes they try, successeless all they prove,
To cure the secret sore of lingring love.

Besides—
They waste their strength in the venereal strife,
And to a Womans will enslave their life;
Th' Estate runs out, and mortgages are made,
All Offices of friendship are decay'd;
Their fortune ruin'd, and their fame betray'd.
Assyrian Oyntment from their temples flows,
And Diamond Buckles sparkle at their shooes.
The chearful Emerald twinkles on their hands,
With all the luxury of foreign lands:
And the blew Coat that with imbroid'ry shines,
Is drunk with sweat of their o're labour'd loyns.
Their frugal Fathers gains they mis-employ,
And turn to Point, and Pearl, and ev'ry female toy.
French fashions, costly treats are their delight;
The Park by day, and Plays and Balls by night.
In vain:—
For in the Fountain where their Sweets are sought,
Some bitter bubbles up, and poisons all the draught.
First guilty Conscience does the mirrour bring,
Then sharp remorse shoots out her angry sting,
And anxious thoughts within themselves at strife,
Upbraid the long mispent, luxurious life.
Perhaps the fickle fair One proves unkind,
Or drops a doubtful word, that pains his mind;
And leaves a ranckling jealousie behind.
Perhaps he watches closs her amorous eyes,
And in the act of ogling does surprise;
And thinks he sees upon her cheeks the while,
The dimpled tracks of some foregoing smile;
His raging Pulse beats thick, and his pent Spirits boyl.
This is the product ev'n of prosp'rous Love,
Think then what pangs disastrous passions prove!
Innumerable Ills; disdain, despair,
With all the meager Family of Care:
Thus, as I said, 'tis better to prevent,
Than flatter the Disease, and late repent:
Because to shun th' allurement is not hard,
To minds resolv'd, forewarn'd, and well prepar'd:
But wond'rous difficult, when once beset,

To struggle thro' the streights, and break th' involving Net.
 Yet thus insnar'd thy freedom thou may'st gain,
If, like a fool, thou dost not hug thy chain;
If not to ruin obstinately blind,
And willfully endeavouring not to find,
Her plain defects of Body and of mind.
For thus the *Bedlam* train of Lovers use,
T' inhaunce the value, and the faults excuse.
And therefore 'tis no wonder if we see
They doat on Dowdyes, and Deformity:
Ev'n what they cannot praise, they will not blame,
But veil with some extenuating name:
The Sallow Skin is for the Swarthy put,
And love can make a Slattern of a Slut:
If Cat-ey'd, then a *Pallas* is their love,
If freckled she's a party-colour'd Dove.
If little, then she's life and soul all o're:
An *Amazon*, the large two handed Whore.
She stammers, oh what grace in lisping lies,
If she sayes nothing, to be sure she's wise.
If shrill, and with a voice to drown a Quire,
Sharp witted she must be, and full of fire.
The lean, consumptive Wench with coughs decay'd,
Is call'd a pretty, tight, and slender Maid.
Th' o're grown, a goodly *Ceres* is exprest,
A bed-fellow for *Bacchus* at the least.
Flat Nose the name of Satyr never misses,
And hanging blobber lips, but pout for kisses.
The task were endless all the rest to trace:
Yet grant she were a *Venus* for her face,
And shape, yet others equal beauty share;
And time was you cou'd live without the fair:
She does no more, in that for which you woo,
Then homelier women full as well can do.
Besides she daubs, and stinks so much of paint,
Her own Attendants cannot bear the scent:
But laugh behind, and bite their lips to hold.
Mean time excluded, and expos'd to cold,
The whining Lover stands before the Gates,

169 hold.] hold; *85 92*

And there with humble adoration waites:
Crowning with flow'rs the threshold and the floor,
And printing kisses on th' obdurate door:
Who if admitted in that nick of time,
If some unsav'ry Whiff, betray the crime,
Invents a quarrel straight, if there be none,
Or makes some faint excuses to be gone:
And calls himself a doating fool to serve,
Ascribing more than Woman can deserve.
Which well they understand like cunning Queans;
And hide their nastiness behind the Scenes,
From him they have allur'd, and wou'd retain;
But to a peircing eye, 'tis all in vain:
For common sense brings all their cheats to view,
And the false light discovers by the true:
Which a wise Harlot owns, and hopes to find
A pardon for defects, that run thro' all the kind.
  Nor alwayes do they feign the sweets of Love,
When round the panting Youth their pliant limbs they move;
And cling, and heave, and moisten ev'ry kiss;
They often share, and more than share the bliss:
From every part, ev'n to their inmost Soul,
They feel the trickling joyes, and run with vigour to the Goal.
Stirr'd with the same impetuous desire
Birds, Beasts, and Herds, and Mares, their Males require:
Because the throbbing Nature in their veins
Provokes them to asswage their kindly pains:
The lusty leap th' expecting Female stands,
By mutual heat compell'd to mutual Bands.
Thus Dogs with lolling Tongues by love are ty'd;
Nor shouting boys, nor blows their union can divide:
At either end they strive the linck to loose;
In vain, for stronger *Venus* holds the noose.
Which never wou'd those wretched Lovers do,
But that the common heats of Love they know;
The pleasure therefore must be shar'd in common too.
And when the Womans more prevailing juice
Sucks in the mans, the mixture will produce
The Mothers likeness; when the man prevails,

182 Scenes,] Scenes. *85 92* 183 retain;] retain, *85 92* 191 kiss;] kiss, *85 92*

His own resemblance in the seed he Seals.
But when we see the new begotten race
Reflect the features of each Parents face,
Then of the Fathers and the Mothers blood,
The justly temper'd seed is understood:
When both conspire, with equal ardour bent,
From every limb the due proportion sent,
When neither party foils, when neither foild,
This gives the blended features of the Child.
Sometimes the Boy, the Grandsires image bears;
Sometimes the more remote Progenitor he shares;
Because the genial Atomes of the seed
Lie long conceal'd e're they exert the breed:
And after sundry Ages past, produce
The tardy likeness of the latent juice.
Hence Families such different figures take,
And represent their Ancestors in face and Hair, and make.
Because of the same Seed, the voice, and hair,
And shape, and face, and other members are,
And the same antique mould the likeness does prepare.
Thus oft the Fathers likeness does prevail
In Females, and the Mothers in the Male.
For since the seed is of a double kind,
From that where we the most resemblance find,
We may conclude the strongest tincture sent,
And that was in conception prevalent.
  Nor can the vain decrees of Pow'rs above,
Deny production to the act of Love,
Or hinder Fathers of that happy name,
Or with a barren Womb the Matron shame;
As many think, who stain with Victims Blood
The mournful Altars, and with incense load:
To bless the show'ry seed with future Life,
And to impregnate the well labour'd Wife.
In vain they weary Heav'n with Prayer, or fly
To Oracles, or Magique numbers try:
For barrenness of Sexes will proceed,
Either from too Condens'd, or watry seed;
The watry juice too soon dissolves away,

247 proceed,] proceed. *85 92*

And in the parts projected will not stay;
The too Condens'd, unsould, unwieldy mass
Drops short, nor carries to the destin'd place:
Nor pierces to the parts, nor, though injected home,
Will mingle with the kindly moisture of the womb.
For Nuptials are unlike in their success,
Some men, with fruitful seed some Women bless;
And from some men some Women fruitful are;
Just as their constitutions joyn or jarr:
And many, seeming barren Wives have been,
Who, after match'd with more prolifique men,
Have fill'd a Family with pratling boyes:
And many not supply'd at home with joys,
Have found a friend abroad, to ease their smart,
And to perform the Sapless Husbands part.
So much it does import, that seed with seed
Shou'd of the kindly mixture make the breed:
And thick with thin, and thin with thick shou'd joyn,
So to produce and propagate the Line.
Of such concernment too is Drink and food,
T' incrassate, or attenuate the blood.
  Of like importance is the posture too,
In which the genial feat of Love we do:
For as the Females of the four foot kind,
Receive the leapings of their Males behind;
So the good Wives, with loins uplifted high,
And leaning on their hands the fruitful stroke may try:
For in that posture will they best conceive:
Not when supinely laid they frisk and heave;
For active motions only break the blow,
And more of Strumpets than of Wives they show;
When answering stroke with stroke, the mingled liquors flow.
Endearments eager, and too brisk a bound,
Throws off the Plow-share from the furrow'd ground.
But common Harlots in conjunction heave,
Because 'tis less their business to conceive
Than to delight, and to provoke the deed;
A trick which honest Wives but little need.
Nor is it from the Gods, or *Cupids* dart,
That many a homely Woman takes the heart;

But Wives well humour'd, dutiful, and chaste,
And clean, will hold their wandring Husbands fast,
Such are the links of Love, and such a Love will last.
For what remains, long habitude, and use,
Will kindness in domestick Bands produce:
For Custome will a strong impression leave;
Hard bodies, which the lightest stroke receive,
In length of time, will moulder and decay,
And stones with drops of rain are wash'd away.

From LUCRETIUS
Book the Fifth

Tum porrò puer, &c.

THUS like a Sayler by the Tempest hurl'd
A shore, the Babe is shipwrack'd on the World:
Naked he lies, and ready to expire;
Helpless of all that humane wants require:
Expos'd upon unhospitable Earth,
From the first moment of his hapless Birth.
Straight with forebodeing cryes he fills the Room;
(Too true presages of his future doom.)
But Flocks, and Herds, and every Savage Beast
By more indulgent Nature are increas'd.
They want no Rattles for their froward mood,
Nor Nurse to reconcile them to their food,
With broken words; nor Winter blasts they fear
Nor change their habits with the changing year:
Nor, for their safety, Citadels prepare;
Nor forge the wicked Instruments of War:
Unlabour'd Earth her bounteous treasure grants,
And Nature's lavish hand supplies their common wants.

From Lucretius. 18 hand] hands *85 92*

Theocrit. Idyllium the 18th.
THE *EPITHALAMIUM* OF *HELEN* and *MENELAUS*

TWELVE *Spartan* Virgins, noble, young, and fair,
With Violet wreaths adorn'd their flowing hair;
And to the pompous Palace did resort,
Where *Menelaus* kept his Royal Court.
There hand in hand a comely Quire they led;
To sing a blessing to his Nuptial Bed,
With curious Needles wrought, and painted flowers bespred.
Joves beauteous Daughter now his Bride must be,
And *Jove* himself was less a God than he:
For this their artful hands instruct the Lute to sound,
Their feet assist their hands and justly beat the ground.
This was their song: Why happy Bridegroom, why
E're yet the Stars are kindl'd in the Skie,
E're twilight shades, or Evening dews are shed,
Why dost thou steal so soon away to Bed?
Has *Somnus* brush'd thy Eye-lids with his Rod,
Or do thy Legs refuse to bear their Load,
With flowing bowles of a more generous God?
If gentle slumber on thy Temples creep,
(But naughty Man thou dost not mean to sleep)
Betake thee to thy Bed thou drowzy Drone,
Sleep by thy self and leave thy Bride alone:
Go leave her with her Maiden Mates to play
At sports more harmless, till the break of day:
Give us this Evening; thou hast Morn and Night,
And all the year before thee, for delight.
O happy Youth! to thee among the crowd
Of Rival Princes, *Cupid* sneez'd aloud;
And every lucky *Omen* sent before,
To meet thee landing on the *Spartan* shore.
Of all our *Heroes* thou canst boast alone,
That *Jove*, when e're he Thunders, calls thee Son:

Theocrit. Idyllium the 18th. 7 With *85* (*errata*): Which *85* (*text*)

Betwixt two Sheets thou shalt enjoy her bare;
With whom no *Grecian* Virgin can compare:
So soft, so sweet, so balmy, and so fair.
A boy, like thee, would make a Kingly line:
But oh, a Girl, like her, must be divine.
Her equals, we, in years, but not in face,
Twelve score *Virago's* of the *Spartan* Race,
While naked to *Eurotas* banks we bend,
And there in manly exercise contend,
When she appears, are all eclips'd and lost;
And hide the beauties that we made our boast.
So, when the Night, and Winter disappear,
The Purple morning rising with the year
Salutes the spring, as her Celestial eyes
Adorn the World, and brighten all the Skies:
So beauteous *Helen* shines among the rest,
Tall, slender, straight, with all the Graces blest:
As Pines the Mountains, or as fields the Corn,
Or as *Thessalian* Steeds the race adorn:
So Rosie colour'd *Helen* is the pride
Of *Lacedemon*, and of *Greece* beside.
Like her no Nymph can willing Ozyers bend
In basket-works, which painted streaks commend:
With *Pallas* in the Loomb she may contend.
But none, ah none can animate the Lyre,
And the mute strings with Vocal Souls inspire,
Whether the Learn'd *Minerva* be her Theam,
Or chast *Diana* bathing in the Stream;
None can record their Heavenly praise so well
As *Helen*, in whose eyes ten thousand *Cupids* dwell.
O fair, O Graceful! yet with Maids inroll'd,
But whom to morrows Sun a Matron shall behold:
Yet e're to morrows Sun shall show his head,
The dewy paths of meadows we will tread,
For Crowns and Chaplets to adorn thy head:
Where all shall weep, and wish for thy return,
As bleating Lambs their absent mother mourn.
Our Noblest Maids shall to thy name bequeath

40 *Eurotas*] *Eurota's* 85 92   58 Souls 85 (*errata*): Soul 85 (*text*)   67 head:] head. 85 92

The boughs of *Lotos*, form'd in to a wreath.
This Monument, thy Maiden beauties due,
High on a Plane tree shall be hung to view:
On the smooth rind the Passenger shall see
Thy Name ingrav'd; and worship *Helens* Tree:
Balm, from a Silver box distill'd around,
Shall all bedew the roots and scent the sacred ground;
The balm, 'tis true, can aged Plants prolong,
But *Helens* name will keep it ever young.
Hail Bride, hail Bridegroom, son in Law to *Jove*!
With fruitful joys, *Latona* bless your Love;
Let *Venus* furnish you with full desires,
Add vigour to your wills and fuel to your fires:
Almighty *Jove* augment your wealthy store,
Give much to you, and to his Grandsons more.
From generous Loyns a generous race will spring,
Each Girl, like her, a Queen; each Boy, like you, a King.
Now sleep if sleep you can; but while you rest,
Sleep close, with folded arms, and breast to breast.
Rise in the morn; but oh before you rise,
Forget not to perform your morning Sacrifice.
We will be with you e're the crowing Cock
Salutes the light, and struts before his feather'd Flock:
Hymen, oh *Hymen*, to thy Triumphs run,
And view the mighty spoils thou hast in Battle won.

Idyllium the 23d.

THE Despairing LOVER

WITH inauspicious love, a wretched Swain
Persu'd the fairest Nimph of all the Plain;
Fairest indeed, but prouder far than fair,
She plung'd him hopeless in a deep despair:
Her heavenly form too haughtily she priz'd,
His person hated, and his Gifts despis'd:
Nor knew the force of *Cupids* cruel darts,
Nor fear'd his awful pow'r on humane hearts;

72 Monument,] Monument *85 92*

But either from her hopeless Lover fled,
Or with disdainful glances shot him dead.
No kiss, no look, to cheer the drooping Boy:
No word she spoke, she scorn'd ev'n to deny.
But as a hunted Panther casts about
Her glaring eyes, and pricks her list'ning ears to scout,
So she, to shun his Toyls, her cares imploy'd,
And fiercely in her savage freedom joy'd.
Her mouth she writh'd, her forehead taught to frown,
Her eyes to sparkle fires to love unknown:
Her sallow Cheeks her envious mind did show,
And every feature spoke alowd the curstness of a Shrew.
Yet cou'd not he his obvious Fate escape,
His love still drest her in a pleasing shape:
And every sullen frown, and bitter scorn
But fann'd the fuel that too fast did burn.
Long time, unequal to his mighty pain,
He strove to curb it, but he strove in vain:
At last his woes broke out, and begg'd relief
With tears, the dumb petitioners of grief.
With Tears so tender, as adorn'd his Love;
And any heart, but only hers wou'd move:
Trembling before her bolted doors he stood;
And there pour'd out th' unprofitable flood:
Staring his eyes, and haggard was his look;
Then kissing first the threshold, thus he spoke.
  Ah Nymph more cruel than of humane Race,
Thy Tygress heart belies thy Angel Face:
Too well thou show'st thy Pedigree from Stone;
Thy Grandames was the first by *Pyrrha* thrown:
Unworthy thou to be so long desir'd;
But so my Love, and so my fate requir'd.
I beg not now (for 'tis in vain) to live;
But take this gift, the last that I can give.
This friendly Cord shall soon decide the strife,
Betwixt my ling'ring Love and loathsome life;
This moment puts an end to all my pain;
I shall no more despair, nor thou disdain.
Farewell ungrateful and unkind, I go
Condemn'd by thee to those sad shades below.

I go th' extreamest remedy to prove,
To drink Oblivion, and to drench my Love.
There happily to lose my long desires:
But ah, what draught so deep to quench my fires!
Farewel ye never opening Gates, ye Stones
And Threshold guilty of my Midnight Moans:
What I have suffer'd here ye know too well;
What I shall do the Gods and I can tell.
The Rose is fragrant, but it fades in time,
The Violet sweet, but quickly past the prime;
White Lillies hang their heads and soon decay,
And whiter Snow in minutes melts away:
Such is your blooming youth, and withering so;
The time will come, it will, when you shall know
The rage of Love; your haughty heart shall burn
In flames like mine, and meet a like return.
Obdurate as you are, oh, hear at least
My dying prayers, and grant my last request!
When first you ope your doors, and passing by
The sad ill Omend Object meets your Eye,
Think it not lost, a moment if you stay;
The breathless wretch, so made by you, survey:
Some cruel pleasure will from thence arise,
To view the mighty ravage of your Eyes.
I wish, (but oh my wish is vain I fear,)
The kind Oblation of a falling Tear:
Then loose the knot, and take me from the place,
And spread your Mantle o're my grizly Face;
Upon my livid Lips bestow a kiss:
O envy not the dead, they feel not bliss!
Nor fear your kisses can restore my breath;
Even you are not more pittiless than death.
Then for my Corps a homely Grave provide,
Which Love and me from publick Scorn may hide.
Thrice call upon my Name, thrice beat your breast
And hayl me thrice to everlasting rest:
Last let my Tomb this sad inscription bear,
A wretch whom Love has kill'd lies buried here:
Oh, Passengers *Amintas* Eyes beware.
  Thus having said, and furious with his Love;

He heav'd with more than humane force, to move
A weighty Stone, (the labour of a Team,)
And rais'd from thence he reach'd the Neighbouring Beam:
Around its bulk a sliding knot he throws;
And fitted to his Neck the fatal noose:
Then spurning backward took a swing, till death
Crept up, and stopt the passage of his Breath.
The bounce burst ope the door; the Scornful Fair
Relentless lookt, and saw him beat his quivering feet in Air,
Nor wept his fate, nor cast a pitying eye,
Nor took him down, but brusht regardless by:
And as she past, her chance or fate was such,
Her Garments toucht the dead, polluted by the touch.
Next to the dance, thence to the Bath did move;
The bath was sacred to the God of Love:
Whose injur'd Image, with a wrathful Eye,
Stood threatning from a Pedestal on high:
Nodding a while; and watchful of his blow,
He fell; and falling crusht th' ungrateful Nymph below:
Her gushing Blood the Pavement all besmear'd;
And this her last expiring Voice was heard;
Lovers farwell, revenge has reacht my scorn;
Thus warn'd, be wise, and love for love return.

DAPHNIS

From *Theocritus Idyll.* 27

Daphnis

THE Shepheard *Paris* bore the *Spartan* Bride
By force away, and then by force enjoy'd;
But I by free consent can boast a Bliss,
A fairer *Helen*, and a sweeter kiss.
Chloris. Kisses are empty joyes and soon are o're.
Daph. A Kiss betwixt the lips is something more.
Chlo. I wipe my mouth, and where's your kissing then?
Daph. I swear you wipe it to be kiss'd agen.

Chlo. Go tend your Herd, and kiss your Cows at home;
I am a Maid, and in my Beauties bloom.
Daph. 'Tis well remember'd, do not waste your time;
But wisely use it e're you pass your prime.
Chlo. Blown Roses hold their sweetness to the last,
And Raisins keep their luscious native taste.
Daph. The Sun's too hot; those Olive shades are near;
I fain wou'd whisper something in your ear.
Chlo. 'Tis honest talking where we may be seen,
God knows what secret mischief you may mean;
I doubt you'l play the Wag and kiss agen.
Daph. At least beneath yon' Elm you need not fear;
My Pipe's in tune, if you'r dispos'd to hear.
Chlo. Play by your self, I dare not venture thither:
You, and your naughty Pipe go hang together.
Daph. Coy Nymph beware, lest *Venus* you offend:
Chlo. I shall have chaste *Diana* still to friend.
Daph. You have a Soul, and *Cupid* has a Dart;
Chlo. *Diana* will defend, or heal my heart.
Nay, fie what mean you in this open place;
Unhand me, or, I sware, I'le scratch your face.
Let go for shame; you make me mad for spight;
My mouth's my own; and if you kiss I'le bite.
Daph. Away with your dissembling Female tricks:
What, wou'd you 'scape the fate of all your Sex?
Chlo. I swear I'le keep my Maidenhead till death,
And die as pure as Queen *Elizabeth.*
Daph. Nay mum for that; but let me lay thee down;
Better with me, than with some nauseous Clown.
Chlo. I'de have you know, if I were so inclin'd,
I have bin wo'd by many a wealthy Hind;
But never found a Husband to my mind.
Daph. But they are absent all; and I am here;
Chlo. The matrimonial Yoke is hard to bear;
And Marriage is a woful word to hear.
Daph. A scar Crow, set to frighten fools away;
Marriage has joys; and you shall have a say.
Chlo. Sour sawce is often mix'd with our delight,
You kick by day more than you kiss by night.

Daphnis. 33 What,] What *85 92*

Daph. Sham stories all; but say the worst you can,
A very Wife fears neither God nor Man.
Chlo. But Child-birth is they say, a deadly pain;
It costs at least a Month to knit again.
Daph. *Diana* cures the wounds *Lucina* made;
Your Goddess is a Midwife by her Trade.
Chlo. But I shall spoil my Beauty if I bear.
Daph. But Mam and Dad are pretty names to hear.
Chlo. But there's a Civil question us'd of late;
Where lies my jointure, where your own Estate?
Daph. My Flocks, my Fields, my Wood, my Pastures take,
With settlement as good as Law can make.
Chlo. Swear then you will not leave me on the common,
But marry me, and make an honest Woman.
Daph. I swear by *Pan* (tho' he wears horns you'll say)
Cudgell'd and kick'd, I'le not be forc'd away.
Chlo. I bargain for a wedding Bed at least,
A house, and handsome Lodging for a guest.
Daph. A house well furnish'd shall be thine to keep;
And for a flock-bed I can sheer my Sheep.
Chlo. What Tale shall I to my old Father tell?
Daph. 'T will make him Chuckle thou'rt bestow'd so well.
Chlo. But after all, in troth I am to blame
To be so loving, e're I know your Name.
A pleasant sounding name's a pretty thing:
Daph. Faith, mine's a very pretty name to sing;
They call me *Daphnis*: *Lycidas* my Syre,
Both sound as well as Woman can desire.
Nomæa bore me; Farmers in degree,
He a good Husband, a good Houswife she.
Chlo. Your kindred is not much amiss, 'tis true,
Yet I am somewhat better born than you.
Daph. I know your Father, and his Family;
And without boasting am as good as he
Menalcas; and no Master goes before.
Chlo. Hang both our Pedigrees; not one word more;
But if you love me let me see your Living,
Your House and Home; for seeing is believing.
Daph. See first yon *Cypress* Grove, (a shade from noon;)

56 late;] late? *85 92* 82 *Menalcas*] *Menelaus 85 92*

Chlo. Browze on my goats; for I'le be with you soon.
Daph. Feed well my Bulls, to whet your appetite;
That each may take a lusty Leap at Night.
Chlo. What do you mean (uncivil as you are,)
To touch my breasts, and leave my bosome bare?
Daph. These pretty bubbies first I make my own.
Chlo. Pull out your hand, I swear, or I shall swoon.
Daph. Why does thy ebbing blood forsake thy face?
Chlo. Throw me at least upon a cleaner place:
My Linnen ruffled, and my Wastcoat soyling,
What, do you think new Cloaths, were made for spoyling?
Daph. I'le lay my Lambskins underneath thy back:
Chlo. My Head Geer 's off; what filthy work you make!
Daph. To *Venus* first, I lay these off'rings by;
Chlo. Nay first look round, that no body be nigh:
Methinks I hear a whisp'ring in the Grove.
Daph. The *Cypress* Trees are telling Tales of love.
Chlo. You tear off all behind me, and before me;
And I'm as naked as my Mother bore me.
Daph. I'le buy thee better Cloaths than these I tear,
And lie so close, I'le cover thee from Air.
Chlo. Y'are liberal now; but when your turn is sped,
You'l wish me choak'd with every crust of Bread.
Daph. I'le give thee more, much more than I have told;
Wou'd I cou'd coyn my very heart to Gold.
Chlo. Forgive thy handmaid (Huntress of the wood,)
I see there's no resisting flesh and blood!
Daph. The noble deed is done; my Herds I'le cull;
Cupid, be thine a Calf; and *Venus*, thine a Bull.
Chlo. A Maid I came, in an unlucky hour,
But hence return, without my Virgin flour.
Daph. A Maid is but a barren Name at best;
If thou canst hold, I bid for twins at least.

Thus did this happy Pair their love dispence
With mutual joys, and gratifi'd their sense;
The God of Love was there a bidden Guest;
And present at his own Mysterious Feast.
His azure Mantle underneath he spred,

97 What,] What *85 92* 99 Geer 's *92*: Geer'es *85*

And scatter'd Roses on the Nuptial Bed;
While folded in each others arms they lay,
He blew the flames, and furnish'd out the play,
And from their Foreheads wip'd the balmy sweat away.
First rose the Maid, and with a glowing Face,
Her down cast eyes beheld her print upon the grass;
Thence to her Herd she sped her self in haste:
The Bridegroom started from his Trance at last,
And pipeing homeward jocoundly he past.

Horat. Ode 3. Lib. I
Inscrib'd to the Earl of Roscomon, *on his intended Voyage to* IRELAND

So may th' auspitious Queen of Love,
And the twin Stars, (the Seed of *Jove*,)
And he, who rules the rageing wind,
To thee, O sacred Ship, be kind;
And gentle Breezes fill thy Sails,
Supplying soft *Etesian* Gales,
As thou to whom the Muse commends,
The best of Poets and of Friends,
Dost thy committed Pledge restore:
And land him safely on the shore:
And save the better part of me,
From perishing with him at Sea.
Sure he, who first the passage try'd,
In harden'd Oak his heart did hide,
And ribs of Iron arm'd his side!
Or his at least, in hollow wood,
Who tempted first the briny Floud:
Nor fear'd the winds contending roar,
Nor billows beating on the shore;
Nor *Hyades* portending Rain;
Nor all the Tyrants of the Main.
What form of death cou'd him affright,
Who unconcern'd with stedfast sight,
Cou'd view the Surges mounting steep,

129 Maid,] Maid *85 92*
Horat. Ode 3. Lib. I. 3 wind,] wind *85 92* 4 kind;] kind, *85 92*

And monsters rolling in the deep?
Cou'd thro' the ranks of ruin go,
With Storms above, and Rocks below!
In vain did Natures wise command,
Divide the Waters from the Land,
If daring Ships, and Men prophane,
Invade th' inviolable Main:
Th' eternal Fences over leap;
And pass at will the boundless deep.
No toyl, no hardship can restrain
Ambitious Man inur'd to pain;
The more confin'd, the more he tries,
And at forbidden quarry flies.
Thus bold *Prometheus* did aspire,
And stole from heaven the seed of Fire:
A train of Ills, a ghastly crew,
The Robbers blazing track persue;
Fierce Famine, with her Meagre face,
And Feavours of the fiery Race,
In swarms th' offending Wretch surround,
All brooding on the blasted ground:
And limping Death, lash'd on by Fate,
Comes up to shorten half our date.
This made not *Dedalus* beware,
With borrow'd wings to sail in Air:
To Hell *Alcides* forc'd his way,
Plung'd thro' the Lake, and snatch'd the Prey.
Nay scarce the Gods, or heav'nly Climes
Are safe from our audacious Crimes;
We reach at *Jove*'s Imperial Crown,
And pull the unwilling thunder down.

Horace Lib. I. *Ode* 9

I

BEHOLD yon' Mountains hoary height
Made higher with new Mounts of Snow;
Again behold the Winters weight
Oppress the lab'ring Woods below:

And streams with Icy fetters bound,
Benum'd and crampt to solid ground.

II

With well heap'd Logs dissolve the cold,
  And feed the genial hearth with fires;
Produce the Wine, that makes us bold,
  And sprightly Wit and Love inspires:
For what hereafter shall betide,
God, if 'tis worth his care, provide.

III

Let him alone with what he made,
  To toss and turn the World below;
At his command the storms invade;
  The winds by his Commission blow·
Till with a Nod he bids 'em cease,
And then the Calm returns, and all is peace.

IV

To morrow and her works defie,
  Lay hold upon the present hour,
And snatch the pleasures passing by,
  To put them out of Fortunes pow'r:
Nor love, nor love's delights disdain,
What e're thou get'st to day is gain.

V

Secure those golden early joyes,
  That Youth unsowr'd with sorrow bears,
E're with'ring time the taste destroyes,
  With sickness and unweildy years!
For active sports, for pleasing rest,
This is the time to be possest;
The best is but in season best.

Horace Lib. I. *Ode* 9. 8 hearth *85* (*errata*): heat *85* (*text*)

VI

The pointed hour of promis'd bliss,
  The pleasing whisper in the dark,
The half unwilling willing kiss,
  The laugh that guides thee to the mark,
When the kind Nymph wou'd coyness feign,
And hides but to be found again,
These, these are joyes the Gods for Youth ordain.

Horat. Ode 29. Book 3 Paraphras'd in *Pindarique* Verse; and *Inscrib'd to the Right Honourable* Lawrence *Earl of* Rochester

I

DESCENDED of an ancient Line,
  That long the *Tuscan* Scepter sway'd,
Make haste to meet the generous wine,
  Whose piercing is for thee delay'd:
The rosie wreath is ready made;
  And artful hands prepare
The fragrant *Syrian* Oyl, that shall perfume thy hair.

II

When the Wine sparkles from a far,
  And the well-natur'd Friend cries, come away;
Make haste, and leave thy business and thy care,
  No mortal int'rest can be worth thy stay.

III

Leave for a while thy costly Country Seat;
  And, to be Great indeed, forget
The nauseous pleasures of the Great:
      Make haste and come:
Come and forsake thy cloying store;
  Thy Turret that surveys, from high,
The smoke, and wealth, and noise of *Rome*;

And all the busie pageantry
That wise men scorn, and fools adore:
Come, give thy Soul a loose, and taste the pleasures of the poor.

IV

Sometimes 'tis grateful to the Rich, to try
A short vicissitude, and fit of Poverty:
A savoury Dish, a homely Treat,
Where all is plain, where all is neat,
Without the stately spacious Room,
The *Persian* Carpet, or the *Tyrian* Loom,
Clear up the cloudy foreheads of the Great.

V

The Sun is in the Lion mounted high;
The *Syrian* Star
Barks from a far;
And with his sultry breath infects the Sky;
The ground below is parch'd, the heav'ns above us fry.
The Shepheard drives his fainting Flock,
Beneath the covert of a Rock;
And seeks refreshing Rivulets nigh:
The *Sylvans* to their shades retire,
Those very shades and streams, new shades and streams require;
And want a cooling breeze of wind to fan the rageing fire.

VI

Thou, what befits the new Lord May'r,
And what the City Faction dare,
And what the *Gallique* Arms will do,
And what the Quiver bearing Foe,
Art anxiously inquisitive to know:
But God has, wisely, hid from humane sight
The dark decrees of future fate;
And sown their seeds in depth of night;
He laughs at all the giddy turns of State;
When Mortals search too soon, and fear too late.

VII

Enjoy the present smiling hour;
And put it out of Fortunes pow'r:
The tide of bus'ness, like the running stream,
Is sometimes high, and sometimes low,
A quiet ebb, or a tempestuous flow,
And alwayes in extream.
Now with a noiseless gentle course
It keeps within the middle Bed;
Anon it lifts aloft the head,
And bears down all before it, with impetuous force:
And trunks of Trees come rowling down,
Sheep and their Folds together drown:
Both House and Homested into Seas are borne,
And Rocks are from their old foundations torn,
And woods made thin with winds, their scatter'd honours mourn.

VIII

Happy the Man, and happy he alone,
He, who can call to day his own:
He, who secure within, can say
To morrow do thy worst, for I have liv'd to day.
Be fair, or foul, or rain, or shine,
The joys I have possest, in spight of fate are mine.
Not Heav'n it self upon the past has pow'r;
But what has been, has been, and I have had my hour.

IX

Fortune, that with malicious joy,
Does Man her slave oppress,
Proud of her Office to destroy,
Is seldome pleas'd to bless.
Still various and unconstant still;
But with an inclination to be ill;
Promotes, degrades, delights in strife,
And makes a Lottery of life.
I can enjoy her while she's kind;
But when she dances in the wind,
And shakes her wings, and will not stay,

I puff the Prostitute away:
The little or the much she gave, is quietly resign'd:
Content with poverty, my Soul, I arm;
And Vertue, tho' in rags, will keep me warm.

X

What is 't to me,
Who never sail in her unfaithful Sea,
If Storms arise, and Clouds grow black;
If the Mast split and threaten wreck,
Then let the greedy Merchant fear
For his ill gotten gain;
And pray to Gods that will not hear,
While the debating winds and billows bear
His Wealth into the Main.
For me secure from Fortunes blows,
(Secure of what I cannot lose,)
In my small Pinnace I can sail,
Contemning all the blustring roar;
And running with a merry gale,
With friendly Stars my safety seek
Within some little winding Creek;
And see the storm a shore.

FROM HORACE, *Epod. 2d.*

How happy in his low degree,
How rich in humble Poverty, is he,
Who leads a quiet country life!
Discharg'd of business, void of strife,
And from the gripeing Scrivener free.
(Thus e're the Seeds of Vice were sown,
Liv'd Men in better Ages born,
Who Plow'd with Oxen of their own
Their small paternal field of Corn.)
Nor Trumpets summon him to War
Nor drums disturb his morning Sleep,

From Horace. 1 degree, *92*: degree *85*

Nor knows he Merchants gainful care,
  Nor fears the dangers of the deep.
The clamours of contentious Law,
  And Court and state he wisely shuns,
Nor brib'd with hopes nor dar'd with awe
  To servile Salutations runs:
But either to the clasping Vine
  Does the supporting Poplar Wed,
Or with his pruneing hook disjoyn
  Unbearing Branches from their Head,
  And grafts more happy in their stead:
Or climbing to a hilly Steep
  He views his Herds in Vales afar
Or Sheers his overburden'd Sheep,
  Or mead for cooling drink prepares,
  Of Virgin honey in the Jars.
Or in the now declining year
  When bounteous *Autumn* rears his head,
He joyes to pull the ripen'd Pear,
  And clustring Grapes with purple spread.
The fairest of this his fruit he serves,
  Priapus thy rewards:
Sylvanus too his part deserves,
  Whose care the fences guards.
Sometimes beneath an ancient Oak,
  Or on the matted grass he lies;
No God of Sleep he need invoke,
  The stream that o're the pebbles flies
  With gentle slumber crowns his Eyes.
The Wind that Whistles through the sprays
  Maintains the consort of the Song;
And hidden Birds with native layes
  The golden sleep prolong.
But when the blast of Winter blows,
  And hoary frost inverts the year,
Into the naked Woods he goes
  And seeks the tusky Boar to rear,
  With well mouth'd hounds and pointed Spear.
Or spreads his subtile Nets from sight

32 of this his *92*: of his *85*

With twinckling glasses to betray
The Larkes that in the Meshes light,
Or makes the fearful Hare his prey.
Amidst his harmless easie joys
No anxious care invades his health,
Nor Love his peace of mind destroys,
Nor wicked avarice of Wealth.
But if a chast and pleasing Wife,
To ease the business of his Life,
Divides with him his houshold care,
Such as the *Sabine* Matrons were,
Such as the swift *Apulians* Bride,
Sunburnt and Swarthy tho' she be,
Will fire for Winter Nights provide,
And without noise will oversee,
His Children and his Family,
And order all things till he come,
Sweaty and overlabour'd, home;
If she in pens his Flocks will fold,
And then produce her Dairy store,
With Wine to drive away the cold,
And unbought dainties of the poor;
Not Oysters of the *Lucrine* Lake
My sober appetite wou'd wish,
Nor *Turbet*, or the Foreign Fish
That rowling Tempests overtake,
And hither waft the costly dish.
Not *Heathpout*, or the rarer Bird,
Which *Phasis*, or *Ionia* yields,
More pleasing morsels wou'd afford
Than the fat Olives of my fields;
Than Shards or Mallows for the pot,
That keep the loosen'd Body sound,
Or than the Lamb that falls by Lot,
To the just Guardian of my ground.
Amidst these feasts of happy Swains,
The jolly Shepheard smiles to see
His flock returning from the Plains;
The Farmer is as pleas'd as he
To view his Oxen, sweating smoak,

Bear on their Necks the loosen'd Yoke.
To look upon his menial Crew,
 That sit around his cheerful hearth,
And bodies spent in toil renew
 With wholesome Food and Country Mirth.
This *Morecraft* said within himself;
 Resolv'd to leave the wicked Town,
 And live retir'd upon his own;
He call'd his Mony in:
 But the prevailing love of pelf,
 Soon split him on the former shelf,
And put it out again.

A New SONG

SYLVIA the fair, in the bloom of Fifteen,
 Felt an innocent warmth, as she lay on the green;
She had heard of a pleasure, and something she guest
By the towzing and tumbling and touching her Breast;
She saw the men eager, but was at a loss,
What they meant by their sighing, and kissing so close;
 By their praying and whining
 And clasping and twining,
 And panting and wishing,
 And sighing and kissing
 And sighing and kissing so close.

II

Ah she cry'd, ah for a languishing Maid
In a Country of Christians to die without aid!
Not a Whig, or a Tory, or Trimmer at least,
Or a Protestant Parson, or Catholick Priest,
To instruct a young Virgin, that is at a loss
What they meant by their sighing, and kissing so close!
 By their praying and whining
 And clasping and twining,
 And panting and wishing,
 And sighing and kissing
 And sighing and kissing so close.

III

Cupid in Shape of a Swayn did appear,
He saw the sad wound, and in pity drew near,
Then show'd her his Arrow, and bid her not fear,
For the pain was no more than a Maiden may bear;
When the balm was infus'd she was not at a loss,
What they meant by their sighing and kissing so close;
By their praying and whining,
And clasping and twining,
And panting and wishing,
And sighing and kissing,
And sighing and kissing so close.

SONG

Go tell *Amynta* gentle Swain,
I wou'd not die nor dare complain,
Thy tuneful Voice with numbers joyn,
Thy words will more prevail than mine;
To Souls oppress'd and dumb with grief,
The Gods ordain this kind relief;
That Musick shou'd in sounds convey,
What dying Lovers dare not say.

II

A Sigh or Tear perhaps she'll give,
But love on pitty cannot live.
Tell her that Hearts for Hearts were made,
And love with love is only paid.
Tell her my pains so fast encrease,
That soon they will be past redress;
But ah! the Wretch that speechless lyes,
Attends but Death to close his Eyes.

THRENODIA AUGUSTALIS

A Funeral-Pindarique

POEM Sacred to the Happy Memory of King CHARLES II

Fortunati Ambo, si quid mea Carmina possunt,
Nulla dies unquam memori vos eximet ævo!

I

THUS long my Grief has kept me dumb:
Sure there's a Lethargy in mighty Woe,
Tears stand congeal'd, and cannot flow;
And the sad Soul retires into her inmost Room:
Tears, for a Stroke foreseen, afford Relief;
But, unprovided for a sudden Blow,
Like *Niobe* we Marble grow;
And Petrifie with Grief.
Our *British* Heav'n was all Serene,
No threatning Cloud was nigh,
Not the least wrinkle to deform the Sky;
We liv'd as unconcern'd and happily
As the first Age in Natures golden Scene;
Supine amidst our flowing Store,
We slept securely, and we dream't of more:
When suddenly the Thunder-clap was heard,
It took us unprepar'd and out of guard,
Already lost before we fear'd.
Th' amazing News of *Charles* at once were spread,
At once the general Voice declar'd,
Our Gracious Prince was dead.
No Sickness known before, no slow Disease,
To soften Grief by Just Degrees:
But, like an Hurricane on *Indian* Seas,
The Tempest rose;
An unexpected Burst of Woes:

Threnodia Augustalis. Text from the Harvard copy of the first edition, 1685, (*H*), *collated with the subsequent London editions* (*A, B*) *and the Dublin edition* (*C*), 1685. *See Commentary*
24 *Indian*] *Indians C*

With scarce a breathing space betwixt,
This *Now* becalm'd, and perishing the next.
As if great *Atlas* from his Height
Shou'd sink beneath his heavenly Weight,
And, with a mighty Flaw, the flaming Wall
(As once it shall)
Shou'd gape immense and rushing down, o'erwhelm this neather Ball;
So swift and so surprizing was our Fear:
Our *Atlas* fell indeed; But *Hercules* was near.

II

His Pious Brother, sure the best
Who ever bore that Name,
Was newly risen from his Rest,
And, with a fervent Flame,
His usual morning Vows had just addrest
For his dear Sovereign's Health;
And hop'd to have 'em heard,
In long increase of years,
In Honour, Fame and Wealth:
Guiltless of Greatness thus he always pray'd,
Nor knew nor wisht those Vows he made,
On his own Head shou'd be repay'd.
Soon as th' ill omen'd Rumor reacht his Ear,
(Ill News is wing'd with Fate, and flies apace)
Who can describe th' Amazement in his Face!
Horrour in all his Pomp was there,
Mute and magnificent without a Tear:
And then the *Hero* first was seen to fear.
Half unarray'd he ran to his Relief,
So hasty and so artless was his grief:
Approaching Greatness met him with her Charms
Of Pow'r and future State;
But look'd so ghastly in a Brother's Fate,
He shook her from his Armes.
Arriv'd within the mournful Room, he saw
A wild Distraction, void of Awe,
And arbitrary Grief unbounded by a Law.
God's Image, God's Anointed lay

28 becalm'd *A B*: beclam'd *H*

Without Motion, Pulse or Breath,
A Senseless Lump of sacred Clay,
An Image, now, of Death.
Amidst his sad Attendants Grones and Cryes,
The Lines of that ador'd, forgiving Face,
Distorted from their native grace;
An Iron Slumber sat on his Majestick Eyes.
The Pious Duke—forbear audacious Muse,
No Terms thy feeble Art can use
Are able to adorn so vast a Woe;
The grief of all the rest like subject-grief did show,
His like a Sovereign did transcend;
No Wife, no Brother, such a Grief cou'd know,
Nor any name, but Friend.

III

O wondrous Changes of a fatal Scene,
Still varying to the last!
Heav'n, though its hard Decree was past,
Seem'd pointing to a gracious Turn agen:
And Death's up-lifted Arme arrested in its hast.
Heav'n half repented of the doom,
And almost griev'd it had foreseen,
What by Foresight it will'd eternally to come.
Mercy above did hourly plead
For her Resemblance here below:
And mild Forgiveness intercede
To stop the coming blow.
New Miracles approach'd th' Etherial Throne,
Such as his wondrous Life had oft and lately known,
And urg'd that still they might be shown.
On Earth his Pious Brother pray'd and vow'd,
Renouncing Greatness at so dear a rate,
Himself defending what he cou'd,
From all the Glories of his future Fate.
With him th' innumerable Croud
Of armed Prayers
Knock'd at the Gates of Heav'n, and knock'd aloud;
The first, well meaning rude Petitioners.

70 sat] sate *A B*   97 Croud] Croud, *H A B*

All for his Life assayl'd the Throne,
All wou'd have brib'd the Skyes by offring up their own.
So great a Throng not Heav'n it self cou'd bar;
'Twas almost born by force as in the Giants War.
The Pray'rs, at least, for his Reprive were heard;
His Death, like *Hezekiah*'s, was deferr'd:
  Against the Sun the Shadow went;
  Five days, those five Degrees, were lent
  To form our Patience and prepare th' Event.
The second Causes took the swift Command,
The med'cinal Head, the ready Hand,
All eager to perform their Part,
All but Eternal Doom was conquer'd by their Art:
Once more the fleeting Soul came back
  T' inspire the mortal Frame,
And in the Body took a doubtful Stand,
  Doubtful and hov'ring like expiring Flame,
That mounts and falls by turns, and trembles o'er the Brand.

IV

The joyful short-liv'd news soon spread around,
Took the same Train, the same impetuous bound:
The drooping Town in smiles again was drest,
Gladness in every Face exprest,
Their Eyes before their Tongues confest.
Men met each other with erected look,
The steps were higher that they took,
Friends to congratulate their friends made haste;
And long inveterate Foes saluted as they past:
Above the rest Heroick *James* appear'd
Exalted more, because he more had fear'd:
His manly heart, whose Noble pride
Was still above
Dissembled hate or varnisht Love,
Its more then common transport cou'd not hide;
But like an **Eagre* rode in triumph o're the tide.

* *An* Eagre *is a Tyde swelling above another Tyde, which I have my self observ'd on the River* Trent.

105 Reprive] Reprieve *A B*   were *A B*: was *H*   125 that *A B*: then *H*
126 Friends . . . their friends *B*: Each . . . his friend *H A*

Thus, in alternate Course,
The Tyrant passions, hope and fear,
Did in extreams appear,
And flasht upon the Soul with equal force.
Thus, at half Ebb, a rowling Sea
Returns and wins upon the shoar;
The watry Herd, affrighted at the roar,
Rest on their Fins a while, and stay,
Then backward take their wondring way:
The Prophet wonders more than they,
At Prodigies but rarely seen before,
And cries a *King* must fall, or Kingdoms change their sway.
Such were our counter-tydes at land, and so
Presaging of the fatal blow,
In their prodigious Ebb and flow.
The Royal Soul, that like the labouring Moon,
By Charms of Art was hurried down,
Forc'd with regret to leave her Native Sphear,
Came but a while on liking here:
Soon weary of the painful strife,
And made but faint Essays of Life:
An Evening light
Soon shut in Night;
A strong distemper, and a weak relief,
Short intervals of joy, and long returns of grief.

V

The Sons of Art all Med'cines try'd
And every Noble remedy apply'd;
With emulation each essay'd
His utmost skill, nay more they pray'd:
Never was losing game with better conduct plaid.
Death never won a stake with greater toyl,
Nor e're was Fate so near a foil:
But, like a fortress on a Rock,
Th' impregnable Disease their vain attempts did mock;
They min'd it near, they batter'd from a far
With all the Cannon of the Med'cinal War;

164 Never was *B*: Was never *H A*

No gentle means cou'd be essay'd,
'Twas beyond parly when the siege was laid:
Th' extreamest ways they first ordain,
Prescribing such intollerable pain,
As none but *Cæsar* cou'd sustain:
Undaunted *Cæsar* underwent
The malice of their Art, nor bent
Beneath what e'r their pious rigour cou'd invent:
In five such dayes he suffer'd more
Then any suffer'd in his reign before;
More, infinitely more, than he,
Against the worst of Rebels, cou'd decree,
A Traytor or twice pardon'd Enemy.
Now Art was tir'd without success,
No Racks cou'd make the stubborn malady confess.
The vain *Insurancers* of Life,
And He who most perform'd and promis'd less,
Even *Short* himself forsook th' unequal strife.
Death and despair was in their looks,
No longer they consult their memories or books;
Like helpless friends, who view from shoar
The labouring Ship, and hear the tempest roar,
So stood they with their arms across;
Not to assist; but to deplore
Th' inevitable loss.

VI

Death was denounc'd; that frightful sound
Which even the best can hardly bear,
He took the Summons void of fear;
And, unconcern'dly, cast his eyes around;
As if to find and dare the griesly Challenger.
What death cou'd do he lately try'd,
When in four days he more then dy'd.
The same assurance all his words did grace;
The same Majestick mildness held its place;
Nor lost the Monarch in his dying face.
Intrepid, pious, merciful, and brave,
He lookt as when he conquer'd and forgave.

VII

As if some Angel had been sent
To lengthen out his Government,
And to foretel as many years again,
As he had number'd in his happy reign,
So chearfully he took the doom
Of his departing breath;
Nor shrunk nor stept aside for death:
But, with unalter'd pace, kept on;
Providing for events to come,
When he resign'd the Throne.
Still he maintain'd his Kingly State;
And grew familiar with his fate.
Kind, good and gracious to the last,
On all he lov'd before, his dying beams he cast:
Oh truly good, and truly great,
For glorious as he rose benignly so he set!
All that on earth he held most dear,
He recommended to his Care,
To whom both heav'n
The right had giv'n
And his own Love bequeath'd supream command:
He took and prest that ever loyal hand,
Which cou'd in Peace secure his Reign,
Which cou'd in wars his Pow'r maintain,
That hand on which no plighted vows were ever vain.
Well for so great a trust, he chose
A Prince who never disobey'd:
Not when the most severe commands were laid;
Nor want, nor Exile with his duty weigh'd:
A Prince on whom (if Heav'n its Eyes cou'd close)
The Welfare of the World it safely might repose.

VIII

That King who liv'd to Gods own heart,
Yet less serenely died than he:

226 heav'n] heav'n, *H A B* 232 on *A B*: in *H* 239 *opening lines of stanzas VIII–XVIII indented in H A B*

Charles left behind no harsh decree
For Schoolmen with laborious art
To salve from cruelty:
Those, for whom love cou'd no excuses frame,
He graciously forgot to name.
Thus far my Muse, though rudely, has design'd
Some faint resemblance of his Godlike mind:
But neither Pen nor Pencil can express
The parting Brothers *tenderness*:
Though thats a term too mean and low;
(The blest above a kinder word may know:)
But what they did, and what they said,
The Monarch who Triumphant went,
The Militant who staid,
Like Painters, when their heigthning arts are spent,
I cast into a shade.
That all forgiving King,
The type of him above,
That inexhausted spring
Of clemency and Love;
Himself to his next self accus'd,
And ask'd that Pardon which he ne're refus'd:
For faults not his, for guilt and Crimes
Of Godless men, and of Rebellious times:
For an hard Exile, kindly meant,
When his ungrateful Country sent
Their best *Camillus* into banishment:
And forc'd their Sov'raigns Act, they cou'd not his consent.
Oh how much rather had that injur'd Chief
Repeated all his sufferings past,
Then hear a pardon beg'd at last,
Which giv'n cou'd give the dying no relief:
He bent, he sunk beneath his grief:
His dauntless heart wou'd fain have held
From weeping, but his eyes rebell'd.
Perhaps the Godlike Hero in his breast
Disdain'd, or was asham'd to show
So weak, so womanish a woe,
Which yet the Brother and the Friend so plenteously confest.

259 inexhausted *A B*: inexhausting *H*

IX

Amidst that silent show'r, the Royal mind
An Easy passage found,
And left its sacred earth behind:
Nor murm'ring groan exprest, nor labouring sound,
Nor any least tumultuous breath;
Calm was his life, and quiet was his death.
Soft as those gentle whispers were,
In which th' Almighty did appear;
By the still Voice, the Prophet knew him there.
That Peace which made thy Prosperous Reign to shine,
That Peace thou leav'st to thy Imperial Line,
That Peace, oh happy Shade, be ever thine!

X

For all those Joys thy Restauration brought,
For all the Miracles it wrought,
For all the healing Balm thy Mercy pour'd
Into the Nations bleeding Wound,
And Care that after kept it sound,
For numerous Blessings yearly shour'd,
And Property with Plenty crown'd;
For Freedom, still maintain'd alive,
Freedom which in no other Land will thrive,
Freedom an *English* Subject's sole Prerogative,
Without whose Charms ev'n Peace wou'd be
But a dull quiet Slavery:
For these and more, accept our Pious Praise;
'Tis all the Subsidy
The present Age can raise,
The rest is charg'd on late Posterity.
Posterity is charg'd the more,
Because the large abounding store
To them and to their Heirs, is still entail'd by thee.
Succession, of a long Descent,
Which Chastly in the Channells ran,
And from our Demi-gods began,
Equal almost to time in its extent,

288 Voice *B*: Sound *H A*

Through Hazzards numberless and great,
Thou hast deriv'd this mighty Blessing down,
And fixt the fairest Gemm that decks th' Imperial Crown:
Not Faction, when it shook thy Regal Seat,
Not Senates, insolently loud,
(Those Ecchoes of a thoughtless Croud)
Not Foreign or Domestick Treachery,
Could warp thy Soul to their Unjust Decree.
So much thy Foes thy manly Mind mistook,
Who judg'd it by the Mildness of thy look:
Like a well temper'd Sword, it bent at will;
But kept the Native toughness of the Steel.

XI

Be true, O *Clio*, to thy Hero's Name!
But draw him strictly so
That all who view, the Piece may know,
He needs no Trappings of fictitious Fame:
The Load's too weighty: Thou may'st chuse
Some Parts of Praise, and some refuse:
Write, that his Annals may be thought more lavish than the Muse.
In scanty Truth thou hast confin'd
The Vertues of a Royal Mind,
Forgiving, bounteous, humble, just and kind:
His Conversation, Wit, and Parts,
His Knowledge in the Noblest, useful Arts,
Were such, Dead Authors cou'd not give;
But habitudes of those who live;
Who, lighting him, did greater lights receive:
He drain'd from all, and all they knew;
His Apprehension quick, his Judgment true:
That the most Learn'd, with shame, confess
His Knowledge more, his Reading only less.

XII

Amidst the peaceful Triumphs of his Reign,
What wonder if the kindly beams he shed
Reviv'd the drooping Arts again,
If Science rais'd her Head,

322 Decree. *A B*: Decree, *H*   327 thy] the *C*   347 he *A B*: be *H*

And soft Humanity that from Rebellion fled;
Our Isle, indeed, too fruitful was before;
But all uncultivated lay
Out of the *Solar* walk and Heav'ns high way;
With rank *Geneva* Weeds run o're,
And Cockle, at the best, amidst the Corn it bore:
The Royal Husbandman appear'd,
And Plough'd, and Sow'd, and Till'd,
The Thorns he rooted out, the Rubbish clear'd,
And blest th' obedient Field.
When, straight, a double Harvest rose;
Such as the swarthy *Indian* mowes;
Or happier Climates near the Line,
Or Paradise Manur'd, and drest by hands Divine.

XIII

As when the New-born Phœnix takes his way,
His rich Paternal Regions to Survey,
Of airy Choristers a numerous Train
Attend his wondrous Progress o're the Plain;
So, rising from his Fathers Urn,
So Glorious did our *Charles* return;
Th' officious Muses came along,
A gay Harmonious Quire like Angels ever Young:
(The Muse that mourns him now his happy Triumph sung)
Even *they* cou'd thrive in his Auspicious reign;
And such a plenteous Crop they bore
Of purest and well winow'd Grain,
As *Britain* never knew before.
Tho little was their Hire, and light their Gain,
Yet somewhat to their share he threw;
Fed from his Hand, they sung and flew,
Like Birds of Paradise, that liv'd on Morning dew.
Oh never let their Lays his Name forget!
The Pension of a Prince's praise is great.
Live then thou great Encourager of Arts,
Live ever in our Thankful Hearts;
Live blest Above, almost invok'd Below;
Live and receive this Pious Vow,

353 Heav'ns *B*: Heavens *H A*   371 like *B*: of *H A*

Our Patron once, our Guardian Angel now.
Thou *Fabius* of a sinking State,
Who didst by wise delays, divert our Fate,
When Faction like a Tempest rose,
In Death's most hideous form,
Then, Art to Rage thou didst oppose,
To weather out the Storm:
Not quitting thy Supream command,
Thou heldst the Rudder with a steady hand,
Till safely on the Shore the Bark did land:
The Bark that all our Blessings brought,
Charg'd with thy Self and *James*, a doubly Royal fraught.

XIV

Oh frail Estate of Humane things,
And slippery hopes below!
Now to our Cost your Emptiness we know,
(For 'tis a Lesson dearly bought)
Assurance here is never to be sought.
The Best, and best belov'd of Kings,
And best deserving to be so,
When scarce he had escap'd the fatal blow
Of Faction and Conspiracy,
Death did his promis'd hopes destroy:
He toyl'd, He gain'd, but liv'd not to enjoy.
What mists of Providence are these
Through which we cannot see!
So Saints, by supernatural Pow'r set free,
Are left at last in Martyrdom to dye;
Such is the end of oft repeated Miracles.
Forgive me Heav'n that Impious thought,
'Twas Grief for *Charles*, to Madness wrought,
That Question'd thy Supream Decree!
Thou didst his gracious Reign prolong,
Even in thy Saints and Angels wrong,
His Fellow Citizens of Immortality:
For Twelve long years of Exile, born,
Twice twelve we number'd since his blest Return:
So strictly wer't thou Just to pay,
Even to the driblet of a day.

Yet still we murmur, and Complain,
The Quails and Manna shou'd no longer rain;
Those Miracles 'twas needless to renew;
The Chosen Flock has now the Promis'd Land in view.

XV

A Warlike Prince ascends the Regal State,
A Prince, long exercis'd by Fate:
Long may he keep, tho he obtains it late.
Heroes, in Heaven's peculiar Mold are cast,
They and their Poets are not form'd in hast;
Man was the first in God's design, and Man was made the last.
False Heroes made by Flattery so,
Heav'n can strike out, like Sparkles, at a blow;
But e'r a Prince is to Perfection brought,
He costs Omnipotence a second thought.
With Toyl and Sweat,
With hardning Cold, and forming Heat,
The Cyclops did their strokes repeat,
Before th' impenetrable Shield was wrought.
It looks as if the Maker wou'd not own
The Noble work for his,
Before 'twas try'd and found a Masterpiece.

XVI

View then a *Monarch* ripen'd for a Throne.
Alcides thus his race began,
O're Infancy he swiftly ran;
The future God, at first was more than Man:
Dangers and Toils, and *Juno*'s Hate
Even o're his Cradle lay in wait;
And there he grappled first with Fate:
In his young Hands the hissing Snakes he prest,
So early was the Deity confest;
Thus, by degrees, he rose to *Jove*'s Imperial Seat;
Thus difficulties prove a Soul *legitimately* great.
Like his, our Hero's Infancy was try'd;
Betimes the Furies did their Snakes provide;

433 form'd] made *C* 435 Heroes] Heroes, *B*
452 *om. C* 456 *legitimately B*: legitimately *H A*

And, to his Infant Arms oppose
His Father's Rebels, and his Brother's Foes;
The more opprest the higher still he rose:
Those were the Preludes of his Fate,
That form'd his Manhood, to subdue
The *Hydra* of the many-headed, hissing Crew.

XVII

As after *Numa*'s peaceful Reign,
The Martial *Ancus* did the Scepter wield,
Furbish'd the rusty Sword again,
Resum'd the long forgotten Shield,
And led the *Latins* to the dusty Field;
So *James* the drowsy *Genius* wakes
Of *Britain* long entranc'd in Charms,
Restiff and slumbring on its Arms:
'Tis rows'd and with a new strung Nerve, the Spear already shakes.
No Neighing of the Warriour Steeds,
No Drum, or louder Trumpet, needs
T' inspire the Coward, warm the Cold,
His Voice, his sole Appearance makes 'em bold.
Gaul and *Batavia* dread th' impending blow;
Too well the Vigour of that Arm they know;
They lick the dust, and Crouch beneath their fatal Foe.
Long may they fear this awful Prince,
And not Provoke his lingring Sword;
Peace is their only sure Defence,
Their best Security his Word:
In all the Changes of his doubtful State,
His Truth, like Heav'ns, was kept inviolate,
For him to Promise is to make it Fate.
His *Valour* can Triumph o'r Land and Main;
With broken Oaths his Fame he will not stain;
With Conquest basely bought, and with Inglorious gain.

XVIII

For once, O Heav'n, unfold thy Adamantine Book;
And let his wondring *Senate* see,
If not thy firm Immutable Decree,

480 their] the *C* 484 Their *A B*: The *H*

At least the second Page, of strong contingency;
Such as consists with wills, Originally free:
Let them, with glad amazement, look
On what their happiness may be:
Let them not still be obstinately blind,
Still to divert the Good thou hast design'd,
Or with Malignant penury,
To sterve the Royal Vertues of his Mind.
Faith is a Christian's and a Subject's Test,
Oh give them to believe, and they are surely blest!
They do; and, with a distant view, I see
Th' amended Vows of *English* Loyalty.
And all beyond that Object, there appears
The long Retinue of a Prosperous Raign,
A Series of Successful years,
In Orderly Array, a Martial, manly Train.
Behold ev'n to remoter Shores
A Conquering Navy proudly spread;
The *British* Cannon formidably roars,
While starting from his Oozy Bed,
Th' asserted Ocean rears his reverend Head;
To View and Recognize his ancient Lord again:
And with a willing hand, restores
The *Fasces* of the Main.

PROLOGUE and EPILOGUE to *ALBION AND ALBANIUS*

PROLOGUE *To the* OPERA

FULL twenty years and more, our lab'ring Stage
Has lost, on this incorrigible age:
Our Poets, the *John Ketches* of the Nation,
Have seem'd to lash yee, ev'n to excoriation:

494 strong *B*: great *H A*
Prologue and Epilogue. Text from Albion and Albanius: An Opera, *1685, collated with the editions of 1687 and 1691*

But still no sign remains; which plainly notes,
You bore like Hero's, or you brib'd like *Oates*.
What can we do, when mimicking a Fop,
Like beating Nut-trees, makes a larger Crop?
Faith we'll e'en spare our pains: and to content you,
Will fairly leave you what your Maker meant you.
Satyre was once your Physick, Wit your Food;
One nourisht not, and t'other drew no Blood.
Wee now prescribe, like Doctors in despair,
The Diet your weak appetites can bear.
Since hearty Beef and Mutton will not do,
Here's Julep dance, Ptisan of Song and show:
Give you strong Sense, the Liquor is too heady;
You're come to farce, that's Asses milk, already.
Some hopeful Youths there are, of callow Wit,
Who one Day may be Men, if Heav'n think fit;
Sound may serve such, ere they to Sense are grown;
Like leading strings, till they can walk alone:
But yet to keep our Friends in count'nance, know,
The Wise *Italians* first invented show;
Thence, into *France* the Noble Pageant past;
'Tis *England*'s Credit to be cozn'd last.
Freedom and Zeal have chous'd you o'er and o'er;
'Pray' give us leave to bubble you once more;
You never were so cheaply fool'd before.
Wee bring you change, to humour your Disease;
Change for the worse has ever us'd to please:
Then 'tis the mode of *France*, without whose Rules,
None must presume to set up here for Fools:
In *France*, the oldest Man is always young,
Sees *Opera's* daily, learns the Tunes so long,
Till Foot, Hand, Head, keep time with ev'ry Song.
Each sings his part, echoing from Pit and Box,
With his hoarse Voice, half Harmony, half Pox.
Le plus grand Roy du Monde, is always ringing;
They show themselves good Subjects by their singing.
On that condition, set up every Throat;
You Whiggs may sing, for you have chang'd your Note.
Cits and Citesses, raise a joyful strain,
'Tis a good Omen to begin a Reign:

Voices may help your Charter to restoring;
And get by singing, what you lost by roaring.

EPILOGUE *To the* OPERA

AFTER our *Æsop*'s Fable, shown to day,
I come to give the Moral of the Play.
Feign'd Zeal, you saw, set out the speedier pace;
But, the last heat, *Plain Dealing* won the Race:
Plain Dealing for a Jewel has been known;
But ne'er till now the Jewel of a Crown.
When Heav'n made Man, to show the work Divine,
Truth was his Image, stampt upon the Coin:
And, when a King is to a God refin'd,
On all he says and does, he stamps his Mind:
This proves a Soul without allay, and pure;
Kings, like their Gold, should every touch endure.
To dare in Fields is Valour; but how few
Dare be so throughly Valiant to be true?
The Name of Great, let other Kings affect:
He's Great indeed, the Prince that is direct.
His Subjects know him now, and trust him more,
Than all their Kings, and all their Laws before.
What safety could their publick Acts afford?
Those he can break; but cannot break his Word.
So great a Trust to him alone was due;
Well have they trusted whom so well they knew.
The Saint, who walk'd on Waves, securely trod,
While he believ'd the beckning of his God;
But, when his Faith no longer bore him out,
Began to sink, as he began to doubt.
Let us our native Character maintain,
'Tis of our growth, to be sincerely plain.
T' excel in Truth, we Loyally may strive;
Set Privilege against Prerogative:
He Plights his Faith; and we believe him just;
His Honour is to Promise, ours to Trust.
Thus *Britain*'s Basis on a Word is laid,
As by a Word the World it self was made.

To my Friend Mr. J. Northleigh, *Author of the* Parallel. *On his Triumph of the British Monarchy*

SO *Joseph* yet a youth, expounded well
The bodeing Dream, and did th' event foretell,
Judg'd by the past, and drew the Parallel.
Thus early *Solomon* the Truth explor'd,
The Right awarded, and the Babe restor'd.
Thus *Daniel*, e're to Prophecy he grew,
The perjur'd Presbyters did first subdue,
And freed *Susannah* from the canting Crew.
Well may our Monarchy Triumphant stand
While warlike *JAMES* protects both Sea and Land,
And under covert of his sev'n-fold shield,
Thou send'st thy shafts to scowre the distant Field.
By Law thy powerful Pen has set us free,
Thou study'st that, and that may study thee.

To the Pious Memory Of the Accomplisht Young LADY Mrs Anne Killigrew, Excellent in the two Sister-Arts of Poësie, and Painting. An ODE

I

THOU Youngest Virgin-Daughter of the Skies,
Made in the last Promotion of the Blest;
Whose Palmes, new pluckt from Paradise,
In spreading Branches more sublimely rise,
Rich with Immortal Green above the rest:
Whether, adopted to some Neighbouring Star,

To my Friend, &c. *Text from* The Triumph of Our Monarchy, *1685*
To the Pious Memory, &c. *Text from* Poems by Mrs Anne Killigrew, *1686, collated with* Examen Poeticum, *1693*

Thou rol'st above us, in thy wand'ring Race,
Or, in Procession fixt and regular,
Mov'd with the Heavens Majestick Pace;
Or, call'd to more Superiour Bliss,
Thou tread'st, with Seraphims, the vast Abyss:
What ever happy Region is thy place,
Cease thy Celestial Song a little space;
(Thou wilt have Time enough for Hymns Divine,
Since Heav'ns Eternal Year is thine.)
Hear then a Mortal Muse thy Praise rehearse,
In no ignoble Verse;
But such as thy own voice did practise here,
When thy first Fruits of Poesie were giv'n;
To make thy self a welcome Inmate there:
While yet a young Probationer,
And Candidate of Heav'n.

II

If by Traduction came thy Mind,
Our Wonder is the less to find
A Soul so charming from a Stock so good;
Thy Father was transfus'd into thy Blood:
So wert thou born into the tuneful strain,
(An early, rich, and inexhausted Vain.)
But if thy Præexisting Soul
Was form'd, at first, with Myriads more,
It did through all the Mighty Poets roul,
Who *Greek* or *Latine* Laurels wore,
And was that *Sappho* last, which once it was before.
If so, then cease thy flight, *O Heav'n-born Mind!*
Thou hast no Dross to purge from thy Rich Ore:
Nor can thy Soul a fairer Mansion find,
Than was the Beauteous Frame she left behind:
Return, to fill or mend the Quire, of thy Celestial kind.

III

May we presume to say, that at thy Birth,
New joy was sprung in Heav'n, as well as here on Earth.

11 Abyss:] Abyss. *86 93* 12 is *93*: be *86* 32 wore,] wore. *86 93*

For sure the Milder Planets did combine
On thy Auspicious Horoscope to shine,
And ev'n the most Malicious were in Trine.
Thy Brother-Angels at thy Birth
Strung each his Lyre, and tun'd it high,
That all the People of the Skie
Might know a Poetess was born on Earth.
And then if ever, Mortal Ears
Had heard the Musick of the Spheres!
And if no clust'ring Swarm of Bees
On thy sweet Mouth distill'd their golden Dew,
'Twas that, such vulgar Miracles,
Heav'n had not Leasure to renew:
For all the Blest Fraternity of Love
Solemniz'd there thy Birth, and kept thy Holyday above.

IV

O Gracious God! How far have we
Prophan'd thy Heav'nly Gift of Poesy?
Made prostitute and profligate the Muse,
Debas'd to each obscene and impious use,
Whose Harmony was first ordain'd Above
For Tongues of Angels, and for Hymns of Love?
O wretched We! why were we hurry'd down
This lubrique and adult'rate age,
(Nay added fat Pollutions of our own)
T' increase the steaming Ordures of the Stage?
What can we say t' excuse our *Second Fall*?
Let this thy *Vestal*, Heav'n, attone for all!
Her *Arethusian* Stream remains unsoil'd,
Unmixt with Forreign Filth, and undefil'd,
Her Wit was more than Man, her Innocence a Child!

V

Art she had none, yet wanted none:
For Nature did that Want supply,
So rich in Treasures of her Own,
She might our boasted Stores defy:

71 wanted none: *93*: wanted: none *86* (*text*): None. *86* (*errata*)

Such Noble Vigour did her Verse adorn,
That it seem'd borrow'd, where 'twas only born.
Her Morals too were in her Bosome bred
By great Examples daily fed,
What in the best of Books, her Fathers Life, she read.
And to be read her self she need not fear,
Each Test, and ev'ry Light, her Muse will bear,
Though *Epictetus* with his Lamp were there.
Ev'n Love (for Love sometimes her Muse exprest)
Was but a *Lambent-flame* which play'd about her Brest:
Light as the Vapours of a Morning Dream,
So cold herself, whilst she such Warmth exprest,
'Twas *Cupid* bathing in *Diana*'s Stream.

VI

Born to the Spacious Empire of the *Nine*,
One would have thought, she should have been content
To manage well that Mighty Government:
But what can young ambitious Souls confine?
To the next Realm she stretcht her Sway,
For *Painture* neer adjoyning lay,
A plenteous Province, and alluring Prey.
A Chamber of Dependences was fram'd,
(As Conquerors will never want Pretence,
When arm'd, to justifie the Offence)
And the whole Fief, in right of Poetry she claim'd.
The Country open lay without Defence:
For Poets frequent In-rodes there had made,
And perfectly could represent
The Shape, the Face, with ev'ry Lineament;
And all the large Demains which the *Dumb-sister* sway'd,
All bow'd beneath her Government,
Receiv'd in Triumph wheresoe're she went.
Her Pencil drew, what e're her Soul design'd,
And oft the happy Draught surpass'd the Image in her Mind.
The *Sylvan* Scenes of Herds and Flocks,
And fruitful Plains and barren Rocks,
Of shallow Brooks that flow'd so clear,
The Bottom did the Top appear;

97 the Offence] th' Offence *93*

Of deeper too and ampler Flouds,
Which as in Mirrors, shew'd the Woods;
Of lofty Trees with Sacred Shades,
And Perspectives of pleasant Glades,
Where Nymphs of brightest Form appear,
And shaggy Satyrs standing neer,
Which them at once admire and fear.
The Ruines too of some Majestick Piece,
Boasting the Pow'r of ancient *Rome* or *Greece*,
Whose Statues, Freezes, Columns broken lie,
And though deface't, the Wonder of the Eie,
What Nature, Art, bold Fiction e're durst frame,
Her forming Hand gave Feature to the Name.
So strange a Concourse ne're was seen before,
But when the peopl'd Ark the whole Creation bore.

VII

The Scene then chang'd, with bold Erected Look
Our Martial King the sight with Reverence strook:
For not content t' express his Outward Part,
Her hand call'd out the Image of his Heart,
His Warlike Mind, his Soul devoid of Fear,
His High-designing Thoughts, were figur'd there,
As when, by Magick, Ghosts are made appear.
Our Phenix Queen was portrai'd too so bright,
Beauty alone could Beauty take so right:
Her Dress, her Shape, her matchless Grace,
Were all observ'd, as well as heav'nly Face.
With such a Peerless Majesty she stands,
As in that Day she took the Crown from Sacred hands:
Before a Train of Heroins was seen,
In *Beauty* foremost, as in Rank, the Queen!
Thus nothing to her *Genius* was deny'd,
But like a Ball of Fire the further thrown,
Still with a greater Blaze she shone,

118 fear. *93*: fear *86* 124 Feature to *93*: Shape unto *86* 128 sight *93*: Eye *86* 139–41 As . . . the Queen! *93*: *86 has*
As in that Day she took from Sacred hands
The Crown; 'mong num'rous Heroins was seen,
More yet in Beauty, than in Rank, the Queen!

And her bright Soul broke out on ev'ry side.
What next she had design'd, Heaven only knows,
To such Immod'rate Growth her Conquest rose,
That Fate alone its Progress could oppose.

VIII

Now all those Charmes, that blooming Grace,
The well-proportion'd Shape, and beauteous Face,
Shall never more be seen by Mortal Eyes;
In Earth the much lamented Virgin lies!
Not Wit, nor Piety could Fate prevent;
Nor was the cruel *Destiny* content
To finish all the Murder at a Blow,
To sweep at once her Life, and Beauty too;
But, like a hardn'd Fellon, took a pride
To work more Mischievously slow,
And plunder'd first, and then destroy'd.
O double Sacriledge on things Divine,
To rob the Relique, and deface the Shrine!
But thus *Orinda* dy'd:
Heav'n, by the same Disease, did both translate,
As equal were their Souls, so equal was their Fate.

IX

Mean time her Warlike Brother on the Seas
His waving Streamers to the Winds displays,
And vows for his Return, with vain Devotion, pays.
Ah, Generous Youth, that Wish forbear,
The Winds too soon will waft thee here!
Slack all thy Sailes, and fear to come,
Alas, thou know'st not, Thou art wreck'd at home!
No more shalt thou behold thy Sisters Face,
Thou hast already had her last Embrace.
But look aloft, and if thou ken'st from far,
Among the *Pleiad's* a New-kindl'd Star,
If any sparkles, than the rest, more bright,
'Tis she that shines in that propitious Light.

148 its *93*: their *86*

X

When in mid-Aire, the Golden Trump shall sound,
  To raise the Nations under ground;
  When in the Valley of *Jehosaphat*,
The Judging God shall close the Book of Fate;
  And there the last Assizes keep,
  For those who Wake, and those who Sleep;
    When ratling Bones together fly,
From the four Corners of the Skie,
When Sinews o're the Skeletons are spread,
Those cloath'd with Flesh, and Life inspires the Dead:
The Sacred Poets first shall hear the Sound,
  And formost from the Tomb shall bound:
For they are cover'd with the lightest Ground
And streight, with in-born Vigour, on the Wing,
Like mounting Larkes, to the New Morning sing.
There *Thou*, Sweet Saint, before the Quire shalt go,
As Harbinger of Heav'n, the Way to show,
The Way which thou so well hast learn'd below.

To my Ingenious Friend, Mr. Henry Higden, Esq; On his Translation of the Tenth SATYR OF JUVENAL

THE *Grecian* Wits, who *Satyr* first began,
Were Pleasant *Pasquins* on the Life of Man:
At Mighty Villains, who the State opprest,
They durst not Rail; perhaps, they Laugh'd at least,
And turn'd 'em out of Office with a Jest.
No Fool could peep abroad, but ready stand
The *Drolls*, to clap a *Bauble* in his Hand:
Wise *Legislators* never yet could draw
A *Fopp* within the Reach of Common-Law;
For Posture, Dress, Grimace, and Affectation,
Tho' Foes to *Sence*, are Harmless to the *Nation*.

187 Dead:] Dead; *86 93*

To my Ingenious Friend, &c. *Text from Higden's* A Modern Essay on the Tenth Satyr of Juvenal, *1687*

Our last Redress is Dint of *Verse* to try;
And Satyr is our *Court* of *Chancery*.
This Way took *Horace* to reform an Age
Not Bad enough to need an Author's Rage:
But Yours,* who liv'd in more degen'rate Times,
Was forc'd to fasten Deep, and woorry Crimes:
Yet You, my Friend, have temper'd him so well,
You make him Smile in spight of all his Zeal:
An Art peculiar to your Self alone,
To joyn the Vertues of Two Stiles in One.
Oh! were your Author's Principle receiv'd,
Half of the lab'ring World wou'd be reliev'd;
For not to Wish, is not to be Deceiv'd!
Revenge wou'd into *Charity* be chang'd,
Because it costs too Dear to be *Reveng'd*:
It costs our *Quiet* and *Content of Mind*;
And when 'tis compass'd, leaves a Sting behind.
Suppose I had the better End o' th' Staff,
Why shou'd I help th' ill-natur'd World to laugh?
'Tis all alike to them, who gets the Day;
They Love the Spight and Mischief of the *Fray*.
No; I have Cur'd my Self of that *Disease*;
Nor will I be provok'd, but when I please:
But let me half that *Cure* to You restore;
You gave the *Salve*, I laid it to the *Sore*.
Our kind Relief against a Rainy Day,
Beyond a Tavern, or a tedious Play;
We take your Book, and laugh our Spleen away.
If all Your *Tribe*, (too studious of *Debate*)
Wou'd cease false Hopes and Titles to create,
Led by the *Rare Example* you begun,
Clyents wou'd fail, and *Lawyers* be undone.

* *Juvenal.*